Canon, Theology, and
Old Testament
Interpretation

Canon, Theology, and Old Testament Interpretation

ESSAYS IN HONOR OF BREVARD S. CHILDS

Edited by
Gene M. Tucker,
David L. Petersen,
and Robert R. Wilson

FORTRESS PRESS   Philadelphia

Library of Congress Cataloging-in-Publication Data

Canon, theology, and Old Testament interpretation.

Bibliography: p.
1. Bible. O.T.—Criticism, interpretation, etc.
2. Bible. O.T.—Theology. 3. Bible. O.T.—Canon.
4. Childs, Brevard S. I. Tucker, Gene M. II. Petersen,
David L. III. Wilson, Robert R., 1942–
IV. Childs, Brevard S.
BS1171.2.C36 1988   221.6   87–45908
ISBN 0–8006–0854–2

3048L87   Printed in the United States of America   1–854

Contents

Contents

Part II. The Interpretation of the Torah and the Former Prophets

Part III. The Interpretation of Prophetic Texts

Contents

Contributors

Bernhard W. Anderson, Princeton Theological Seminary (Emeritus)
James Barr, Christ Church, Oxford University
Bruce C. Birch, Wesley Theological Seminary
Ronald E. Clements, King's College, London
George W. Coats, Lexington Theological Seminary
Erhard S. Gerstenberger, University of Marburg
Paul D. Hanson, Harvard University, The Divinity School
Jörg Jeremias, University of Munich
Burke O. Long, Bowdoin College
James Luther Mays, Union Theological Seminary in Virginia
Roy F. Melugin, Austin College
David L. Petersen, The Iliff School of Theology
Marvin H. Pope, Yale University (Emeritus)
Alexander Rofé, Hebrew University
John Van Seters, University of North Carolina at Chapel Hill
Gerald T. Sheppard, Emmanuel College, Toronto
W. Sibley Towner, Union Theological Seminary in Virginia
John B. Trotti, Union Theological Seminary in Virginia
Gene M. Tucker, Candler School of Theology, Emory University
J. William Whedbee, Pomona College
Robert R. Wilson, The Divinity School, Yale University

Preface

This volume is presented with respect and affection to Brevard S. Childs by his colleagues in the field of Old Testament studies, on the occasion of his sixty-fifth birthday. For more than three decades, Childs, through his teaching and his publications, has significantly influenced many scholars and, through them, the reading of the Bible in the United States and abroad. This volume is intended to celebrate his lifelong devotion to clarity about method in biblical study, concern for providing critically founded interpretation of the biblical text, and dedication to the articulation of the canon's theological perspective. The contributors have attempted to honor Childs by furthering the discussion of issues that have been at the center of his own work: biblical theology, hermeneutics, and specific topics throughout the Old Testament canon.

Except for four years as Professor of Exegesis and Old Testament at Mission House Seminary (1954–58), Childs has spent his entire teaching career at Yale University. Since 1981 he has been Holmes Professor of Old Testament Criticism and Interpretation at Yale Divinity School, with appointments in the University's Graduate School, the Department of Religious Studies, and the Department of Near Eastern Languages and Civilizations as well. He was educated at the University of Michigan (A.B. and M.A.), Princeton Theological Seminary (B.D.) and the University of Basel (Th.D.). Both of his Michigan degrees were in history, but even then his interest in the Old Testament was evident.

At Princeton he concentrated in biblical studies, and continued to improve his facility with German and French, which he had first developed while serving in the U.S. Army in Europe. Among the academic awards he received at Princeton were the Samuel Robinson Prize and the Old Testament Fellowship. The latter helped finance his first year of graduate study at the University of Basel.

All of Brevard Childs's nine books have been highly influential. The first, *Myth and Reality in the Old Testament* (1960), emerged from his Basel dissertation. It was a religio-historical and theological investigation of important aspects of biblical thought in the wider context of the ancient Near East. His second book, *Memory and Tradition in Israel* (1962), was a broadly based theological word study, and his third, *Isaiah and the Assyrian Crisis* (1967), was a historical and theological investigation of traditions in the Book of Isaiah. In *Biblical Theology in Crisis* (1970) he reviewed the history of the so-called biblical theology movement in American scholarship and called for a different approach, one that would address more directly the canonical shape and contents of the biblical text. That was followed by what many have judged to be one of the most significant Old Testament commentaries written in the United States, *The Book of Exodus: A Commentary* (1974). In that volume he began to apply his canonical approach, analyzing each unit in terms of the issues usually addressed in commentaries, but asking other questions as well. He broadened the consideration of the history of interpretation to include the full range of treatments of the particular parts of the Book of Exodus in the church and the synagogue, took into account the use of those texts in the rest of the canon, and focused the theological issues and implications of each unit. His *Introduction to the Old Testament as Scripture* (1980) was the mature statement of his canonical approach. Declining to be bound by the traditional academic specializations he then published *The New Testament as Canon: An Introduction* (1984). His most recent volume is *Old Testament Theology in a Canonical Context* (1985).

In addition he has published dozens of articles and reviews, writing both for his colleagues in biblical studies and for a wider audience. A full list of his publications concludes this volume.

Childs has been an active member of the Society of Biblical Literature, serving for five years as the book review editor of its *Journal of Biblical Literature.* He is an honorary member of the British Society for Old Testament Study, and was for many years a member of the editorial board of the journal *Interpretation*. Among the distinguished lectureships he has given are the Sprunt Lectures at Union Theological Seminary in Virginia, the Gray Lectures at Duke University, the Jackson Lectures at Southern Methodist University, and the Stone Lectures at Princeton Theological Seminary. His honors and awards include a Guggenheim Fellowship, an American Council of Learned Societies Fellowship, a National Endowment for the Humanities Research Fellowship, and a Fulbright Fellowship. The University of Aberdeen honored him with the D.D. degree in 1981.

A volume that represented the full range of Childs's scholarly interests and contributions would be far broader than the present one. While most of his publications focus upon the Old Testament, his work has touched other parts of the theological curriculum, some facets of it deeply. In addition to his introduction to the New Testament, he has incorporated into many of his publications studies of the history of both Christian and Jewish biblical interpretation from the earliest to modern times, and he has frequently addressed normative theological and ethical issues as well.

This volume, however, has been limited to the field in which Childs has worked most extensively, the theory and practice of the interpretation of the Hebrew Scriptures, and to contributions from a few of his many friends and colleagues working in that discipline. Each contributor was asked to prepare an essay that would focus upon an issue in Old Testament theology or hermeneutics, either in direct conversation with Childs's work or emerging from the issues of theology and interpretation that have concerned Childs in his research and teaching. The contributors were invited to address these general themes from the perspectives of their own research and reflection. What we present here is a volume that intends to advance the dialogue on the theory and practice of Old Testament interpretation. The essays in Part I, Canon and Theology, address methodological and theological issues. Those in the other three parts take up specific exegetical problems that have theological dimensions or implications, ranging from the first part of the Old Testament canon to the last.

The explicitly methodological and theological essays reflect diverse approaches. In "The Theological Case against Biblical Theology," James Barr offers a critique of biblical theology from the perspective of systematic theology. Erhard Gerstenberger's "Canon Criticism and the

Meaning of *Sitz im Leben*" examines a canonical approach from the point of view of form critical and sociological research and emphasizes the importance of the interpreter's own social setting. Paul D. Hanson's hermeneutical essay, "Biblical Interpretation: Meeting Place of Jews and Christians," argues that both the substance of the Bible and the history of the relationship between Jews and Christians call for a dialogical process of interpretation. Roy F. Melugin shows how exegesis that is sensitive to the canonical shape of the material will be both literary and historical. Two essays, those of Robert R. Wilson and Bruce C. Birch, examine issues in the emerging discussion of Old Testament ethics. David L. Petersen considers the history of the idea of monotheism and the theological implications of that discussion.

Although they employ different exegetical methods, all of the essays on specific problems within the canon are sensitive to the broader theological implications of interpretation, and most keep a canonical perspective in view. John Van Seters shows how source and redaction critical conclusions have a bearing on the theology of the Pentateuch. George W. Coats investigates the tradition of Moses as healer and its echoes throughout the entire canon. Ronald E. Clements considers a similar theme, the healing of the blind and the lame, discerning that it reveals patterns in the prophetic canon. Both J. William Whedbee and Burke O. Long demonstrate how literary analysis opens up theological meaning in narrative texts.

Acknowledging that the final form of the text has priority in the interpretation of a biblical book, Jörg Jeremias shows through a redaction critical investigation of Amos 3—6 how the history of the composition of the text is important for the interpretation of its final form. Bernhard W. Anderson's essay considers similar issues with regard to Isaiah 5—10. Gene M. Tucker's study of the law in the eighth-century prophets, primarily traditio-historical in approach, is a contribution to the theology of both those prophets and the legal traditions. Both Alexander Rofé and Gerald T. Sheppard contribute to the complex issue of the reliability and authority of prophetic figures and prophetic words.

All three of the essays on texts in the Writings consider the importance of canonical location and shape for the understanding of those texts. According to W. Sibley Towner, reading Daniel 1 in the framework of the canon rather than against a hypothetical cultural or historical context uncovers significant aspects of the story's meaning.

Preface

Choosing to analyze Psalm 118 because of its established liturgical settings in Judaism and Christianity, James L. Mays shows the rich meaning of the text in its various canonical and historical horizons. Marvin H. Pope's point of departure is the early disputes concerning the sanctity or canonicity of the Song of Songs. He argues that resolution of the issue turned on both the interpretation and the judgment of the book's purpose and theological significance. He also reviews the history of the interpretation of the book in Judaism and Christianity and suggests the implications of following one or another of the alternative interpretations that have emerged in that history.

Few scholars have done more than Brevard Childs to stimulate dialogue concerning theological issues in the interpretation of the Old Testament, or to contribute to that dialogue. The contributors and editors hope that this volume will enhance such dialogue between the canon and its interpreters.

The editors are grateful to Fortress Press, and particularly to John A. Hollar and Harold W. Rast, for their encouragement and support of this publication project honoring Brevard S. Childs.

GENE M. TUCKER
DAVID L. PETERSEN
ROBERT R. WILSON

Abbreviations

AB	Anchor Bible
AOAT	Alter Orient und Altes Testament
ASSR	*Archives des sciences sociales des religions*
ATANT	Abhandlungen zur Theologie des Alten und Neuen Testaments
ATD	Das Alte Testament Deutsch
BA	*Biblical Archaeology*
BAT	Die Botschaft des Alten Testaments
BDB	F. Brown, S. R. Driver, and C. A. Briggs, *Hebrew and English Lexicon of the Old Testament*
BEvT	Beiträge zur evangelischen Theologie
BFCT	Beiträge zur Förderung christlicher Theologie
BHS	*Biblia hebraica stuttgartensia*
BHT	Beiträge zur historischen Theologie
Bib	*Biblica*
BK	*Bibel und Kirche*
BKAT	Biblischer Kommentar: Altes Testament
BR	*Biblical Research*
BWANT	Beiträge zur Wissenschaft vom Alten und Neuen Testament
BZAW	Beihefte zur *ZAW*
CTM	*Concordia Theological Monthly*
EB	Etudes biblique

Abbreviations

EncJud	*Encyclopaedia judaica* (1971)
ET	English translation
FOTL	The Forms of the Old Testament Literature
FRLANT	Forschungen zur Religion und Literatur des Alten und Neuen Testaments
GBS OTS	Guides to Biblical Scholarship, Old Testament Series
HBT	*Horizons in Biblical Theology*
HDB	*Harper's Dictionary of the Bible*
HKAT	Handkommentar zum Alten Testament
HSM	Harvard Semitic Monographs
HTR	*Harvard Theological Review*
IB	*Interpreter's Bible*
ICC	International Critical Commentary
IDB	G. A. Buttrick, ed. *Interpreter's Dictionary of the Bible*
Int	*Interpretation*
JAAR	*Journal of the American Academy of Religion*
JB	*Jerusalem Bible*
JBL	*Journal of Biblical Literature*
JPOS	*Journal of the Palestine Oriental Society*
JSOT	*Journal for the Study of the Old Testament*
JSOTS	*JSOT* Supplements
KAT	E. Sellin, ed. Kommentar zum Alten Testament
KeHAT	Kurzgefaßtes exegetisches Handbuch zum Alten Testament
KHC	Kurzer Hand-Kommentar zum Alten Testament
KJV	*King James Version*
LXX	Septuagint
MHUC	Hebrew Union College Monographs
NEB	*New English Bible*
NJPSV	*The New Jewish Publication Society Version*
NT	New Testament
NTS	*New Testament Studies*
OBT	Overtures to Biblical Theology
Or	*Orientalia* (Rome)
OT	Old Testament
OTL	Old Testament Library
OTS	*Oudtestamentische Studiën*
RevScRel	*Revue des sciences religieuses*
RSV	*Revised Standard Version*

Abbreviations

SBLASP	Society of Biblical Literature Abstracts and Seminar Papers
SBLDS	Society of Biblical Literature Dissertation Series
SBS	Stuttgarter Bibelstudien
SBT	Studies in Biblical Theology
SWBAS	The Social World of Biblical Antiquity Series
TBü	Theologische Bücherei
TEV	*Today's English Version*
TLZ	*Theologische Literaturzeitung*
TQ	*Theologische Quartalschrift*
TUMR	Trinity University Monographs in Religion
VT	*Vetus Testamentum*
VTSup	Vetus Testamentum, Supplements
WBC	Word Biblical Commentary
WMANT	Wissenschaftliche Monographien zum Alten und Neuen Testament
ZAW	*Zeitschrift für die alttestamentliche Wissenschaft*
ZBK	Züricher Bibelkommentare
ZTK	*Zeitschrift für Theologie und Kirche*

Part I

CANON AND THEOLOGY

1

The Theological Case against Biblical Theology

JAMES BARR

In his important work *Biblical Theology in Crisis*, published in 1970, Brevard Childs chronicled the decline and fall of the Biblical Theology Movement, at least as it had been, and especially in the United States. The failure of the movement left the entire prospects of biblical theology in a state of crisis, and Childs's own proposal for an approach totally based on the canon is intended as a response to that crisis. The canon was the way forward to a renewed biblical theology. Moreover, in his later works, which develop the canonical approach in greater detail, the primacy of theology is repeatedly emphasized. He claims again and again that the canonical approach is truly "theological." The adjective "theological" seems to be the highest of all superlatives: to be theological is the best that one can be. This emphasis seems to be a continuation, and indeed an even greater heightening, of the ethos and impulse of the older biblical theology.

A number of writers objected to Childs's depiction of biblical theology. It had, of course, been a many-sided and not a homogeneous affair, as Childs very well knew, and some averred that they could not see any unity in it at all, surely a sign of myopia.[1] Historically, Childs's delineation of it was very well done. A more reasonable objection, especially now and with the advantage of hindsight, is the argument that biblical theology never really fell into crisis but has continued in fairly full productivity on the continent, in the Roman Catholic world, and in the developing countries, if not in the United States.[2] This seems to be very largely true, but with a qualification that will shortly be mentioned. Examples are to be seen on all sides. In OT theology it once looked as if von Rad's great work had cast a pall of silence over all possible competitors; but in the 1970s and 1980s there has been a lively series of fresh approaches to the same genre: Clements, Fohrer, W. H. Schmidt, Terrien, and Zimmerli, for example. Important new essays about the subject of biblical theology have come from writers like Gese, H. H. Schmid, and Stuhlmacher. Monographs continue to appear on subjects close to the traditional interests of biblical theology. In spite of all that the present writer said about the word-study method, two, if not more, theological dictionaries of the OT have been added. They were careful to avoid misuse of words, but in other respects continued the tradition of this type of work. Nor, indeed, is it always clear that the lessons about semantics and meanings of words were really learned. In this respect a work like H. W. Wolff's *Anthropology of the Old Testament* (German 1973, English 1974) continues very much the atmosphere of the older biblical theology.

It is thus difficult to maintain that biblical theology had somehow come to a stop. It seems, on the contrary, to have continued on rather smoothly, if we measure it in terms of productivity alone. This in itself does not constitute any criticism of the analysis that Childs made. But it does make a difficulty for a consequence that he may have drawn. He gave the impression that, biblical theology having fallen into crisis, it could not make any progress except through a completely fresh start: The canonical approach was thus the only way forward. This seems not to be so. On the contrary, all the evidence is that the canonical approach is only one possibility among several that are being actively pursued. Indeed, some initiatives that could well count as biblical theology point in a very different direction. Consider, for example, H. H. Schmid's approach, concentrating upon creation and integrating this with the world of ancient religion with its myths and its emphasis on order. Obviously biblical theologians would have to debate the merits of such different proposals, but it is manifest that, insofar as a stage of biblical theology exists, it is occupied by a quite varied set of possibilities and no one of them can claim to be the only possible continuant of the tradition of the subject.

The crisis of biblical theology lay not, therefore, in the cessation of its activities, but in its loss of status, its loss of prestige, the loss of its power to persuade. This factor has not been sufficiently considered in the discussion and was scarcely touched on by Childs himself in *Biblical Theology in Crisis*.[3] The fact is that the fall from grace of biblical theology was welcomed with warm acclamation by a very large number of leading theologians; its demise, if it was a demise, was greeted with cordial accents of joy. It is this fact, more than any other, that makes it true to speak of a decline and fall of biblical theology. It was not so much that the activities that had been attempted under this heading ceased to go on—as we have seen, they continued rather serenely on their way—but the sort of authority that biblical theology had seemed to wield, its ability to carry the day, its power to coerce opinion and to overwhelm arguments coming from any other sector of theological opinion, was definitely and irrevocably destroyed. Henceforth arguments based upon biblical theology were no longer to be proof against arguments based on other considerations within theology. They were no longer to be above criticism. In this respect almost all currents within serious theology greeted the demise of the older biblical theology with relief and delight. But the importance of this reaction has still to be properly evaluated within any discussion of biblical theology.

Why did this happen? Why did biblical theology not discern that there were important theological reasons against its own enterprise? The reason can be easily stated: It was against *history*, not against *theology*, that biblical theology thought it had to justify itself. Biblical theology, of course, was not entirely against the historical reading of scripture, and it took for granted certain standard historical-critical positions, for instance, the then-standard datings of Deuteronomy or Daniel. In a certain limited sense, therefore, biblical theology could be seen as in alliance with the historical reading of the Bible. But the main thrust of its argumentation was in the opposite direction. It was quite wrong to suppose that historical research into the Bible could lead to wholesome theological results. Nothing was more vehemently opposed than the idea that the biblical scholar should be primarily a historian. Biblical theology expected to be attacked from the side of those who stood for the historical tradition in biblical studies. It expected this attack, and it discounted it, for it thought it could easily overcome it. It could overcome it by arguing that the Bible was itself a theological document, that theological insight was needed for the understanding of it, and that purely historical research could not succeed in producing relevant theological results from it. These arguments succeeded because most of the constituency of biblical scholars and clergy was intrinsically sympathetic to them. What was not taken into account to anything like the same degree was the possibility that there would be strong and valid *theological* arguments against the whole program of biblical theology. Biblical theology did not sufficiently consider the possibility that theology, as theology, would be hostile to the claims it made. The revelation of this hostility, more than any other factor—more, for example, than its own internal contradictions—ruined the apparently successful career of biblical theology as it was.

What, then, were the basic theological reasons against the claims of biblical theology? Nowhere, perhaps, were these expressly stated, and to this extent we have to imagine for ourselves what was in people's minds but not made explicit at the time. Surely the core of the difficulty lay in the very idea of "biblical theology" itself. Naturally, biblical theology was difficult to define and included a number of competing interests, and everyone knew this. But almost all ideas of biblical theology had one common characteristic. For it, the only target, the only horizon, the only criterion, and the only arbiter must be the Bible. What other standard, what other organizing principle, could it have? Almost inevitably this meant that any sort of theology for which there existed any sort of authority, any sort of consideration at all, apart from the Bible or alongside the Bible, must be uneasy in its relations with biblical theology. This does not mean that biblical theologians thought that biblical theology in itself decided everything. They commonly accepted that there were realms of systematic theology, of contact with modern thought, and so on, that could well be important. But they could not enter into these realms, they could not expressly approach these questions, as long as they remained within the methods and the purview of biblical theology as such.

Suppose we were to say that the defining horizon of biblical theology is the Bible, but that the defining horizon of theology as such is God in Jesus Christ?[4] Would these not be different things, and organized in different ways? At least in principle they might be very different. They would easily coincide only on one assumption, namely, that the circle defined by the Bible and the circle defined by God are identical. In other words, there are *no* factors other than the Bible itself that count in the understanding of God. This position might in itself be true but it undoubtedly excludes the possibility of many kinds of theology.

This was central to the theological case against biblical theology: it was intrinsically one-sided. It did not necessarily oppose in principle, but was methodologically unable to handle, numerous kinds of questions that most theologians considered very important. It thereby came necessarily to favor those theological directions that thought that questions of these kinds should not be taken up at all. In this respect, as was very obvious to everyone at the time, biblical theology stood close to the general movement of neo-orthodoxy and assisted it in its warfare against other theological directions.[5]

This point can be made more specific. One central neo-orthodox position was the drastic rejection of natural theology. Biblical theology would appear, in principle, to belong clearly to revealed theology and to stand on the opposite side of the line from natural theology. (This will not necessarily always remain so, but it is easy to understand that it then seemed natural.) Again, neo-orthodoxy sought to minimize the role of the traditional apologetic questions: How do we know that this is true of God? How can we tell whether this or that really happened? There was no standing point from which one could approach such questions, and the attempt to create such a standing point was disastrous to theology. Biblical theology might not understand these reasonings, but operationally it could hardly help taking the same direction. It could hope or aspire to tell us what was the viewpoint of the Bible, but it could not discuss whether that viewpoint was valid, for it had no ground on which to stand in doing so; it could state and estimate the importance that the Bible attached to events reported, but it could not say how far these events were historically true, for that endeavor belonged to the historical approach from which it wanted to distance itself. Neo-orthodoxy insisted that "the Scriptures," that is, the books of the accepted canons, were the valid written form of the Word of God and thereby authoritative in a degree not comparable with any other human cultural manifestation; biblical theology was operationally restricted to the Bible and could scarcely avoid supporting that conception. Thus individual biblical theologians might distance themselves from the position of one like Barth, but the whole nature of their operation seemed to conform to the general trend of neo-orthodoxy much more than to any sharply different theological direction. Theologians thus felt that biblical theology was a partisan movement, lined up on one side of a series of disagreements that were really a matter for doctrinal theologians to discuss among themselves. The biblical theology movement tended to short-circuit what should have been an open and many-sided discussion.

This in itself would not have been so bad, but biblical theology made it much worse by appearing to furnish scientific evidence to support the neo-orthodox points of view.[6] This was paradoxical. The prevailing tendency in biblical theology was to diminish all claims that historical scholarship on the Bible was scientific. It tended to emphasize the ideology-laden character of all historical work, thereby justifying the theological approach to the Bible as equal or superior to the historical. But biblical theology in effect did much worse. It may not have used the word "scientific" but it made sure of producing that impression. The masses of etymologies, Hebrew words, and delineations of Hebrew concepts worked in effect to provide *hard evidence*, as it was supposed to be, in favor of generally neo-orthodox points of view. Thus neo-orthodox convictions that should really have had the value of hypotheses, or of convictions set forth for examination, quickly acquired the air of being founded upon a mass of central biblical evidence. The technicality of the grounds on which this evidence was elaborated tended to put it beyond the reach of many doctrinal theologians and thus make fair examination difficult. Competent theologians felt that discussion was frustrated. When it eventually transpired that much of the technical apparatus, the Hebrew roots and meanings of Greek words, had been seriously incompetent all along, doctrinal theologians were correspondingly infuriated. They felt that they had been cheated by biblical theology.

Another defect lay in the fact that biblical theology seemed to separate theology from its classical roots. It did, of course, clearly affirm the Bible as the central and original source. But the mode in which it established the coherence of the Bible, through emphasis on its peculiar Hebraic culture and through drastic opposition to the thought of the Greek world, even if it was valid for the NT (which is surely disputable, to put it mildly), could not be valid for the patristic world in which the great theological doctrines were actually worked out. To be sure, within biblical theology itself opinions differed in these regards. Some, perhaps more logically, thought that everything that was Hellenic was wrong; others somehow found it possible to combine constant polemics against Greek thought on the one hand with wholesale acceptance of the patristic use of Greek categories on the other. But to many this was too difficult and confusing. The main natural trend of biblical theology was to produce a serious separation between the NT and the patristic age. But for anyone whose starting point lay in that age, for anyone for whom the patristic period is the real creative period for *theology*, this point of view was deeply distressing.

We have seen that biblical theology tended, intentionally or unintentionally, to side with the neo-orthodox opposition both to natural theology and to apologetic discussion. This in itself might not have been so serious, were it not that biblical theology in itself seemed to undertake these same activities but in a hidden way. The idea that Hebrew thought and culture furnished a logic within which the theological interconnections became clear and lost their contradictoriness was something like a natural theology of a new kind. The demonstration of the coherence of all the biblical material seemed to work like a kind of apologetic. It did not prove that events had happened, perhaps, but it created a web of connections that seemed, in an analogical way, to remove difficulties of belief and make the total biblical material seem more convincing and credible. This suggested that biblical theology was intent on doing in a secret and hidden way what it overtly said should not be done. This was damaging, not because it was wrong to do these things, but because it was theologically inhibiting to do them in this way.

Biblical theology, therefore, was felt to have unduly restricted the range of choices that should have been made openly available through theological discussion. Added to this was one final question about biblical theology that by implication may be more serious than any of those already mentioned, namely, the feeling that biblical theology at its best was still not really *theology*. It was a mode of organizing and interlinking the biblical material that differed indeed from the historical mode; but that in itself did not make it into theology. Theology could never be simply an organization of the biblical material, in whatever mode or on whatever level, but must be the construction, criticism, and refining of *our* concepts of God in Christ and in the church. For such a theological task the biblical material would be of extreme importance, but no amount of consideration of the biblical material, in whatever mode, would in itself perform that task. In relation to making actual theological decisions, biblical theology thus actually took us no farther forward than purely historical exegesis did. In fact, it made the position worse, because its own self-designation as "theology" and its own clearly expressed theological values only made it look all the more like theology when in fact it was not theology at all. The most advanced biblical theologies did not reach as far as the point at which actual theological thinking began. The whole strenuous effort to establish that biblical theology was distinct from historical exegesis had been unimportant. In relation to real theology, if one of them was merely preparatory, then so was the other.

These, I suggest, are the arguments against biblical theology that were active in the minds of many theologians.

To have stated the existence of these arguments, however, is not to have shown whether they are valid or invalid. Can biblical theology defend itself against them? Or, perhaps better, instead of defending itself, should it admit to some such faults and promise to try to mend its ways in the future? But if it is to do better in the future, what alterations of course will it have to make? And what can be learned from these criticisms that will be to the benefit of biblical theology? Is there something here that, if recognized, might overcome some of the present tensions and conflicts that affect relations between biblical studies and theology?

The most obvious point that most readers will take from the arguments as presented is that these differences represent very different understandings of what theology really is. This is indeed so. If doctrinal theologians think that theology should have God as its horizon, and not the Bible, it means that they have a different idea of how theology should be constructed; if they think that the most "theological" of the arguments of biblical theology are still not really theological, then this represents a quite different idea of what counts as theology.

But where does this lead us? These are indeed disagreements, but if so they have to be resolved at the level of doctrinal theology. Biblical theologians can hardly presume to instruct doctrinal theologians in what does or does not constitute theology. Why so? Not because doctrinal theologians cannot be wrong. The reason is obvious. Biblical theologians, as biblical theologians, do not dispose of material that will enable them to judge and decide the question. They may have the *competence*—most biblical theologians have been quite well trained in doctrinal theology—but they do not have the *material* to which they can turn. For the Bible itself, strictly speaking, has no concept of *theology* as such and gives no direct guidance about it. Any decision about what is or is not theology depends on going outside the circle of directly *biblical* guidance. But this means that it must be a question of entirely open discussion in the general realm of doctrinal and philosophical theology. If this is denied, it means that the first of the charges against biblical theology is true and that it is, and has been, a partisan discipline, seeking to support one particular doctrinal understanding.

For what if doctrinal theology wants to go in a quite different direction from that favored by biblical theology? What, for instance, if biblical theology should tend to minimize the importance of historical research but doctrinal theology should maintain that Christianity is a historical religion and that the most useful thing that biblical scholarship can do for theology is to assemble and clarify the historical evidence, both about events and about the meanings of texts? What if biblical theology insists that the entire canon is the only horizon for interpretation, but doctrinal theology says that all past theology has in fact worked with a selection of emphases from within the canon and that it still has to work with some such inner canon, overt or implied? What if biblical theology works out a biblical mode of thinking, which will provide the mental matrix for faith, but doctrinal theology says that it has to live in contact with modern philosophy and does not really want any scheme that will bypass that contact? What if biblical theology exerts itself to achieve synthesis at all costs and at the end of it doctrinal theology says, Thank you very much, but what we really want to know is the background and intention behind some central individual texts? What if doctrinal theology wants to set out the possibilities for faith in the modern world and has no intention of being totally bound by biblical precedent, whether presented synthetically or analytically?

Putting these questions serves to disengage two main extreme possibilities for biblical theology: either it is dogmatically interlinked, or it is essentially independent.

Let us suppose, first, that it is independent. It does not seek to have a normative or a prescriptive function. Such matters are dealt with by theology proper, doctrinal theology. Biblical theology is descriptive. It tells us how things are within the Bible, or (more historically expressed) within biblical times. Powerful scholars in the field have argued the case in just this way. In modern times, for instance, both Eichrodt and Stendahl have done so in their very different ways. Earlier on, J. P. Gabler, in the first proper study of the matter, had made the same point. According to this view, biblical theology should be descriptive and should have no dogmatic interlinkage. It would be ancillary, providing to dogmatic theology the biblical material suitably processed; it would not worry about the way in which the normative theological sciences used that material.

This understanding has an admirable purity but its weakness is that it is unrealistic. Most biblical theology has drawn ideas and inspiration from older dogmatic traditions; still more, it has had dogmatic aims and purposes. To say this is not to say that descriptive objectivity is impossible—that is not at all so. But such objectivity has, as a matter of fact, seldom been achieved, and not surprisingly so, for it has seldom been seriously aimed at. Yet its virtues quickly become evident when we consider the alternative, namely, the minatory or hortatory conception of biblical theology. Biblical theology, seen in this way, has real interlinkage with doctrinal theology. It gets some of its inspiration from theology, and it aspires to direct theology in a certain direction. It says, We got something from you to start us off, and now we want you to go this way rather than some other way. The emphasis is not so much on the origin as on the purpose. When it is said, as one well-known viewpoint puts it, that biblical theology is a Christian discipline and belongs entirely within the Christian theological enterprise, this means not so much that "Christianity" will direct the operation—for much of Christianity, if permitted, would direct it quite otherwise—but rather that the operation seeks to persuade Christianity to go in one way rather than in another way. Its goal is to establish a certain doctrinal position within Christianity.

Much more of biblical theology, one may suspect, has been thus motivated than has been motivated by the ideal of objective description. Thus those who said in the early days of biblical theology that such theology belonged to the realm of Christian dogmatics and not to real biblical scholarship were not so far wrong as was felt by those who at the time were infuriated by such remarks, including the present writer. Yet, however much this view of biblical theology may be justified by factual experience, there are severe limits to the degree to which it can be accepted as a correct and adequate statement of the nature of the subject. For one thing, few scholars have been willing to reveal their purposes so crudely; and not without reason. Much writing on the edges of biblical theology urged, surely foolishly, that scholars should reveal their presuppositions—a demand that was most disobeyed by those who most strongly expressed it. For who, really, would be favorably impressed by a book that openly confessed from the beginning that it was written to satisfy certain partisan ends and that all selection of material had been motivated by this aim?

Thus the hortatory or minatory account of biblical theology also has severe limitations. The success of biblical theology has largely lain in the degree to which works written within it have been able to transcend this kind of motivation; in the degree to which they have been able to furnish ideas, information, and guidance that could be used with profit within other schemes of thought and other motivations than that which the author supported; in the degree to which they recognized the limits of their purpose and the extent of the biblical evidence that might point in other directions. Thus, however strong the minatory or hortatory motivation of particular biblical theologians, the strength of their contributions is likely to be proportionate to the degree to which they are prepared for the possibility that their admonitions will not be accepted. Or, conversely stated, if biblical theology is to accept that it is dogmatically interlinked as a matter of principle—as in part it often is as a matter of fact—then it will have to accept that that means also a reduction of its influence and effectiveness.

Where then lies the true justification for the existence of any biblical theology at all? Neither the purely descriptive, nor the dogmatically purposive account can do it justice. And, if we accept that doctrinal theology is not bound to follow the same direction in which biblical theology seems to point, what can be the purpose of biblical theology at all?

It seems that biblical theology is best understood as a necessity, a valid and inevitable expression of the nature of biblical scholarship. Most biblical scholarship is theological and always was. A continuum spreads through the three distinguishable stages: biblical criticism, biblical theology, and doctrinal theology. Biblical theology certainly always had a large overlap of interest with doctrinal theology even if it could be distinguished in some important way. More important, biblical theology was very closely linked with the entire tradition of critical scholarship. It was thus mistaken to think of biblical theology as standing in contrast with older critical scholarship. On the contrary, it was the other side of the same coin. The consciousness of biblical theology as a subject awoke later and tended to be very aware of its difference from earlier critical scholarship. But this is typical of such closely paired movements of thought; they were still the two sides of the same coin. The biblical theology of the forties and fifties seemed at the time to be very different, but it developed very easily out of the older critical scholarship, for it too had always been a search for a sort of biblical theology, but one formed in a somewhat different way.

That this is so is shown by one significant fact. There was never any real *anti-critical* biblical theology; none of the really conservative people who rejected critical scholarship contributed anything to biblical theology. Biblical theology—and this is one of the things it deserves to be proud of—was always an experimental movement; it was looking for the true theology of the Bible because that theology was not already known. Conservatism basically rejected critical scholarship because, for it, the theological meaning of the Bible was something already given, fixed, and known. Only where there was critical scholarship was there anything for biblical theology to be about. The works that conservative scholars have written in the area of biblical theology are mere reiterations of some traditional dogmatic point of view, or secondhand and second-rate rehashes of what has been said by major scholars on the basis of critical scholarship, or a mixture of the two.[7]

If this is so, then it is mistaken if biblical theology defines itself primarily in terms of oppositional contrasts to other aspects within biblical scholarship. Its relation to these other aspects—textual, historical, comparative, and the like—is more suitably expressed in terms of interdependence rather than of contrast. The degree and nature of its contrast vis-à-vis doctrinal theology has been less explored but is likely to be more important in its ultimate effects. For too close an alliance with particular doctrinal trends can only damage the reputation and the effect of biblical theology. Moreover, too much insistence on the "theological" character of biblical theology can only encourage the impression that all essential theological decisions are already given and present in the Bible. The effect of this can be, among other things, to encourage those for whom an essentially *religious*, rather than a *theological*, devotion to the shapes and contours of the Bible takes the place of actual theological thinking.

This article has been written on moderate assumptions. It has assumed that biblical theology in some recognizable form will continue and that the question lies in finding its right proportions in relation to adjacent disciplines. The theological case against biblical theology, as it has thus far been discussed, is a reasonable and moderate theological case, to which a reasoned and constructive response may be given. It should not be ignored, however, that much more severe opposition to biblical theology does exist, and it would not be right to leave the subject without a moment's consideration of that harsher aspect. This harsher rejection of biblical theology is manifested on two sides:

On the one side biblical theology has been felt to be a dishonest evasion of the real problems of the modern world. As Houlden puts it, "Some have gone so far as to see biblical theology as an almost wilful refusal to face the profound theological difficulties of our times, in effect a retreat into a citadel which has proved all too vulnerable."[8] Houlden quotes the thoughts of Don Cupitt in *The World to Come.* According to Cupitt, neo-orthodoxy ("a sort of sophisticated fundamentalism") and biblical theology used the doctrine of revelation to justify a very sharp division between Christianity and other religions. "Other faiths were just mythological expressions of human religiosity," and through this approach Christianity was able for several decades to fend off unwelcome questions "by projecting them all on to other faiths and asking none of them of itself, a classic diversionary tactic."[9]

Cupitt does not amplify this, but by implication he seems to be saying that the whole approach of biblical theology was intrinsically dishonestly biased. The way in which it described the theological world within the Bible, and contrasted it with the environing world of religion, was chosen, molded, and guided by the purpose of protecting Christianity from honest comparison with the rest of the religious world. Whether or not this is fair to all the older biblical theology will not be discussed here; but clearly any future biblical theology would wish to avoid even the supposition that it was so motivated and guided. The estimate expressed by Cupitt is likely long to cast its shadow over the development of the subject.

The other side of the opposition lies in the conservative evangelical world. Biblical theology exercised a softening and limiting effect upon this movement during its time of prosperity. Otherwise, it would have been a cruder and harsher fundamentalism. Biblical theology's ideas of essentially personal revelation softened the edges of harsh questions about the truth or falsity of the Bible; it provided for many a route toward a moderate acceptance of mildly critical concepts; it was able to valorize many warm and attractive biblical concepts that would have been quite inaccessible to hard traditional orthodoxy. Whatever its weaknesses, it was much more biblical and much more powerfully Christian than anything that conservative Protestantism and evangelicalism had to offer.

Today, however, we must admit, if we are realistic, that almost all of this has vanished. The values that were then perceived are still active and beneficent in some ecumenical thinking, in Roman Catholic theology, in some liturgical reform, and in some of the developing countries; but in the field of conservative evangelical Christianity in the English-speaking world they are largely unrecognized and unknown. Biblical theology had placed the emphasis upon the *theological power and religious appeal* of the biblical concepts, which by their nature were different from our own categories and our own logic. All this was rejected because people preferred a reversion to "our" categories, that is, the eighteenth-century categories in which conservative evangelicalism had conceptualized all the questions.[10] The tactical advantages of insisting on decisions in *our* categories outweighed the values of theological concepts that could not be clearly defined without an exploratory journey of the mind. Thus the concepts that were so familiar in the older biblical theology—time and history in the Bible, the Hebrew conception of soul and body, truth as personal relation, the covenant as a dynamic relationship—all of these are unknown or unvalued, for they are subordinated to the harsh confrontations of inerrancy: the Bible, true or false? Yes or no? Revelation denied, or revelation affirmed (with no question asked about the biblical credentials of the concept of revelation)? All these concepts meant something only where two conditions were fulfilled: That there should be some degree of understanding for fresh scholarly exploration in the Bible, and along with it a certain degree of theological flexibility that today, in large tracts of the religious world, no longer exists. Thus the absence of the focus that the older biblical theology furnished has powerfully contributed to the extreme polarization of opinion between "conservative" and "mainstream" positions that is so obvious in many countries today. Moreover, it means that any continuing program that revives the term "biblical theology" is likely to be understood and interpreted in a way, and above all in an ethos and atmosphere, very different from that which was implied in biblical theology as it was before. Unless any continuation of biblical theology is linked with a reaffirmation of the two conditions mentioned above, namely, the presence of some theological flexibility and the need for free scholarly exploration in the Bible, it will simply be subordinated to existing conservative religious categories and will do nothing to affect the attitudes associated with them.

If the loss of the older biblical theology has accentuated these difficulties, it may be thought that biblical theology is not to blame for this, and that the blame rests rather on those who made criticisms of it. But I do not think so. It was not the *decline* of biblical theology that brought about this situation; rather, it was the fact that biblical theology, even in its best times, never really made any deep impression on inherited conservative attitudes. It could be used by conservative tendencies for a time, or used in conjunction with them by some who belonged in a sense to both; but when it came to a decision the older conservative convictions turned out to be much more powerful; and the main conservative constituency and its categories had remained underground or remained untouched throughout. Thus the decline of biblical theology did not affect the conservative evangelical constituency much. Most of them had never believed in it more than marginally, if at all. Its decline affected the situation more because mainstream theology in its use of the Bible from now on emphasized biblical theology less and the critical understanding of the Bible more; hence the increased intensity of conflict.

If there is to be future progress in biblical theology, it is to be hoped that it will take care to avoid misunderstanding on either side of the dilemma just outlined. On the one hand it should make it clear that important theological questions lie open beyond the range of biblical theology, and that biblical theology is not a form of retreat from the modern world into a biblical myth. On the other hand it should make clear its own solidarity with the entire range of biblical scholarship and associated disciplines and its assurance that no useful work in biblical theology is attainable without that solidarity. Both of these requirements, in any case, seem to follow our discussion of the principles of the subject as set out in the earlier part of this article.[11]

Brevard Childs is a great person and a great friend, and one whose paths of thinking have been interwoven with my own throughout the development of modern biblical theology. It is a great pleasure to dedicate this essay to his honor.

NOTES

1. See esp. the crusty and ill-tempered book of James D. Smart, *The Past, Present and Future of Biblical Theology* (Philadelphia: Westminster Press, 1979).

2. On these and other aspects, see the well-balanced article "Biblical Theology" by J. L. Houlden, *The Westminster Dictionary of Christian Theology* (ed. A. Richardson and J. Bowden; Philadelphia: Westminster Press, 1983; British title, *A New Dictionary of Christian Theology*) 69–71.

3. Childs's section on "The Pressure from Without" (*Biblical Theology in Crisis* [Philadelphia: Westminster Press, 1970] 82–87) is a perfectly good survey; but it concentrates mainly on the impact of changing social circumstances and the like. I have in mind a wider and more traditional current of opposition to biblical theology which had long been there and is likely to remain as a problem for any future biblical theology. Not only Childs, but protagonists of biblical theology in general, have tended to understate the significance of this opposition. Smart, *Past, Present and Future,* gives the impression that *any* query or doubt about biblical theology is absolutely wrong.

4. Childs, *Biblical Theology,* 87, mentions a somewhat similar formulation from Gilkey; but he gives the impression that this is a rather individual and idiosyncratic suggestion, and that the majority of theologians are rather asking, Where do we go from here in the use of the Bible? (p. 91). I think that Gilkey in this stands for a much wider spectrum of theologians, and that for most of them the use of the Bible, essential as it is, is dependent upon the kind of theological structures that are based upon the Bible but are not necessarily derived from the Bible.

5. "Neo-orthodoxy" is highly appropriate as an "amorphous category" (the words of Childs, *Biblical Theology,* 78). I find it absurd when Smart attacks him for producing "confusion" (one of Smart's favorite terms) by using this useful term; see Smart, *Past, Present and Future,* 24ff.

6. The appearance of "scientific" scholarship, imparted to biblical theology by the fact that it chiefly involved biblical scholars rather than dogmaticians, is mentioned by Houlden, "Biblical Theology," 69. Later criticism was to show, he says, how heavily this "scientific" work was loaded with presuppositions. The opinion voiced by Houlden was certainly widely held.

7. This point is well expressed by K. Grayston in his review of Donald Guthrie's *New Testament Theology* in *Theology* 85 (Sept. 1982) 374–76. What Guthrie really does "is to fit the New Testament testimonies into a predetermined doctrinal position. . . . In many ways he does not need the New

Testament at all: he knows what the doctrine is and how the New Testament can be shown to support it. Reading the New Testament can never tell him anything new now that his book is written." Similarly also H. Räisänen in a review of Guthrie's book in *TLZ* 110 (1985) 889–90.

8. Houlden, "Biblical Theology," 70.

9. Don Cupitt, *The World to Come* (London, SCM Press, 1982) 22.

10. A good example is the importance attached to the contrasting pair of categories "natural" and "supernatural." To traditional biblical theology it was simply obvious that this contrast, far from being biblical, was false to the Bible and deeply contradictory of it. It is a manifest inheritance from eighteenth-century theological controversy. Yet many conservative evangelicals today seem quite unaware of this argument and consider that an insistence on "the supernatural" is both proper to Christian theology and consonant with their own emphasis on the authority of the Bible.

11. In case it should be thought that I exaggerate the extent of doubt among theologians about the whole idea of biblical theology, I should mention the section by Dietrich Ritschl (certainly a truly "biblical" theologian) entitled "The fiction of a 'biblical theology' " in his *The Logic of Theology* (Philadelphia: Fortress Press; London: SCM Press, 1986), 68–69 (German original, *Die Logik der Theologie* [Munich: Chr. Kaiser, 1984], 98ff.). According to Ritschl, very little of the Bible is "theology," and in comparison with major theologies like the doctrine of the Trinity even the Pauline letters are theology only in "the inauthentic sense of the word."

2

Canon Criticism and the Meaning of *Sitz im Leben*

ERHARD S. GERSTENBERGER

Since the early 1960s, Brevard Childs has made major contributions in his attempt to move beyond an old and biased biblical theology to a new, academically sound, and open-minded theology of the Christian community. While his program is inspiring it also has its disconcerting aspects. What does it mean to take seriously the decision concerning canon made by the primitive church, and consequently to base modern exegesis on the *canonical* texts? Does this approach provide a secret opening for fundamentalism, the seductive opportunity to harmonize biblical conflicts of faith, to level out historical, cultural, and social discrepancies, to homogenize the biblical message—and in the interest of whom? Is this the heretical lust for clarity and unquestioned authority (cf. Exodus 32 in its canonical shape)? Such is by no means the case with Brevard Childs's own work. But would others recognize the dangers of his approach, reducing his careful analytical work to a slogan?

Instead of analyzing the impressive work of Brevard Childs in order to discover its strengths and possible weak points, I propose here to reflect freely on one central issue at stake in a canonical approach, namely, the situational fixation of the Word of God, its incarnation in the social history of humankind. These unpretentious thoughts from a distance are meant as a small contribution to an intercontinental dialogue with my former teacher, present friend, and beloved colleague.

Word and Reality

Every word, whether spoken or chanted, written or televised, repeated or freshly coined, has its proper context that determines its meaning. There is no such thing as a free-floating word without any solid contextual roots, although loose bits of language occasionally may leave that impression. The soil of all meaningful human articulation is in their interaction; that is, words and language grow from social intercourse. To articulate words is, by definition, to communicate. Soliloquies in themselves are of no interest. If, however, they fall prey to the neighbor's curiosity they immediately enter the realm of communication. All this means that unless we grasp the communicative situation of any word or phrase we are unable to understand it correctly. Words are like bones: They seem rather unattractive and provide little nourishment without their flesh and meat.

At the same time we must appreciate the mobility of words and language. If we talk about "roots" and "soil" in regard to linguistic communication we do not mean to suggest any kind of petrifaction or sclerosis. On the contrary—in fulfilling their purpose, words are in motion all the time. They are vehicles of meaning, bridging space, time, and other gaps of differentiation. This means nothing more and nothing less than: Words are uttered in order to travel from one life situation to another, taking with them signals and calling for reactions to their place of origin. Such mobility does not mean that words are therefore vagabonds. As soon as a word reaches its addressee it becomes corporal and social again, taking its place, as it were, in the new texture of personal and communal relations. This place will differ more or less from the place occupied earlier in the speaker's world. Yet words do create ties between environments, those of speakers or writers and those of hearers or readers. And what about their signification? Do words accumulate meaning on their journeys? To the contrary, they are unloaded and reloaded every now and then like trucks that operate between various ports of destination.

It seems that the mobility of words causes major problems for the modern exegete. The interpreter of the OT in particular constantly deals with words and texts coming from a thousand-year history of a distant and ancient people. These texts have been transmitted through the ages without interruption by communities of faith, and largely within the worshiping assembly. The texts have changed their life situations innumerable times. Together with these shifts, naturally, there occurred transmutations of meaning. How can we deal with these ancient witnesses? Looking at the long chain of transmission and of tradents of text and meaning, I cannot help but think that each station where a text incorporated itself, from the beginning to the present day, is worth serious consideration. It is difficult to imagine that any particular time or interpretation acquired or set forth a—or "the"—normative meaning. Why is that so?

Each historical situation has its own dignity and importance which may not be used one against the other. Speaking in traditional theological terms we may put it this way: God addresses humanity, taking its situation with utmost seriousness, no matter how humble and restricted the addressee's life might be. In fact, according to the Bible, God prefers the lowly situations of his weak and lost partners. Consequently, there certainly are no situations of power and glory to be singled out as guidelines for the interpretations of others. Considering the nature of the biblical God we might think of those situations of salvation and liberation typical of the biblical story. Could they be normative for our theological interpretations? Perhaps, but for the time being we should recognize the essential parity between all situations in which God has acted. Neither Exodus nor prophets, neither imperial Israel nor exilic dispersion provide an authoritative pattern for OT theology. The criteria for our interpretations, and eventually for our text preferences (cf. biblical pericopes and lectionaries) invariably emerge through a delicate interplay between present-day exigencies and interests on the one hand and biblical witness on the other.

How can the exegete become aware of that formative reality behind the text? Readers of the Bible always have felt the need to place its words within their contexts, to be sure. The collocation has been different, however, in varying times and schools of thought. In the past, a very popular mode of planting ancient texts into their respective realities was their personalization. To determine the supposed speaker or author of a given word was considered sufficient. Thus the psychic reality of the individual author became all-important. What did he feel when he spoke or wrote these words? Sunday school exegesis up to this day quite often asks this question and by asking it already strikes a juncture between the ancient situation and today's life experiences. Other approaches to the reality underlying ancient texts include the archaeological claim that hard and fast evidence drawn from Palestinian or other ancient Near Eastern sites may be essential in locating or even proving certain biblical texts. Furthermore, all the ethnographic, linguistic, historical, and religious research in the biblical and related fields have had as their main purpose to provide the real background for the words and the Word of the Holy Writ.

In spite of all these efforts modern exegetes have been haunted, among other things, by their failure to realize fully and adequately the elusive *Sitz im Leben* of the biblical words and therefore to miss their real meaning. For this reason, modern form criticism, cult-functional analysis, and sociological investigation in OT research since H. Gunkel and S. Mowinckel turned its attention to social customs and institutions. The true background for biblical texts, they argued, is neither individual personalities nor abstract culture but human interaction in definable institutions. Recurring rites and procedures prompted by the exigencies of group life are the matrix for the origin and—still more important—the transmission and regular use of those texts that have come down to us in the Bible. Much recent research in anthropology, linguistics, and folkloristics would support this view.

The individualistic and historicist way of text analysis thus is modified, opening up to include broader, communal views. History, it seems, acquires a new dimension. It is no longer only a punctual and abstract affair, connected to previous and subsequent events by threads of cause and effect. Rather, it is the continuous experience of groups of people. The foundations of history, in fact, are the various social groupings and their interactions. Social history, then, becomes the primary concern for those who want to elucidate the background of biblical texts. The basic idea is that human interaction tends to become ritualized, and that ritualized interaction produces patterns of speech that can be classified. The modern exegete, of course, starts with textual analysis. By way of inference from its patterns and by comparing relevant life situations in similar societies the interpreter may be able to recover the true *Sitz im Leben* of given texts.

Types of Life Situations in the Old Testament

The OT indeed confronts us with a great variety of life situations. There are synchronic diversities in that contemporary groups established themselves from various local or social perspectives, and there are diachronic variations resulting from successive transformations of social bodies. The modern exegete has to follow up both lines of coordinates and determine as closely as possible the exact position of each given text.

In general and according to research done so far, we may expect the following main areas of life to be represented in OT texts: cult and cultic offices, educational processes, juridical proceedings, warfare and military activities, family life and strife, entertainment and celebration. All these are part of the synchronic level of affairs. Other areas find only occasional expression in extant OT literature, so that they hardly may be considered, from an OT perspective, as text producing: for example, daily labor, household affairs and the daily life of women, magical operations, applied sciences like architecture or navigation, and diplomatic correspondence. Although countless texts must have existed in these fields, they did not enter significantly into OT tradition.

On the diachronic level we have to take account most of all of a sequence of nomadic, tribal, urban, imperial, and ecclesiastical forms of organization, all of which left their stamps on OT tradition. But the OT as a whole cannot be understood as being exclusively tied to any one of these stages of Israel's social history. Moreover, special historical events, identifiable through names and places, sometimes have left their mark, but all of them—from the times of Moses to those of Ezra—have been substantially dissolved into the extant documents of Israel's faith.

The redactional processes, of course, demand special attention in this context. The text-producing situations brought forth the compositions of words and provided the first *Sitz im Leben* for their repeated use. Gradually, continued interest in the customary, useful, and effective texts stimulated their collection, and, to a certain degree, their authorization by the group. Thus collections of laws, proverbs, hymns, tales, and so on came together in order to be used for determined, ritualized purposes. Speaking in broad terms, we may locate these partial and functional collections of OT genres in the preexilic period. Each tradition-building group acted on its own and within a particular area of life; no normative ambitions for the whole of Israel were involved. (I would include here the authentic deuteronomic reform texts, if there are any.)

A significant change took place in exilic and postexilic times. A restored, theocratic community gathered together all the relevant traditions of old, joining them in the holy Torah that became the supreme norm for all areas of communal and private life. "Prophets" and "Writings," being lesser parts of the canon of authoritative writings, followed in due course. Is this "canon decision" of the early Jewish community to be regarded as the pivotal event, the point at which the OT text finally was created? Are all the preceding productions and uses of text merely preparatory to the authorization of the written Torah under Ezra?

The answer must be in the negative. First of all, the community that created the Torah was a particular one. It was by no means the standard, eternal social or ecclesiastical organization decreed by God for all times and all peoples. Therefore, its decisions, no matter how important they have proved to be, do not have binding force. Theologically speaking, the revelatory value of the canonized text produced by the early Jewish community is neither higher nor lower than that of those texts which originated in former stages and groups. Second, the collection of authoritative material was no homogeneous affair, because existing groups and tensions did not simply disappear in postexilic Israel. Remaining tensions include those between the exiled elite and those left in Judah, between rich and poor, clerics and laity, women and men. There were even factions within the dominating clergy (cf. Numbers 16). The emerging canon could not be a uniform or unilateral document, nor a univocal authority. Third, the older traditions that were brought together in the Torah were quite diverse, like stones from different quarries. No matter how diligently polished by selective and redactional policies, they remained witnesses of distinctive earlier experiences with God.

Consequently, the formation of the Torah was a very normal process of text production. A particular group, in this case the early Jewish community in its various locations and social shapes, used older materials in an updated form in order to articulate its own existence, conduct worship services, educate young people, administer justice, and so on. The focal point of all activities probably was the assembly of the congregation. Here all vital concerns met, and here the authoritative will of Yahweh was experienced in the reading of scripture. Divine instructions for the members' life, admonitions, chastisement, absolution, and comfort occurred in the assembly. Thereafter, the Word of God accompanied the members into their daily routines, being remembered, restudied, and rehearsed whenever necessary. In a broad sense, Torah reflects its *Sitz im Leben,* the early Jewish congregation.

Community, Authority, and Canonicity

All biblical words have their specific place of origin—their *Sitz im Leben*—and their own transmission history. What made these words and texts so worthy to be transmitted through generations? Apart from their function within the group, or rather through it, the communities expressed their experience with the savior God, Yahweh. The words that tell about encounters with him have been constantly reused, not because they were sacred words, but because they carried promise and hope to advance new encounters with him and new salvation experiences.

The main contents of all Israelite experiences with Yahweh may be epitomized in the word "solidarity." Israel's desire, at all levels, during all the historic periods, and in all social groupings, was to maintain itself within that life-giving solidarity of God. What Israelites longed for was love through justice and peace. For the early Israelite this implied a very strong emphasis on the welfare of one's own group. In fact, we may discern in OT literature an annoying, because egocentric, hunger for that equity and order that favors one's own group. Yahweh most of all is a God who maintains the social position and structure of his followers. This side of the coin is in fact firm evidence of the Word's incarnation in social structures. There is another side which shows a God who corrects crimes and faults, who sides with those who are weak or have been wronged, who invites in the outsiders and the uprooted. These features for their part prove that God has not been suffocated in a society's concerns with itself.

If the central message within the varying testimonies of the OT is that of a helpful God, then the search for the "authority" of the texts is altogether wrong. Water in the desert has no authority but it fertilizes the ground and makes it blossom. Thus the biblical texts have no authority but they open up paths toward real human life in a wholesome social environment. They thus testify to the reign of God, and in being used and reused in their proper places they bring about that reign. Admonitions within the Bible to heed and to practice the Word are nothing else than tentatives—justified by special circumstances—to keep the community of faith together, and thus keep in contact with the living God. Coercion comes not from the Word, but from its ecclesiastical administrators.

Decisions about canon, besides being plain text-producing mechanisms, may be necessary in certain moments in the history of a given community of faith, if taken in self-defense and in order to establish the group's identity. But they must not claim universal validity, and, in fact, such decisions never have had the force of an absolutely binding restriction. If they ever became laws to be strictly obeyed, as in times of fierce orthodoxy, they certainly seriously hampered God's activities and his revelatory solidarity with new groupings of believers.

The Christian community renewed and modified the early Jewish community's decision concerning the canon. But it certainly was an arduous, ambivalent, and never totally conclusive development that led to the Christian canon of Scripture. In the beginning we find a great deal of unrestrained, joyful use of OT Scripture on the part of small, struggling congregations. At the end canon becomes a powerful weapon in the imperial church's battle against dissidents. Yet one should also recognize the fact that Christianity's decisions concerning the canon accompanied that remarkable transition of the old Jewish faith in Yahweh to the lower strata of the Hellenistic Roman society. In this regard the emerging new canon (in open conflict with a shorter Jewish canon) signifies the production of meaningful texts for the Christian community. It happened, as it were, by using and remodeling the holy texts of the forebears.

The Sitz im Leben *of the Exegete*

In the European hermeneutical discussion there is hardly ever any reference to the exegete's real predisposition, that is, to the interpreter's affiliation with certain social, economic, ethnic, sexual, political, or cultural groups. This is very strange indeed, because one no less than Rudolf Bultmann long ago called attention to the prime importance of "preconceived ideas" in all interpretive proceedings. But Bultmann actually limited preconception to intellectual, emotional, and religious dispositions. The *Sitz im Leben* of the exegete did not enter his considerations. This is very different with some Latin American theologians of our time. They point out vehemently the Babylonian Captivity of theology and church, naturally including exegesis. They sharpen our eyes so that we may realize our being tied up in oppressive systems of tremendous economic (and military, political, and social) power. Feminist exegetes discover the sexist interpretation of the male majority of their colleagues. Black interpreters unmask a predominantly white and therefore racist reading of the Bible. In short, every exegete is a child of his or her own environment, bringing along her or his own world view and experiences when approaching the biblical texts.

There is no fault in this well-known and little-heeded fact, let alone that there is absolutely no help against it. There is no fault (the only fault being the failure to admit this entanglement with one's situation); on the contrary, the exegete's situational dependence is a prerequisite for any successful exegesis. The presence of God, experienced in biblical situations and testified to in biblical texts, strives to reincarnate itself in present-day milieus. It is necessary to prepare today's *Sitz im Leben* for this re-incarnation. Exegetes are in a better position than most to make themselves and their contemporaries aware of the character and limits of their own situation. It is the community of readers of the Bible who become aware of their own environment, its structures, anxieties, hopes, vicissitudes, and barriers. The present economic and political, as well as the cultural and religious, texture of society at large and its subdivisions is the frame to be investigated. The Christian community and its relation to coexisting groups and institutions need to be clarified. In short, present-day social reality (including the global aspects of world population) has to be scrutinized by the modern exegete because this reality is the only one that can become the vessel for the biblical proclamation of the reign of God. A number of issues should be considered in this effort to survey the ground for such proclamation.

First of all, we note a great many differences between reality today and reality in OT times. Science and industrial techniques have changed the world. Social relations have undergone substantial transformations. Psychological conditions and outlooks at least superficially have been modified. Cultural patterns have been in constant flux. Educational systems and contents were revolutionized. The list could go on. On the other hand, the exegete certainly can recognize more than a few similarities between old and new situations. After all, these analogies give rise to our hopes that ancient messages of the reign of God may find an echo in our own times. Similarities not only include the inner life of the person, what has been called the "eternal humankind," but the functioning of social relations, the basic modes of how people construct their social systems and keep them going.

Perhaps the central theological question today is, indeed, How can the old messages of solidarity between God and humanity be implanted in our contexts? Or better, Does there exist a desire in our societies for justice and love, a desire analogous to that reflected in the Bible? Certainly there does. Exegetes of the OT are in an exceptionally favorable position to find in their own world longings for peace and equity that closely resemble those of the OT tradition. To tell the truth, some of these sentiments may even come from OT roots. In any case, they are extant today around the globe in all true movements of liberation, emancipation, and humanization. It seems that these favorable developments sprang up—just as in OT times—in opposition to oppression, racism, sexism, exploitation, military expansion, or ecological devastation. Exegetes, just by looking at their own contemporary situation, are liable to exclaim, The reign of God is at hand! Their work with the biblical texts should be greatly enhanced by this discovery of analogous dimensions in the present day.

To be sure, today's life situations also exercise a normative function. They predispose exegetes to ask predetermined questions and to find fixed answers according to what they and their groups expect from the texts. This restrictive role of *Sitz im Leben* is much easier to recognize in historical texts than in our own text-producing interpretation. Nonetheless, the exegete's living conditions and experiences today have a tremendous influence on his or her work, often exceeding by far all possible ancient decisions concerning the canon. Exegesis then becomes eisegesis, and the truths extrapolated from the texts are identical to those values forged within the exegete's own community. Such a state of affairs is untenable. It signifies nothing else than an absolutization of one's own position and privileges. The whole world becomes centered, and immutably so, in one's own group, value system, social or ethnic order, and all other values, especially all the "others," become subordinate or subservient to one's own proper interests. The exegete, when falling into this temptation, in fact becomes "like God." The dialogue with the testimonies of biblical faith, so indispensable for a historical—that is to say, limited—existence, proves impossible at this point. Equally barred is the exchange with differing contemporary communities of faith. Once again: No text-producing (interpreting) situation may impose itself on others; God is acting in all of them.

Yet there cannot be denied the right of a theological proposition that insists also on the positive function of the exegete's contextuality. The parameters of our present world are destined to receive the proclamation of the reign of God. If so, the structure of contemporary reality gives some sort of orientation as to the path and goal of biblical exegesis. The exegete and his or her community pose *their* problems, ask *their* questions, open *their* lives in the face of a God who is ready to help now. This means that the dialogue with the ancient (and contemporary) witnesses invariably is directed back and forth, but certainly aims at the present-day situation. Thus, biblical texts stimulate and correct modern theological reflection, and necessarily so, because no single interpretation or confession of faith could ever express the full truth about God and the world. Taken this way, all the biblical witnesses retain their independence. Each one of them, including those of layers of texts and stages of textual tradition, has its word to say, not being subject to anybody's supervision. We, the interpreters living in the dying twentieth and the coming twenty-first century after Christ, are entrusted responsibility for our churches and states, and for all of humankind. The signs of the times are fairly obvious. Thus we should do our work of interpretation, taking with equal seriousness the witnesses to God's action right near to us—as did the OT prophets— and the witnesses from the remote past of the biblical people.

Conclusions

Each "word" or "text" that is a document of faith points to its proper *Sitz im Leben* where God's action has been experienced. In interpreting texts we must consider immediately the reality behind the text. Text without reality does not exist. Strangely enough, however, our own reality becomes involved in exegesis and theology. We are not "objective" researchers, if any such person exists at all. We bring our visions with us and deposit them into our interpretations, which become new texts· about the presence of that savior God of old. Mysteriously, the communication between today's interpreters and ancient believers is through the experience of social reality. And if we need any orientation as to which texts to read and how to read them we have to find our canon in our time. Canon originally means "orientation" and not "coercion." The old orientation-seeking decisions of our Jewish and Christian forebears were valid only for their respective times and environments. They always had to be revised, and in fact they often were. Moreover, no community of faith ever lived exclusively on canonized literature. But contemporary orientation is highly necessary in order that fresh encounters with the living God may find articulation in new texts of faith.

BIBLIOGRAPHIC NOTE

The following works were consulted in the preparation of this paper: R. Albertz, *Persönliche Frömmigkeit und offizielle Religion* (Stuttgart: Calwer Verlag, 1978); J. Miguez Bonino, *La fe en busca de eficacia* (Salamanca, 1977); W. Brueggemann, *The Psalms and the Life of Faith* (JSOTS 17; Sheffield, Eng.: JSOT Press, 1980); G. Casalis et al., *Bibel und Befreiung* (Freiburg/Munster, 1985); B. S. Childs, *The Book of Exodus* (Philadelphia: Westminster Press, 1974); idem, *Introduction to the Old Testament as Scripture* (Philadelphia: Fortress Press, 1979); M. Clevenot, *Approches matérialistes de la Bible* (Paris: Editions du Cerf, 1976); J. S. Croatto, *Exodus: A Hermeneutics of Freedom* (Maryknoll, N.Y.: Orbis Books, 1981); Chr. Hardmeier, *Texttheorie und biblische Exegese* (BEvT 79; Munich: Chr. Kaiser Verlag, 1978); J. H. Hayes, ed., *Old Testament Form Criticism* (TUMR 2; San Antonio: Trinity University Press, 1974); F. Houtart, *Religion et Modes de Production Precapitalistes* (Brussels: Editions de l'Université de Bruxelles, 1980); R. Knierim, "Old Testament Form Criticism Reconsidered," *Int* 27 (1973) 435–68; D. A. Knight and G. M. Tucker, eds., *The Hebrew Bible and Its Modern Interpreters* (Philadelphia: Fortress Press; Chico, Calif.: Scholars Press, 1985); C. Mesters, *Por tras das palavras* (vol. I; Petropolis: Editora Vozes, 3rd ed. 1977); C. Mesters et al., *A Biblia como memoria dos pobres* (Estudos Biblicos 1; Petropolis: Editora Vozes, 1984); J. L. Segundo, *Liberación de la teología* (Buenos Aires: Ediciones C. Lohlé, 1975); E. Tamez, *La Biblia de los oprimidos* (San José, Costa Rica: Apdo, 1979); R. de Vaux, *Les institutions de l'Ancien Testament* (vol. I, Paris: Editions du Cerf, 2d ed. 1961; vol. II, Paris: Editions du Cerf, 1960).

3

Biblical Interpretation: Meeting Place of Jews and Christians*

PAUL D. HANSON

The contribution of biblical studies to the theological reflection of religious communities is perceived in different ways. For some, biblical scholarship is responsible for establishing the most reliable possible form of the text of Scripture and for elucidating what it meant in its original setting, so as to offer a firm foundation for the constructive activities of theologians.[1] Others, while acknowledging that role, go further and expect biblical scholars to address normative issues of faith and ethics from the perspective of the biblical sources, though within this group opinions differ regarding the point at which the biblical scholar's work ends and the theologian's or ethicist's begins. Virtual unanimity prevails, however, on the next level of theological reflection—that dealing with the fundamental presuppositions and principles informing the theological task. Here biblical scholars traditionally have left the discussion to their colleagues in theology and the philosophy of religion.

This essay argues for the involvement of biblical scholars also on that third level. The potential contribution they have to make to fundamental questions concerning theological method stems directly from the primary materials of their discipline. For in the Bible we detect the occurrence of a paradigmatic shift in the manner in which

*This essay is dedicated to an esteemed teacher and friend whose many valuable lessons to his students included the importance of careful attention to Jewish scholarship in Christian biblical exegesis.

matters of ultimacy were addressed in antiquity. It is a shift, moreover, that is directly relevant to the current discussion dealing with theological method.

In the wider world within which the Bible arose, it is possible to recognize an almost universal understanding of religious values and truths to which the earliest Hebrews and their offspring took bold exception. According to that widespread view, religious truth was transmitted by the gods to humans in the form of myths and laws. Its source was thus not human, but divine, being mediated to the community in question by special agents, especially kings and priests. Humans were instructed in this eternal, divine truth through the annual ritual reenactment of the myth, that is, the divine drama ordering and securing reality; it was their obligation to accept the truth of the myth and the laws and institutions it prescribed as an unquestioned aspect of their religious and civil duty.

The paradigmatic shift in the manner of perceiving religious truth that occurred in ancient Israel was of revolutionary significance for the development of human thought. The primary locus of religiously significant events switched from the heavenly realm to the realm of human experience. Yahweh, the God of Israel, was encountered by human slaves amidst their experiences of oppression and bondage; the salvation offered by the religious cult was political deliverance from slavery to freedom; and the world view and values of the community were preserved and handed down not in the form of an eternal myth, but of a historical epic, a narrative recounting and interpretation that by definition was open-ended and subject to amplification and change on the basis of new experiences and reflection. What this revolutionary development accomplished was the transfer of religious warrants from a metahistorical and superhuman realm to the realm of human experience and historical consciousness. Though mythic elements never disappeared completely, and indeed during periods like the late Second Temple Period staged a comeback in apocalyptic circles, the primary orientation of religion in the Bible shifted from the mythopoeic to the historical, with the result that processes of historiography and narrative creativity came to terms with the element of temporality as never before in the ancient cultures of the Near East.

The implications of this shift were far-ranging. (1) Religious authority was no longer ascribed unquestioningly to kings and priests deemed entrusted by the deity/ies with eternal heavenly secrets, but was associated with the loyalties and imperatives arising within the believing community as an aspect of its experience of God's presence within its temporal existence. (2) Religious truths and values were no longer grasped as immutable expressions of a divine order that was to be imitated within the social and cultic structures of the human community, but were drawn inferentially by the community of faith from mundane experiences within which it believed God's presence could be discerned and God's purpose and will could be perceived. (3) The division between the holy and the profane no longer was drawn as a separation between divine essential being and human existential being, but as a moral division cutting across all facets of human experience and calling for an integration of divine righteousness and mercy into all areas of life.

As we move to consider how the shift from a mythic to a historical paradigm bears on contemporary theological issues, it is important to emphasize that we are dealing with a polarity that is less a literal description than a heuristic tool of analysis. The great myths of the ancient Near Eastern world were not utterly lacking in a historical element. In the most common Mesopotamian cosmogonic myth, for example, the role of the exalted hero shifts from Enlil to Marduk and finally to Assur as a result of changes in the international balance of power. By the same token, mythic notions like the divine council and the origin of covenant law in divinely inscribed (or dictated) tablets are familiar to readers of the Hebrew Bible. What we are describing, though, is a shift in the *dominant* mode of perceiving truth, and here it is clear that historical consciousness became a force in Jewish thought to a degree unprecedented among the neighbors of early Israel. This in turn lent a dynamic dimension to biblical religion that empowered peasants to challenge pharaohs, prophets to repudiate priests, scribes to revise laws, and, in general, a people to maintain a remarkable openness to God's new thing to be experienced in their common life. In terms of the literary development of Israel's sacred writings, this historical consciousness led to a lively process of reinterpreting the received heritage in the light of new experiences and to a reshaping of narrative traditions as expressions of a vivid sense of God's presence within the temporality of human existence.

Paradigmatic shifts do not only move in one direction. Religious consciousness can become remythologized as quickly as it had been historicized. Hence the enormous appeal of apocalypticism and gnosticism within the biblical period, especially during times of crisis and uncertainty. The myth promises certainty. It commends truth with an absolutist claim. It eliminates uncertainty, ambiguity, and incompleteness, and offers sure ground for asserting the infallibility of one's position over against the error of those subscribing to other positions.

In general, the early history of Christianity can be seen as a continuation of the historical orientation of Jewish faith. God's presence continued to be experienced within historical events, the future remained important as the people reflected on the relation of God's sovereignty to changing human experiences and insights, Torah was related ever anew to new circumstances, stories were retold so as to give expression to developing understanding, and other stories were added to bring out meanings earlier obscure or hidden. All of this is in harmony with phenomena observable within the earlier history of Israel, and with parallel phenomena occurring within Judaism. The controversies occurring within the fledgling church document the ambiguities and uncertainties that are inevitably a part of a faith reckoning seriously with its particular location in history and its own temporality, and the stand taken by Paul and others against the triumphalism and atemporality of gnostic enthusiasts is a significant chapter in the ongoing struggle to maintain the moorings of faith in the world of human experience. But powerful forces were present to heighten the mythological elements in gospel tradition to the detriment of the historical orientation and the epic-narrative mode. Historical developments, many of them harsh and unrelenting, led increasing numbers not to a renewed grappling with their theological significance but to a renewed fascination with a realm unsullied by the ambiguities of life in the world. For example, disappointments over the failure of God's universal dominion of peace and justice to be fulfilled by the mission of the one they named Messiah prompted less reflection on the significance of the implied contradiction than mythologizing declarations that Christ had established a spiritual kingdom immediately ecstatically accessible to those who would deny the reality of their bodily existence. From the struggles of the first two centuries of Christianity, subsequent ages inherited a deep-seated conflict between mythic and historical understandings of the Gospel.

In the long history of that conflict, a pattern of features developed that threatened to convert a biblical narrative of the covenant relationship between God and the human family into a mythical drama that obliterated the theme of patient waiting and suffering as a part of the life of a people bearing witness to God's righteousness in an imperfect world.[2] Over the course of many centuries a view unfolded that obscured an epic-narrative understanding of revelation in favor of an abstract notion of truth construed in terms of inerrancy and infallibility. The early gospel portrayed the Jewish teacher Jesus of Nazareth whose courageous witness to God's reign led to his tragic death. The mythologized version of the gospel portrayed an otherworldly redeemer figure who summoned believers out of this world into a heavenly bliss. It is this otherworldly, individualized, and asocial version of Christianity that we see presented today as an absolute truth-claim immune to criticism and untroubled by rival religious perspectives within a pluralistic society: God has granted the truth to Reverend X in the form of a Bible that is inerrant and infallible, which Bible Reverend X can interpret for his followers with absolute certainty in relation to all matters. This makes Christ available to those followers as a personal possession guaranteeing both their earthly prosperity and their heavenly salvation, even as it assures the damnation of all those who do not accept the truth as thus presented. While most Christians of the mainstream denominations will not identify themselves with this understanding of the gospel message, elements of it are very widespread and certainly not limited to so-called sectarian groups.

Before criticizing this manner of presenting Christian faith, its benefits must be recognized. At a time when individuals are being confronted with an array of religious options as vast as those of the first century, an absolute claim to truth dispelling the ambiguities implied by human historicality and temporality has tremendous appeal. For the one suspending all doubt and wholeheartedly embracing the truth-claims of a mythologized version of Christianity, a means may be found for ameliorating the threats of uncertainty arising out of a modern cultural setting presenting the individual with a vast array of religious options and with experiences that offer conclusive proof in favor of none of them. But within our religiously plural world, what is the cost paid by the individual or the community that establishes its own security by renouncing self-criticism and historical consciousness and denying the questions and insights of people of other orientations and perspectives?

Because this question is so broad, we shall limit our focus in the remainder of this essay to one aspect of our pluralistic environment, namely, the interaction between Judaism and Christianity. Though sharing much both by way of historical tradition and present values, the lives of many Jews and Christians are affected by the differences between the two faiths and especially by the ways in which those differences are understood. Focusing on the relation between Judaism and Christianity thus can be instructive in its own right and illustrative of the larger problem of the interrelationships between people of different religions or life orientations.

The choice of the relationship between Judaism and Christianity moreover is not one made out of an attitude of scholarly detachment. It is pressed upon us by our own particular history. The treatment of Jews by Christians over a period of almost two thousand years contains a message for Christians, and it is one of the most urgent tasks of Christian theology to explicate the nature of that message. It is not sufficient to place the blame on the Nazis; the German church was too deeply implicated in the tragedy. It is not sufficient to place the blame solely on German Christians; Christians of many lands failed to act on the basis of ominous signs and even specific information. It is not enough to treat the problem as a recent one; the anti-Judaism that was the fertile ground for modern anti-Semitism has a history reaching back to the early church.[3] The evidence points to a cause lying close to the heart of Christianity, one expressed in a set of assumptions that constitute one of the darkest sides of church history: Jews who do not convert to Christianity are not saved; Jews are responsible for the death of Christ; Judaism is based on a crude legalism according to which salvation must be earned by humans; God's covenant with Israel was annulled by God's covenant with the New Israel in Christ. This tradition of lies has grown over the centuries and offered the evil-intentioned open opportunity to oppress, persecute, and murder Jews in the name of religion. Culminating in Auschwitz, Dachau, and the other death camps, Christian cruelty toward Jews must be traced to its roots. Modern European history teaches us that it is not enough to lament past mistakes and pass resolutions prohibiting their recurrence. The Holocaust followed close on the heels of the emancipation of Jews in the "enlightened" nations of Europe, for legal emancipation had not been accompanied by an emancipation of the heart of Christianity from bondage to the disease of anti-Judaism and bigotry.

Especially within a religious tradition that takes history and human experience seriously, that dark legacy cannot be ignored. Franz Mussner makes this programmatic statement in a book published in 1979: " 'Auschwitz' performs a hermeneutical function. For the [resulting] conversion of thought implies a new understanding (*Verstehen*)."[4] One year before the publication of Mussner's book, I had included the Holocaust in a diagram of paradigmatic revelatory events with the same intent of claiming that it comes as a somber bearer of an elemental message to people of faith.[5]

The history of the relationship of Christians to Jews thus behooves us to reconsider basic issues of theological hermeneutics, that is, that area of theology concerning the means by which a community relates to its religious tradition and applies it to matters of contemporary faith, values, and practice. The object of hermeneutical reflection is to foster understanding, that is, a life orientation based on beliefs and values that are trustworthy and good. Hermeneutical reflection involves two dimensions, namely, presuppositions (what in German is called *Vorverständnis*), and an appropriate process of interpretation.

Presuppositions, as that which we bring to the sources being studied, have a great deal of influence on interpretation. And that influence may be of a positive or a negative nature, depending on whether it facilitates our grasping the spirit and meaning of a text, or inhibits proper interpretation. As an obvious negative example, if we harbor a latent anti-Judaism or anti-Semitism, the results of our interpretation will be distorted and erroneous. We will magnify instances of prejudice, overlook elements of self-criticism, and read our sickness of soul into the meaning of the ancient texts. As a corrective to such error, regret for past wrongs and a general feeling of good will are not sufficient. What is further called for is a close examination of our system of belief analogous to psychoanalysis, in which root causes of outward maladies are sought out and analyzed with intent to change the depth-level structure of personality. In its classical form, psychoanalysis is a method combining both imaginative and rigorously historical dimensions aimed at reconstructing both the historical facts of the individual's past and the history of that individual's interpretation of his or her past (i.e., the person's own story), all in the hope of creating a critical self-awareness that can become the basis for a more healthful life orientation. Where root problems are instead rationalized and covered over by outward patterns of seeming normalcy, they are liable to erupt in yet uglier forms.

Some would use considerations such as the above to argue that one who would properly understand the past must seek to rid the investigation of all presuppositions. Contemporary writers on the subject, however, point to the futility of such a notion, since all interpretation is influenced by the views of the interpreter, whether on a conscious or subconscious level. The constructive way to deal with presuppositions involves subjecting them to a rigorous critique informed by an awareness of their specific location in time and space, which is to say, their temporality and the limits within which they operate. This attitude toward presuppositions is fully in keeping with the historical orientation and narrative mode of the biblical writings. It is also congruous with the notion of revelation as occurring within the realm of human experience. And finally, it holds promise of fostering a hermeneutical process that does not force dialogue between different perspectives, but embraces dialogue as an essential aspect of critical self-understanding.

The second dimension involved in hermeneutical reflection is an appropriate and consistently applied process of interpretation. This process, involving far more than the application of technical linguistic skills, grows out of one's understanding of both the nature of textual composition and transmission and the nature of the human's ability to understand the meaning and significance of texts from the past. Specifically in the case of interpreting the classics of Judaism and Christianity, methods vary widely. Recent scholars have been particularly creative in developing new methods, such as structuralism, the new literary criticism, feminism, and social history. Each of these methods has contributed to our ability to understand the past more adequately. It is regrettable, however, that these developments have gone their separate ways, with protagonists ignoring other methods or claiming the superiority of one over all others. For example, those adopting the historical-critical method often look with disdain at methods paying special attention to narrative qualities of texts. By the same token, those taking a literary approach often discredit practitioners of historical criticism as being insensitive to the creative ingredient in all literary activities, both ancient and modern. If we are to take advantage of the insights of various of the modern interpretive innovations, an approach must be found that is sensitive to the multiple dimensions of a literary work.

In the case of biblical interpretation, an adequate process of interpretation must include three distinct dimensions. We can call the first the historical dimension, which locates the text in the world of its origin. This dimension in turn has two aspects, in recognition of the fact that the texts we are treating are located in both a world of external particulars and a creative process. The first aspect of the historical dimension is construction of the historical, political, social, and economic setting (or settings) of the text, that is, the traditional endeavor of historical criticism. Though the ancient setting of a text is never fully recoverable, due to both the incompleteness of the data given by the text and the subjective nature of all interpretation, the recovery effort forces the interpreter to take into account the text's original home as an important aspect of its essential character.

The second aspect of the historical dimension is construction of the narrative, that is, the recovery of the creative interpretation of the world presented to us by the text's "author." This aspect is universally recognized in the case of texts classifiable as fiction. What must be recognized further is that so-called historical texts also include this aspect, inasmuch as historical writings also manifest the creative interpretation of the writer. By integrating these two aspects, the historical dimension of interpretation sets in motion a dialectical process fostering sensitivity to both the givenness of the text's ancient setting and its world of meaning and values.

This dialectical process can be carried out, however, only if the interpreter is conscious of a second dimension of the interpretive process, what we might call the critique of presuppositions. Unless one is self-critical of one's own involvement in recovering the meaning of a text, the results will be distorted, and the possibility of discussing that meaning with others much diminished. Even as the text's location in a specific time and place is an important dimension in interpretation, so is the interpreter's awareness of the specific time and place that she or he occupies. Involved are both a clear awareness of the presuppositions one personally holds and a consciousness of the influence exerted by one's particular social/religious/ideological setting. The result will be an awareness of the limits imposed upon one's own interpretive efforts by one's particular background and home, which in turn will create an openness to the contributions of those coming from different settings.

The third dimension of the interpretive process is theological construction, that is, the creative effort to bring the world of the text and the world of the interpreter together in a process of enhancing understanding. Partners in this process are the text, offering from its original setting a distinct witness to ancient events and their interpretation, and the interpreter, conscious within the modern setting of both personal presuppositions and of the enrichment to be gained from engagement with those interpreting the text from other perspectives. Theological construction within this dialogical context seems fitting in relation to the biblical writings, since it can be viewed as an extension of the historical consciousness that began to develop in early Israel. It functions as a restraint to the tendency to remythologize the Bible by muting the temporality and historical particularity of the biblical writings through locating text and interpreter outside of the historical process. It rather identifies temporality and particularity as hallmarks of biblical faith and seeks to allow the development of faith to continue within a new setting.

Though there is not space to develop the above suggestions into a full statement, I shall conclude by noting several implications growing out of such a three-dimensional process of interpretation as they bear on biblical studies within a Jewish-Christian context.

(1) It is undeniable that Jews have repeatedly been victimized by sweeping Christian historiographies that do injustice to Jewish history and experience. Two such historiographies, romanticism and idealism, have many of the features of mythology that we have discussed above. A rigorous historical orientation serves as a corrective vis-à-vis such potentially dangerous reconstructions of the past.

Romantic historiography releases the interpreter from important aspects of the first two dimensions of the interpretive process with serious consequences for the third. The givenness of the text and its world are not acknowledged with due respect. Along with a blurring of the particularities of ancient text and world comes a distortion of the essential dynamics of the text. The nitty-gritty of inner-community conflicts, political maneuverings, power plays, accommodations to ruling classes, as well as episodes of courage and faith, are flattened into a sweeping reconstruction of the past that is so dominated by the views of the interpreter as to mute the voice of text. This abuse is abetted by failure to exercise an adequate critique of presuppositions. The results of romantic historiography can be illustrated by the history-of-Jesus research, since it has placed at the center of the piety of countless Christians over the ages a Jesus whose Jewishness has been completely obliterated and supplanted by sentiments and values from later cultures.

Idealist historiographies for their part force historical evidence into conformity with a concept of historical process according to which each stage of history is surpassed by the next, culminating in the system of the protagonists. Hegelianism is commonly cited as the prime example of such historiography, with its picture of Enlightenment Germany as the culmination of the entire history of Judaism and Christianity. But the influence of this type of historiography is far-reaching, and can be recognized at the base of most Christian theologies, both biblical and systematic. Accordingly, the exodus is judged to be superseded by Calvary, God's covenant with Israel by God's New People in Christ, the Old Testament by the New, the Law by the Gospel, and so on. The end result of such supersessionist typology is that Judaism is regarded as essentially dead, whereas God's whole future is seen bound up with Christianity. The historical orientation that we commend seeks instead to evaluate the history of Judaism and of Christianity critically and within their own particularities. Modern presuppositions and faith commitments will not be denied, but will be brought into dialogue with texts respected in their own right, both in relation to their historical settings and their creative narrative content and structure. This approach, integrating self-criticism and a respect for the autonomy of classics of the past, will restrain patterns of meaning brought from subsequent ages. It will insist that larger patterns of meaning, be they historiographic, ideological, or theological in nature, must be demonstrated as being in harmony with the biblical materials themselves, though by virtue of the dialogical nature of all interpretation, they will of course move beyond ancient settings and meanings by participating in the world and setting of the interpreter and his or her community.

(2) Even as the particularities of the biblical text's world and "author" will be taken seriously, so too will the full range of contemporary realities be part of the interpretive process, especially within the third dimension of theological construction. This serious attention to tem-

porality and particularity is in keeping with the biblical concept of a God present in human history and experience, and discernible to the faithful within their specific settings. It is also in keeping with the stringent ethical monotheism of biblical faith, according to which God's purposes in the world are in keeping with God's own nature as a holy, righteous, and compassionate Being. This means that even the most cherished symbols and beliefs of a community of faith are not exempted from criticism based on their relation to contemporary issues of justice and mercy. For example, Christians must not plead immunity to the queries raised by Jews regarding the manner in which a particular Christology functions vis-à-vis people of other faiths.[6] Such queries arise out of concerns basic to biblical faith and must be answered within the context of real life rather than in abstract, ahistorical (i.e., mythic) categories that belie the historical orientation of the Bible. Jewish perceptions of the truthfulness or untruthfulness of Christian teachings cannot be expected to exclude considerations drawn from elements of anti-Judaism in parts of the New Testament, vilification of Jews by classical Christian writers, and the deep wounds of pogroms and the Holocaust. And Jewish responses to the messianic titles attributed by Christians to Jesus cannot be expected to overlook the historical evidence that the peace, justice, and healing that traditionally have been an essential part of the promises associated with the messianic kingdom have not yet materialized. For Christians to resort to a mythic orientation by claiming that fulfillment of messianic prophecies has occurred on a transcendent level removed from the general category of human experience is a form of special pleading that both betrays the historical orientation of biblical religion and is destructive of honest dialogue between Jews and Christians.

(3) A historical orientation and a sensitivity to the literary qualities of Scripture and tradition also imply a relativizing of all theological formulations. Positively, this affirms the genuineness of the grounding of biblical faith in human experience. Negatively, it affirms the limits of human understanding, especially when dealing with questions of ultimate meaning. To make absolute claims for one's theological formulations is to shift from a historical and self-critical mode of understanding to a mythic one. On the other hand, to accept that all theological formulations are relativized implies both an affirmation of the historical setting of all human religious experience and the truth of the aniconic principle of the first tablet of the Decalogue. It also sets

the context for a proper understanding of a dimension of contemporary religious experience that has pressed itself forcibly on the minds of many, the dimension of religious pluralism. Whereas the religious homogeneity that characterized traditional societies left most believing persons untroubled by the truth claims of others, today people are growing increasingly aware of the teachings and world views of other religions and life orientations. Specifically regarding our topic, Christians find themselves in a very different position vis-à-vis Judaism when they come to know the latter not as an abstraction or a category out of a remote and dimly understood past, but as the faith of friends and neighbors living courageously and compassionately out of their religious traditions. The fact that diversity is a natural and inevitable aspect of a historically grounded faith has powerful bearing on dialogue between Jews and Christians. Differences can be examined closely in the expectation that some aspects of biblical faith will be preserved more adequately in one of the traditions than in the other, a fact all the more to be expected given the diversity that characterizes the biblical writings themselves. Christians, for example, have learned, largely through conversation with religious Jews, how inadequate has been their understanding of the social dimensions of righteousness. Similarly, Torah is slowly being recovered as a dynamic expression of God's faithfulness to God's people, indivisible in its embodiment of God's justice and mercy. One of the important tasks of theology within the context of Jewish-Christian dialogue thus becomes that of enriching its understanding of life in relationship with God within the family of all humans by drawing freely on the richness of *both* Jewish and Christian traditions. To do so need not be threatening to the identity of either group, insofar as historical particularity is accepted freely as a natural aspect of Jewish and Christian faith. The implications this understanding of relativity and diversity has for the question of proselytizing are of particular importance if dialogue is to be genuine. For Christians, Judaism comes to be understood as a living witness to God's ongoing presence in the world. As a historical faith, Judaism both preserves aspects of biblical tradition lost to or weakened in Christianity and possesses rich postbiblical traditions. It becomes a matter of deepest concern that Judaism's witness be strengthened through understanding and support rather than threatened by aggressive Christian missionary activity.

(4) The fact that groups within both Judaism and Christianity will

reject aspects of the interpretive process outlined above raises the question of how one adopting such a process might relate to those maintaining nonrelativist, absolutist claims for their religious traditions. In relation to such people, it is necessary to acknowledge that the difference is located on a fundamental presuppositional level and that on that level it is not possible to gain a transcendent perspective from which to render definitive judgments. What is called for instead is an awareness of the location of historically oriented methods of study within world views that are as much influenced by specific historically determined factors as any other, and a willingness to place them impartially alongside other positions, be they orthodox, fundamentalist, liberal, or whatever, as legitimate objects of criticism. This will help foster an ability not only to understand other positions historically, but also empathetically to appreciate them as responses to specific circumstances that have integrity in their own right as they seek to order and interpret life for their respective groups. What we must strive for is thus an understanding of other positions in their historical particularity and, as it were, from within their own presuppositions, an understanding fostered by the realization that our own historical orientation is also one held from within, rather than from some universal Archimedean point transcending historical limits and particularities. Hopefully this way of viewing diversity will point beyond the hermeneutical impasse currently hindering interreligious dialogue, and indicate that all stand to gain from a vision of religious cooperation within which we learn from each other without diminishing what is unique and true on any side of the dialogue.

(5) While it is to be hoped that we have made a case for a process of interpretation that combines historical and literary sensitivities with a critique of presuppositions and a dialogical approach to theological construction, one final implication must be made explicit so as to guard against a common misconception. Terms like "historical orientation," "critique," and "relativizing" are often taken to suggest a reduction of theology to anthropology or sociology. In many cases this impression is valid. In the case of the process envisioned here, however, it would be a violation of acknowledged limitations to exclude as categorically impossible or illegitimate religious experiences relating to transcendent or divine reality. A historical orientation insists that all religious experiences are contextualized within the realm of human experience and history, but it does not set limits on the range or nature

of those experiences. Perhaps the most central theme of the biblical writings is that life's deepest meaning is discerned at those points where humans encounter God's presence in the context of mundane activities. The orientation we have described, accordingly, does not seek to remove human discernment of the transcendent as a category of religious experience, but to insist that this discernment occurs as an aspect of historical experience and human creativity rather than as a phenomenon removed from temporality and the restraints and limits of human existence. The problem with myth, therefore, lies not in the fact that it describes transcendent reality, but in its unbiblical conception of the relation of transcendence to the human realm. Mythologization of biblical faith thus errs in two directions: It obliterates the persistent biblical theme of God's genuine involvement in human experience; and it reduces divine Reality by translating it into the frozen spatial idiom of myth. A historical orientation, in contrast, recognizes the authentically temporal and human dimension to divine revelation even as it acknowledges the ultimate inaccessibility of divine mystery to human discernment. Accordingly, the category of experience of transcendent reality is thoroughly consistent with a historical orientation and declares an openness to the rich diversity of experiences of divine presence found within all religious groups. In acknowledging elements of both divine presence and divine hiddenness in such experiences, it deems proper a human response of doxology leading to a life of humble dedication to the well being of all members of the human family, even as it deems triumphalist responses a misconstruction of both the radical historicality of God's presence among humans and the limits of human perception in grasping the nature of divine being and purpose. The sobering thought that even the highest moments of religious experience remain thoroughly human experiences subject to the full range of human limits and errors should have a unifying and humanizing effect as people of different faiths share their most precious histories and stories with one another.

NOTES

1. Influential in the advocacy of this position has been Krister Stendahl's article "Biblical Theology," *IDB*, 1.418–32.

2. Ronald F. Thiemann has recently charted the way toward recapturing the significance of the narrative mode of revelation found in the Bible, a mode long obscured by foundational theologies. Discussion with him has greatly en-

riched my understanding of the compatibility of historical-critical and narrative approaches to the study of ancient texts, when those approaches are properly defined.

3. Important steps toward identifying and analyzing anti-Judaic elements in the New Testament have been taken by two Catholic scholars, Rosemary Ruether, *Faith and Fratricide* (New York: Seabury Press, 1974), and Daniel J. Harrington, S.J., *God's People in Christ: New Testament Perspectives on the Church and Judaism* (OBT 1; Philadelphia: Fortress Press, 1980).

4. Franz Mussner, *Traktat über die Juden* (Munich: Kösel-Verlag, 1979) 16.

5. Paul D. Hanson, *Dynamic Transcendence: The Correlation of Confessional Heritage and Contemporary Experience in a Biblical Model of Divine Activity* (Philadelphia: Fortress Press, 1978) 55.

6. Particularly helpful in bringing such queries to the attention of Christians is Eugene B. Borowitz's recent study, *Contemporary Christologies: A Jewish Response* (Paramus, N.J.: Paulist/Newman Press, 1980).

4

Canon and Exegetical Method

ROY F. MELUGIN

No one has done more to keep biblical theology alive in the past decade and a half than Brevard Childs. His concern that biblical interpretation in the Christian community be executed in ways appropriate for Christian theology has been the dominant focus of his scholarly career. It is well known that, for him, canon is the proper context for engaging in theologically oriented exegesis. It is also widely known that his proposals have generated a lively debate, especially concerning the concept of canon as the primary context for interpretation and over his advocacy of centering upon the final or "canonical" form of the text.

The purpose of this essay is not so much to debate Childs's claim for primacy of canon as the context for interpretation in the church as to focus primarily on which methods of exegesis might be appropriate if canonical context is deemed important. In particular, I propose to examine the contention that the final form of the text is the most appropriate object of interpretation.

We must not neglect entirely, however, an explanation of why a canonical approach is proper. James Barr's recent critique of canon hermeneutics necessitates our addressing this question briefly, even though this is not the primary concern of my essay.[1] Although Childs may have overemphasized the significance of canon, the importance of a generally accepted body or canon of scripture can scarcely be overlooked. While it is true that the communities of faith in the biblical period did not find authorization for their faith and life primarily through a canon of scripture,[2] the fact remains that the church soon came to possess a widely accepted group of books that it regarded as scripture. Different ecclesiastical groups, to be sure, exhibit differences in the list of books considered to be scripture, but what is important is that there was a definite trend to accept a rather large number of books—ultimately called a canon—as the primary authoritative writings for the community of faith. The acceptance of such a collection of books as authoritative has been decisive for the church's subsequent theological activity, for the church has taken seriously the fact that a certain group of books are accepted as scripture, despite the fact that the list has not always been the same.

An important corollary to the idea of canon is the recognition that usage of biblical passages, books, or themes in the church must take place in the context of the body of scripture as a whole.[3] This does not necessarily entail the conviction that every part of the canon is on an equal footing with every other part. It is hard to imagine indeed how everything in a canon of scripture could in practice be accorded equal significance. Some aspects inherently take precedence over others in the Christian community, for example, "new covenant" over the covenant with Israel, the reappraisal of the Mosaic law in the Christian community, or the insistence that in Jesus Christ the division between Jews and Gentiles is broken down. Moreover, value judgments must be made with regard to conflicting textual precedents, for example, Ezra versus Jonah on attitudes toward Gentiles, or the hierocratic Ezekiel 40—48 versus a more visionary Trito-Isaiah.[4] Despite the inevitability of giving priority to some aspects of scripture over others, the acceptance of a relatively large and diverse body of texts within a canon of scripture indicates the appropriateness of examining and evaluating the whole of scripture when making theological judgments.[5]

If, then, we are to take the church's canon of scripture as an important frame of reference for interpretation, what approaches to the text are suitable for that enterprise? Childs answers that the "canonical form" of the text should be the primary object of interpretation, for it is in this form that it manifests itself in the church's canon of scripture.[6]

James Barr has objected to what he sees as methodological confusion precipitated by a move from the understanding of canon as a list of books accepted as scripture to the theological conviction that these books must be interpreted in final, that is, canonical form.[7] The first, he argues, does not necessarily entail the second. Barr is quite right about the logic of the matter, but he does not fully appreciate the relationships between a canon of scripture and the form of the writings it contains. It is admittedly misleading to speak of the "final form of the text," for biblical texts never reached a totally fixed form. Textual criticism is a witness to that fact. Nevertheless, canons of Christian scripture are collections of texts in the form of biblical books. That is why there is a certain prima facie case to be made for a synchronic analysis of biblical books.

Not only has the final form of the text traditionally been considered as normative, but interpretation in the church has quite often occurred without giving primary attention to original setting or purpose. Paul Ricoeur considers this to be proper, because an utterance, once committed to writing, becomes autonomous from both authorial intention and the understanding of its original audience.[8] Indeed, meaning, according to Ricoeur, is to be found in the text itself and in the "world" the text portrays.[9] Childs also assumes that the meaning of texts for the Christian community does not reside in a text's generating context but rather in the canonical form of the text as it is used again and again in the church's ongoing life.[10]

There is much to be said for this view. The very fact that certain books have been treasured as scripture by a religious community locates the interpretation of scripture in the text itself. Indeed, biblical books, interpreted synchronically, have often spoken powerfully to the church and transformed its life. Such an insight taken alone, however, is an oversimplification of the ways in which biblical texts may impart meaning to the church. Texts frequently bear witness to the divine-human relationship in particular historical circumstances, so that it may quite properly be said that there is meaning for the church in the original or at least earlier contexts that the texts reflect. Thus there may sometimes be good theological reasons, based on the witness of the text in canonical form, to concern ourselves with contexts that are earlier than those that produced the final shape of the text. There is furthermore at least one other context in which interpretation of the Bible takes place, namely, the context of the biblical interpreter and that interpreter's own community. It is insufficient to contend that the text itself, in canonical form, is a timeless whole, which, in that form, presents itself to the church in every time and circumstance.[11] The text is not simply a "timeless entity" that floats free of any context save its own structure and content. In every historical situation in the life of the church, scripture is interpreted afresh. Moreover, these changing contexts of the interpreting community affect the way the church interprets scripture. It is proper indeed that the context of the interpreting community should be a factor in the exegetical process itself.

Thus there are at least three contexts with which theologically oriented exegesis might concern itself: (1) the text itself as a synchronic entity, (2) the generating contexts that the texts reflect, and (3) the context of the interpreter and the interpreter's community.[12] Let us examine each of these in turn.

Literary Context: The Text as Synchronic Entity

Childs's biblical theology reveals an awareness that traditional historical-critical methods must be replaced to a large degree by approaches better suited for synchronic analysis. Thus he sometimes employs techniques that are similar in some respects to New Criticism, rhetorical criticism, and analysis of the structure of the text in final form. A canonical approach differs, he says, from such strictly literary approaches by investigating biblical texts from the vantage point of an ongoing faith community rather than from aesthetic perspectives.[13] Such a distinction is proper, but interpretive methods that originated for one purpose might conceivably be useful for a different aim. A theologically sensitive synchronic analysis of biblical books should be open to test the value of any method that deals with texts synchronically.

Synchronic analyses of texts may profitably include study of the structure of biblical books. Childs's emphasis on the canon has already led him in that direction. He sees the Book of Genesis, for example, not primarily through the classic Wellhausian analysis of sources, but rather by observing the role of the repeated genealogical formula, "These are the generations of . . ." (2:4; 5:1; 6:9; 10:1; 11:10, 27; 25:12, 19; 36:1[9]; 37:2).[14] Yet his analysis of structure is somewhat undeveloped when compared with George Coats's structural analysis of Genesis.[15]

We saw above that Childs mentions New Criticism and rhetorical criticism as tools which share with canon exegesis a concern for the text in its present form. Yet he does not make use of such methods as fully as he might. I shall illustrate by comparing his analysis of Exod.

1:1—2:10 with that of James Ackerman. Childs demonstrates a certain awareness of the literary artistry of the text: (1) The Egyptian king is portrayed not as the son of Re but as a "clever despot who sets out to convince his supporters of his plan."[16] (2) The fact that there are only two midwives is related to the "poetic character of the narrative." (3) The narrator "underplays" the situation connected with the order given the midwives by the king by omitting both a spoken threat and a narration of the answer of the midwives. The crafty answer to the king's accusation of disobedience shows the stupidity of the supposedly wise monarch. Indeed, "the frail resources of two women have succeeded in outdoing the crass power of the tyrant."[17] (4) The narrator of the birth of Moses (chap. 2) says nothing of the events of chapter 1, for the reader is allowed to make the connection. (5) The presence of Moses' sister in the story is a literary device for joining the theme of the mother and child with that of princess and child. Furthermore, the sister "tempers the harshness of the exposure by keeping watch at a distance."[18] (6) The princess is a means by which the king's evil plan has once again been undone, for the child is rescued from danger by the daughter of the person who issued the command.

Childs's sensitivity to the artistic form of the text is quite visible, but this sensitivity is more fully developed by James Ackerman.[19] Ackerman, like Childs, recognizes the connection between the opening of the Book of Exodus and the creation account in Genesis, but Ackerman focuses more on the artistry of the language. He points out that Exod. 1:7 introduces the text in "stately, deliberate, repetitive language" by means of a "series of five verbs which supplement one another and intensify the effect, explaining Pharaoh's fear and setting into motion the oppressive measure he undertakes."[20] This becomes apparent in Ackerman's translation of the text:

> And the Israelites *were fruitful,* and they *teemed,* and they *multiplied,* and they *became vast* in exceeding abundance, so that the land *was filled* with them.

Not only does the narrative use these verbs to set the stage for Pharaoh's "fearful acts" that follow, but it also uses them to point back to the language of the Book of Genesis, where God uses similar verbs to bless the man and the woman (Gen. 1:28) and where Noah (a new Adam) is the recipient of a similar five-verb blessing (Gen. 9:1–2). This connection is made in order to show that the multiplying of the

Israelites in Egypt is a result of the "mysterious purposes and hidden presence of God."[21] The narrative employs a five-word repetitive pattern later on:

> So the Egyptians made the Israelites *serve* with harshness; and they made their lives bitter with hard *service,* with mortar and with bricks and with all the *service* in the fields. And all their *service* which they *served* for them [was done] with harshnesss. (Exod. 1:13–14)[22]

The "monotonous, drumlike repetition" elicits from the reader a sense of the deadly character of slave labor. This repetition also suggests that the reader consider the contrast between forced service under Pharaoh and the five-word description of fruitful life (Exod. 1:7), which is "wrought by the quiet power of the hidden God."[23]

Ackerman points to another connection between the exodus narrative and the Book of Genesis, namely, a deliberate use of language that connects this narrative with that of the Tower of Babel:

> In both there is an emphasis on human ingenuity. Both are introduced by the interjection *haba* "come now," with the main verb in the Hebrew cohortative, "let us," followed by *pen* "lest," describing the situation which the protagonists are seeking to avoid. Both stories refer to building activity and describe similar building materials. Both stories stress that man's proud wisdom and purposive activity are in vain, and can lead to his own destruction, when they run counter to the order of things as perceived by Israel. In each story man's purposive activity precipitates a divine counterreaction which results in redemptive dispersion, first in Abraham, and then in Israel. . . ."[24]

At the climax of the Babel narrative, God's descending *(yārad)* to destroy the tower and to scatter the population suggests that he might descend to help Israel in Egypt. After all, God had promised that he would descend *(yārad)* with Jacob to Egypt (Gen. 46:4). The reader's expectation is fulfilled; at the burning bush Yahweh states that he has *descended* to deliver his people (Exod. 3:8), and at Sinai he *descends* to act on behalf of his people.

Ackerman cites still another example of a deliberate connection between this exodus narrative and the Book of Genesis. The word for the basket into which Moses is placed is the same Hebrew word for the ark by which Noah and his family were delivered from the flood. In Exodus the threat of death comes from Pharaoh rather than God, and the victims are the Israelites in Egypt instead of the entire human race. But the aim is similar: just as the whole world is saved through Noah, so also the enslaved Israelites were to be delivered "from the spiritual death of bondage and oppression."[25]

Childs recognizes the theme of God's use of what is weak in the world to frustrate the plans of the powerful king of Egypt, but Ackerman penetrates even more deeply the way in which this theme is developed artistically. Ackerman sees the women as intentional symbols of God's mysterious and hidden power by which worldly rulers are undone by those who are utterly devoid of power. The midwives are engaged in an "uneven conflict" with the mighty king, but their deceit is a part of the purposes of God.[26] They, who symbolize what is weakest in the world, succeed in thwarting the power of the oppressor because the power of God stands hidden but nevertheless at work in their activity of deception. Pharaoh's daughter and Moses' sister also— "mere women"—are further means of Pharaoh's undoing.[27]

Ackerman's analysis is scarcely the work of a canonical critic. His intentions are clearly aesthetic and not explicitly theological. But he most certainly is working with the final form of the text, and his interpretation allows insights into its theological meaning in ways that Childs's less artistic approach does not illumine. This is no criticism of the impressive contribution by Childs to biblical interpretation; it is rather a contention on my part that synchronic analysis of texts must include the insights of literary criticism.

Generating Context and the Value of Historical Method

Historical method has been invaluable in helping us understand the culture and religion of the biblical communities. Many scholars have considered historical method to be theologically significant as well. Childs, however, argues that the attempt to tie theological meaning to generating context cuts off the interpreter from the ongoing significance of texts for the community of faith in every epoch of its life.[28]

Childs is quite correct in saying that the theological significance of scripture lies in its ability to speak to the community in every age. He is by no means alone in his contention that the meaning of texts is not determined primarily by original context.[29] Nevertheless, strong theological reasons remain for reaffirming the value of historical criticism. The scriptures themselves testify to the historical character of divine activity. The Book of Hebrews affirms that "in many and various ways God spoke to our fathers . . . but in these last days . . ." (Heb. 1:1).

Luke-Acts presupposes a history of salvation.[30] So also does the Apostle Paul.[31] The same can be said of the narrative material in the Pentateuch (Tetrateuch) and the Deuteronomistic history.

Because the scriptures bear witness to the interaction between God and human beings in particular historical situations, theologically oriented exegesis may quite properly concern itself with the contexts out of which these testimonies arose. To understand the Gideon narrative, for example, out of the context of tribal life and holy war is to set the narrative into a framework of the historical activity of God. We would undoubtedly lose a great deal theologically if we were to abandon attention to such historical activity, for it helps us better interpret the Bible's own theological witness.[32]

Historical inquiry is theologically important for yet another reason. There is need for better comprehension of the power of religious language in shaping history itself. Philosophers have long understood the role of language in describing or representing reality, but we are now coming to recognize that language also creates reality and, in so doing, is a factor in making history.[33] The potential power of a presidential address to mold history is obvious, but so also is the force of religious rhetoric in creating new directions in human history.

Walther Zimmerli has argued in this connection that the language of promise in Israel was an important power in the molding of Israelite history and religion.[34] Promises create an expectation of fulfillment at some future time; thus the language of promise is a language relating to history—a history that unfolds between the time of the giving of the promise and the time of its fulfillment. The Bible presents God as making promises that are to be fulfilled in history, for example, the promise of the land, the promise of many descendants for Abraham, and the promise to David concerning his messianic offspring. One of the characteristics of this language of promise is that a promise, once fulfilled, retains its character as promise.[35] The promise of the land, long after its fulfillment in the original occupation of the land, continued to function as promise: in the exile the ancient promise, originally fulfilled when the land was first occupied, functioned once again as promise to be fulfilled in the return from Babylon. The original referent of the promise does not exhaust its meaning; it can acquire ever new meanings throughout the course of history.

It is important to recognize that promises not only create certain understandings about history but also that promises have force since they are critical factors in molding human behavior. Behavior can be formed in response to promises; thus promises can be said to shape history. Because Haggai and Zechariah, for instance, saw the Davidic dynastic promise being fulfilled in Zerubbabel, they encouraged the postexilic community to respond in an appropriate way. Indeed, they interpreted the ancient promise so that they shaped history in a very definite way. That same promise in another time was a major factor in molding a new historical direction as the early church saw that ancient promise fulfilled in Jesus. In still another time, it helped to form the understanding and the behavior of Jews in the circumstances of Bar Kokba's revolt. As a result, Nathan's promise to David began an entire history that emerged by means of the community's ongoing interpretations and reinterpretations of this promise.

Inquiry concerning the history of biblical promises can have considerable theological significance for the contemporary church. The history of the interpretation of messianic promises up through the time of early Christian reflection, for example, shows a reinterpretation of the ancient promise in such a way that messianic activity can no longer be understood in the church apart from the Isaianic servant whose sufferings are seen as fulfilled in Jesus Christ. The recognition that this reinterpretation was achieved in history through the power of language can help us discover how subsequent reinterpretations of the ancient messianic promises have further shaped our contemporary theological understandings. And in so asking, we will inevitably discover that the reinterpretations of prior theological understandings often emerge out of a dialogue involving the biblical texts themselves, certain other theological views which have developed in history, and the particular situations in which fresh interpretation takes place. In sum, this dynamic involves (1) the text itself, (2) the history that encompasses both the text's origin and the history of its usage, and (3) the situation of the interpreting community in which the most recent interpretation takes place.

Zimmerli's essay was limited to the language of promise, but his approach might well be applied to other kinds of speech-acts as well, for example, laws, proverbs, pareneses. These too were reinterpreted over time. Surely a better understanding of the character and process of reinterpretation of the church's most sacred traditions could aid us immensely in comprehending the historical character of the usage of our most paradigmatic religious traditions. Once again, then, we might better comprehend how to employ historical study to explore the possible relationships between the Bible and its use in our own historical situation.

The Text and the Situation of the Interpreter's Community

The most basic function of scripture in the community of faith is its role of addressing the church in every age and circumstance so that the covenant people may live faithfully before God. Historical analysis or synchronic study of the "world of the text" should not remain ends in themselves, if the purpose of biblical interpretation is to shape the life of the contemporary church. All theologically oriented exegesis should have as its ultimate aim the illumination and transformation of the interpreting community in the contexts in which it seeks to be faithful.

Throughout the history of the church, interpretation of scripture has occurred in particular contexts for the purpose of aiding the church in those contexts. Paul, for example, interpreted the Abraham narrative for the churches of Galatia in order to deal with the controversy over the law (Gal. 3:6–18). Martin Luther interpreted the writings of Paul in such a way that the indulgence question could be seen from the vantage point of the categories of righteousness by faith versus righteousness by works of the law. The writings of Paul, addressed specifically to the issue of righteousness in the context of the Jewish law, were thus reinterpreted by Luther to speak to a new situation in the life of the church. For both Paul in his use of Abraham and Luther in his use of Paul, the context in which interpretation took place was a significant factor in the way Scripture was interpreted.

It is certainly proper for interpreters to adopt methods of exegesis that are suitable for the circumstances in which the interpretations are to be used. Bultmann, for instance, was concerned that the claims of scripture had become inaccessible to many moderns because of the mythological world view of the biblical writers. He used the philosophy of Heidegger as a means for opening the door to an understanding of scripture so that, in a particular epoch, the gospel could be proclaimed with understanding on the part of its hearers. A careful reading of his essay on Romans 7[36] shows that the exegesis itself is formulated, in part, within the framework of that existentialist intellectual tradition. Phyllis Trible, representing a different concern in the church's life, interprets the narrative of the Garden of Eden from the standpoint of a feminist critique.[37] The questions that she puts to the text are derived from the context in which many contemporary Christian women find themselves. Certain methods of interpretation have been chosen because the author considers them appropriate to the particular task to which she has addressed herself. Robert Jewett has undertaken a study of the Epistle to the Hebrews out of a conviction that its message may be especially suited to a twenty-first century America "caught between reactionary efforts to restore old myths of America as the Redeemer Nation on the one side, and nihilistic ventures that convey a loss of morale and of any sense of limits on the other."[38]

It would undoubtedly be profitable to analyze the strengths and weaknesses of the interpretations of scholars whose exegeses are explicitly intended for the church in a particular context, but such an enterprise would lead us beyond the limits of this essay. It is more important here to indicate how critical it is for scholarship to pay attention to the relationships between exegesis and the contexts in which such interpretation occurs. It is of great benefit, for example, when interpreters who are concerned with problems of poverty and political oppression address the text with methods derived from sociology, economics, and political theory.[39] Or, to cite another example, there may be value, in a society dominated by a variety of secular myths (e.g., the John Wayne myth, the Horatio Alger myth, the myth of Manifest Destiny), for the development of an exegesis exploring critically the Bible's mythical patterns, to the end that Christians may be aware of authentic alternatives to popular cultural myths.[40] Such work would require the development of a theory of myth adequate for both biblical literature and the modern cultural situation. There is always the risk that methodologies from the social sciences might be applied to texts from antiquity in an inappropriate way or that myth may be defined in such a way that it obscures rather than illumines. Nevertheless, interpretive enterprises that are addressed to the needs of the contemporary church, if they are undertaken with care, should prove useful.

Conclusion

The main focus of this essay has been to evaluate Childs's contention that the text should be interpreted primarily in its final or canonical form. He has made an important contribution to biblical interpretation by arguing that the text's theological significance for the church is not to be located in its original meaning but rather in the church's continuing use of the text in every age. Moreover, his insight that the church's scriptures exist in the form of completed books is a significant contribution as well. This essay has attempted to build upon Childs's insights by contending that meaning for the church cannot be located in the canonical text alone. Rather, meaning in a text is profoundly related to history. Of primary importance is the historical situation in which the community must use the text. However, there is also a prior history of textual meaning, which has conditioned the possibilities of meaning for the contemporary interpreting community. All of these factors affect the text's interpretation. Moreover, these contexts must be held together in the total task of theological exegesis. Although individual exegetical projects may focus on only one context, the total activity of scriptural interpretation in the church should embrace them all.

This essay is indebted to the thought of Brevard Childs. He has inspired his students to be serious about the theological character of exegesis, and his writings in biblical theology have stimulated a dialogue that surely will continue to benefit the church.

NOTES

1. James Barr, *Holy Scripture: Canon, Authority, Criticism* (Philadelphia: Westminster Press, 1983), chaps. III, V.

2. Ibid., 65ff.

3. Brevard Childs, *Biblical Theology in Crisis* (Philadelphia: Westminster Press, 1970) 97ff.

4. See Paul Hanson, *The Dawn of Apocalyptic* (Philadelphia: Fortress Press, 1975) 71–76.

5. Childs, *Biblical Theology in Crisis,* 99.

6. Childs, *Introduction to the Old Testament as Scripture* (Philadelphia: Fortress Press, 1979) 75–79.

7. Barr, *Holy Scripture,* 75–81.

8. Paul Ricoeur, *Essays on Biblical Interpretation* (Philadelphia: Fortress Press, 1980) 99.

9. Ibid., 100.

10. Childs, *Introduction,* 75–79.

11. It is not "timeless" in the sense of an eternal entity that has nothing to do with history, but rather in the sense of a relatively fixed text that is the object of interpretation in every age.

12. Much attention has been given to original setting, but there has been

less reflection given to the settings in which the contemporary interpreter works.

13. Childs, *Introduction,* 74.

14. Ibid., 145–50.

15. George W. Coats, *Genesis* (FOTL I; Grand Rapids: Wm. B. Eerdmans, 1983).

16. Brevard Childs, *The Book of Exodus* (Philadelphia: Westminster Press, 1974) 15.

17. Ibid., 17.

18. Ibid., 18.

19. James Ackerman, "The Literary Context of the Moses Birth Story," *Literary Interpretations of Biblical Narratives* (ed. K. R. R. Gros Louis, J. S. Ackerman, and T. S. Warshaw; Nashville: Abingdon Press, 1974) 74–119.

20. Ibid., 76.

21. Ibid., 77.

22. Ibid., 83.

23. Ibid., 84.

24. Ibid., 81.

25. Ibid., 91.

26. Ibid., 87–88.

27. Ibid., 95.

28. Childs, *Introduction,* 79.

29. The New Critics and Paul Ricoeur are noteworthy examples of interpreters who exhibit a degree of similarity with Childs on this point.

30. Hans Conzelmann, *The Theology of St. Luke* (trans. G. Buswell; New York: Harper & Brothers, 1960) 14–17.

31. See, e.g., Gal. 3:6–29.

32. I do not believe Childs would disagree with this argument, but he does not sufficiently emphasize the point.

33. J. L. Austin, *How to Do Things with Words* (Cambridge: Harvard University Press, 1962); Donald D. Evans, *The Logic of Self-Involvement* (London: SCM Press, 1963).

34. Walther Zimmerli, "Promise and Fulfillment," *Essays on Old Testament Hermeneutics* (ed. C. Westermann; English trans. ed. J. L. Mays; Atlanta: John Knox Press, 1980) 89–122.

35. Ibid., 112.

36. Rudolph Bultmann, "Romans 7 and the Anthropology of Paul," *Existence and Faith* (trans. S. M. Ogden; New York: Living Age Books, 1960) 147–57.

37. Phyllis Trible, *God and the Rhetoric of Sexuality* (Philadelphia: Fortress Press, 1978) 72–143.

38. Robert Jewett, *Letter to Pilgrims: A Commentary on the Epistle to the Hebrews* (New York: Pilgrim Press, 1981) 15.

39. See Norman K. Gottwald, "Biblical Theology or Biblical Sociology?" *Radical Religion* 2 (1975) 42–57. See also his major work, *The Tribes of*

Yahweh: A Sociology of the Religion of Liberated Israel (Maryknoll, N.Y.: Orbis Books, 1979) 705–9.

40. See Robert Jewett, *The Captain America Complex: The Dilemma of Zealous Nationalism* (Philadelphia: Westminster Press, 1973), for a fascinating discussion of the relationships between biblical traditions and certain mythical themes in American culture.

5

Approaches to
Old Testament Ethics

ROBERT R. WILSON

I

Much of the credit for the current revival of interest in the subject of
OT ethics must go to Brevard Childs. Although to date he has not
written a book on the topic, in his seminal work *Biblical Theology in
Crisis,* he noted that while American Christianity has been intensely
interested in the problems faced by Christians trying to make ethical
decisions in today's world, there have been few attempts to explore the
contributions that the Bible might make to solving these problems.
With a few exceptions, the so-called Biblical Theology Movement was
unable to provide clergy and laity with an approach to biblical theology that was helpful in dealing with ethical dilemmas, and even at
the scholarly level the movement fostered little interaction between
professionals in ethics and Bible. Indeed, at the time Childs wrote he
could accurately say, "There is no outstanding modern work written in
English that even attempts to deal adequately with the Biblical material as it relates to ethics."[1] To be sure, scholars who write in the field
of ethics frequently discuss the role of Bible, usually the NT, in ethical
decision making, and people who are actually making ethical decisions
often try to ground them rather vaguely in the Bible, but from Childs's
standpoint as a biblical scholar these efforts are hardly adequate. At
the same time, Childs recognized that much of the blame for this state
of affairs has to be assigned to biblical scholars themselves, who in
recent years have avoided taking up the question of the relevance of

their studies for the living of the Christian life. This was particularly true in the case of OT scholars. At the time Childs wrote, the most recent book in English devoted exclusively to the subject of OT ethics was J. M. P. Smith's *The Moral Life of the Hebrews,* which was published in 1923.[2]

Childs's own solution to the problem was to focus on what he perceived to be the central ethical problem of the Bible itself: knowing the will of God. This problem is by no means an easy one to solve. Although the Bible insists that God's will is not secret but has been revealed to the community of faith, there are numerous and sometimes conflicting witnesses to what God's will actually is. The Bible itself does not provide a systematic way for dealing with these conflicts but leaves that task to the community of faith. According to Childs, this task can best be accomplished by undertaking a twofold investigation of the full range of biblical witnesses that bear on any given ethical dilemma. The first stage of the investigation is the description of all of the witnesses in their complexity and diversity. The second stage is tracing the inner movement of the witnesses within the biblical canon. Although Childs feels that this sort of investigation will not necessarily provide definitive solutions to ethical problems, it will delineate the canonical boundaries within which a solution might lie. For Childs, the canon is the context within which the ethical inquiry must take place.[3]

In recent years specialists in both Bible and ethics have taken up the discussion where Childs left it and in particular have tried to deal with the methodological problems involved in using the Bible in ethical decision making. From the standpoint of OT studies, the most noteworthy of these recent treatments are the general discussion of hermeneutical issues in Bruce C. Birch and Larry L. Rasmussen's *Bible and Ethics in the Christian Life* and the full-scale monographic treatment in Walter C. Kaiser, Jr.'s *Toward Old Testament Ethics.*[4]

The work of Birch and Rasmussen is important not only because of its original contribution to the discussion but also because it provides a useful survey of the ways in which modern scholars, particularly specialists in ethics, have tried to deal with the diversity of biblical witnesses which Childs noted. These proposals by ethicists differ greatly in detail. However, once this diversity is recognized, it is possible to point to features that they have in common. First, most ethicists would claim that the Bible contains explicit moral laws or commands which are still binding on the Christian community. Second, most would also suggest that scripture can be the source of moral ideals, which are either explicit in the texts or can be deduced from them. Third, some ethicists suggest that the Bible provides examples of proper responses to God's laws and commands. Finally, many scholars would argue that the Bible is simply one of the factors that influence ethical decision making. Other forces also act on individuals as they attempt to live a moral life.[5]

On the basis of these hermeneutical guidelines for the way in which the Bible is used by communities of faith, Birch and Rasmussen go on to suggest that the most effective way to use scripture is to employ it to shape the moral identity of Christians and the churches of which they are a part. Within the context of the community of faith, the Bible is a source of moral laws, "stories, symbols, images, paradigms, and beliefs" that can help shape Christian character.[6] Christian moral decisions, then, are simply those that are made by people whose characters have been formed within the church. The Bible plays a role in this process of character formation, but it is not the only force at work, and it is often difficult to isolate the various influences that cause a person to make a decision in a particular way.

Birch and Rasmussen's work may well provide an important insight into the way that ethical decisions are actually made. However, it is also important to note some of the problems that are associated with the various ways in which ethicists (and others) have used scripture. First, while most scholars would agree with the general notion that the Bible's own explicit moral laws and commands remain authoritative for the community of faith, numerous problems of interpretation still remain. To take the most obvious case, there is still much basic disagreement about which of the Bible's explicit commands constitute moral law and which do not. The OT itself does not provide separate legal categories for laws dealing with such diverse topics as homicide, theft, ritual purity, the regulation of feasts and offerings, and the treatment of enemies and heretics. All of these regulations are subsumed under the general heading "law," and all are considered equally binding on the Israelite community. Yet most modern Christian interpreters (and some Jewish interpreters) feel compelled to impose categories on the biblical material and then to argue that only certain categories of law are authoritative for the moral life. However, the grounds for distinguishing moral laws from other types of laws are not always consistent or clear. For example, Christian ethicists often try to separate moral laws from the ritual laws that governed ancient Israel's cult and then argue that the former are binding on modern Christians while the latter are not. This sort of distinction leaves ambiguous the status of laws such as those governing the treatment of heretics (Deuteronomy 13) or the laws mandating the extermination of certain types of enemies during a holy war (Deuteronomy 20). Although these are religious laws in that they govern Israel's relationship to God, they cannot be classified, strictly speaking, as ritual laws and so cannot be said to lack authority on such grounds. Nevertheless, they are laws that most Christians would be reluctant to regard as binding. Often laws such as these are rejected on the grounds that they were the products of particular groups and historical situations, but such an argument could be used against any of the biblical laws. In the end these laws, along with others that deal with current issues such as homosexuality and abortion, are likely to be considered un-authoritative primarily because they are at odds with the interpreting community's current standards of morality, standards that of course vary from time to time and from community to community. When the rejection of laws occurs on grounds such as these, then in fact the Bible is not being used consistently as the source of moral norms but is simply being invoked to support ethical principles that have been arrived at in other ways. The dilemma of how to use the Bible's legal material responsibly is a difficult one to solve, but there is clearly a need to develop hermeneutical guidelines if the selection, rejection, and interpretation of laws is not to become completely subjective.

Although many ethicists and OT scholars have focused their attention on the legal corpus when they have considered the problem of how to use the Bible's explicit commands in ethical decision making, some attention also needs to be given to other areas of scripture in which moral imperatives appear. For example, the prophets are often seen as the high point of Israel's ethical development, and their teachings are taken by many Christian interpreters to play a special if not a preeminent role in shaping the modern moral conscience. Yet the prophets also used their divine authority to advocate mass murder and to proclaim God's delight in the destruction of Israel's enemies (e.g., 1 Kings 18—19; Isaiah 13—19). Ethical maxims such as those now found in Proverbs have also been interpreted as a source of moral guidance. However, some of these maxims also seem to be designed to create and support a stratified, hierarchical social system of a sort that the prophets condemned and that many modern Christians would find difficult to accept.[7] Again, it would appear that some principle of selectivity must be employed if this sort of material is to be used in shaping the moral life.

A second area in which further hermeneutical work is needed is the use of the OT as a source of moral ideals. One way in which ethicists have tried to solve some of the complex problems involved in using the OT's legal material has been to extract from the text one or more great moral principles, such as "love" or "justice," and then to use these principles as guidelines for making ethical decisions. There is nothing inherently wrong with this procedure, but there is always the danger that the great principle will turn out to be whichever great principle is in the forefront of theological thinking at the moment (e.g., shalom). Some attention needs to be given to the problem of how to extract moral principles from biblical writers who did not usually present their thoughts in abstract terms. This is particularly true in the case of the prophets, who usually delivered oracles concerned with particular political, social, and religious situations. The general moral principles, if any, that underlie these oracles are not always obvious, and their use in generating modern moral norms needs to be carefully controlled if the risk of subjectivity in interpretation is to be minimized.

Finally, interpreters have long noted the problems involved in using biblical stories as examples of appropriate human responses to God's ethical demands.[8] Almost every biblical character (Abraham, David, Ruth) usually does something that would normally be considered inappropriate moral behavior in both ancient and modern communities of faith. Even the presumably safe principle of *imitatio dei* is difficult to apply, given the stories about God's treatment of Pharaoh (Exodus 3—14) or Isaac (Genesis 22).

Many of these problems are discussed in great detail in Kaiser's monograph, although not everyone will agree with his conclusions. After giving a detailed history of prior treatments of the subject, Kaiser concentrates on the problem of interpreting God's commands, the one area where most would agree that the OT contributes to shaping the moral life. He solves the problem of selectivity by arguing that Israel's moral law must be distinguished from its civil and ceremonial law. According to Kaiser, this distinction is an ancient one, and even the rabbis agreed that the moral law always had precedence over the other types. Furthermore, all laws, whatever their weight, contain a moral principle. This moral principle can be uncovered even in specific, contextually bound laws, although to do so sometimes necessitates the study of parallel laws both inside and outside scripture.

Using a complex set of interpretive guidelines, Kaiser then sets out an interpretation of Israel's moral laws. According to him, these are (1) the Decalogue (Exod. 20:1–17; Deut. 5:6–21), (2) the Covenant Code (Exod. 20:22—23:33), (3) the Holiness Code (Leviticus 18—20), and (4) the core of Deuteronomy (Deuteronomy 12—25). These codes share the underlying moral principle that Israel is to be holy as God is holy, and this principle can in turn become the basis for further ethical reflection.[9]

Space will not permit a detailed critique of Kaiser's discussion. It is sufficient at this point to note that his reasons for including some laws in the category of "moral law" and excluding others are not always clear. This is particularly true in the case of the Covenant Code, which contains ritual law (Exod. 20:24–26, the law of the altar) and civil law (Exodus 21—22, damages) as well as moral law. The same is true of Deuteronomy, which Kaiser analyzes as moral law by arguing that the core of Deuteronomy is organized on the principle of the Decalogue. Furthermore, by elevating the notion of God's holiness to the status of a legal principle, Kaiser is forced to explain away stories such as the account of the divine hardening of Pharaoh's heart (Exodus 3—14), stories that call God's own holiness into question.[10]

II

Although recent work on OT ethics has raised enough substantive and hermeneutical issues to keep biblical scholars occupied for some time to come, there is one potentially fruitful area of research that has yet to be investigated in detail. Although much research has been devoted to the history and interpretation of Israel's laws, little attention has been paid to the way that the legal system actually functioned in Israelite society. In the case of laws that are intended to regulate ethical behavior, this means that there has been almost no attempt to investigate how ancient Israelites actually used their own moral laws. Yet information on this point would not only add to our understanding of Israel's life and culture, but it might also help modern communities of faith to understand more clearly what is involved in living a moral life governed by biblical law.

Although scholars have long noted cases where later biblical writers have harmonized, clarified, or specified earlier laws, little attention has been paid to the way in which Israelites applied their laws when they made ethical decisions and moral valuations.[11] The reason for this neglect is clearly the limited amount of evidence that can be brought to bear on the question. A complete study would require a thorough knowledge of the way in which individuals in Israel made their everyday decisions, and such detailed sociological knowledge is simply not available. However, there is one OT source that can at least supply some hints about the process: the Deuteronomistic History.

Scholars generally agree that the Deuteronomistic History (Joshua through Kings) is informed by roughly the same theological views as those that underlie the Book of Deuteronomy. For our purposes, it does not matter whether Deuteronomy and the rest of the history were written by the same individual or group at one time or whether some version of the core of Deuteronomy predates the remainder of the history. It is only necessary to assume that some version of Deuteronomy was the lawcode accepted as authoritative by the writer(s) of the history, an assumption with which most scholars would agree. If the Book of Deuteronomy was the lawcode of the Deuteronomists, then it should be possible to test the degree to which the code informed their ethical decision making by looking at whether or not it influenced their moral and theological evaluations of characters described within the history. These explicit and implicit evaluations are usually considered to be the hallmark of the Deuteronomistic History, and scholars often accuse the Deuteronomists of judging the characters in their narratives by rigidly applying to them the principles of the Deuteronomic law.[12] If this is so, then we could say that the Deuteronomic law had a marked influence on the way in which the Deuteronomists evaluated the behavior of others. We could further expect the Deuteronomists to have believed that the law ought to be rigidly applied when they made their own ethical decisions. A brief look at the Book of Deuteronomy and the narratives about Israel's early monarchy will help us to determine whether or not this was so. It is important to repeat that we are not interested in how the characters in the narratives actually acted or in the degree to which their actions can serve as moral paradigms for the modern reader. Rather we are concerned only with the way in which the Deuteronomistic historians evaluated the characters' actions and the role Deuteronomic law played in that evaluation.

We do not need to rehearse here the entire contents of Deuteronomy, but it is necessary to point out certain crucial features of the law. Like the covenant code, the book gives a special place to the Decalogue (chap. 5), pointing out that it was given by God directly to the people at Sinai and was not mediated through Moses, as was the rest of the law. The Decalogue is followed by Deuteronomy's central theological affirmation that Israel has only one God, Yahweh. The people are to love and worship only Yahweh and are not to be tempted by the gods of the nations which Yahweh will drive out before Israel during the conquest of the land. If Israel obeys Yahweh's commands, especially the command to worship only Yahweh, then the people will live long in the land. If Israel does not obey, then they will be removed from the land (Deuteronomy 6—11).

These moral laws are contained in what scholars usually consider to be the introductory exhortation of the book. When the writers turn to the specific statutes that are to be binding on Israel when it enters the land, the text becomes more specific and more closely resembles a standard lawcode (Deuteronomy 12—25). Like other lawcodes, the Deuteronomic code begins with a law concerning the altar and the appropriate place of worship. Non-Israelite altars are to be destroyed, and God is to be worshiped only in the one place which "the Lord your God shall choose." There offerings must be brought, and only there can legitimate sacrifice take place. Animals can be slaughtered and eaten outside of the central sanctuary, but such killing must be considered profane slaughter rather than sacrifice (Deuteronomy 12). The law of the altar is followed by laws dealing with what might be considered "high treason" against the Deuteronomistic state. The people are warned against anyone who entices them to worship other gods. It makes no difference whether the enticement comes from a prophet who speaks in the name of the Lord or from a family member or from the riffraff of the cities. Everyone who advocates the worship of other gods is to be killed (Deuteronomy 13).

After the laws governing treason, the Deuteronomists turn to various laws dealing with social conduct, property, and the practice of ritual (Deuteronomy 14—16). For our purposes we need only note one peculiar feature of these laws. In Deuteronomic law the poor of the land are the responsibility of the whole people. Every three years the people are to bring a special tithe in order to provide for the Levites, the orphans, and the widows, that is, everyone who has no resources and has no one else to support them (Deut. 14:28–29). In normal ancient Near Eastern practice, provision for the poor would have been the responsibility of the king, and they would in fact have become wards of the state.[13]

The peculiar status of the king in Deuteronomic law is further emphasized in the laws that deal with the roles of officials in the Deuteronomic state (Deut. 16:18—18:22). Judges are to be appointed locally by the people, and there is to be no royal control of the judicial system at the local level (Deut. 16:18–20). When cases cannot be decided locally, they are referred to the central sanctuary, where they are adjudicated by the Levitical priests and a judge appointed for that purpose. Again, the king is curiously absent from judicial proceedings even at the appellate level (Deut. 17:8–13). Control of the cult is completely in the hands of the priests, and the Levitical priests have the right to make sacrifices at the central shrine whenever they choose to do so (Deut. 18:1–8). The king seems to have no cultic or ritual functions in Deuteronomic law, a sharp contrast with the situation elsewhere in the ancient world, where kings routinely took part in cultic celebrations. The chief teacher of law in the Deuteronomic state is to be the prophet "like Moses," who transmits God's word to the people and functions as an intermediary between the people and Yahweh. The king plays no role in religious teaching (Deut. 18:9–22).

It should come as no surprise, then, that the Deuteronomic laws governing kingship provide for extremely limited royal power (Deut. 17:14–20). It is indeed legitimate for the Israelites to have a king, but in practice he is to have almost no role in governing the nation. He must be a native Israelite. Foreign-born kings are not permitted, and Israelites may not acknowledge the sovereignty of foreign kings, for to do so would be the equivalent of making the people return to slavery in Egypt. The king may have no standing army and may not enter into foreign alliances in order to increase his military strength. This provision is further underlined by Deuteronomy's elaborate provisions for an ad hoc army staffed by volunteer troops and officers (Deuteronomy 20). The king is not to "multiply wives for himself, lest his heart turn away" (Deut. 17:17) and is prohibited from amassing enough money to support an army or a royal court. The only positive task assigned to the king is that he is to make a personal copy of the Deuteronomic law, which is kept by the Levitical priests, and is to read in it all his days so that he will not become overly impressed with his royal status. In short, Deuteronomy envisions a monarchy whose power is sharply limited. If this view is accepted by the Deuteronomistic historians, then we should expect these laws to influence the historians' evaluations of Israel's kings. Weak kings should be praised to the degree that they conform to the law, and strong kings should be condemned for not conforming.

A brief examination of the historians' treatment of Israel's early monarchy suggests that the situation is not so simple as we might expect. The Deuteronomists' treatment of Saul incorporates much earlier material, some of which is promonarchical and some of which is antimonarchical, but there can be no doubt about the historians' overall point of view. As the narratives have been edited, it is clear that monarchy per se is evaluated negatively because it represents a rejection of Yahweh's kingship over Israel (1 Samuel 7—8; 10:17-27; 12). At first glance this evaluation of kingship seems to be in keeping with the laws of Deuteronomy, but in fact the historians here go considerably beyond the demands of Deuteronomic law, which does permit kingship but limits it severely.

About Saul himself, the historians have nothing to say that is good. Out of a reign that lasted either twelve or twenty-two years, they choose to concentrate on three events that illustrate Saul's violation of the Deuteronomic laws regulating kingship. In 1 Samuel 13 Saul is condemned for violating the prophet Samuel's instructions and for taking for himself priestly authority. In 1 Samuel 14 Saul is condemned for not punishing his son Jonathan for violating a prohibition against eating during the holy war, even though the text reports that Saul was in fact willing to impose the punishment but was prevented from doing so by the people. Finally, Saul is condemned for violating Deuteronomy's holy war laws that provided for the devotion of captured people and property to Yahweh (1 Samuel 15). According to the historians, these three legal violations led Yahweh to reject Saul from being king over Israel and to replace him with David. In its evaluation of Saul, the historians apply the Deuteronomic law rigidly and leave no room for mitigating circumstances, even though in each case sensitive readers can sympathize with Saul's predicaments and understand why he took the course of action that he did.

However, when they turn to the narratives about David, the historians treat him in a completely different way. Although in the Throne Succession Narrative the Deuteronomic editors have preserved narratives that are critical of David (2 Samuel 7—1 Kings 2), the overall perspective of the narrative is that David remains the divinely chosen king who becomes the paradigm for all future Judean rulers. This evaluation of David's conduct is made in spite of the fact that he violated most of the Deuteronomic laws governing kingship. Early in his career he strengthened his political power by making marriage alliances with a number of important families throughout the land, and after he captured Jerusalem and made it his capital he arranged similar marriages with important Jebusite families in the city (2 Sam. 3:2–5; 5:13–16). He clearly took on priestly functions when he put on a priestly garment, the ephod, and danced before the ark as it was brought into Jerusalem (2 Samuel 6). Before he became king, he gathered around him a private army to aid his ascent to the throne, and after he established his royal power he used the same army to maintain his position (1 Sam. 22:1–2). He set up the beginnings of a bureaucracy, which included military commanders and royally appointed priests, at least some of whom were not Levites (2 Sam. 8:15–18). None of these acts is condemned by the historians, although they do express mild disapproval of some of his political murders, particularly his slaughter of the house of Saul, and his adultery with Bathsheba. Instead, David continues to be positively evaluated throughout the remainder of the Deuteronomistic History.

It is difficult to discern why the historians applied the Deuteronomic law strictly to Saul but loosely to David. It is possible to make some guesses, but none of them are certain. It may be that the historians had positive feelings about David because he installed their ancestor Abiathar as one of the two high priests in Jerusalem (2 Sam. 8:15–18). If so, their moral valuations of David may have been colored by their own political and religious interests. It may be that they were bound by a positive evaluation of David in the traditions they received and felt that they could not modify that evaluation. However, it is also worth noting that they also received positive evaluations of Solomon's reign but did not shrink from condemning his reign and laying upon him the blame for the revolt of the northern tribes and the establishment of the Northern Kingdom (1 Kings 11). Finally, it may be that the Deuteronomists simply liked David. There is ample testimony to the king's charisma and his ability to acquire and retain supporters even during the darkest days of his reign (2 Sam. 15:13–23). If this is the reason for the historians' treatment of David, then it is clear that they have let their personal feelings influence the way that they applied their own law.

Although we cannot reconstruct all of the details, it seems safe to conclude that, at least in the narratives we have examined, factors other than allegiance to the Deuteronomic law have played a role in the moral valuations that the historians have made of characters in the narrative. Historical, sociological, and theological factors, as well as other influences, presumably mediated through Deuteronomic tradition, may well have been involved in shaping the way in which the writers applied the moral law to the characters in the stories. To summarize the situation succinctly, the Deuteronomic law appears to have been only one of the influences on the historians' evaluations of Saul and David. Specific historical circumstances and perhaps a particular understanding of the whole Deuteronomistic tradition itself may also have been involved.

On the basis of the material we have examined, it is impossible to determine whether or not the Deuteronomists' evaluations of Saul and David are typical of the way they normally made ethical evaluations and applied the Deuteronomic law. But if an examination of other stories in the history shows that the same complex influences were involved in other moral valuations as well, then it might be safe to suggest that the situation in ancient Israel was much like the situation sketched by Birch and Rasmussen. The law—in this case the Deuteronomic law—played a role in the formation of the character of the Deuteronomists, but it was not the only factor involved in that process of formation. Other factors were influential as well, and for this reason the law was applied differently in different situations. In the end the legal tradition could not be incorporated woodenly into the process of making ethical decisions but had to be evaluated along with other ethical influences case by case. The Deuteronomists made their moral valuations on the basis of what they had become, and they acted in accord with the way that they had been shaped by both tradition and the particular situations in which they found themselves.

NOTES

1. Brevard S. Childs, *Biblical Theology in Crisis* (Philadelphia: Westminster Press, 1970) 124.

2. J. M. P. Smith, *The Moral Life of the Hebrews* (Chicago: University of Chicago Press, 1923).

3. Childs, *Biblical Theology in Crisis,* 123–38. Cf. his more recent treatment in *Old Testament Theology in a Canonical Context* (London: SCM Press, 1985) 51–91, 204–21.

4. Bruce C. Birch and Larry L. Rasmussen, *Bible and Ethics in the Christian Life* (Minneapolis: Augsburg Pub. House, 1976); Walter C. Kaiser, Jr., *Toward Old Testament Ethics* (Grand Rapids: Academic Books, 1983).

5. Birch and Rasmussen, *Bible and Ethics in the Christian Life,* 45–78.

6. Ibid., 104.

7. For a discussion of the ethical principles underlying Proverbs, see Brian W. Kovacs, "Is There a Class-Ethic in Proverbs?" in *Essays in Old Testament Ethics: J. Philip Hyatt, In Memoriam* (ed. James L. Crenshaw and John T. Willis; New York: Ktav, 1974) 171–89.

8. See, e.g., Roland H. Bainton, "The Immoralities of the Patriarchs according to the Exegesis of the Late Middle Ages and of the Reformation," *HTR* 23 (1930) 39–49.

9. Kaiser, *Toward Old Testament Ethics,* 1–78.

10. For examples of this procedure, see ibid., 247–69.

11. For a thorough discussion of the history of legal interpretation within the Bible itself, see Michael Fishbane, *Biblical Interpretation in Ancient Israel* (Oxford: Clarendon Press, 1985) 91–277.

12. See, e.g., the representative discussion of Robert H. Pfeiffer, *Introduction to the Old Testament* (New York: Harper & Brothers, 1941) 379–83.

13. For a thorough discussion of the legal responsibilities of kings in Israel and in the rest of the ancient Near East, see Hans Jochen Boecker, *Law and the Administration of Justice in the Old Testament and Ancient Near East* (Minneapolis: Augsburg Pub. House, 1980); and Keith W. Whitelam, *The Just King: Monarchical Judicial Authority in Ancient Israel* (Sheffield, Eng.: JSOT Press, 1979).

6

Old Testament Narrative and Moral Address

BRUCE C. BIRCH

The OT is not a document of abstract reflection about matters of God and faith in the time of ancient Israel. It is the story of God's encounter with Israel and the various responses that engendered. More accurately, the OT is composed of stories about God and Israel which the community has now preserved in the canon as parts of a larger story. It is, of course, the narrative traditions that most obviously preserve the character of story, but even the non-narrative traditions must be understood in the context of Israel's story and the roles played by various subgroups within that story (priests, prophets, sages, poets, or apocalypticists).

Until recently biblical story has not been highly valued as a source for Christian ethics. This has been especially true in the use of the OT as a moral resource. Christian ethicists who have treated the OT materials at all have focused largely on texts with explicit moral content, usually of a propositional or admonitional character. The Decalogue has, of course, received a good deal of attention as a central text for any biblically based ethic.[1] The preaching of the prophets, with its heavy moral and social content, has also received a good deal of attention. Even here the message of the prophets has been used frequently as a source for important ethical principles, such as justice, without adequate attention to the sociohistorical context of the prophetic message or the significance of the place of individual prophets in Israel's story.

The OT is dominated by its storytelling traditions. With respect to God that story begins with the creation of the cosmos and extends to the dawn of God's new age at the end of time. Within the sweep of that divine story major focus falls on Israel's story as a community called into being by divine initiative. It begins with the promise to the ancestors and ends (as far as the Hebrew canon is concerned) with the persecutions under Antiochus IV Epiphanes. Relatively little of the literature of the OT stands outside this story framework and does not need to be understood with reference to the stories of God and Israel. The Book of Proverbs may be an example. Other books that do not refer explicitly to the God/Israel stories nevertheless find it necessary to tell stories that create worlds of their own as framework to their contributions, for example, the Book of Job and the Song of Songs.

In spite of the centrality of the narrative storytelling traditions in the OT, they have seldom been considered for their moral address. How do these stories of the biblical communities of faith impact on our efforts as the church to live life faithfully in our modern world? What does it mean that these traditions have been handed on to us as more than mere ancient stories but as scriptural canon?

It is curious that attention to the moral address of OT narrative should be so lacking, since the telling of biblical stories from generation to generation has been such a common form of biblical influence on Christian lives. Indeed, with respect to the OT, where general ignorance of biblical content is more widespread than with the NT, the arresting drama and power of OT stories (e.g., creation, crossing the sea, David and Goliath, Daniel) have kept any knowledge of the OT alive for many.

This neglect of OT narrative has been part of a general loss of appreciation for the narrative structure of biblical texts in general, as the important work of Hans Frei[2] has demonstrated. Nevertheless the NT has suffered less from this neglect of its narrative features than has the OT, especially where its use as an ethical resource is concerned. In the NT the central theological and moral focus is on the person of Jesus Christ. His birth, life, death, and resurrection, his story, are the very heart of the NT witness, and the narratives that convey that story, the gospels, cannot be avoided. Even during the scholarly "eclipse of biblical narrative" which Frei describes, the story of Jesus remained widely known and highly regarded among church people, while the Old Testament is not now at all well known among church people.

Especially with respect to the use of the Bible for Christian ethics,[3] the New Testament narrative, the story of Jesus, has remained more central than is true for the OT. In crucial ways Jesus does model moral behavior for Christians, whether that be in the popular pietistic slogan "Let me live the whole week through, asking what would Jesus do," or in more sophisticated moral analyses such as John Howard Yoder's *Politics of Jesus.*[4] None of the OT characters model moral behavior in such a consistent and intentional way. Their stories reflect all the ambiguities and complexities of human experience and the struggle to find and live out faith relationships to God in the midst of life. Even the faith community, Israel, does not merely model for the church a moral norm for the faith community. The stories are often of Israel's faithlessness as well as its faith, and many periods are represented by narratives that reflect differing moral viewpoints on events (e.g., the rise of kingship). Unlike the gospel presentations of Jesus, the simple presentation of normative models for the moral life cannot be the function of OT narrative.

Narrative Theology and the Ethics of Story

Recent developments in contemporary ethics and theology have brought new attention to the central importance of narrative and story for the Christian faith.[5] Insights from this work must preface any effort to recover the moral address of OT narrative.

The categories of narrative and story are intertwined. As a literary structure narrative requires "the presence of a story and a storyteller."[6] A story may be defined as "an account of characters and events in a plot moving over time and space through conflict toward resolution."[7] Story is distinguished from history by deferring to the plotting vision of the narrator. Historical elements may be incorporated and even crucial to the story but the empirical presentation of events is subordinated to the movement of the plot toward resolution and the meaning thereby conveyed.

In a now-classic essay Stephen Crites articulated a fundamental insight now assumed by virtually all work on narrative and story, namely, that human experience itself is inherently narrative in form.[8] The experience of our lives flows continuously with developments, conflicts, and resolutions. We do not experience our lives as isolated points or moments. The present cannot be isolated and analyzed, for in doing so it has already become the past and is incorporated into individual or corporate stories. Alasdair MacIntyre has been especially influential in his rebuke of "modern philosophy's version of disconnected, isolated, and action-oriented individuals who live without meaning and have no place to go."[9]

> In what does the unity of an individual life consist? The answer is that its unity is the unity of narrative embodied in a single life. . . . The unity of a human life is the unity of a narrative quest.[10]

Abstract analysis of human experience may be valuable but only if it is remembered that it is abstracted from the more durational character of life. The wholeness of human experience and the meaning to be derived from it are more suitably spoken of in narrative form. "The implication of this view is that without a story that is both faithful to our ongoing experiences and actions, and examined critically for its truthfulness, we cannot be fully human."[11]

All persons find identity by learning and developing their own story, becoming conscious of its dimensions and adding to it as life goes on through adulthood. Obviously we are shaped by contact with the stories of our families and of significant individuals who influence our lives. Our own life stories also come into contact with the stories of communities and cultures. These stories have power as they have resonance with who and what we most essentially are as human beings. If we cannot see ourselves in the stories we encounter, they have little power to shape or transform us. Great stories are those that address us, draw us in as a part of larger stories beyond our own selves, act as a corrective to the distorted stories that seek to claim us, and give new meaning to our own stories. The biblical stories of the Christian faith tradition are such great stories. Their enduring power over the centuries and the rich stories of the church born out of the influence of the biblical story are ample witness to their greatness, but if we lose the ability to remember and tell those stories we also lose their power. Our lives participate in the plot of many stories. The power of biblical stories is their ability to help us see the many stories of our lives as part of larger stories which integrate our life story into stories of ultimate meaning. "Virtually all our basic convictions about the nature and meaning of our lives find their ground and intelligibility in some sort of overarching, paradigmatic story."[12] For Christians that larger story has been the biblical story. In spite of theologians' renewed interest in biblical narrative there is a significant need to recover the importance of biblical narrative, especially that of the OT, in the life of the church.

One of the most important developments in contemporary Christian ethics is a renewed emphasis on the formation of Christian character as of equal importance alongside the shaping of Christian conduct.[13] It makes a difference which stories interact with our personal story to form identity and mold character. When we cease to know or tell the biblical stories and the stories of our faith traditions growing out of the biblical stories, we are likely to be shaped, whether consciously or not, by cultural, national, ethnic, or ideological stories without the corrective of religious values. No amount of appeal to abstract principles of Christian ethics and no calls to Christian decision making and action based on those principles will be of much use if the shaping influence of our biblical faith stories is not a formative part of our identity. Is it any wonder that, ignorant of the biblical story, thousands of well-intentioned people buy the thinly disguised American nationalism story peddled by many media evangelists as a substitute for biblical faith?

Christian ethics is not just the abstract application of a decision-making process. Moral life flows from the way in which we engage the world, and this engagement is structured by our vision, the way we see the world as persons of faith. The biblical story has shaped the Christian way of seeing, not in terms of analytical discourse, but in the concreteness of time and place and people. We recognize something of our own lives and their meaning before God in the stories of those times and places and people.

> As in all good storytelling, we recognize ourselves in the depiction. Not the concept of liberation but the journey out of Egyptian bondage, not an essay on the teleological suspension of the ethical but Isaac and Abraham on Mount Moriah, not the penal substitutionary theory of the atonement but the blood of Jesus on Golgotha, not an exposition of the motif of Agapé but the open arms of the running father. Would a historical God speak to us in any other way than through history first and then in the "history-like" accounts of biblical narrative, the extraordinary in the ordinary?[14]

Biblical story captures the sin and grace, the evil and the good, the death and life that encounter us at every turn in our own lives and names them in the language of faith. It removes them from the abstract and names them in narrative terms that intersect with our own experience. None of this can happen if we remain ignorant of or remote and removed from the biblical story and its moral power. It is the purpose of this essay to address that concern with respect to OT narrative in particular. How shall we understand the moral address of OT narrative in its multiple facets? How then do we foster a recovery of OT narrative as a moral resource in the life of the church?

The Moral Function of Old Testament Narrative

In OT narrative we are confronted with testimony to the experience of reality in ways that address us because of the narrative quality of our lives. Because this is the testimony of a faith community, the narratives *disclose* a reality that unfolds in relationship to God, whose story the community seeks to tell as it is intertwined with the community's own story. In the encounter with God the community understands itself to have been *transformed,* and some of its stories seek to effect the same transformative power in those encountering the stories.[15] Within these two broad categories OT narrative is as multivalent as is human experience. Thus, when considering these narratives for their moral address, it should be clear that they do not lead easily to moral prescription or principle, although many would use them in that way.

Consider first that the OT contains narratives intended to disclose reality. They have the power to reveal the reality of the narrator's experience in ways that make deeper and more meaningful our own experience of reality. We encounter in these stories testimony to what is really real and enduring—about our own humanity, about the God who encounters us in the midst of our humanity, about the community called into being from that encounter, about the world where that community seeks to live faithfully, and about the purposes toward which God moves community and world. OT stories are not susceptible to neat typology or glib analysis because our lives are not like that. This becomes one of the strengths of OT narrative. We don't see there idealized reality but our own. This can, of course, be both comforting and disturbing since our lives include both comfort and disturbance. Robert Alter reminds us that OT narrative at its best "honors ambiguity, acknowledges complexity, and presupposes indeterminacy."[16]

OT stories disclose reality in different ways. Some stories actually create worlds or realities in the telling.[17] Such stories establish their own framework of reality and invite the reader or hearer into that world for the purpose of disclosing there a meaningful word. It is obvious that both of the creation narratives that open the Book of Genesis are stories that disclose reality by creating worlds. Each of these narratives (Gen. 1:1—2:4a; 2:4b–25) characterizes the divine reality responsible for an ordering of the cosmos, the nature of that cosmos, the role of humanity within that cosmos, and the relationship of humanity to the Creator. But in the stories these characterizations are completely different between the two. We are not required to adjudicate the claims of each to truth. Each communicates its truth within the world it sets up. We are invited into these worlds to receive the disclosure of their truth. To the degree that these stories disclose a reality that rings true to our own experience, their truth can be incorporated into our story. We need not stay in the worlds they create or harmonize their worlds so that they are explainable in terms of our own story of reality. We can incorporate the different truths of the divine as transcendent and intimate, of humanity as created in the divine image and as related to all of creation, and of creation as good but also containing the responsibility of choice and its consequences.

There are OT narratives other than creation stories that create worlds. The narrative opening of Job creates a world absolutely essential for the context of tension (some would say irony) in which the unfolding dialogues of Job find their meaning. The Song of Songs creates a timeless world of its own for the poetry of lovers. The poetry would lose much of its power if forced into some more mundane and common reality. Its world suggests a world open to love which can be disclosed in the midst of, perhaps even in spite of, the other stories of reality out of which we live.

Most narratives that disclose reality do not in themselves seek to set up the worlds of reality out of which they operate. Most narratives are actions or plots which assume a world and seek to describe events and characters in that world. In doing so they may deepen our own experience of reality, and that deepening may be enhanced by study and reflection on the stories so that we better understand the reality they assume and can therefore be more open to disclosure within that reality. The episode of Moses encountering God out of the burning bush in Exodus 3 is a good example. This narrative is not concerned to establish a world. It assumes a world that includes both the sociopolitical realities of bondage and the religious experience of theophany on a sacred mountain. This narrative is much more concerned with the beginning of a plot line which moves through successive episodes to climax in the deliverance of the Hebrew slaves in the wondrous event of the crossing of the sea. To enter this story is, however, to find in its plot important disclosures concerning the nature of divine reality and human vocation in relation to that divine reality.

The disclosing of reality resides in both the story and the storyteller. After reading Phyllis Trible's retelling of the story of the Book of Ruth,[18] this writer wondered how he could ever have read that story and failed to see so many things. The failure was not in the story, a story of women's courage in a man's world which has been fixed in its text for centuries, but in the eyes with which the story was read and the understanding with which it was received. Hearing the story of Ruth told so many times with Boaz as hero and Ruth as rescued victim imposes another story even upon our reading of the text. It is thus well to remember that in our efforts to be open to the disclosure of reality from the narratives of the OT we must be prepared to be critical in our examination of the stories we bring with us and may well impose on the biblical story.

If OT narrative discloses reality, it can also have the power to transform us in that disclosure. If narratives can create worlds, they can also overturn them. Here the emphasis is on stories that shake us in the world of our own stories. In the encounter with some narratives, we are reoriented. The journey through our own life experience is no longer the same because of our encounter with the biblical story. Some of the intentional use of story in pedagogy and preaching in the life of the church seeks to heighten this transformative quality.

Any OT narrative is potentially transformative, but it appears possible to distinguish several different ways in which narratives exercise transformative power. Certain stories are experienced as perennially transformative. To mark this quality such stories may be referred to as salvation stories. In the OT the Exodus story (Exodus 1—15) is the most important of these. Israel understood clearly that this story was not just descriptive of a moment in past history. Almost from the beginning this story was cut loose from its historical moorings and treated as a story that addressed the reality of Israel's life in every generation and did so with the transforming power to make each generation the Exodus generation. Such events and the stories that preserve them have been referred to as "reservoirs of meaning."[19] Each time the pattern of distress become deliverance, the gift of God's life-giving grace, is experienced as Exodus story in the experience of a new generation, then the story itself grows in meaning and power. It is enhanced by all of the transforming moments that flow from the story and yet become part of the story and its power. Other OT narratives also function as salvation stories. The well-known credos (e.g., Deuteronomy 26 and Joshua 24) and salvation history Psalms such as 78 or 136 call to mind and celebrate those transforming stories. Perhaps the clearest example of Israel's understanding of the ability of some stories to transform subsequent generations is Moses' reference to the story of covenant making on Mt. Sinai when he is speaking to the generation about to enter the promised land: "Not with our fathers did the Lord make this covenant, but with us, who are all of us here alive this day" (Deut. 5:3). In a similar fashion these stories have continued to have transformative power throughout the centuries of the church's continued telling of them. They can continue to exercise power as paradigm stories of transforming power if they are told and reflected upon in light of our own experience.

Other OT narratives can have transforming power but do not become central salvation stories. For example, there are stories of transformation to new life that invite the reader or listener to similar transformation. The story of Jacob in general, the episode of Jacob's wrestling with the night visitor (Gen. 32:22ff.) in particular, is a story of transformation to new life. This narrative could be dismissed as one of those most bizarre and remote from our own experience unless we attend carefully to the transformation taking place. Jacob is fearfully facing encounter with his alienated brother Esau. In wrestling with "a man" through the night, Jacob, the controller, cannot seize control but instead is injured, given a new name which points toward community, and sent limping away from the place he calls "face of God," for he has come to see God present in this struggle. When he meets with Esau the following day, he is embraced and not assaulted, and Jacob cries, "Truly to see your face is to see the face of God." To be open to the moral address of this story and its power to transform our lives is to see how often we, like Jacob, must pass through struggles and risk injury in order to be able to see the face of God in the face of our alienated brothers and sisters. It is to face God's encounter with our own controlling natures in the human struggles which refuse to be controlled.

Other stories transform by shattering our illusions, overturning our worlds. Crossan has shown this quality as a prominent feature of the parables of Jesus.[20] Although the parable form is not as common in the OT, a good example is Nathan's parable in confronting David in 2 Samuel 12. Nathan's dramatic and shattering declaration, "Thou art the man!" has continually left its ancient context to shatter illusions of those who thought their self-serving actions to be secret but who had not reckoned with God. A nonparable example of this type of illusion-shattering story is the story of Tamar in Genesis 38. In this narrative a resourceful woman seeking to be faithful to her familial obligations in the face of Judah's failure to fulfill his executes a plan to conceive a child by Judah himself. When she is discovered to be pregnant she is charged with the capital offense of adultery and about to be burned. When Judah is confronted at the last moment with the truth that he is the father he unexpectedly declares of Tamar, "She is more righteous than I." In this story worlds are overturned for ancient and modern community. Righteousness is on the side of one who subverted the rules, the laws. We are forced to rethink our own institutionalization and domestication of the good and to consider the risks that genuine righteousness might demand of us. In Tamar, we are invited to look for insight to those pressed to the margins of our societies as Tamar, a woman, was marginal in her patriarchal world.

The Recovery of Moral Address in Old Testament Narrative

The concern to recover the moral address of OT narrative exists only among those who regard the Bible as scripture and therefore as authoritative in some way for the community of faith. In the following suggestions for matters of concern in such a recovery, the church (or the synagogue) is assumed as the context.[21]

If the moral power of biblical stories is to be preserved and passed on, there is an urgent need to reassess the way in which biblical exegesis is taught to church leaders in the theological schools and to lay people in the life of the local church. In particular we need to become more aware of the limits of historical-critical method in biblical studies. For several generations this method has been taught by many as the sum total of the exegetical task. It was assumed that this method properly and rigorously applied could successfully recover the objective meaning of texts. Since its focus was most frequently on authorship, historicity, and the development of literary traditions, the results of historical-critical work were frequently the fragmenting of texts without a concern for their meaning as a whole. The result has been the blunting of the moral address of the biblical story by the fragmenting of the story itself. There is little moral power left in looking at the literary pieces of a text and discussing their meaning in isolation from one another, but seldom was the meaning of the whole discussed.

Of equal concern is the way in which the claim to objectivity in historical-critical method places the experience of hearing or reading an OT narrative at arm's length from one's own experience. Biblical story has moral power as it intersects our own story, and in those intersections the stories become intertwined. Objective method seeks to avoid this. In 1962 Krister Stendahl argued that the task of the biblical theologian is properly limited to the "descriptive," whereas the "normative" meaning of scripture is not the province of biblical theology.[22] This represented the triumph of a view first introduced by Gabler in 1827 that descriptive theology must be sharply divided from the work of constructive theology.[23] Biblical scholars at the time of the Stendahl article largely believed they were engaged in describing the history and faith of the communities of the Bible in an objective and value-free fashion through the use of historical-critical methods. They viewed this task as detached from the claim of confessing communities that these materials were scripture and somehow authoritative for modern faith. This approach still predominates, and one still hears talk of "what a text meant" and "what a text means," as if the two were separable and one could legitimately choose to work only on the former. Brevard Childs recently wrote:

> It is far from obvious that an appeal of objectivity will resolve the hermeneutical issues. Nor is it evident that the subjective presuppositions of the interpreter can only be regarded as a negative factor. . . . It is a false dichotomy which contrasts objective analysis with subjective presuppositions. The issue is rather the quality and the skill with which presuppositions are brought to bear on the biblical material. In sum, one of the major issues for developing a new biblical theology lies in rethinking the sharp distinction which Gabler first introduced into the field when he separated descriptive from constructive theology. The two aspects of biblical theology belong together.[24]

Feminist[25] and third-world scholars[26] have taught us to recognize that there are no truly objective methods or interpretations. Texts address us in multiple ways because of the multiple perspectives brought by the interpreters in their encounter with the biblical stories. Not only is this inherently true, but this interaction of text and experience, the biblical story with our own story, is to be valued, encouraged, taught, and critically reflected upon. OT narrative cannot become a resource for the moral shaping of our lives if its story is not allowed to intersect our own story. Cultivated, false objectivity is precisely the sort of exegesis that will not allow this to happen. It is for this reason that so many pastors will candidly admit that the biblical study methods they were taught in seminary do not help them bridge the gap between analyzing a text and claiming it (or being claimed by it) for preaching or teaching in the life of the church. It is indeed important to master certain critical tools including those of the historical-critical method, but beyond this critical task there must be encouragement and training in methods that will allow us to be encountered by the biblical story and to foster such encounter in others.

A second area important in the recovery of the moral address of OT story is an increased awareness of the multiple layers of storytelling that are necessarily a part of the unique character of those OT narratives that seek to claim us as part of scripture. The truth of these stories cannot be limited to any one of these layers. They must all be heard and reflected upon.

The first of these is the narrator's voice in the story itself—the witness who gives testimony to the characters, events, and conflicts of Israel's story and God's story. This immediate voice in the literary structure of the narrative itself gives us access to its vision of reality and the demand for response that flows from it. "Events, characters, time, place, action, surprise, tension, resolution, plot, narrator—they are all there in the stories of Scripture."[27] Sometimes the narrator's voice can be identified with specific times or places or interests, and the story may be heard as testimony to particular points of view (e.g., the contributions of the Deuteronomic historian). This may enhance our encounter with a given narrative or group of narratives, but it should be clear that meaning and truth in our encounter with OT stories do not depend on such determinations.

A second level present in the OT stories is the level of the community that preserved and passed on these particular stories. The OT canon itself represents the judgment of the ancient Hebrew community of faith concerning which stories deserve to be preserved and retold.[28] The canon is itself the testimony of the community on the stories judged to be true—those stories that have the power to disclose and transform the reality of our lives. We can only briefly suggest some functions of canon that bear on the moral address of OT narrative.

One of the issues with which Christian ethics must perennially struggle is the issue of self-deception. We have a tendency to tell false stories about ourselves because the truth is not always easy or simple or unambiguous. Hauerwas calls truthful stories "continually discomforting."[29] When we deceive ourselves, we choose safe stories that make no demands and expect nothing in return, that fit comfortably with the stories we have already chosen for ourselves. The OT canon is a part of the faith community's antidote to self-deception. Without the canon and its insistence that the canon's total witness is authoritative, we could comfortably select our own collection of stories in accord with our previously shaped story. The canon is the collection of stories that break through our self-deceptions and make the demands on us that come from bearing the promise of Abraham and Sarah, receiving the gift of Exodus deliverance, becoming the alternative community of covenant, and being enabled to sing the Lord's song in a strange land. We are forced to deal with stories of judgment as well as hope, folly as well as wisdom, sin as well as grace, death as well as life. We encounter the profound and the simple, the obscure and the plain. It is important not to limit the canon to our own selections in it. This would be to risk that our own self-deceptions will perpetuate themselves and shut out challenging or threatening stories. We must ask, for example, why stories like that of Tamar (Genesis 38) are almost unknown. It may be that their perspective on righteousness is threatening, even subversive. It is not only their presence in the canon but their resonance through the canon that makes their claim on us clear.

This reminds us of another function of canon. Narratives no longer stand alone but are caught up as episodes in larger stories, juxtaposed to one another in complementary or tension-making ways, or edited in new and revealing patterns. Those biblical communities who passed on the OT stories did not experience them as discrete and isolated episodes because they had experienced the interaction of those stories in their own lives and faith. The canonical shape and placement of stories is as important as the story-episodes themselves in hearing the moral address aimed at us by the biblical communities. Why does the whole Hebrew canon begin with Genesis 1, a creation story not shaped in its present form until the time of Babylonian exile? Is this portrait of God intended as necessary prelude to the more particularized story of Israel and the God of that particular people? Why is the upbeat Horatio Alger tale of Joseph interrupted by the story of Tamar in Genesis 38? Is it to remind us of the ambiguities of righteousness, lest the Joseph story seem too glib? Why is the story of the rise of kingship in Israel filled with the contradictory perspectives of judgment and grace? Can it be that tearing these apart into early and late sources does violence to the message of moral ambiguity and struggle that attend the grasping of sociopolitical power apart from trust in God? The canon is the shape of the community's corporate story encompassing the voices of particular narrators.

One final function of the canon must be briefly mentioned. For the contemporary community of faith seeking the moral address of scripture, the canon provides a common ground of moral reflection which allows our separate story-formed identities to speak to one another. Sharing the common canonical story allows us to speak across cultural, ethnic, and class barriers. As an example, would we in North American churches be nearly as challenged by liberation theology if it were only addressed in the terms of analytical theological discourse? Part of the unavoidable power of its challenge comes from its retelling of biblical stories such as the Exodus deliverance story in ways that tell us how those stories have intersected their own experience. Speech out of such intersections reaches us because even when our personal story is remote from the dispossessed we share the biblical story, and its retelling gives us vision and access to the experiences of the retellers. The canon thus provides an important framework for moral discourse.

This final point actually takes us to a third level through which OT story comes to us, alongside the voice of the narrator and the witness of the biblical community in the shape of the canon. It is the level of the tradition (or traditions) through which the OT stories come to us. By the time we hear the biblical story, it has been retold through many generations. So we never hear it without being affected by all those retellings. Preaching and teaching in the church mediate the biblical story, but not without contributing witness to some segment of the tradition which testifies to encounter with the biblical story over many preceding generations. Often these generations of witness enrich us, but sometimes they deceive us and distort the biblical story (e.g., the preaching to justify slavery prior to the Civil War). Thus our traditions are never to be confused with the biblical story itself but always are to be judged by our own faithful encounter with scripture itself. Further, both biblical story and the traditions of our retelling are to be critically reflected upon in the belief that God's story is still being lived in our own time and experience and ever new insights might still flow from our encounter with a living Word.

NOTES

1. Walter Harrelson, *The Ten Commandments and Human Rights* (Philadelphia: Fortress Press, 1980), is an excellent treatment of the Decalogue as an ethical resource, and it makes use of much of the extensive literature available on the Decalogue.

2. Hans Frei, *The Eclipse of Biblical Narrative: A Study in Eighteenth and Nineteenth Century Hermeneutics* (New Haven: Yale University Press, 1974).

3. For general understandings of the dynamics involved in the use of the Bible for Christian ethics, see Bruce C. Birch and Larry L. Rasmussen, *Bible and Ethics in the Christian Life* (Minneapolis: Augsburg Pub. House, 1976); and Thomas Ogletree, *The Use of the Bible in Christian Ethics* (Philadelphia: Fortress Press, 1983).

4. John Howard Yoder, *Politics of Jesus* (Grand Rapids: Wm. B. Eerdmans, 1972).

5. This article is deeply indebted to a number of key works in what has become a rather large bibliography on narrative and story. An especially helpful survey article is Gabriel Fackre, "Narrative Theology: An Overview," *Int* 37 (1983) 340–52. In ethics the works of Stanley Hauerwas have been especially helpful. See *A Community of Character* (Notre Dame, Ind.: University of Notre Dame Press, 1981); *Truthfulness and Tragedy* (Notre Dame, Ind.: University of Notre Dame Press, 1977); and *The Peaceable Kingdom* (Notre Dame, Ind.: University of Notre Dame Press, 1983). In narrative theology key works that have informed this essay are Terrence W. Tilley, *Story Theology* (Wilmington: Michael Glazier, 1985); George Stroup, *The Promise of Narrative: Recovering the Gospel in the Church* (Atlanta: John Knox Press, 1981); Michael Goldberg, *Theology and Narrative* (Nashville: Abingdon Press, 1982). In biblical studies John Dominic Crossan, *The Dark Interval: Towards a Theology of Story* (Nile, Ill.: Argus Communications, 1975); and Robert Alter, *The Art of Biblical Narrative* (New York: Basic Books, 1981) have been especially important.

6. Robert Scholes and Robert Kellogg, *The Nature of Narrative* (London: Oxford University Press, 1966) 4.

7. Fackre, "Narrative Theology," 341.

8. Stephen Crites, "The Narrative Quality of Experience," *JAAR* 39 (1971) 291–311.

9. This particular characterization of MacIntyre's argument is from Ron Large's "Story and Ethics: The Moral Dimension of Narrative" (unpublished paper, 1986).

10. Alasdair MacIntyre, *After Virtue: A Study in Moral Theory* (Notre Dame, Ind.: University of Notre Dame Press, 1981) 203.

11. Tilley, *Story Theology,* 26.

12. Michael Goldberg, "Expository Article: Exodus 1:13–14," *Int* 37 (1983) 389.

13. See the works of Hauerwas cited in n. 5, as well as Birch and Rasmussen, *Bible and Ethics in the Christian Life,* chap. 3.

14. Fackre, "Narrative Theology," 346. Fackre is himself citing Frei, *Eclipse,* 11 for the suggestion that biblical narrative is "history-like."

15. Fackre distinguishes disclosive and transformative aspects of biblical narrative ("Narrative Theology," 345), although he is in no way responsible for the descriptions of types within those broad categories as suggested here.

16. Alter, *Art of Biblical Narrative,* as characterized by Fackre in "Narrative Theology," 345.

17. Tilley (*Story Theology,* 40ff.) uses a similar category, "stories that set up worlds," although he calls such stories "myths." This is potentially confusing given the various ways in which that term has been used.

18. Phyllis Trible, "A Human Comedy," *God and the Rhetoric of Sexuality* (Philadelphia: Fortress Press, 1978).

19. The phrase is from Paul Ricoeur but is used effectively in discussing the Exodus story by J. Severino Croatto, *Exodus: A Hermeneutics of Freedom* (Maryknoll, N.Y.: Orbis Books, 1981).

20. Crossan, *Dark Interval.*

21. Many of these remarks may well apply to Jewish communities of faith but there will also be some differences. This essay will speak only out of this author's experience in dealing with these issues in the life of Christian churches.

22. Krister Stendahl, "Biblical Theology, Contemporary," *IDB* 1:418ff.

23. Johann Philip Gabler, "Oratio de iusto discrimine theologicae biblicae et dogmaticae regundisque recte utriusque finibus," *Kleine theologische Schriften* (ed. Th. A. Gabler and J. G. Gabler; Ulm, 1831) 2.179–98.

24. Brevard S. Childs, "Some Reflections on the Search for a Biblical Theology," *HBT* 4 (1982) 5–6.

25. E.g., Elizabeth Schüssler Fiorenza, "Toward a Feminist Biblical Hermeneutics: Biblical Interpretation and Liberation Theology," *The Challenge of Liberation Theology* (ed. B. Mahan and L. Dale Richesin; Maryknoll, N.Y.: Orbis Books, 1981) 108ff.

26. Juan Luis Segundo, *The Liberation of Theology* (Maryknoll, N.Y.: Orbis Books, 1976).

27. Fackre, "Narrative Theology," 346.

28. I am greatly indebted to the work of Brevard S. Childs and James A. Sanders for increasing my understanding of the canon and its importance.

Representative of their work is Childs, *Introduction to the Old Testament as Scripture* (Philadelphia: Fortress Press, 1979); and Sanders, *From Sacred Story to Sacred Text* (Philadelphia: Fortress Press, 1987).

29. Hauerwas, *Truthfulness and Tragedy,* 95.

7

Israel and Monotheism:
The Unfinished Agenda

DAVID L. PETERSEN

In scholarly circles, it has not been fashionable to speak about ancient Israel, at least for most of its history, as embodying a monotheistic religion, if by that we mean what most dictionaries offer as a basic definition of monotheism, namely, the belief that there is only one God. This negative judgment is presented in such standard reference works as *The Interpreter's Dictionary of the Bible:* "It is highly doubtful whether Israel's faith in the Mosaic period should be called monotheistic."[1] B. Anderson then goes on to suggest that monotheism does, in fact, develop in Israel by the sixth century. Such monotheism is, he maintains, evident in the poetry of Isaiah 40—55. This thesis about the development of monotheism in Israel has been typical of much recent biblical scholarship.[2]

Moreover, one senses that the issue of monotheism in Israel is relatively unimportant in recent discussions of Old Testament theology. Such a judgment seems as relevant for relatively recent volumes, those by Reventlow and Clements for example, as it does for the earlier tomes of von Rad and Eichrodt.[3] Instead, the matter appears to have been relegated to treatments of the history of Israel, and even there the issue remains, for the most part, marginal.[4]

This lack of attention is unfortunate, and for a variety of reasons. First, Yahwism, the religion of ancient Israel, embodies theological traditions that eventuate in distinctly monotheistic formulations, whether one discerns them in Yahwism itself or later, in Judaism,

Christianity, and Islam. Hence, it is incumbent upon those who specialize in the study of Yahwism to address the topic for an audience that includes, at the minimum, historians of religion and theologians, those for whom the topic has remained significant. Second, considerable and incisive work has been devoted to the study of monotheism outside the arena of biblical scholarship. Such work illumines substantively the issues that discussion of monotheism involves. And yet, biblical scholars remain unfamiliar with their colleagues' research in this area.[5] Third, the issue of monotheism entails theological implications. The matter does not involve, exclusively, the description of one or another historical period and the number of deities Yahwism allows. Rather, the very nature of Israel's deity, and the way we think about him, are at stake.

In this paper I hope to identify the constitutive issues that reflection on Yahwism properly involves and, in so doing, to suggest which sectors of the discussion are likely to be profitable and which are not. By dint of this analysis, I intend to demonstrate that discussion of monotheism is important and deserves further and careful study.

I

I begin by classifying the various general theories that have made up the larger discussion of monotheism. One may use three catchwords to encapsulate the various approaches: evolution, devolution, and revolution. Numerous thinkers in the post-Renaissance period have argued for the existence of a primitive monotheism *(Urmonotheismus)*. Those include Herbert of Cherbury, Joseph-François Lafitau, Voltaire, Andrew Lang, and Wilhelm Schmidt.[6] All articulated a position exemplified by Voltaire and the romantics who followed him when he wrote, "I venture to believe . . . that men began by knowing a single God and that latter human weakness adopted a number of deities." I would characterize this view as devolution. From an earlier and positively valued form of religious behavior, that is, monotheism, there developed a less sophisticated and ignoble form, polytheism. In OT circles, this view is represented by M.-J. Lagrange, who maintained that primitive Semitic worship entailed the veneration of El, a deity that later evolved into a variety of subsidiary gods.[7]

An early and alternate argument provides what I would label the evolutionary postulate. The Scottish philosopher David Hume wrote in 1757, "If we consider the improvement of human society from rude beginnings to a state of greater perfection, polytheism or idolatry was, and necessarily must have been, the first and most ancient religion of mankind."[8] This side, too, did not lack for advocates. Auguste Comte, the French positivist, announced a series of stages that culminated in monotheism: fetishism, polytheism, and then monotheism.[9] Not dissimilarly, E. B. Tylor, an anthropologist, argued for the following stages: animism, polytheism, and then monotheism.[10] A variant form of this schema, polytheism, henotheism, and then monotheism, has been widely influential and may be associated with the name of Wellhausen.[11] That monotheism is a development out of a prior and polytheistic religious climate has, I think, been the ruling notion in OT studies.

The work of Morton Smith and Bernhard Lang is a refinement of this evolutionary hypothesis. Both Smith and Lang identify a "Yahweh-alone movement" within a larger polytheistic and syncretistic Israelite environment. Though their work is similar, Smith's approach locates Israelite belief sociologically whereas Lang tends to focus on political factors.

Smith argues that beginning in the ninth century B.C.E. "there was a newly important element in the situation: the demand that all Israel worship Yahweh and Yahweh alone."[12] Elijah and Elisha appear as leaders of a Yahweh-alone movement. Hosea too belongs at the head of this group, as a "fanatical representative."[13] The raison d'être of this movement is apparently, for Smith, theological: "At the heart of the system is the teaching of the Yahweh-alone prophets: Yahweh's jealous love for Israel"; since Yahweh loves Israel, he is concomitantly jealous for Israel's exclusive love in return.[14] Over time, that is, by the end of the monarchic period, "the Yahweh-alone party became in effect a new religion, and a new kind of religion."[15] Israel became "a people . . . united essentially by its agreement to worship Yahweh alone, united by its contempt for all other gods, a contempt soon expressed as denial of their existence. . . ."[16] For Smith, monotheism evolves. It evolves from a group, one might say sectarian, movement into a more all-encompassing social phenomenon. Moreover, some of the prophets, according to Smith, were instrumental in initiating and articulating that monotheistic perspective.

Lang, in an essay that builds on the approach of Smith by speaking of a Yahweh-alone group, also adopts an evolutionary perspective, though Lang describes the process at one place as "a chain of revolutions."[17] He identifies five phases in which Yahwism moves from polytheism, "the oldest form of Israelite religion" to monotheism, which Lang thinks may be identified in the writings of Deutero-Isaiah.[18] Of key importance to Lang's essay is the notion of temporary monolatry, a situation in which God is appealed to, especially in times of crisis. This is a religious practice identified by van Selms not only in Israel, but elsewhere in the ancient Near East.[19] For Lang, "Yahweh-alone worship can be understood as a crisis-cult which is continued beyond the actual crisis situation."[20] Moreover, this Yahweh is a God unusual in the ancient Near East since he is not linked to others by kinship ties. For example, he has no spouse, parent, or child, and Lang highlights this aspect of Yahweh in a nice turn of phrase: "The lonely Yahweh becomes the only Yahweh."[21] According to Lang, the break-through to monotheism occurred partly as a result of a latent mono-theism (so Lohfink) and partly as a result of the influence of Zoroastrian monotheism (so Vorländer), but discrete historical cir-cumstances were important too: "While Judah as a political entity is shattered by a super-power, the idea of the only God is born."[22] Monotheism is then, according to Lang, fundamentally an answer to political exigency.

The aforementioned notion of an evolution from polytheism to monotheism has been challenged incisively by, among others, Pet-tazzoni. Pettazzoni maintains: "If we contemplate the monotheistic religions . . . we find that every one of them arises as a new religion out of a previously-existing polytheistic environment"; but, for Pettazzoni, this is not a natural evolution, but rather a revolution, often the work of a religious reformer.[23] He states, "Monotheism presupposes poly-theism by the very fact of denying it," and then further, "far from developing out of polytheism by an evolutionary process, monotheism takes shape by means of a revolution." One might add that Gottwald's notions about the origins of Yahwism in Israel as a "mono-Yahwism" are not inconsistent with some of Pettazzoni's views.[24]

In sum, there are three quite distinct models for understanding the place of monotheism vis-à-vis other religious formulations. One of these schemata, the so-called evolutionary viewpoint, has dominated Hebrew Bible studies. Nonetheless, it is important for scholars to recognize that other theoretical options are available.

II

A second nexus of issues involves the question of whether or not monotheistic religions existed elsewhere in the ancient Near East, and whether, if they did exist, they might have influenced the development of monotheism in Israel. This diffusionist approach is most often found in discussions of the possible connection between the Amarna religion of Akhnaton and so-called Mosaic Yahwism. There is a vast bibliography. Perhaps the most famous, if not best informed, articulation of the thesis concerning Egyptian influence on Yahwistic religion is Freud's *Moses and Monotheism*.[25] The Egyptian connection is not, however, the only option. Now the Ebla documents provide a whole new arena for discussion. Pettinato stresses a move away from polytheism toward monotheism in the religious climate documented in the Ebla inscriptions.[26] There is also germane material from Mesopotamian sources (both Sumerian and Akkadian) that is conveniently summarized and assessed by Hartman.[27] Then, as indicated earlier, there is a considerable literature on the potential impact of Zoroastrian religion on Israel during the Persian period.[28] Finally, the Kenite hypothesis for the inception of monotheism in Israel is conveniently summarized by Rowley.[29]

In all these investigations scholars attempt to discern a monotheistic, henotheistic, or monolatrous element in Yahwism that may be traced to some prior or antecedent religious environment. In my judgment, no scholar has yet been able to identify palpable monotheistic influence upon the religion of ancient Israel.

III

A third arena of discussion involves two related questions: (1) whether Israel ever was monotheistic, and (2), if it was, when it became monotheistic. There is, as one might expect, a considerable range of answers to these questions. As for the first, most scholars will allow that Israel did at some point become monotheistic. Renan, and more recently Oldenburg, maintain that monotheism, that is, the veneration of a single Semitic God, predates Israel.[30] For Albright, the Mosaic period seems to represent the first impulse of monotheism in Israel.[31] Maag argued that the desert, the wilderness or the so-called nomadic environment, was the context out of which Yahwism arose.[32] Von Rad rather clearly points to the time of the tribal league, the amphictyony, as the point of origin for monotheistic Yahwism in Israel.[33] Interestingly no one seems willing to argue that monotheism arose during the period of the United Monarchy. This situation is in some ways surprising since one might expect a correlation between the presence of an imperial ruler in Israel and a single strong deity for the state. Causse and Procksch, and apparently Smith, maintain that monotheism may be observed for the first time in Israel in the ninth century, especially in the work of Elijah and Elisha.[34] Wellhausen is the most prominent spokesperson for the view that Israelite monotheism developed in the eighth century, particularly in the work of the eighth-century prophets.[35] Other scholars, such as R. H. Pfeiffer, trace the origins of monotheism to the sixth century, where it can be seen especially in the literature of Deutero-Isaiah. They argue that the exile provided the context for the development of monotheism in Israelite religion.[36] After surveying such scholarship, one senses a certain futility in attempting to define *the* century during which time Israel became monotheistic.

IV

A fourth range of issues in the discussion of monotheism involves the critical vocabulary. In the current discussion there are four important descriptors: polytheism, henotheism, monolatry, and monotheism. The first and last terms are reasonably clear. Monotheism is regularly used to describe a religion in which the adherents express belief in the existence of and venerate only one high god. In contrast, polytheism may be described as a religion in which adherents believe in the existence of and venerate a variety of important deities. It is, of course, the case that these descriptors have minimal value in offering truly significant statements about particular religions, since ancient Sumerian, Amerindian, and Hindu religions all could be construed as polytheistic according to the above definition.

Henotheism and monolatry are more complex. Henotheism, a term often attributed to Max Müller, was, according to Pettazzoni, used early on by Welcker, and, possibly, by Schelling, to mean "a rudimentary monotheism."[37] The term henotheism has more recently been used to describe "belief in or worship of one god without denying the existence of others."[38] It does seem to be the case that henotheism grew out of an evolutionary concept that sought to identify and label a stage of "practical monotheism" prior to the development of "true monotheism."

Typical definitions of monolatry do not differ much from those just offered for henotheism. So, for example, the *Oxford English Dictionary* defines monolatry as "the worship of one god where other gods may be supposed to exist." This definition is attested, according to the dictionary, in the work of William Robertson Smith in 1881. That OT scholar wrote, "The religion of the Old Testament is no mere natural variety of Semitic monolatry." According to the same entry in the *Oxford English Dictionary,* the term was apparently used by Wellhausen, to whom Huxley attributes it in 1886. On the basis of nineteenth- and twentieth-century scholarly writings, I find it difficult to distinguish between the meaning and the usage of these two terms. They do, however, appear to have different origins. Henotheism is a term that was first used significantly with regard to Greek sources and their implications for study of monotheism, whereas the term monolatry developed currency within OT studies and their contributions to reflection about monotheism. Interestingly, henotheism was apparently first used within a context in which primal monotheism was understood to have existed, whereas monolatry was used to describe a stage between an original polytheism and later monotheism. However, both terms now refer to a context in which one main deity is venerated but the existence of other deities is not denied. In sum, it does not seem to make a great deal of difference which term is used.

A review of recent discussions reveals that scholars do attempt more precision than is allowed by appeal to either monolatry or monotheism. So, for example, one finds with considerable regularity the following sorts of language: implicit monolatry, explicit monolatry, implicit monotheism, and latent monotheism. Nonetheless, this use of a vocabulary does not appear to have resulted in significant conceptual clarity.

V

Having surveyed theories of origin, questions of influence on and the status of Yahwism as expressing monotheism, and critical vocabulary for such discussions, I now propose to address a range of topics that I would describe in summary fashion as the implications of monotheism. Some years ago, Rowley pointed in this direction when he wrote, "Religion is to be tested by the character, not merely the number of the gods. . . ."[39] The implications of monotheism have been addressed in a variety of ways by scholars surveying all so-called monotheistic religions as well as by scholars surveying only one monotheistic religion. Moreover, these scholars have used a wide variety of perspectives, psychology, sociology, literary studies, and theology among them. The pursuit and interplay of these perspectives should provide for fruitful and creative work on monotheism in biblical studies.

First, some would argue that monotheism has distinctive psychological implications. Monotheism, that is to say, the veneration of a sole deity, was the subject of considerable reflection by Sigmund Freud. Best known here is Freud's *Moses and Monotheism,* though he did in fact write on the topic in a variety of other settings. Stemberger has recently devoted an extensive study to "'Der Mann Moses' in Freud's *Gesamtwerk."* In that study, she contends that "monotheism is, according to the psychoanalytic judgment, the original form of religion. It is the restoration of the primal form of parent-child relationship. . . . After the Oedipal phase, when the real father is a rival, God is projected as the ideal father. And after the father is killed as a result of the Oedipal rivalry, the father figure is deified. Jewish monotheism comprises a restoration of the original relationship of child to father."[40] According to Stemberger, for Freud the Israelite-Jewish developments in monotheism entailed progress in the history of religion since they create a psychologically healthy state and a religious world view that could accommodate the critical Oedipal struggle. For both personal reasons (Freud was a Jew) and the larger psychological issues of the Oedipal crisis, Freud argued strongly on behalf of the value of monotheistic religion within the context of psychology.

Second, Paul Ciholas, in an essay entitled "Monothéisme et violence," has broached in interdisciplinary fashion psychological and sociological as well as history-of-religions issues.[41] Ciholas has argued that there is a direct correlation between monotheistic religions and the presence of violence. There is of course an aspect of the dangerous, namely, violence, and the sacral inherent in all religions. However, the notion of a jealous and sole deity enhances this general tendency such that violence appears to function more importantly in monotheistic than in nonmonotheistic systems. Ciholas goes so far as to maintain that monotheistic formulations, rather than eliminating violence, have immortalized it. It is therefore not surprising that missionary zeal and violent eschatology often appear as regular features of a monotheistic religion. Such features, Ciholas maintains, are true of all monotheistic formulations and not simply of Yahwistic monotheism.[42]

In a related matter, the relation between Yahwism as a monotheistic system and power has been noted and assessed by a number of feminist thinkers. They have argued that the presence of a sole powerful and male deity has direct implications for gender relationships among those who venerate the deity. Such implications eventuate in greater power for male adherents and in less status for and even oppression of female adherents.[43]

A third way of construing monotheism is to focus directly on sociological concerns. Gottwald has done this within the confines of OT studies. Monotheism, or to use his term, "mono-Yahwism," is a corollary to a new, egalitarian form of social organization. There is, Gottwald maintains, a correlation betwen mono-Yahwism and egalitarian social order, just as there is a correlation between a polytheistic Canaanite religion and multiple social strata. The oneness of God seems to entail a oneness in society. Gottwald writes, "Such an insight suggests not only that mono-Yahwism was a function of socio-political egalitarianism, but that in some senses at least socio-political egalitarianism was a function of mono-Yahwism."[44] He continues, "Yahweh's uniqueness lay in the fact that he was the symbol of a singleminded pursuit of an egalitarian tribal social system."[45] For Gottwald, mono-Yahwism had distinct social entailments. It would be interesting to determine the validity of this thesis about monotheism and the other monotheistic systems as well. The question then would be, Was early Christianity or was early Islam egalitarian in a way similar to that of early Yahwism?

Guy Swanson, a sociologist, challenges implicitly Gottwald's claims about monotheism and society. Swanson, in a rigorously argued analysis of fifty different societies including ancient Israel, attempted to discover social correlates to various types of theological formulation. He was able to identify a strong positive correlation between "the presence of hierarchy of three or more sovereign groups in a society" and monotheistic affirmations.[46] Put another way, only certain sorts of societies have regularly produced monotheistic religions; and they are not the simplest forms of society. Such a conclusion, that a considerable degree of social complexity, which is articulated morphologically as hierarchy, is necessary for monotheism stands in significant contrast to the notion of Gottwald, for whom an unstratified egalitarian society is the birthplace of a monotheistic religion. (Swanson's work also strikes a decisive blow against the notion of primitive monotheism.)

Fourth, we move to the matter of literary perspectives. Robert Alter, in his influential *The Art of Biblical Narrative,* has suggested that a monotheistic religion may eventuate in a form of literary expression different from texts that emanate out of a polytheistic environment. He writes:

> The underlying biblical conception of character, as often unpredictable, in some ways, impenetrable, constantly emerging from and slipping back into a penumbra of ambiguity, in fact has greater affinity with dominant modern notions than do the habits of conceiving character typical of the Greek epics. The monotheistic revolution, in consciousness, profoundly altered the ways in which man as well as God was imagined, and the effects of that revolution probably still determine certain aspects of our conceptual world more than we suspect.[47]

Alter seems to imply that monotheistic systems allow for greater freedom for the deity and concomitantly for human characters as well. One must note here that monotheism affords not only freedom but a certain ambiguity and obscurity, both for the human and the deity, as the Book of Job clearly attests. It would be interesting to determine whether this aspect of the deity or of human characters obtains in other monotheistic systems in a way more pronounced in polytheistic systems.[48]

Fifth, and finally, monotheistic formulations involve profoundly important theological issues. Henri Corbin has made a very strong case for this situation in the case of Islam.[49] The situation in Israel is, I think, best put in the following way: Yahweh must perform in a variety of roles. In the legal context, one may observe Yahweh performing as prosecutor, judge, court of appeal, and executioner. If one thinks diachronically, Yahweh appears to have taken on various roles of ancient Near Eastern deities. In addition, we may observe clearly this accumulation of roles by comparing the creation and the flood narratives of the Bible to creation and deluge epics from the ancient Near East. I would suggest Yahweh, in certain cases, has assumed complementary roles; in other cases, he has enacted conflicting roles. First, the complementary role. In Genesis 1, Yahweh enacts the role of creator of the cosmos, the role that Marduk plays in the Enuma Elish. And yet, in both Genesis 1 and 2, especially Genesis 2, Yahweh enacts the role of the creator of humanity, the *belet-ili* role as that occurs in the Atra-hasis epic. Despite this apparent lumping of disparate roles onto one deity, one does not here sense a problem. There is no reason that the creator of the cosmos cannot also create humanity. Enuma

Elish, in fact, at one point attributes both types of creative activity to Marduk. Put another way, Yahweh's taking on these several creative roles represents an accumulation of complementary roles.

Not so with the Yahweh in Israelite flood traditions. In the Mesopotamian flood stories, conflict between the Enlil and Enki figures is an essential element in the plot. They stand in fundamental opposition on the wisdom of the flood as well as other such attempts to rid the earth of humanity. One causes the flood, the other helps humanity survive. And yet, in the Israelite versions, Yahweh takes on both the Enlil and Enki roles. He causes the flood and he enables humans to survive. To this extent, Yahweh has assumed conflicting roles. Conflict concerning the flood, in Israel, exists within the deity rather than between two opposing deities.

This confusion over the flood within the person of the deity is enhanced by literary tensions within the Israelite flood stories themselves. The so-called priestly version emphasizes the cosmic character of the flood. Here the flood lasts over one year, represents the collapse of the heavenly vault so that the primeval waters wash down over the created space, and involves a recreation of the cosmos and an attendant covenant. Clearly for this writer the flood was a terribly significant and positive event.[50]

The so-called Yahwistic version presents quite a different tack. This writer, who usually tells a good story, does not perform well here. From his perspective the flood achieves no good purpose since, for him, the reason for the flood is the same as the reason for no more floods. This writer had to tell the story but he apparently did not think Yahweh as single primary deity could take on easily the roles of two conflicting deities. One senses that, for this writer, the role of flood perpetrator was one role that Yahweh should not have assumed.[51]

In Mesopotamia there were many gods and rather uniform stories about those gods as actors in creation and flood. In Israel, by contrast, there was one primary deity, Yahweh. That deity had taken on many and disparate roles; hence it became natural, perhaps even necessary, to include multiple versions of stories in order to explore his complex character.

Yahweh, because he has performed the roles of conflicting deities as those occur in a multi-deity system, has a very complex character. Such complexity seems manifest in numerous OT episodes in which Yahweh must change his mind, shift tactics, or simply disappear from the human scene. In not dissimilar fashion, one senses that the deity in Jewish, Christian, and Muslim traditions is equally, if not more, complex, having to perform as agent of both judgment and salvation. In sum, Yahwism, as an exemplar of monotheistic-like formulations, involves considerable theological complexity.

VI

Attention to the work of other scholars can help biblical scholars think about monotheism using a variety of models: evolution, devolution, and revolution. Literary, sociological, psychological, and theological issues arise prominently when one reflects upon monotheistic or monolatrous religion. If monotheistic religions inherently involve violence, point to a particular form of social organization, or present us with especially complex deities, then we have truly begun to address the character of a religion, and not simply the number of its deities. It remains difficult indeed to gainsay that the theological complexity of Yahweh is in significant measure a function of that deity's role in an essentially monotheistic system. And since this system was of seminal importance for Judaism, Christianity, and Islam, reflection on the implications of a mono-Yahwism constitutes a desideratum for Old Testament scholars.

In sum, discussion of Yahwism and monotheism may involve much more than identifying moments of origin, points of contact with prior monolatrous or monotheistic religions, and refinements in critical vocabulary. In fact, such discussion may even move from the descriptive task, namely, indicating the ways in which Yahwism relates to monotheistic and/or polytheistic formulations, to more normative questions, namely, the ways in which one may think about a monotheistic Israelite faith and literature within religious communities today. J. Sanders's reflections about the Hebrew Bible as "a monotheizing literature" are germane: "To monotheize ... is not to progress or evolve toward monotheism, but rather to struggle within and against polytheistic contexts to affirm God's oneness, both in antiquity and today."[52] Clearly, the unfinished agenda may involve both the careful analysis of Yahwism as ancient religion as well as the appropriation of that faith's dynamics for the contemporary scene.

NOTES

1. B. Anderson, "God, OT Views of," *IDB* 2.427. Cf. F.-L. Hossfeld, "Einheit und Einzigkeit Gottes im frühen Jahwismus," *Im Gespräch mit dem*

dreieinen Gott. Elemente einer trinitarischen Theologie. Festschrift zum 65. Geburtstag von Wilhelm Breuning (ed. M. Böhenke and H. Heinz; Dusseldorf: Patmos Verlag, 1985) 57–74; F. Stolz, "Monotheismus in Israel," *Monotheismus in alten Israel und seiner Umwelt* (ed. O. Keel; Fribourg: Verlag Schweizerisches Katholisches Bibelwerk, 1980) 143–83.

2. Cf. J. Barr, "Monotheism," *HDB* 652.

3. So H. G. Reventlow, *Problems of Old Testament Theology in the Twentieth Century* (Philadelphia: Fortress Press, 1985); R. Clements, *Old Testament Theology: A Fresh Approach* (Atlanta: John Knox Press, 1978). Both von Rad and Eichrodt downplay the importance of the monotheism discussion, though for differing reasons. Von Rad views the matter as an improper attempt to discern what is central in Israel's theological traditions: "Monotheism as such was not a thing in which Israel of herself would have taken any particular interest—she did not measure herself by it or make it a touchstone, as she did with the first commandment" (*Old Testament Theology* [New York: Harper & Row, 1962] 1.211; cf. vol. 2.298 [1965]). Eichrodt writes: "Hence for us today the problem of monotheism in the religion of Israel is very far from being a burning issue as it was for earlier generations, when on the answer to this one question very often depended one's decision about the rightness or otherwise of the Old Testament revelation as a whole" (*Theology of the Old Testament* [Philadelphia: Westminster Press, 1961] 1.220). Cf., however, the significant attention that R. Knierim devotes to the issue of monotheism and pluralism in the OT ("The Task of Old Testament Theology," *HBT* 6 [1984] 25–57): "We have a fundamental problem with the evidence for monotheism in the Old Testament's theological pluralism" (p. 30). Not unrelated is J. Sanders's notion of the canon's tendency "to monotheize" ("Hermeneutics in True and False Prophecy," *Canon and Authority: Essays in Old Testament Religion and Theology* (ed. G. Coats and B. Long; Philadelphia: Fortress Press, 1977) 40.

4. So H. Ringgren, *Israelite Religion* (Philadelphia: Fortress Press, 1966) 99, 307. Cf., for a related discussion, F. Smith-Florentin, "Du monothéisme biblique: émergence et alentours," *ASSR* 59 (1985) 5–16.

5. This situation is exemplified by the absence of a reference to Pettazzoni's seminal article (see n. 6) in H. Vorländer, "Der Monotheismus Israels als Antwort auf die Krise des Exils," *Der einzige Gott. Die Geburt des biblischen Monotheismus* (ed. B. Lang; Munich: Kösel Verlag, 1981) 84–113.

6. For a convenient review of positions and initial citations of Voltaire, Hume, and Comte, see R. Pettazzoni, "The Formation of Monotheism," *Reader in Comparative Religion: An Anthropological Approach* (ed. W. Lessa and E. Vogt; New York: Harper & Row, 1965) 34–39. A more recent survey may be found in B. Lang, "Neues über die Geschichte des Monotheismus," *TQ* 163 (1983) 54–58. On the issue of a primitive monotheism, see esp. W. Mühlmann, "Das Problem des Urmonotheismus," *TLZ* 78 (1953) 705–18; and, more generally, P. Radin, *Monotheism among Primitive Peoples* (New York: Bollingen, 1954).

7. M.-J. Lagrange, *Études sur les religions semitiques* (EBib; Paris: Lecoffre, 1903).

8. David Hume, *The Natural History of Religion,* as cited by Pettazzoni, "Formation of Monotheism," n. 6.

9. Auguste Comte, *Cours de philosophie positive,* as cited by Pettazzoni, "Formation of Monotheism," n. 6.

10. E. B. Tylor, *Primitive Culture* (New York: Harper & Brothers, [1871] 1958).

11. J. Wellhausen, *Prolegomena to the History of Ancient Israel* (New York: World-Meridian, [1927] 1957).

12. M. Smith, *Palestinian Parties and Politics That Shaped the Old Testament* (New York: Columbia University Press, 1971) 23.

13. Ibid., 35–36.

14. Ibid., 45.

15. Ibid., 55.

16. Ibid., 56.

17. B. Lang, *Monotheism and the Prophetic Minority: An Essay in Biblical History and Sociology* (Sheffield, Eng.: Almond Press, 1983) 56. Cf. his more recent and concise presentation, "Zur Entstehung des biblischen Monotheismus," *TQ* 166 (1986) 135–42.

18. Lang, *Monotheism and the Prophetic Minority,* 20, 45.

19. A. van Selms, "Temporary Henotheism," *Symbolae Biblicae et Mesopotamicae Francisco Mario Theodoro de Liagre Böhl dedicatae* (ed. M. Beck et al.; Studia Francisci Scholten Memoriae Dedicata 4; Leiden: E. J. Brill, 1973) 341–48).

20. Lang, *Monotheism and the Prophetic Minority,* 35.

21. Ibid., 20.

22. Ibid., 54. See n. 5 above on Vorländer. N. Lohfink, "Gott und die Götter im Alten Testament," *Theologische Akademie* 6 (1969) 50–71. Cf. N. Lohfink's other valuable discussions, "Das Alte Testament und sein Monotheismus," *Der eine Gott und der dreieine Gott. Das Gottes Verständnis bei Christen, Juden, und Muslimen* (ed. K. Rahner; Schriftenreihe der Katholischen Akademie der Erzdiözese Freiburg; Munich: Schnell & Steiner, 1983) 28–47; "Zur Geschichte der Diskussion über den Monotheismus im Alten Israel," *Gott der Einzige. Zur Entstehung des Monotheismus in Israel* (ed. H. Haag; Quaestiones Disputatae 104; Freiburg: Herder, 1985) 9–25.

23. Pettazzoni, "The Formation of Monotheism," 37.

24. N. Gottwald, *The Tribes of Yahweh: A Sociology of the Religion of Liberated Israel, 1250–1050 B.C.E.* (Maryknoll, N.Y.: Orbis Books, 1979) 616.

25. S. Freud, *Moses and Monotheism* (London: Hogarth, 1939). See for the Egyptological perspective T. Peters, "Monotheism and Kingship in Ancient Memphis: A Study in Egyptian Mythology," *Perspectives in Religious Studies* 4 (1977) 160–73; E. Hornung, "Monotheismus im pharonischen Agypten," *Monotheismus im Alten Israel,* 83–97; E. Hornung, *Conceptions of God in*

Ancient Egypt: The One and the Many (Ithaca, N.Y.: Cornell University Press, 1982).

26. G. Pettinato, "Polytheismus und Henotheismus in der Religion von Ebla," *Monotheismus im Alten Israel,* 31–48.

27. B. Hartmann, "Monotheismus in Mesopotamien?" *Monotheismus im Alten Israel,* 49–81; see also J. Finkelstein, "Bible and Babel: A Comparative Study of the Hebrew and Babylonian Religious Spirit," *Commentary* 26 (1956) 431–44.

28. So, e.g., Vorländer, "Der Monotheismus Israels," 103–6.

29. H. H. Rowley, "Moses and Monotheism," *From Moses to Qumran: Studies in the Old Testament* (New York: Association Press, 1963) 35–63.

30. E. Renan, as cited by B. Lang, "Neues über die Geschichte des Monotheismus," 58; U. Oldenburg, *The Conflict between El and Ba'al in Canaanite Religion* (Supplementa Numen, Altera Series Dissertationes Ad Historian Religionum Pertinentes 3; Leiden: E. J. Brill, 1969) 174–84.

31. W. Albright, *From the Stone Age to Christianity: Monotheism and the Historical Process* (Garden City, NY: Doubleday Anchor Books, 1957) 27.

32. V. Maag, *Kultur, Kulturkontakt und Religion. Gesammelte Studien zur allgemeinen und alttestamentlicher Religionsgeschichte* (Göttingen: Vandenhoeck & Ruprecht, 1980).

33. Von Rad, *Old Testament Theology.*

34. See Rowley's discussion of these figures, "Moses and Monotheism," 35.

35. J. Wellhausen, *Prolegomena to the History of Ancient Israel.*

36. R. H. Pfeiffer, *Religion in the Old Testament* (New York: Harper & Row, 1961).

37. Pettazzoni, "The Formation of Monotheism."

38. Albright's work tends in this direction, so his use of the term "tribal or national henotheism" (*From the Stone Age to Christianity,* 192).

39. Rowley, "Moses and Monotheism," 39.

40. B. Stemberger, " 'Der Mann Moses' in Freud's Gesamtwerk" *Kairos* 16 (1974) 161–25.

41. P. Ciholas, "Monothéisme et violence," *RSR* 69 (1981) 325–54.

42. R. Girard (*Violence and the Sacred* [Baltimore: Johns Hopkins University Press, 1977]) makes a more general claim about the relation of violence and religion, especially within the ambit of primitive religion. "Every god, hero and mythic creature so far encountered, from the sacred African king to Chief Pestilence of the Tsimshians, embodies the interplay of violence projected by an act of generative violence" (p. 250).

43. See, e.g., C. Keller, *From a Broken Web: Separation, Sexism, and Self* (Boston: Beacon Press, 1986); and J. Ochshorn, *The Female Experience and the Nature of the Divine* (Bloomington: Indiana University Press, 1981).

44. Gottwald, *The Tribes of Yahweh,* 16.

45. Ibid., 693.

46. G. Swanson, *The Birth of the Gods: The Origin of Primitive Beliefs* (Ann Arbor: University of Michigan Press, 1960).

47. R. Alter, *The Art of Biblical Prose* (New York: Basic Books, 1981) 129.

48. H. Gunkel presaged Alter's work by arguing that no myth is possible in a monotheistic setting (*The Legends of Genesis* [New York: Schocken Books, 1969]).

49. H. Corbin, "La paradox du Monothéisme," *Oneness and Variety* (ed. A. Portmann and Rudolf Ritsema; Eranos Yearbook 1976; Leiden: E. J. Brill, 1980) 69–133. Cf. J. Sawyer, "Biblical Alternatives to Monotheism," *Theology* 87 (1984) 172–80.

50. Cf. another classic instance of tension within the deity discussed by J. Sanders, *Canon and Community: A Guide to Canonical Criticism* (Philadelphia: Fortress Press, 1984) 51.

51. D. Petersen, "The Yahwist on the Flood," *VT* 26 (1976) 438–46. Cf. Finkelstein, "Bible and Babel," 438–40 on the moral and perspectival implications of monotheism.

52. Sanders, *Canon and Community,* 52.

Part II

THE INTERPRETATION OF
THE TORAH AND THE
FORMER PROPHETS

8

"Comparing Scripture with Scripture": Some Observations on the Sinai Pericope of Exodus 19—24

JOHN VAN SETERS

The tradition of the giving of the Law to Moses at Sinai now occupies so central a place in the Pentateuch and became so important in the religion of Judaism that the problems of interpretive models and principles and the history of the tradition's development have been a rather constant preoccupation of biblical scholarship. The key to these problems for the last century has always been seen to lie with the "oldest" form of the tradition, the JE strata of the Sinai pericope of Exodus 19—24. Only after the difficult hermeneutical problems of the unit have been solved by the methods of source-critical analysis or the application of form-critical models of covenant or theophany is any consideration given to "later" levels of the tradition, especially in Deuteronomy. This study will argue that such an approach is faulty and that we must return to the ancient hermeneutical principle of "comparing scripture with scripture," but in a historical-critical manner.

The literary and form-critical analysis of the Sinai pericope of Exodus 19—24 has been one of the most difficult and controversial problems of Pentateuchal studies.[1] Many schemes have been proposed to account for the difficulties of these chapters but few have won very widespread acceptance. In German scholarship the recent tendency has been toward viewing more and more of the narrative elements in these chapters as late additions by a series of redactors with an increasing skepticism about getting back to the early Yahwistic or

Elohistic sources.[2] A good deal of the problem has to do with the extent of the so-called Deuteronomistic passages and their place within the unit as a whole. This has led to a new interest in a comparison between the theophany accounts in Exodus and Deuteronomy, but as I hope to show, this comparative analysis has not been extensive enough. One result of such comparison, primarily on the level of terminology, has been to create a new "proto-Deuteronomic" source or editor placed between the work of the Yahwist or Elohist and that of Deuteronomy.[3] The problem with this position is that it first uses all the criteria of Deuteronomistic influence to identify the new source and then it denies that the source thus identified is Deuteronomic. That hardly seems reasonable, especially when nothing seems to be gained by an earlier date. If a proto-Deuteronomic source exists at all, then it must be established by literary criteria other than its similarities to Deuteronomy. Otherwise proto-Deuteronomy may simply be another name for J or E.

If influence from Deuteronomy and the Deuteronomistic tradition is admitted, then it still remains necessary to demonstrate either that this is part of a late editing of the earlier text or that it represents the perspective of the whole pre-Priestly narrative in Exodus 19–24. The latter option represents the view of those who advocate a late Yahwist who is himself post-Deuteronomistic and exilic in date.[4] This view goes beyond the identification of a few Deuteronomistic phrases to a much broader comparison with the Deuteronomistic tradition.

Source Analysis

We may begin by addressing briefly the source analysis of the text. The chronological framework in 19:1 is widely recognized as Priestly and is clearly an addition to v. 2, which includes the awkward repetition of arriving at Sinai. In the unit vv. 3–8 there is a fluctuation in the use of the divine name but this cannot be made to work as a source criterion and is best disregarded.[5] The presence of Deuteronomistic language in this unit has led in the past to suspicions that at least part of these verses was a later addition, but how to distinguish the addition from the basic text on other grounds has never been made clear. There is an apparent problem of repetition between v. 8b and v. 9b that some have used to argue for a duality of sources (although v. 8b would hardly be an editorial addition in that case). Verse 9b, however, clearly refers back to v. 8a and reports the statement of the people to the deity. So the problem must lie in v. 8b, which has the curious expression. "Moses *brought back (wayyāšeb)* the words of the people to Yahweh," which may represent a corruption in the text for an original reading, "and Moses *returned (wayyāšob)* to Yahweh," omitting the phrase, "the words of the people *('et dibrê hā'ām)*." The repetition of this phrase from v. 9b could be accounted for on the basis of homoeoteleuton. Verse 9a introduces a standard Yahwistic theme, that of the legitimation of Moses as mediator, as seen in Exodus 3 and 14, and it also anticipates the theme of the people hearing Yahweh speaking with Moses in an especially impressive way. To this matter we will return below.

Verses 10–15 constitute a set of cultic instructions, first by Yahweh to Moses and then by Moses to the people, but this section is not a unity. The original instruction consisted of vv. 10–11, 13b and has to do with consecrating the people so that they might ascend the mountain at the time of the theophany, and these instructions are relayed to the people (vv. 14–15).

In contrast, vv. 12–13a have to do with consecrating the mountain as a sanctuary with the strictest taboos so that the people could not ascend. This part of the instructions is not carried out in vv. 14–19. But, in vv. 20ff. when Moses ascends the mountain again he receives a divine reprimand since these directives of vv. 12–13a have not been enforced. The instructions are further elaborated in terms of the priests who are viewed as separate from the people and part of the consecrated realm. So vv. 12–13a and vv. 20–25 clearly belong together. Furthermore, the incongruity of the whole unit of vv. 20–25 with what precedes is obvious: *(a)* v. 20 repeats the statement of v. 18 about Yahweh coming down but in v. 20 all signs of the theophany have disappeared and the dialogue returns to the matter of preparations; *(b)* there is no public legitimation of Moses as suggested in v. 9 as the point of Moses' role in the theophany, only a reprimand; *(c)* Moses is still going up and down the mountain giving instructions in the middle of the theophany. The interest here is Priestly, even to the point of anticipating the later laws regarding the holiness of the sanctuary and the priestly office. Consequently, the basic presentation is in vv. 2–11, 13b–19 which I identify as J; vv. 1, 12–13a, 20–25 are Priestly additions.

The unit in 19:16–19 deals with the theophany and has its sequel in 20:18ff., which contains the people's reaction to the theophany.[6]

Consequently, I follow Childs, among others, in regarding 20:18ff. as a literary continuation of 19:19 and all of this I would assign to the Yahwist.[7] The Ten Commandments with its obvious Priestly editing in the law of the Sabbath in v. 11 will be assigned to this source. The sources are as follows:

J =   2–11,   13b–19,   18–26
P = 19:1,   12–13a,   20–25; 20:1–17

Comparisons with Deuteronomy

The separation into two sources does not solve all the difficulties of chapters 19 and 20 for there still exist some rather remarkable features in the Yahwistic account that are hard to explain. An alternate solution is to appeal to a diversity of oral traditions behind the present account, but such conjectures are difficult to control. It would seem preferable to first exhaust the possibility of comparison with extant biblical traditions before conjecturing about such hypothetical sources. This suggests the need to compare the Exodus account of Sinai with the treatment of the Horeb theophany in Deuteronomy. An important beginning was made by Childs in his exploration of Moses' role as mediator, and this was carried further by Nicholson in his treatment of Exod. 20:22–23.[8] But the scope of these comparisons is still too narrow for a complete discussion of the issues. It is my view that an analysis of the structure and form of Exodus 19–20 as compared with Deuteronomy 4 and 5 will prove very rewarding. (See table, 116–17.)

First of all, it has always seemed curious that the theophany in Exod. 19:16–19; 20:18–21 and the subsequent giving of the law in 20:22ff. should be preceded by an earlier dialogue between God and Moses (19:3–6) in which it is assumed that the covenant, including a series of laws, has already been given and which the people agree to obey (vv. 7ff.). Yet, if we compare chap. 19 in terms of its structure with Deut. 5:1ff., we find in the latter an exhortation by Moses to keep the laws which are then associated with the covenant at Horeb, and this reference to laws and covenant comes before the recounting of the actual event of theophany and the giving of the commandments in vv. 4ff. Since in Deuteronomy the speech of Moses is all recapitulation of past events mixed with present exhortation, the order of these items does not constitute a problem. Furthermore, historical recapitulation of events as a basis for exhortation is a regular feature of Deuteronomy.

After the events of Horeb are recounted in 5:4–31 the exhortation to obedience is resumed. This same pattern is found again in Deuteronomy 4. Verses 1–2 contain an exhortation to keep the commandments followed by a historical recapitulation used as a warning: "Your eyes have seen what Yahweh did at Baal-peor" (v. 3), followed by still further exhortation to keep the law (vv. 4–8). Within this exhortation is a reference to Israel's special place among the nations. Deuteronomy 4:9ff. repeats the pattern again. It begins with exhortation that leads right into recapitulation, "lest you forget the things which your eyes have seen" (v. 9), followed by a detailed account of the Horeb theophany and the giving of the law (vv. 10–14), and further exhortation (vv. 15ff.). Moses' speech also recalls the events of the exodus (vv. 20, 34, 37) as evidence of divine election.

In Exod. 19:3ff. the same pattern emerges. Yahweh commands Moses to give an exhortation to the people (v. 3b). The first element of the exhortation is historical recapitulation: "You have seen what I did to the Egyptians . . ." (v. 4), and this is followed by a command to keep the covenant. This, in turn, is followed by a reference to Israel's special place among the nations in language very similar to Deut. 4:20. [9] As in Deuteronomy 4 this introductory parenesis is followed by the account of the theophany and the giving of the law. For Deuteronomy the exhortation to keep the commandments preceding the actual description of the giving of the law is no problem since the style of presentation in chaps. 4 and 5 is recapitulation long after the event. But for Exodus 19, which purports to be a description of the event itself, this creates havoc with the temporal sequence of events. I believe one must explain this by the fact that the author of Exodus 19 depended too heavily upon Deuteronomy for his structuring of the introductory dialogue and disregarded the narrative consequences.

This artificiality in J's structuring of the narrative can be seen in another feature of Exodus 19—24. It has often been observed that Moses goes up and down the mountain an inordinate number of times (even if we regard vv. 20–25 as a later P addition). The solution to this problem of Moses' frequent trips does not lie in the proliferation of sources, either oral or written. If we compare Exodus with Deuteronomy we note that no mention is made of Moses going up and down the mountain in chaps. 4 and 5, although 5:5, 27, 31 could be construed to hint at this. Yet it is clear that for Deuteronomy "standing near Yahweh" (5:31) refers to Moses' constant communion with the

Comparison of Exodus 19—20 with Deuteronomy 4—5

Exodus 19—20		Deuteronomy 4		Deuteronomy 5	
19:2	Encamped at Sinai.				
3a	Moses climbs the mountain.				
3b	God commands Moses to exhort the people.	1–2	Moses exhorts the people.	1	Moses exhorts the people.
4–6	Historical recapitulation of the exodus, exhortation to keep the covenant, become God's special people (comparison with the nations).	3–8	Historical recapitulation of Baal-peor, exhortation to keep the Law (comparison with the nations). Pattern repeated in 9–20 and 30–40 (God's special people, v. 20).	2–5	Historical recapitulation of Horeb event, exhortation to keep the Law = covenant made at Horeb.
7–8	Moses goes down the mountain and relays the exhortation. The people agree to obey. Moses returns to God on the mount.				
9	Legitimation of Moses' authority as reason for theophany.			5	Theophany is reason for Moses as mediator.
10–11, 13b–15	Preparations for the assembly.	10a	"Assemble the people" to hear the words of Yahweh and fear him.	22	Reference to the assembly at Horeb.

Comparing Scripture with Scripture

	Exodus 19—20		Deuteronomy 4		Deuteronomy 5
16–19, 20:18	The Theophany: people at the foot of mountain, thunder, lightning, cloud, smoke, fire, *the sound of the shofar.*	11–12	The Theophany: people at the foot of the mountain, fire, darkness, cloud, gloom, *the sound of words.*	4–5	People do not go up the mountain, fire, cloud, gloom, *great voice,* darkness.
[20:1–17	The ten commandments (P).]	13a	Covenant = ten words.	6–21	Ten commandments.
		13b	Written on two stone tablets.	22b	Written on two stone tablets.
18–19	People's fear and petition for intervention by Moses.			24–27	People's fear and request for Moses' intervention (of v. 5) for the rest of the laws.
20	Reasons for theophany: test and fear leading to obedience.	10	Fear and obedience, (36) discipline.	29	Fear and obedience.
21	The people stand at a distance but Moses draws near to God in the gloom.			30–31	The people return to their tents but Moses is commanded to draw near to God after the theophany.
22–23	Connection is made between theophany and 1st and 2d commandments.	12–19	Connection between theophany and 2d commandment.		
24ff.	All the laws and statutes are given at Sinai.	14	Moses commanded by God to teach the laws "at that time."	31	Moses is told by God to receive the rest of the commandments.

117

deity throughout the wilderness journey, since these commandments and statutes were only finally delivered to the people in the land of Moab. Nevertheless, Deuteronomy does suggest a series of dialogues between the deity and Moses that were at least thought to be related to the Horeb revelation: (1) a divine command to assemble the people at Horeb (4:10); (2) the giving of the Ten Commandments to Moses and the people together (4:12ff.; 5:6ff.); (3) the dialogue between Moses and the deity alone (4:14; 5:28ff.). The Yahwist, in his effort to turn the Deuteronomic recapitulation into a narrative of events in time and space, simply connected every occasion of dialogue by a separate trip up and down the mountain. Even the motif of initial exhortation is made into a divine speech (Exod. 19:3–6) and the occasion of a trip up and down the mountain. This is followed by a separate trip for instructions about the assembly (vv. 9ff.), then the theophany in which Moses and the people together hear Yahweh (vv. 16ff.), and after the theophany in 20:21 another trip by Moses up the mountain to receive all the commandments *at that time* (cf. Deut. 4:14). The complete artificiality of the mountain-climbing motif should make it clear that it is not part of the original tradition. The only ascent that is significant, and probably the origin of this motif, is the one in which Moses climbs the mountain to obtain the two tablets of stone (Deut. 5:22b; 9:9ff.). But this trip in J (24:12–13) has become entirely redundant by Moses writing the book of the covenant in Exod. 24:4. To this we will return below.

The description of the theophany itself in Exod. 19:16–19 has been a prime target for source division because it contains a mixture of volcano and storm motifs, v. 16 reflecting a thunderstorm and v. 18 a volcano. But 20:18 combines both motifs while 20:21 mentions the "thick darkness" that is part of the volcano motif (J) in a supposed E text. Any effort to divide these two motifs cuts across the alternating use of the divine names. Thus the two source criteria would seem to cancel each other out. Deuteronomy, by contrast, is quite consistent in using volcano motifs (4:11ff., 15, 33, 36; 5:4ff., 22–26), with great emphasis upon God speaking to the people "from the midst of the fire." The fire is closely associated with the other elements of the volcano motif so that in fact God's speaking can be heard coming from the cloud and the thick darkness as well (5:22–23). Nicholson has argued that the Deuteronomist in Deuteronomy 4 has developed the theophany a stage further so that the fire reaches to the heart of heaven

(4:1) and Yahweh can be said to speak to his people "out of heaven" as well as out of the fire (v. 36).[10]

In Exodus 19 the essential theophany phenomena have become detached from the mountain so that God himself is spoken of as coming or descending from heaven upon the mountain in a thick cloud (v. 9) and in the fire itself (v. 18). It is in this way that God speaks to his people "from heaven" (20:22), the combination of motifs having been taken over directly from Deut. 4:36.[11] For J the thick cloud and the fire have become symbols of the divine presence quite separate from the mountain and from the features of volcano and storm as they are in the pillar of fire and the pillar of cloud. The whole direction of the development of the symbolism is clear. It moves from its simplest form in Deuteronomy 5 to the idea of transcendence in Deuteronomy 4 ("from heaven"), to the cloud and fire as symbols in the Yahwist. P develops the imagery a stage further by identifying the cloud and the fire with the "glory" *(kābôd)* of Yahweh.

It is, however, in the act of divine speaking that the most significant difference between Exodus and Deuteronomy appears. Deuteronomy, on the one hand, stresses that the people actually heard the Ten Commandments "in a loud voice" *(qôl gādôl,* 5:22), but while they heard the "sound" *(qôl,* 4:12), they did not see any form. This becomes the basis for the discussion throughout the chapter that God is not to be represented by any human form or any likeness in nature (4:15ff.). It is the law, epitomized in the Ten Commandments, and not an image, that becomes for Deuteronomy the primary symbol of the divine presence.

Exodus, on the other hand, does not indicate that the people actually heard the Ten Commandments, especially if 20:18 is viewed as the original continuation of 19:19. Instead the Yahwist lays all the emphasis on the hearing of a sound *(qôl),* but in this case it has become the sound of a trumpet. This feature of the trumpet blast is completely absent from Deuteronomy but it is central to the theophany in Exodus (19:13b, 16, 19; 20:18). There is no indication that this sound came from the camp. On the contrary, it is of divine origin, mysterious and terrifying in nature, and the high point of the theophany. Exodus 19:19 states, "While the sound of the trumphet grew louder and louder Moses would speak and God would answer him in the sound [of the trumpet]."[12]

This means that in the Exodus-Yahwist account the people did *not* hear distinct words, much less the Ten Commandments. The theophany is primarily symbolized by the trumpet sound. It is only after this event that Moses approaches God to receive all the commandments together (20:21ff.; cf. Deut. 5:4ff., 27).[13] The Yahwist makes no distinction between the two types of laws and so they appear in a rather mixed form in what follows in Exod. 20:23ff., and all are given at Sinai.[14]

Furthermore, the introduction of the trumpet sound suggests a cultic setting and this agrees well with the instructions in Exod. 19:10–11, 13b–15. But this should not be construed as the original *Sitz im Leben* of the tradition. Instead, it is a literary elaboration by the Yahwist of the much simpler assembly in Deuteronomy which was only a gathering to hear the law. One might even suggest that the Yahwist's intention is to construct a rather sophisticated etiology for the cultic use of the *shofar* as symbolic of the divine presence.[15] This special consecration of the entire people in preparation for their encounter with the deity relates directly back to the designation of the people as a "kingdom of priests" in 19:6. For the Yahwist there is no need for a special priesthood. The Priestly writer in vv. 12–13a and 20ff. is compelled to revise J's presentation by shifting the emphasis of sanctity to the mountain and by consecrating only the priests as distinct from the rest of the people.

As indicated above, Exod. 20:18 is the direct continuation of 19:19 and tells how the people reacted to the theophany with fear. They then request (20:19) that Moses act as intermediary on their behalf lest they die, and this again corresponds to a similar request in Deut. 5:24–27. In Deuteronomy this request by the people comes after the giving of the Ten Commandments and is the *beginning* of Moses' role as mediator, explaining why it was necessary. In Exodus the whole purpose of the theophany was to *confirm* Moses' role as mediator (19:9) so that the divine speaking was directed toward Moses during the theophany. Moses had already become the mediator for the people through his call in Exodus 3. So the best the Yahwist could do was to combine the two ideas by letting the people experience the theophany as the sound of Yahweh speaking to Moses, but the substance of the divine speech had to be mediated entirely through Moses.[16]

In Exod. 20:20 Moses responds to the people's request by stating the reasons why God has come in the theophany: (1) in order that God might test them, and (2) that they might fear God and thus refrain from sinning. This last motive of the fear of God leading to obedience is strongly suggested by Deut. 5:23–27 and explicitly stated in v. 29, as well as in Deut. 4:9–10. The theme of God's testing seems to correspond to the divine discipline in Deut. 4:36.

After the people experience the theophany, Moses approaches God to receive the commandments (Exod. 20:21). Similarly, in Deut. 5:28ff. after the people request Moses' intervention, God agrees to their request and commands Moses to "stand here by me, and I will tell you all the commandments . . ." (v. 31). These are to be given to the people before they enter the land. Here again, in spite of the similarity in structure there is a critical distinction between Exodus and Deuteronomy—in Exodus additional commandments are given to the people at Sinai and just at this point during the theophany. These laws are represented by 20:23—23:33, which are then written down by Moses in the Book of the Covenant (Exod. 24:4). In Deuteronomy the Ten Commandments are given at Horeb, but the rest of the statutes and ordinances are given during the course of the subsequent travels and comprise the Book of the Law (Deut. 28:64; 31:24).

The beginning of the laws in Exod. 20:22–23 has a rather curious form and structure that calls for some explanation, and here I refer again to the study of Nicholson for the full development of this observation.[17] In v. 22 Yahweh says to Moses, "Thus shall you say to the Israelites: 'You have seen that from heaven I spoke with you.'" This corresponds, as we have seen, to the hortatory style of Exod. 19:3 and also to that of Deuteronomy 4. But the reference to speaking "from heaven" is unusual since it stands rather abruptly alongside the divine speaking in the elements of the theophany. Yet in Deut. 4:36 we have this same speaking "from heaven" set in parallel structure to God's speaking from the midst of the fire. The Yahwist has followed the same theme here.

This introductory statement in Exod. 20:22 is followed by the command: "You shall not make gods of silver to be alongside of me and you shall not make for yourselves gods of gold." The connection between this commandment in v. 23, which is a conflation of the first and second commandments of the decalogue, and the hortatory statement in v. 22 is not immediately clear until one compares Deut. 4:12, 15ff. where Moses in his exhortation lays out the argument that since the Israelites only heard God at Horeb but did not see any form they are not to make images like the other nations. Further, in Deut. 4:32ff.

it is also argued that the singularity of God's speaking in the theophany and of his action in the exodus demonstrates that there is no other deity besides him. The Yahwist must assume these arguments in the implied connection between 20:22 and 23. As in the case of Exod. 19:3ff., the Yahwist has turned an exhortation in Deuteronomy into a divine speech to introduce a series of laws.

Up to this point I am in agreement with Nicholson, except that he wishes to ascribe Exod. 20:22–23 to a Deuteronomistic redactor separate from what has preceded. His argument for doing so is that in the preceding unit (20:18–21) the fear of Yahweh resulted from seeing the theophany, whereas in v. 22 and in Deuteronomy the emphasis is on the speaking of Yahweh as the source of fear. But I do not think this distinction can be maintained. In Exod. 20:19 it is specifically God's speaking that the people regard as such a threat to life (as in Deut. 5:24–27). As we have seen, this divine speech in Exodus was expressed in the mysterious sound of the *shofar,* which is the most prominent element of the theophany. Furthermore, the whole point of the theophany, as stated in 19:9, is "that the people may hear when I speak with you and therefore believe in you forever." The emphasis on hearing God speak is the same as in Deuteronomy; it is only the form of that speech and what is actually heard that has been modified. This means that Exod. 20:22–23 is not a redactional addition whose purpose is to explain the insertion of the decalogue before 20:18–21 (so Nicholson). Instead it introduces a quite new series of laws, the Book of the Covenant. The decalogue in Exod. 20:1–17 with its introduction in Exod. 19:20–25 is a Priestly addition taken over from Deuteronomy with some modifications, especially in the Sabbath law.

The Law of the Altar

The law of the altar in Exod. 20:24–26 follows quite naturally from the prohibition of images in v. 23. The assumption that this law is primitive, pre-Deuteronomic reform and therefore precedes the centralization of worship is virtually universal among scholars. The text is also the major reason for dating the Covenant Code as a whole to an early period. There are, however, some problems with this view, both literary and otherwise.

The law itself is in vv. 24a, 25–26 and it mentions only one altar. Only in the interpretation in v. 24b does the notion of more than one altar come into consideration. The law does not seem to have any bearing on the construction of altars during the monarchy. The only texts that refer to a similar type of altar construction are Josh. 8:31 and Deut. 27:5ff., and both of these are part of post-Deuteronomistic additions. One should note that in all three instances, and also in Exod. 24:3ff., the building of the altars is in close association with the promulgation of the law. This law of the altar actually stands outside of the code of laws that begins with 21:1ff. In Deuteronomy the law of centralization of sacrifice also comes at the beginning of the code.

The main issue for interpreting the whole lies in Exod. 20:24b, which contains the troublesome phrase *hizkîr šem*. The usual meaning is to "invoke the name" of the deity. It occurs with this sense in 23:13 in a prohibition against invoking the name of other gods. In all other examples (Isa. 26:13; 12:4; Ps. 45:18; Josh. 23:7; Amos 6:10; Isa. 48:1; Ps. 20:8) it always has to do with an act by Israel and never by Yahweh.[18] So it is a little puzzling to understand why Childs, in his commentary, wants to render the phrase in 20:24 in the sense: "In every place where I [Yahweh] reveal my name. . . ."[19] The most obvious conclusion is to read, with the Syriac, the verb in the second singular: "In every place where you invoke my name I will come to you and I will bless you." This would be in harmony with the general usage. But invoking the name does not require an altar and stands as an alternative to cultic activity. One is reminded of 1 Kings 8 where prayer may be rendered before the altar but also in distant places quite cut off from the central sanctuary. This statement in Exod. 20:24b is a major shift from the law of the central sanctuary in Deuteronomy 12 where the emphasis is on God choosing the place to set his name and the people coming to that place with the produce with which God has already blessed them. The text is late and probably exilic in date.

The law of the altar would allow for a simple reconstruction of the altar in Jerusalem with its cult in the exilic period.[20] At the same time it stresses that God is not limited by such a provision. There is nothing particularly primitive about this law.

The Covenant Ritual at Sinai

The account of the inauguration of the covenant at Sinai in Exod. 24:3–8 has received a great deal of discussion and scrutiny. Since it has been most recently treated by Nicholson I will use his work as my point of departure.[21] Nicholson, in turn, builds on the works of L.

Perlitt and E. Kutsch, who should also be mentioned here.[22] Perlitt, who regaøled Exod. 19:3b–8 as a late Deuteronomic addition, saw evidence of the same hand in Exod. 24:3–8, particularly in the phraseology of Moses reporting the commands of the deity to the people and their pledge of obedience (24:3, 7b with 19:7–8). The notion of the Book of the Law/Covenant is likewise Deuteronomic in origin. But Perlitt tried to isolate an earlier substratum because of the reference to the "young men" as assistants to Moses, and certain other features which he viewed as evidence of the primitive nature of the ritual. Kutsch accepted Perlitt's argument for the Deuteronomistic character of the unit but regarded the whole piece as a unity with none of it pre-Deuteronomic. Nicholson argues in a similar fashion for its completely unified character.[23]

I accept the arguments both for the unity of Exod. 24:3–8 and for its Deuteronomic character and wish to focus primarily upon the matter of the ritual's meaning. Nicholson is certainly correct in viewing the significance of the blood being sprinkled upon the people as an act of consecration to make them holy, just as priests are consecrated (Exod. 29:20ff.; Lev. 8:22–30). He states:

> Those over whom the blood of Yahweh's sacrifice is cast now belong peculiarly to him, and are thereby also solemnly commissioned to his service, just as the consecration of priests was a commissioning to the office of priest.[24]

This immediately suggests a very close link with Exod. 19:6 and the idea that the people are holy and a "kingdom of priests."

Nicholson also follows Childs in making the connection between the announcement of the covenant in 19:5 and its completion in the ritual in 24:3–8. This would seem to confirm in the strongest way that both Exod. 19:3b–8 and 24:3–8 belong to the same hand and are late Deuteronomistic in date. But just at this point Nicholson wants to draw a distinction between the two and suggests that 24:3–8 is, in fact, proto-Deuteronomic and 19:3b–8 a later Deuteronomistic interpretation of 24:3–8. The proposal seems rather forced, but the reasons that compel him to this earlier date for 24:3–8 are twofold.

First, Deuteronomy does not contain any such ritual and it seems unlikely that a Deuteronomistic writer would have added it. If, however, one acknowledges that within Exod. 19:3b–8 the notion of a "kingdom of priests" is also not Deuteronomic but later in date, since it is paralleled in Isa. 61:6, then the same can be said for the blood ritual of Exod. 24:3–8. The idea of a "holy people" is Deuteronomic. It is the creation of a special ceremony of consecration by which to actualize the idea that is new.

Second, Nicholson regards 24:3–8 as closely tied to the Book of the Covenant and as a way of including the code in its present context. But since the Book of the Covenant cannot be dated apart from its context and since we have argued that the introduction to the laws in 20:21–26 is equally post-Deuteronomic in character, there is no reason to view 24:3–8 as early because of its association with the Book of the Covenant.

If we turn to Deuteronomy we note that the covenant is instituted by the people assembling at the mountain to hear the divine commands. Only after witnessing the theophany do they vow to hear and obey whatever words of Yahweh Moses mediates to them (Deut. 4:10a; 5:2–27). In Exod. 19:9–11, 13b–15 the people not only prepare to hear the divine speech but they must be especially consecrated and ritually pure as if to anticipate the special nature of the ceremony in 24:3–8. The institution of the covenant now includes not only hearing the words of the law through Moses, conflating both the Sinai covenant and the Moab covenant, and the vow to obedience, but also the particular act that makes Israel the holy people of God. The whole account in J is a tightly constructed unity.

Thus Exod. 24:3–8 does not represent a repeatable cultic act to which parallels may be found. It is a special hybrid that has been created by the author as an etiology for a set of ideas derived from the Deuteronomic tradition. It is meant to symbolize and actualize the unique covenant-making event at Sinai, including the inauguration of Israel as the holy people of God.

If we follow the practice of most commentators and exclude Exod. 24:9–11 as belonging to another source,[25] then Exod. 24:12–15a would follow directly on 24:8 and provide a transition to the story of the golden calf in Exodus 32.[26] But if these two units, 24:3–8 and 12–15a, are taken together, there is a problem. The tablets of stone and their content would appear to be redundant since the laws are now contained in a book written by Moses. Once again we need to compare the motif of the stone tablets with Deuteronomy.

The original version of the stone tablets is certainly the one in Deut. 5:22 where it is clear that there were two tablets of stone on which were written the Ten Commandments, inscribed by God and given to Moses. It is only at a much later point in time that Moses wrote the rest of the laws in a book and delivered them to the people in the land of Moab (Deut. 31:9–13, 24–27). We have seen above that in Exod. 24:3–8 J has combined both the words *(dĕbārîm)* and the ordinances *(mišpātîm)* in the Sinai revelation and put them in Moses' book at that time. In the divine tablets of stone in Exod. 24:12, which are no longer two in number, he also includes "both law and commandment," that is, the whole revelation of law as if the divine copy is meant to correspond with what Moses has written. This was J's way of dealing with both of D's traditions of a book and tablets of stone now connected with only one covenant.[27]

Deuteronomy does not say in 5:22 where and when Yahweh gave the tablets to Moses, although the context suggests that it was rather soon after the initial Horeb event. This is only related in Deut. 9:9 in connection with the molten calf episode, where it states that Moses went up the mountain to receive the two tablets of stone containing "all the words that Yahweh had spoken with you on the mountain out of the midst of the fire on the day of assembly." Since Moses' absence from the people while on the mountain to receive the tablets of stone is vital as a transition to the golden calf story, it had to be included between 24:3–8 and the other episode in chap. 32.

Summary and Conclusion

The above comparison with Deuteronomy could be supplemented with a consideration of Exodus 32 and Deuteronomy 9—10, but we must bring this study to a close.[28] To summarize the observations made above:

(1) The Deuteronomistic character of the text of Exodus 19—24 cannot be limited to a few redactional touches. Much more significant is a comparison of the compositional structures of Exodus and Deuteronomy.

(2) This structural comparison shows that the simple picture in Deuteronomy as reflected in the rather repetitive style of recapitulation and exhortation has been made more complex by the Yahwist in Exodus. The latter has created narrative scenes out of hortatory passages and changed some of Moses' speeches into divine speeches with each unit in the structure made a separate scene marked off by its own time and space, usually a trip up and down the mountain.

(3) The Yahwist has changed the deity's proclamation of the Ten Commandments to the people to the sound of the *shofar,* symbolizing the divine presence. This seems to provide an etiology for a known cultic practice.

(4) The Yahwist has also transformed the event from a simple convocation to hear the law, as in Deuteronomy, into a ceremonial event with careful preparation and a final solemn act of consecration and sacrifice, all of this without priesthood. This covenant making in Exod. 24:3–8 is a hybrid construction symbolizing and explaining the origin of the people and their special character.

(5) The Yahwist faced a real problem with Deuteronomy's presentation of Moses' inauguration as a mediator only after the giving of the Ten Commandments, since in J's view he had served as mediator from the time of his call through all the events that ultimately brought the people to Sinai. So he had to interpret the divine speaking and the events in such a way that even during the theophany and the giving of the law at Sinai, Moses continued to act as mediator. The Sinai events were meant to confirm that role.

(6) The Yahwist does not distinguish between the Ten Commandments given at Sinai-Horeb and the rest of the laws. They are all grouped together and given at one time. P represents a compromise. He reintroduces the Ten Commandments again as a separate group, but also has most of the laws given at Sinai. Yet he still allows for the development of laws on the journey after Sinai.

(7) The structural and thematic comparison between Exodus and Deuteronomy greatly simplifies the literary problems that have bedeviled scholars and point strongly in the direction of a late date for the Yahwist in the exilic period.

These observations have important implications for the history of Israel's religion. There is no longer any basis for supporting the notion of a *preexilic* Sinai theology of law and covenant. It is possible that the giving of divine law was first associated with Moses and the wilderness period by the Deuteronomic reformers in the late monarchy, but there is no evidence that this notion rested on a cultic tradition of a covenant renewal festival or law making. The understanding of Israel as a covenant community is an exilic, and primarily a diaspora, form of corporate identity that became significant for Israel's religious life only after the demise of the monarchy and the state. Zion was *not* the heir of Sinai, as commonly suggested,[29] but Sinai the heir of Zion.

NOTES

1. For a survey of the problems see Brevard S. Childs, *The Book of Exodus* (Philadelphia: Westminster Press, 1974) 340ff.; see also H. H. Schmid, *Der sogenannte Jahwist* (Zürich: Theologischer Verlag, 1976) 83ff.

2. See esp. the work of L. Perlitt, *Bundestheologie im Alten Testament* (WMANT 36; Neukirchen-Vluyn: Neukirchener Verlag, 1969) 156–238.

3. A position most recently advocated by A. Phillips, "A Fresh Look at the Sinai Pericope," *VT* 34(1984) 39–52, 282–94.

4. See the work by Schmid in n. 1. Also M. Rose, *Deuteronomist und Jahwist* (ATANT 67; Zürich: Theologischer Verlag, 1981); J. Van Seters, "Confessional Reformulation in the Exilic Period," *VT* 22(1972) 448–59.

5. See the statement by Childs, *Exodus,* 349. For a denial of this criterion in Exodus as a whole see F. V. Winnett, *The Mosaic Tradition* (Toronto: University of Toronto Press, 1949) 20ff.

6. The division of these verses into two different sources (J and E) has been motivated in the past by the fluctuation in the use of the divine name, but once this criterion is abandoned as inadequate for source division then there is no good reason to see more than one source in this unit. See Childs, *Exodus,* 349; cf. M. Noth, *Exodus* (Philadelphia: Westminster Press, 1962).

7. Childs, *Exodus,* 351ff.

8. See ibid.; E. W. Nicholson, "The Decalogue as the Direct Address of God," *VT* 27 (1977) 422–33.

9. For a discussion of the Deuteronomistic language of Exod. 19:3b–8 see E. W. Nicholson, *God and His People* (Oxford: Clarendon Press, 1986) 166–67. His discussion of parallels with Deutero-Isaiah and the echo of the phrase "a kingdom of priests" in Trito-Isaiah (Isa. 61:6) also speaks for a late date.

10. Nicholson, "Decalogue as the Direct Address of God," 424ff.

11. Cf. ibid., 428ff.

12. Reading *baqqôl* with the article. Scholars have usually missed the point of this text by not seeing the connection betwen this "sound" and the sound of the *shofar,* so they debate whether the *qôl* refers to thunder or to the sound of words. See Childs, *Exodus,* 343.

13. It is assumed by most scholars dealing with the Exodus account that the earliest version must have contained the decalogue. But according to our analysis it does not fit into the Yahwistic scheme and therefore was added by P with minor modifications. This calls for some comment on Deut. 5:5. Childs (*Exodus,* 351ff.) points out that the verse suggests a mediatorial role for Moses during the theophany itself and this seems to contrast with v. 4 and the rest of Deuteronomy 5 which suggests that the people themselves heard the ten words without the need of a mediator and only requested a mediator after

the theophany. He therefore takes the verse as a clue to an older tradition and finds this in Exod. 20:18ff. by following those scholars who transpose these verses to a position before the decalogue. But there are many problems with this solution: (1) If there is no decalogue in J then no transposition is needed. (2) Does the *dêbar yhwh* (or possibly *dibrê yhwh* as in *BHS*) in Deut. 5:5 suggest the decalogue? That is by no means necessary. (3) The emphasis on the fire in Deut. 5:5 corresponds more to the D tradition than to that of sound in Exod. 20:18. (4) The circumstantial clause in Deut. 5:5 must depend on the preceding so that it can hardly be older but it could be younger and a modification. (5) The expression "at that time" (Deut. 5:5) would seem to be fairly precise as locating Moses' role as mediator within the theophany. But in Deut. 4:14 the same expression "at that time" is used to refer to the giving of laws subsequent to the theophany as in 5:31. It seems to me that the whole style of recapitulation does not allow one to make such strict distinctions in the sequence of events. We have the same problem with Deut. 5:22b which appears temporally out of place. On the other hand, the remarks about a dialogue between God and Moses in Exod. 20:21 may have been influenced by both Deut. 4:14 and 5:5.

14. This combination seems to be confirmed in Exod. 24:3ff. where it states that Moses repeated to the people both the "words of Yahweh" *(dibrê yhwh)* and the "ordinances" *(mišpāṭîm)* and then wrote them both in a "book of the covenant."

15. One could also make a case for Yahweh's appearance to Moses in the burning bush (Exodus 3) as reflecting the tradition of God's speaking from the fire. Here the burning bush could be viewed as representing a menorah which often resembles a burning tree. We may in fact have a parallel etiology for the menorah as a symbol of the divine presence. On the *shofar* and menorah as symbols of the deity in later Judaism see E. R. Goodenough, *Jewish Symbols in the Greco-Roman Period* (New York: Pantheon Press, 1954) 4.71–98, 167–94.

16. On the relationship of Deut. 5:5 to this text see above n. 13.

17. See Nicholson, "Decalogue as the Direct Address of God," 428ff.

18. See the discussion by Brevard Childs, *Memory and Tradition in Israel* (SBT 37; Naperville, Ill.: SCM Press, 1962) 12–13.

19. Childs, *Exodus,* 466.

20. See Ezra 3:2ff.

21. Nicholson, *God and His People,* 164–78.

22. Perlitt, *Bundestheologie im Alten Testament,* 190–203; E. Kutsch, *Verheissung und Gesetz: Untersuchung zum sogenannten "Bund" im Alten Testament* (BZAW 131; Berlin: Walter de Gruyter, 1973) 80–89.

23. Nicholson, *God and His People,* 169–71. Nicholson's basic difference with Kutsch has to do with the latter's interpretation of the blood rite. Cf. Kutsch, *Verheissung und Gesetz,* 82ff.

24. Nicholson, *God and His People,* 172. See also E. Ruprecht, "Exodus 24, 9–11 als Beispiel lebendiger Erzähltraditionen aus der Zeit des babylonischer Exils," *Werden und Wirken des Alten Testaments: Festschrift*

für Claus Westermann zum 70 Geburstag (ed. Rainer Albretz, Hans-Peter Müller, Hans Walter Wolff, and Walther Zimmerli [Göttingen: Vandenhoeck & Ruprecht/Neukirchen-Vluyn: Neukirchener Verlag, 1980] 165ff.).

25. See E. Ruprecht, "Exodus 24, 9–11 als Beispiel lebendiger Erzähltraditionen," *Werden und Wirken des Alten Testaments,* 138–73; E. W. Nicholson, *Exodus and Sinai in History and Tradition* (Oxford: Basil Blackwell, 1973); idem, "The Interpretation of Exodus XXIV 9–11," *VT* 24 (1974) 77–97; idem, "The Antiquity of the Tradition in Exodus XXIV 9–11," *VT* 25 (1975) 69–79; idem, "The Origin of the Tradition in Exodus XXIV 9–11," *VT* 26 (1976) 148–60.

26. I include v. 15a with this source, especially if the subject includes Joshua as it does in the codex Vaticanus of the Greek text. V. 18b is also part of this source.

27. Those scholars who attempt to view part of the end of v.12 as secondary create greater problems than they solve. Such an addition could not belong to either Dtr or P because they both regard the content of the tablets as the Ten Commandments.

28. For the present see my remarks in "Histories and Historians of the Ancient Near East: The Israelites," *Or* 50(1981) 172–74.

29. See recently J. D. Levenson, *Sinai and Zion: An Entry into the Jewish Bible* (Minneapolis: Winston, 1985).

9

Healing and the Moses Traditions

GEORGE W. COATS

According to the Yahwist, God created humans for intimacy, for special relationships that would flower in the garden established by God for their support.[1] But the humans broke that intimacy by disobeying God's instructions. And as a consequence, they lost their place in God's garden. The instrument for the tragic event that broke the intimacy in the garden was the serpent. "The serpent was more subtle (*'ārûm*) than all the creatures of the field which the Lord God had made." This introduction to the scene (Gen. 3:1) shows that the serpent is not a personification of Satan, a primordial being coeternal with God. The serpent is one of the creatures from the field, subtle to be sure, but simply a creature. Indeed, the text establishes the creaturely status of the serpent with a subtle word play. The serpent is *'ārûm*. The humans are *'ᵃrûmmîm*. That subtle serpent poses the question that effects the broken intimacy between the man and the woman, and then between the humans and God. "Did God say, 'You shall not eat from any tree of the Garden'?"

In defense of God's instructions, the woman explains to the serpent that only one tree has been forbidden. But the serpent objects: God's instructions hide the truth about the tree. So the woman eats and gives the fruit to the man. And he eats. With that event of rebellion, intimacy disappears. God responds to this act of rebellion by expelling the humans from the garden. The following folk etiologies explain the woman's pain in childbirth, the man's work to earn food for life, and the serpent's form that requires crawling as the consequence of the rebellion. But no reference to the serpent as essentially evil appears. Thus, the principal question about the tradition sharpens: In what manner does later tradition alter the shape of the fate for the man and the woman? And what role does the serpent play in that process? The man must always work to obtain food for his family. The woman must always bear pain in childbirth. The serpent must always crawl in the dust without legs. But can the lost intimacy be restored? And if so, what role does the serpent play in the process?

For the Yahwist, an important step in the journey occurs under the leadership of Moses. The people of Abraham's family had become strangers in a foreign land. And in that foreign land, they had fallen into slavery. Under incredible oppression, even a pogrom matched in cruelty only by the heralds of Herod, the descendants of Abraham cry to God for relief from their slavery. God heard that cry and responded, "I have seen the affliction of my people who are in Egypt and have heard their cry because of their taskmasters; I know their sufferings, and I have come down to deliver them out of the hand of the Egyptians . . ." (Exod. 3:7–8). And in the same act, he sent Moses to effect their redemption from slavery: "Come, I will send you to Pharaoh that you may bring forth my people, the sons of Israel, out of Egypt." Armed with a validation of his commission expressed in the very name of God, a validation that promised the immediate presence of God to Moses and to the people, Moses addressed his own people, confronted Pharaoh, and then led the people from their oppression into the wilderness.[2]

In the wilderness, the people bind themselves to God in a new act of intimacy. A covenant at Sinai gives the people the means for living in intimacy with God, with nature, and with themselves. But the problems posed by overt acts that break the intimacy also arise. At the sea, the people rebel against Moses and against God. At the mountain, their golden calf brings the covenant to ruin. And only Moses' intercession saves the rebels. Away from the mountain, into the wilderness again, the people continue their rebellion. So the question posed by the narrative is sharp: What will God do now?

Various motifs in the Moses traditions constitute the basis for an answer to this question. The Moses figure functions as a model for the suffering servant of Second Isaiah.[3] And, of course, the suffering servant establishes an essential model for the NT's presentation of

Jesus. Moses, the intercessor, prefigures the picture of Jesus who intercedes with a petition specifically for the unity of the disciples, a unity established by a messiah who could be both new David and new Moses.[4]

One motif out of the Moses tradition that effects the shape of the suffering servant appears under the rubric of healing. In the Moses tradition, healing events can involve a serpent image. And within the Moses traditions, the sorry saga of broken humanity continues. What will God do now about restoring intimacy for the human community? God destroyed that community once in a flood of cosmic proportions. God scattered them over the face of the earth with no means for communication. But then God moved to bless these human creatures. Abraham could have been the open door for all of the world (so Gen. 12:1–3). But how can God use a broken family to bring blessing to all of the world's people? God gave the people a covenant through Moses. But they rejected it. And as a result, the rebels could not enter the land of promise. But there is another motif, namely, the conviction that God will heal the people. God will heal them at the depth of their lives, their relationships, not lightly as if superficial surgery would solve the problem (so Jer. 6:14; 8:11). Ironically, that healing process in the Moses traditions relates to the serpent.

In the wilderness traditions, the narratives appear regularly under the stamp of the murmuring tradition, although an older, more positive form of the tradition may report Israel's faithful obedience during a bridal period in the wilderness.[5] Exodus 15:22–26, a tale, reports a particular crisis in the sequence. From the event at the sea, the people moved under Moses' leadership three days without water. Then they came to Marah, a place where water was available. But they could not drink that water because it was bitter. Rebellion follows. Moses intercedes before God, and God shows him the way to solve the problem. Implicit in the crisis is a threat of death for the people from thirst in a hostile wilderness (so Exod. 16:3). The resolution thus meets not only the threat of rebellion against Moses' leadership but also the threat of imminent death. Verses 25b–26 probably represent a Deuteronomistic expansion of the tale.[6] The expansion suggests that intimate relationship with God could be restored by keeping the law. But the content of the restored intimacy is characterized explicitly in terms of healing. The diseases God put on the Egyptians will not affect the Israelites. In this pericope, the promise establishes God's response to the rebellion. Instead of death from the diseases of the Egyptians, life would come from God for those obedient to the covenantal law. That promise motivates the epithet for God: "I am Yahweh your healer." Healing belongs to God. Moses functions here as the mediator, the instrument for God's healing act.[7] But specifically, healing is an alternative to the diseases that attacked the Egyptians. Those diseases were fatal, just as God's response generally to the rebellion in the wilderness was fatal (so Num. 14:35). Deuteronomy 28:60 reflects the same tradition in opposite dress. A threat warns Israel that failure in keeping the law will bring the diseases of Egypt. Those diseases mean death for Israel (so vv. 61, 63). Ironic for the description, the disease that brings the death now represents an intimacy for the Israelites. "They [the diseases] shall cleave to you" (v. 60). The word is the same verb as the one that describes the intimate relationship between a husband and a wife (so Gen. 2:24). But the event that proffers God's healing comes to the Israelites through the hand of Moses, the man of God. Whether the act of throwing the tree into the water or proclaiming the new law, the instrument of God's healing comes from Moses. Moses pulls his people from the threat of death back to life.

Two texts in the Moses traditions relate the healing event more directly to the action of Moses himself. In Num. 12:1–16, a legend, Miriam and Aaron challenge Moses' unique authority for leading the people. Verse 3 identifies Moses as a man of integrity, the validated leader of the people.[8] Then the remaining section of the legend shows what Moses' integrity as leader looks like. God responds to the challenge by striking Miriam with leprosy. Moses intercedes for her, despite the fact that her challenge threatens his position before the people. The content of this intercession is of critical importance for study of the healing motif. Aaron petitions Moses for the intercession on behalf of Miriam, vv. 11–12. And in the petition, he identifies Miriam's plight as death: "Let her not be as one dead...." Moses reponds to Aaron's petition with intercession addressed to the Lord. "Heal her, O God, I beseech thee." The Lord responds by giving Moses the proper ritual for restoring Miriam to the community. When the ritual was properly executed, then the healing occurred.

The same conclusions noted for the first pericope apply here as well: (1) The healing event belongs to God. (2) Moses effects God's healing by intercession and, in this case, properly carrying out the ritual. (3) The healing restores the one at death's door, isolated from the community by some kind of strife, to intimacy within the community. Miriam's return to the community marks the resumption of Israel's wilderness march under the leadership of Moses and, through Moses, under the leadership of God. Return to the community, the result of healing effected by Moses, constitutes restored intimacy for its members. One step toward paradise regained results in continuation of the wilderness march.

The second text that relates the Moses traditions directly to the healing event, and thus to a reconciled community for God's people, appears in Num. 21:4–9. This tale describes an attack on the Israelites in the wilderness by fiery serpents. In this case, the wilderness crisis is not the cause for rebellion among the people but rather its result. The fiery serpents, as the instrument of God's wrath, attack the rebels who have rejected Moses because of problems with food, water, and the worthless manna (v. 6). And the consequence of their bite was death (so v. 6). In response to the crisis, Moses intercedes for his rebellious people. And God accedes to his petition. The instructions to Moses call for construction of a bronze serpent *(nᵉḥaš nᵉḥōšet)* erected on a pole *(nēs)*. There is some connection between this Nehushtan and the rod of God in Moses' hand that turns into a serpent *(neḥaš)* before the Israelites and the Egyptians. Moreover, there appears to be an ironic relationship between the bronze serpent *(naḥaš)* and the serpent who challenges Eve in the garden *(naḥaš)*. In addition, the bronze serpent becomes a symbol of Moses' position as leader of the people (cf. 2 Kings 18:4). But the important point here is that the symbol functions as an instrument for healing. People bitten by the serpent and thus doomed to die had but to look at the symbol and, *ex opere operato,* death would be converted into life. The key verb for healing does not appear in this pericope. But the process is the one described elsewhere as healing. Death is converted into life (so v. 9). The irony in the scene must not be missed. The serpent is an instrument of death. But, by the miracle of ritual, the bronze serpent becomes an instrument of life.

Moreover, the new life effected by the healing event with Moses' bronze serpent, the resolution of the rebellion against Moses and God, would enable the Israelite community to be restored. The event of healing brings new life not only to the body, a process of the natural world, but also to the community, a process of the social world. This healing process restores relationships of intimacy between the rebels and Moses, between the leader and the led. As a gift of God, the healing event restores relationships between the rebels and God. The healed community does not enjoy the intimacy of the garden, the peace of Isaiah's paradise, at least not yet. But it anticipates that kind of life. Healing effected by the bronze serpent ironically as the opposite of the serpent's gift to humanity in the garden, prefigures the messianic kingdom where no hurt can be found in all of God's holy mountain. "As Moses lifted up the serpent in the wilderness, so must the son of man be lifted up, that whoever believes in him may have eternal life" (John 3:14). As a foretaste of that kingdom, the bronze serpent stands as a symbol of reconciliation between Moses and David, the north and the south, the suffering servant and the messiah. For the Yahwist, the Moses who heals points toward restored intimacy for all of God's people. Does the presence of the bronze serpent in the Jerusalem temple at least until the time of Hezekiah not point to some sign of that reconciliation (so 2 Kings 18:4)?

There is another dimension in the serpent tradition with its role of healing the broken intimacy within the people of God. Through the serpent Moses calls his people not only from broken intimacy to a new sense of community, but also from death to life. Elijah, a new Moses in the wilderness, intercedes for the son of a widow. And the child lived. But the new life stands not only for restored nature in the body of the child. "Elijah took the child...and delivered him to his mother" (1 Kings 17:23). With the restoration of life for the dead child, there is restoration of intimacy within the family, within the community.[9] Elisha responds to the cry of the Shunammite woman whose son died in her arms. And again, the ritual of healing effected by this disciple of Elijah, this new Moses, brings healing, life, even resurrection for the dead.[10]

The suffering servant poem from the Second Isaiah depicts the death of the new Moses (Isa. 53:8).[11] But the death of this particular servant did not occur for his own rebellion. He carried the rebellions of his people. And the result was death, like Moses cut off from the promised land, like Moses "stricken for the transgressions of my people." But the critical point is that the salvation offered the people of God by this new Moses is explicitly healing. "With his stripes we are healed." The death of the servant brings healing, restoration to the people.

I suggest, therefore, that a critical root in the OT for understanding the proclamation of reconciliation is the picture of Moses, the healer who brings restored intimacy to the community by healing their diseases, their wounds, their strife, and their rebellion. Indeed, I suggest that resurrection motifs in OT traditions must be understood in relationship to the healing paradigm, rooted essentially in the Moses traditions. The point can be defended generally from the verb itself. In Deut. 32:39, the verb relates to its negative pole, "to wound." But the pair, "I wound and I heal," stands synonymously parallel to a resurrection statement: "I kill and I make alive." Psalm 30:3–4 makes the same point: "O Lord my God! I cried to you for help, and you healed me. O Lord, you have brought up my life from Sheol, restored me to life from among those gone down to the pit." In Jer. 33:6, the promise "I will heal them" stands in contrast to the threat in v. 5, "to fill them with dead bodies of men whom I shall smite in my anger and my wrath." In John 3:14, following a Son of man saying that connects resurrection and ascension to an explicit tradition about the preexistence of the Son of man, the Moses tradition appears. "As Moses lifted up the serpent in the wilderness, so must the Son of Man be lifted up, that whoever believes in him may have eternal life." Son of man theology is obviously present. But what does the Moses theology contribute to the saying? The function of the symbol, by virtue of its history within the Moses tradition, is clear. The Son of man, lifted up like Moses' serpent in the wilderness, is an instrument of healing. The dominant point is that like the Israelites in the wilderness, the people who see, the disciples of Christ, will also be healed. The broken intimacy shared by all with the people of the garden can be converted into reconciliation, restored intimacy, and peace with God, with fellow humans, and with the world. The glorification of Jesus, the resurrection that heals the broken body, heals the broken body of the disciples as well. Looking at the bronze serpent brings healing to the Israelites in the face of death from the bite of the wilderness serpents. Believing in the crucified, glorified new Moses brings healing to the body of Christ. Indeed, that healing carries a promise for eternal life.

Yet, where does this healing happen? For Israel, rebellion in the wilderness continued to the border of the land. Apostasy at Baal-peor marked the land not simply as the symbol of God's presence with the people but as the place of their worst apostasy (Josh. 22:17). For the Yahwist, intimacy is related to the figure of David (so Num. 24:7–9, 17). And for the Chronicler, that notion of intimacy is confirmed. For Deuteronomy, the place for intimacy must be associated with Moses

(Deut. 26:5–11; Josh. 24:1–28). But the contrast between appeal to David and appeal to Moses highlights a fundamental point of strife in the community of God's people. Is the dream for restored intimacy anything more for the OT than the dream of the Yahwist?

Josiah tried to realize that dream. Something of a new David, Josiah launched a reform built around proclamation of a new Mosaic law. Indeed, an apparent goal for the reform must have been the unity of the people under the new law of Moses. But Josiah died at Meggido, and the attempt at reform proved to be little more than an appetizer (2 Kings 22—23). The gospel interprets Jesus as new David and new Moses together.[12] Just as Josiah worked for unity among the people of God, so Jesus prays for the unity of the people of God (John 17). Indeed, Jesus died on a lonely hill, just as Josiah did. Does not the event require still further projection toward the future? This projection focuses precisely in the resurrection, an event of healing for the body of Christ. Precisely in the resurrection, reconciliation occurs. Intimacy is restored for humanity, the world with humanity, and humanity with God. The resurrection brings healing to the whole body of Christ.

But still humanity is divided. The resurrection is not the fulfillment of healing for the whole body of Christ, the restoration of intimacy for the community. It only prefigures that healing. As prolepsis, it promises incredible good news. Broken humanity can be healed. But where does humanity share the fruit of that good news? In the Eucharistic sacrament, the unity of the healed body of Christ stands most sharply in the light of God's word. The sacrament effects the healed body of Christ, the place of restored intimacy for God's people, the new Garden of Eden. And its symbol is as ironic as the Mosiac bronze serpent. The serpent was a creature of death, representing broken intimacy for those who look at it in obedience to its command for disobedience. It symbolized punishment for rebellion against Moses and against God. Yet, it becomes the symbol of life, representing restored intimacy for those who look at it in obedience to the word of God through Moses. The symbols of the sacrament are symbols of violence, rejection, broken intimacy, death. Broken bread stands for a broken body. The wine stands for spilled blood. But in the sacrament, these symbols become the symbols of peace, harmony, restored intimacy, healing, new life in resurrection. In the sacrament, the healing of the body of Christ occurs in advance of the final new creation.

The serpent facilitates an act that destroys human intimacy. The bronze serpent facilitates a healing process that restores intimacy. Ritual can effect new community. Yet the risk of performing the ritual without the appropriate intimacy raises questions about the healing process. In effecting the healing by ritual, exploitation may occur. When confronted with exploitation, someone must raise a prophetic voice of protest. Jeremiah objects to the prophets of his day: "They have healed the wound of my people lightly, saying, 'peace, peace,' when there is no peace" (6:14; 8:11). The same point can be found throughout the prophetic traditions (so Ezek. 13:10, 16; Mic. 3:5).

Interestingly, there is some connection between the healing process at home in the Moses tradition and the healing process linked to the so-called false prophets.[13] The following points show a common tradition:

First, the verb associated with the action of the so-called false prophets is the same as the one that appears in the two key units of the Moses traditions: $r\bar{a}p\bar{a}$? The object of that verb is "wound." A wound is a prelude to death, a condition that stands in sharp contrast to healing, a condition that calls for the healing process (so Jer. 15:18; 30:12; Mic. 1:9; Nah. 3:19). In the case of the prophets attacked by Jeremiah, the threats in 6:14 and 8:11, "the wound of the people," become death for those who fall under the Lord's punishment. And ritual cannot resolve the tragedy. The people who would be healed by the ritual of the prophets of peace remain separated from the Lord. Intimacy that would create genuine peace is broken precisely by the failure to execute the ritual properly. Ritual without the intimacy of integrity cannot produce intimacy.

Second, the fruit of the healing process expected by the prophet who pronounces the ritual is "peace," $\check{s}\bar{a}l\hat{o}m$. The character of $\check{s}\bar{a}l\hat{o}m$ is defined by the model of messianic justice and righteousness (so Isa. 11:6–9), although in that text the word $\check{s}\bar{a}l\hat{o}m$ does not appear. An oracle in Isa. 9:1–6 makes the same point. Messianic rule will be marked by righteousness and justice, by $\check{s}^e d\bar{a}q\bar{a}h$ and $mi\check{s}p\bar{a}t$. But the fruit of that model is peace, $\check{s}\bar{a}l\hat{o}m$. And the peace is perpetual, without end. There can be no peace without righteousness and justice. From the perspective of this exploration, there can be no healing, no intimacy, without righteousness and justice. The intimacy produced by the healing process, symbolized by the bronze serpent within the Mosiac tradition, involves a relationship that does not support exploitation. Intimacy is defined by righteousness and justice, signs of the new life effected by healing. There can be no healing without righteousness and justice. Any relationship short of that character approaches slavery.

Third, the condition that calls for healing, that stands in contrast to peace, intimacy with God, nature, and fellow human beings, is not simply a physical disease, although obviously physical disease provokes a call for healing (2 Kings 20:5; cf. also Lev. 13:37; 14:3, 48). The condition is primarily moral. In the wilderness, the people rebel against Moses and against God. That violation brings on the attack by fiery serpents. Healing with the bronze serpent brings not only recovery from physical agony that can lead to death but also recovery from the moral violation represented by the murmuring of the people. Indeed, healing of the moral violation, the rebellion represented by the murmuring, is a prerequisite for the healing of the physical violation (cf. Matt. 9:1–8). Thus, typical prophetic rhetoric involving the healing process calls for repentance (Hos. 6:1; 14:5; Jer. 3:22; Isa. 6:10; 19:22). Restoration of intimacy, return to peace that effects relationships between a person and God, nature, and fellow persons, is not an event that, even by ritual, can be established automatically. To the contrary, such restoration calls for obedience, the sense of integrity lost in the garden of Eden.

One must, however, ask about the negative image of the prophets of peace, who heal the wounds of the people lightly. Is it possible that the prophets of peace, with their ritual for healing, depend on the Mosaic tradition, a tradition that in the proper context might have been seen as a positive force in the Israelite religious life? Not all of the classical prophets condemn the prophets who heal, who call for peace, who effect new intimacy by their ministry.

In Hos. 14:1–8 (Engl.), an example of a prophetic oracle that functions as a proclamation of the healing, a reconciling word of God appears. The oracle has two formal elements. The first, vv. 1–3, contains an address from the Lord through the prophet to the people. The first part of the address, vv. 1–2a, admonishes the audience to repent. The opening verb, "return," calls explicitly for the act of repentance fundamental for the healing process (cf. also Isa. 6:10; 19:22; Jer. 3:22; Hos. 14:4; 2 Chron. 7:14).[14] Moreover, the admonition is supported by an explicit description of the event that has broken the intimacy between the people and their God. Verses 2b–3 then define the confession expected from the people. The confession features a general term for violation of relationships, "iniquity," ʿăwôn. Verse 3 names three concrete examples of the violation: dependency on Assyria, dependency on the power of horses, and definition of still some other object as "our God." Verse 3bß provides a contrast to these acts of dependence on objects other than the Lord. Mercy for the orphan, for the one who has lost a natural source of intimacy, comes from God. This confession reflects acts that have broken the covenant of intimacy, leaving the people without a source of hope for renewal.

The second element in the oracle, vv. 4–8, is the proclamation of healing.[15] God announces God's intention to heal. The object of the healing is explicitly the negative acts of the people that have broken the intimacy of the covenantal relationship. Verse 4b views the act of healing as parallel to an act of love that abolishes God's anger and thus God's power to maintain broken intimacy with the people (like the power to place cherubim at the entrance to the garden). Verse 8 then describes the fruit of healing, a restored relationship between people and God. "They shall return and dwell beneath his shadow. They shall grow grain. They shall blossom as the vine. Their fragrance shall be like the wine of Lebanon." That picture is an effective description of restored intimacy. Indeed, this verse captures the quality of šālôm, even though the word itself does not appear.

The healing described by Hosea occurs as if in response to the confession. Just as a priestly oracle of salvation responds to a lament, so a prophetic oracle of healing responds to a confession of covenant violation and establishes the event of healing, an event whose content restores the intimacy of the covenant relationship. I suggest, then, that this ritual is the event for Israel that accompanies the symbol of the bronze serpent, the event that effects the healing of broken intimacy. It is important to note that this healing oracle occurs in a prophet of the Northern Kingdom, a prophet who alludes to the role of Moses as the prophet who brought Israel out of Egypt (Hos. 12:13). In this regard, Hosea makes more effective use of the Moses traditions than he does of the David complex.[16]

In Isa. 57:14–21, there is no confession of broken intimacy, no admonition to repent introduced by the verb "return," šûb. It may be that the admonition in v. 14 functions in the same way as an admonition to repent (cf. Jer. 42:10; Mal. 1:4). An admonition to build, to prepare the way, to remove obstructions, effects the same kind of ritual that enables intimacy to be restored. Indeed, the description of the worshiper, who participates in the process of preparing the way, as a person of contrite and humble spirit, a point repeated in v. 15b, belongs to the ritual of repentance. Verse 16 promises God's response to the ritual depicted by vv. 14–15. That response is marked as an event of life (v. 16b). Such an event of life stands in contrast to the anger of God, the lawsuit that threatens the people with death. Verse 17 repeats the pattern, but from a new perspective. God describes God's response to the iniquity of the people. The initial response was one of punishment. "I smote him. I hid my face and was angry" (17a). But the people did not change. The punishment did not alter the character of the people. "He went on backsliding in the way of his own heart" (v. 17b).

This oracle poses a severe question. Because of Israel's iniquity, God punished; God removed the divine presence from Israel. There could be no intimacy in that kind of life. But Israel did not repent. Thus, the tradition faces a severe question. What will God do this time? God is not blind. "I have seen his ways." But God acts in an unexpected way. "I will heal him. I will lead him and requite him with comfort, creating for his mourners the fruit of the lips" (v. 18). What follows comprises the content of the healing tradition. "'Peace, peace, to the far and to the near,' says the Lord. 'And I will heal him.'" The fruit of the ritual, the result of the oracle given the backsliding people, is *šālôm*, restored intimacy. In the context of the ritual, but by the word of God, the guilty receive peace, the intimacy lost in the garden. And that gift is explicitly the result of healing.

But the intimacy, the state of being healed, must be marked by integrity. The wicked still toss in the sea of broken intimacy. "The wicked are like the tossing sea, for it cannot rest" (v. 20). Rest comes from restoration of the intimacy lost in the garden. "'There is no peace,' says my God, 'for the wicked'" (v. 21). The notion of *(šabbāt)* is particularly at home in the Sabbath tradition. Perhaps the Sabbath is the most effective ritual for creating intimacy with God. The Sabbath brings healing for a wounded people, restored intimacy for those who strive with God, neighbors, and nature.

Another insight into the moral dimension of healing appears in Third Isaiah. In keeping with the orientation of Isaiah 40—55, with its emphasis on a new exodus, a new wilderness journey, and a new

Moses, Third Isaiah also employs exodus/Moses traditions. The point is particularly prominent in Third Isaiah's focus on the Sabbath. Isaiah 58:1–14 (cf. Num. 15:32–36) employs three structural elements to relate healing, the rest of the Sabbath, with restored intimacy.

First, Isa. 58:1–5 indicts the rebellious people for violating the Sabbath. "They seek me daily and delight to know my ways. . . . They ask of me righteous judgments" (v. 2). Specifically, these people of the broken covenant perform the ritual: fasting, humbling themselves. According to the tradition, the ritual should be effective. But the indictment is explicit. "In the day of your fast, you seek your own pleasure and oppress all your workers. You fast only to quarrel and to fight and to hit with wicked fist" (vv. 3–4a). The ritual, unaccompanied by integrity and intimacy, fails. "Fasting like yours this day will not make your voice to be heard on high" (v. 4b).

Second, in contrast, 58:6–7 describes the ritual that effects intimacy. "Is not this the fast that I choose: to loose the bonds of wickedness, to undo the thongs of the yoke, to let the oppressed go free, and to break every yoke? Is it not to share your bread with the hungry and to bring the homeless poor into your house; when you see the naked, to cover him, and not to hide yourself from your own flesh?" The content of the ritual that serves as the antidote for broken intimacy combines the operation of the ritual with integrity and commitment to a proper relationship.

Third, the result of the combination (vv. 8–9a) is again explicit: "Then shall your light break forth like the dawn, and your healing shall spring up speedily. Your righteousness shall go before you. The glory of the Lord shall be your rear guard." But the capstone of the restored intimacy is the final assertion. "Then you shall call, and the Lord will answer. You shall cry, and he will say, 'Here I am.'" Restored intimacy effected by the healing of God, centered in a ritual on the Sabbath but open to all of God's people wherever they call for an answer, offers the presence of the Lord, the opposite of the experience of the man and the woman expelled from the garden and kept at a distance from the Lord by the terrible cherubim.

Is this image of restored intimacy in the Sabbath ritual not already anticipated by the perceptive redactor who combined the tale of a paradise lost with a priestly account of creation that focuses on the Sabbath as the occasion to celebrate God's creation? But of even more importance is the power of the Sabbath to effect healing and restored intimacy. The tale in Matt. 12:9–14 (and parallels) points just in this direction. "Is it lawful to heal on the Sabbath?" The justification for the event, an event held by Jesus' opposition as a violation of the Sabbath ritual, lies precisely in the integrity of intimate relationships. If a friend has a sheep that falls into a pit on the Sabbath, each person in the audience would stop to help that friend lift the sheep out of the pit. Relationships within the community constitute the crucial norm. Indeed, this norm enables healing to occur. Moreover, the healing in Jesus' ministry occurs precisely as a response to the ritual that restores intimacy. As a result, the proclamation of forgiveness for sin effects healing (so Matt. 9:1–8 and parallels). The same point appears in Paul's admonition to the Corinthians about the holy supper (1 Cor. 11:17–26). Violations of the integrity of the community undercut the operation of intimacy in the ritual. In fact, such violations can leave the community under severe threat. "That is why many of you are weak and ill, and some have fallen asleep." But the ritual with intimacy brings strength and health, indeed, life that provides for the integrity of the individual within the community. Healing, the ritual of the fast, combined with the integrity of intimacy, restores the reality of intimacy for the human community. In that reality, members of the community once again have access to the tree of life. In the intimacy of God's presence, resurrection gives new life to all who see the serpent-servant lifted up, to all who experience the healing that comes from that event and respond with integrity to their fellow humans. With this observation comes a final comment about the history of the healing tradition. Should the resurrection story in the early Christian tradition not be understood as a part of the OT tradition history concerning healing, specifically as it is found in the Moses traditions? The irony of the Yahwist, which sets the serpent that helped fracture human intimacy in the garden on a pole in order to facilitate restored intimacy in the wilderness, develops decisively in John 3:14–15: "As Moses lifted up the serpent in the wilderness, so must the Son of man be lifted up, that whoever believes in him may have eternal life."[17]

One must be careful at just this point, however. The description of the process might easily degenerate into a circle. Broken intimacy can be resolved by the healing touch of God, effected by the ritual. But the ritual is effective only if it occurs within the intimacy of the community, characterized by the integrity of relationships within the community. The key to the process that effects healing and restored intimacy, that opens the door of healing to the good news of the resurrection, is the moral dimension. In the healing, restoration involves not only physical and social dimensions, but also spiritual dimensions. Healing occurs with the forgiveness of sin. That element comes from God. But it also calls for commitment from the healed person. Intimacy is not a passive state. To be healed is not simply to receive the grace of God's healing touch. Healed intimacy is an active state, a sharing of life in mutual integrity. "Thus you shall call, and the Lord will answer. You shall cry and he will say, 'Here I am.'"

NOTES

1. For a definition of the term intimacy in the context of the Yahwist's presentation of the primeval saga and the stories about the fathers, see George W. Coats, *Genesis, with an Introduction to Narrative Literature* (FOTL 1; Grand Rapids: Wm. B. Eerdmans, 1983) 13–34.

2. Brevard S. Childs, *The Book of Exodus, a Critical, Theological Commentary* (OTL; Philadelphia: Westminster Press, 1974) 178–214.

3. Aage Bentzen, *Messias, Moses redivivus, Menschensohn. Skizzen zum Thema Weissagung und Erfüllung* (ATANT 17; Zurich: Zwingli Verlag, 1948) 16–17.

4. George W. Coats, "Metanoia in Ancient Israel. Clues for Unity and Change," *Midstream* 23 (1984) 185–88.

5. George W. Coats, *Rebellion in the Wilderness. The Murmuring Motif in the Wilderness Traditions of the Old Testament* (Nashville: Abingdon Press, 1968) 16–17.

6. Martin Noth, *Exodus, a Commentary* (OTL; Philadelphia: Westminster, 1962) 129. But see also Childs, *Exodus,* 266–68.

7. Childs, *Exodus,* 270.

8. George W. Coats, "Humility and Honor: A Moses Legend in Numbers 12," *Art and Meaning. Rhetoric in Biblical Literature* (ed. David J. A. Clines, David M. Gunn, and Alan J. Hauser; JSOTS 19; Sheffield, Eng.: JSOT Press, 1982) 99–107.

9. Burke O. Long, *1 Kings, with an Introduction to Historical Literature* (FOTL 9; Grand Rapids: Wm. B. Eerdmans, 1984) 185.

10. For details, see Odil H. Steck, *Überlieferung und Zeitgeschichte in den Elia-Erzählungen* (WMANT 26; Neukirchen-Vluyn: Neukirchener Verlag, 1968) 11–12.

11. Bentzen, *Messias,* 51. For an interpretation of the poem in terms of death, see Claus Westermann, *Isaiah 40—66, a Commentary* (OTL; Philadelphia: Westminster Press, 1969) 256–69.

12. So Coats, "Metanoia." See also Raymond E. Brown, *The Gospel according to John* (2d ed.; AB 29; New York: Doubleday, 1983) 210–15.

13. G. Quelle, *Wahre und falsche Propheten* (BFCT 46; Gütersloh: C.

Bertelsmann, 1952). See also J. Lindblom, *Prophecy in Ancient Israel* (Philadelphia: Muhlenberg Press, 1962) 210–15.

14. Hans Walter Wolff, *Dodekapropheten I; Hosea* (BKAT 14/1; Neukirchen-Vluyn: Neukirchener Verlag, 1961) 302–3.

15. For details, see ibid., 302–9.

16. For details, see Westermann, *Isaiah 40—66*, 21–27.

17. On the origin of the bronze serpent, see H. H. Rowley, "Zadok and Nehushtan," *JBL* 58 (1939) 113–41. My concern here is not whether the bronze serpent was originally a Mosaic symbol or how that symbol might relate to the ark. Rather, the issue is how the symbol appears in the story and how it facilitates the healing process.

10

On Divine and Human Bonds: The Tragedy of the House of David

J. WILLIAM WHEDBEE

Be eternally and unswervingly loyal to the story.
—Isak Dinesen

I

The Samuel narratives about King David continue to attract the admiring attention of scholars, and the flood of attempts either to reconstruct the various stages in the history of traditions or to interpret the theological and narrative artistry of the finished story shows no sign of abatement. The wealth of diverse interpretations illustrates both the evocative power of the original story as well as the morass of theoretical confusion in finding appropriate models for illuminating the material. In this continuing quest for meaning, Brevard Childs has performed a significant service for the scholarly community by calling us back to a concentration on the canonical text.[1] In this move, however, Childs has in fact joined a company of poets, artists, musicians, and at least some literary critics who take the canonical shape of the stories of David as the starting point for reflection. Concentration on the final form of the text does not devalue the tremendous achievements of historical critics who have sought to disentangle the historical David from the thick, tightly woven fabric of legendary and mythic representation; such a focus on the final form simply recognizes the necessity of giving due heed to the present text and of discerning its theological and literary intentions.

I want to interpret once again the story of King David, particularly as recounted in the second half of the Samuel version, an account we can name David's Reign on the Jerusalem Throne (2 Samuel 5— 1 Kings 2). As is well known, this account is conjoined with the story of David's Rise to the Jerusalem Throne (1 Samuel 16—2 Samuel 5). The two accounts probably come together somewhere in 2 Samuel 5, though debates continue concerning the exact ending of the one and the beginning of the other.[2] Second Samuel 5:10 may well be the ending for the story of David's rise to power irrespective of whether or not it is the "original" ending. What does seem clear is that the lines between ending and beginning are blurred within 2 Samuel 5—indeed within that whole spate of heterogeneous materials now gathered in 2 Samuel 5—8, a section that has always given trouble to historians.

In my judgment, rather than an original historical nucleus in 2 Samuel 5—8, one should see here a series of interlocking episodes that are both retrospective and prospective. The most obvious interlocking device is the annalistic report numbering the years of David's reign: "David was thirty years old when he began to reign, and he reigned forty years. At Hebron he reigned over Judah seven years and six months; and at Jerusalem he reigned over all Israel and Judah thirty-three years" (2 Sam. 5:4–5). This report is explicitly retrospective (his past reign in Hebron) and prospective (his forthcoming reign in Jerusalem). Coming immediately after David's successful extension of his rule to include Israel as well as Judah (2 Sam. 5:1–3), it embraces proleptically his reign in Jerusalem. It is most appropriate that the report of his conquest of Jerusalem immediately follows (2 Sam. 5:6–10).

The Deuteronomistic editor welds together the disparate units of 2 Samuel 5—8 into an interlocking and comprehensive presentation in order to bring to a climax various themes at work in David's tempestuous rise to kingship as well as to anticipate central themes in the account of his troubled reign.[3] Taken as an aggregate, the units now provide *seven modes of legitimation* for David's divinely sanctioned rule over all Israel. Since scholars have recognized most of these modes in some form, it will suffice simply to state them programmatically:[4] (1) *Political bonding* between David and Israel, thus legitimizing David's rule over the Northern Tribes as well as Judah (2 Sam. 5:1–3). (2) *Military conquest,* first of Jerusalem (2 Sam. 5:6–10), then of the Philistines, the most serious threat to Israel (2 Sam.

5:17–24), and finally of all the significant enemies of David's kingdom (2 Sam. 8:1–14, a catalogue beginning with the Philistines and ending with the Edomites). One should note the references to divine support in these encounters with Israel's enemies (e.g., 5:10; 5:19–20, 23–25; 8:6, 14), a typical mode of legitimizing royal conquests. (3) *Diplomatic recognition* highlighted by Hiram's gift of a royal residence for the new king, thus confirming in David's mind "that Yahweh had established him as king over Israel, and that he had exalted his kingdom for the sake of his people Israel" (2 Sam. 5:11–12). (4) *Genealogical confirmation* expressed by the list of sons born in Jerusalem, thus sanctioning the link between the Davidic house and the city of David (2 Sam. 5:13–16; cf. the list of sons born in Hebron, 2 Sam. 3:2–5). (5) *Priestly ritual* represented by the processional of the ark of Yahweh to Jerusalem, thus legitimizing Israel's new capital with the old symbol of Yahweh's presence (2 Samuel 6). (6) *Prophetic revelation* disclosed by Nathan's oracle about Yahweh's promise concerning an enduring Davidic dynasty and a new temple (2 Samuel 7), thus offering eternal legitimation for David's kingdom. (7) *Administrative justice,* thus underscoring the just character of Davidic rule over all Israel (2 Sam. 8:15–18).

A quick glance over all these modes of legitimation shows how systematic and comprehensive is the attempt to provide the newly emergent Davidic kingship with all the necessary sanctions imaginable. The divine support could hardly be more dramatically demonstrated according to the available criteria of the tradition. Moreover, this impressive representation of different modes of legitimation lays the groundwork for the central and complex theme of divine and human bonds, a theme that is crucial for understanding the unfolding drama of David's reign in Jerusalem. Indeed, as we turn from the "swing" narrative in 2 Samuel 5—8 to the so-called Succession Narrative (2 Samuel 9—20, 1 Kings 1—2), we will note how often these modes of legitimation are severely tested.

The theme of bonds particularly reveals the decisive pattern at work in the story of David's reign. In fact, it is my thesis that the theme of bonding animates the action of this story from start to finish. By bonding I mean the creation of covenantal relationships that lie on multiple planes but nevertheless intersect in subtle and significant ways. This multifaceted, complex bonding becomes centered in the master metaphor of David's house,[5] which gives concrete focus for the intersection of all the pivotal bonds. The image of house, with its diverse symbolic representations in physical residence, familial relationships, dynastic succession, and royal temple, becomes the context for the forging of bonds and also for the stretching and even breaking of bonds. These bonds represent the vital links among all the significant parts of Israel in the revolutionary experiment with kingship, links between vertical and horizontal (the divine-human bond as revealed in Yahweh's choice of David as shepherd-prince over Israel), and links between past and future (David's house as the new center of time, now anchored to the divine promise of an enduring dynasty—2 Samuel 7).

The primary bond of course is between king and God, a bond traditionally called the Davidic covenant (2 Sam. 7:11–17; 23:5; cf. Ps. 132:12). By means of this divine-human bond, David's kingship lays claim to being the legitimate fulfillment of earlier covenantal promises (see 2 Samuel 7, esp. vv. 23–24). Embedded in this royal covenant is the bond between Yahweh and Jerusalem, which is preeminently symbolized in the processional of the ark of the covenant to Jerusalem (2 Samuel 6). Extensions of these primary bonds focus on the relationship of the king and his people (especially the union of Judah and the Northern Tribes under the Davidic banner—2 Sam. 5:1–3; cf. 20:1–2); the relationship between king and army (the Lord's anointed was to go out and fight Israel's battles—2 Sam. 5:6–10; 5:17–24; 7:9–11; 8:1–14; 10:26–31; 21:15–22); the relationship between David and the house of Saul, especially as epitomized in his oath to Jonathan (1 Sam. 18:1–3; 2 Sam. 9; 16:1–4; 21:7); the relationship between king and other figures in his court (cf. 2 Sam. 7; 8:16–18; 12; 15:31–37; 16:15–23; 20:23–26; 23:8–39); and finally the relationship between king and his family—both in his role as husband to his wives and as father to his children (cf. 2 Sam. 6:20–23; 7:11–16; 11—19; 1 Kings 1—2). David's many sons were to constitute major problems for much of his career as king, particularly those sons who were too eager to replace their father (see below, 2 Samuel 15—19; 1 Kings 1—2).

The underlying problem in the story of David's reign is the delicate character of the different bonds interwoven within the Israelite community; the burning issue is competing and sometimes contradictory loyalties; the terrifying threat is the shattering of these bonds, which will affect not only the private lives of David and his family but also the public welfare of the nation. In the world of David's kingdom, never were John Donne's words more true and applicable: "No man"—or woman—"is an island sufficient to itself." Within the complex hierarchy of bonds—which are both vertical and horizontal, temporal and spatial—lurks the perennial temptation to think oneself somehow removed from the larger network of relationships.

For ancient Israel, human and divine bonds could provide the context for the experience of blessing and freedom and new life; but these same bonds could easily be broken and thus lead to the rupturing of the community, to the unleashing of violence, chaos, and death. Paradoxically, the bonds designed for freedom could become perverted and turned into a form of cruel bondage. What we will see unfolded constitutes a series of threats against all the significant bonds in Israelite society, threats that illustrate vividly the crisis created by the establishment of a permanent royal house. Indeed, all the major modes of legitimating the Davidic house will be seriously strained. The basic question, then, is whether or not the bonds will be sufficiently strong and flexible to withstand powers bent on their destruction. That the whole atmosphere is charged with the possibility of tragedy ought to be clear. Husbands and wives, fathers and sons, brothers and sisters could be swept up and overwhelmed by forces beyond their control. The possibility for violating bonds was ever present and hence the potential for a deadly curse on the house of David.

The narrative develops several subsidiary themes within this overarching framework of bonding. In particular, the theme of determining the legitimate successor to the Davidic throne emerges as one powerful factor. This theme has often dominated the interpretation of the whole narrative so that since Rost's influential work the second part of David's story has been typically called the Succession Narrative—that is, an elaborate answer to the question Who will be David's successor? (cf. 1 Kings 1:20).[6] Interpreters now increasingly see that this is a one-dimensional model which glosses over the richness and complexity of the story.[7] When one focuses on the subtle, intricate patterns of bonded relationships, the succession theme is set within a more appropriate and comprehensive context where its full implications may be better understood.

By concentrating on the interplay and tension between the house of David and the house of Israel, the narrator is able to move back and forth between private and public realms, where explosive desire and personal ambition often come into conflict with communal responsibility. In summary, it is my view that 2 Samuel 5—1 Kings 2 largely unveils a concrete, highly charged representation of "bonds" that may be either broken or kept, bonds that are vital to the total life of Israel under the new order of kingship.

II

The theme of David's friendship with Jonathan resurfaces in 2 Samuel 9. The episode centers on David's keeping a bond from his youth, his covenant of friendship with Jonathan (see 1 Sam. 18:1–3). The king wants to honor that bond and perform reciprocal love *(ḥesed)* to any survivor of the house of Saul and Jonathan. Here the Hebrew word *ḥesed* is crucial, a word that depicts loyal love in the bond of mutual liability and responsibility.[8] Sure enough a survivor is found and brought to the king's table for lifelong care and provision. Whatever ulterior motives David may have had—for example, to keep any potential rebel under close surveillance—his ostensible motive is just and noble: he wants to maintain his bond of friendship to Jonathan even beyond death.

The next story—the David-Bathsheba-Uriah affair (2 Samuel 10—12)—determines the rest of the story of David's reign; it is absolutely crucial for understanding the second half of David's career. We may note initially the dark background for the events in Jerusalem: war again has broken out, this time against the Ammonites (2 Samuel 10). The report of a new war belies the claim of complete rest from the surrounding enemies boldly asserted in 2 Samuel 7 and 8: David must win even more victories in order to extend and maintain his empire. But this battle report is not given for its own sake; rather it provides the necessary background for a seemingly private, all too typical event: the king's seduction of a beautiful woman. One cannot help but observe the implicit contrast with the earlier picture of David who continues to be devoted to his friend Jonathan; we see now a callous, calculating David who simply takes what he wants.

One recalls the scene. It is wartime, and men and women sometimes do strange things in wartime, when raw human need or sheer boredom may surface and make one vulnerable to the whim or passion of the moment. The larger context of the Israelite-Ammonite war gives a violent background for the seemingly private, personal happenings in Jerusalem. Moreover, the laconic opening lines of chap. 11 introduce the dominant narrative mode: the technique of indirection and implicit ironic contrast.[9] "At the turn of the year, when kings go forth to battle, David sent Joab and with him his own guards and all of Israel; and they ravaged the Ammonites, and besieged Rabbah. Meanwhile David was remaining in Jerusalem" (2 Sam. 11:1). Right from the outset we are alerted that King David is fundamentally a man out of place and out of time. Kings normally go to battle in the spring of the year—but King David stays at home. Why? What does this signify? Is it necessary for the king's protection? Is it necessary for the king to be on the home front to attend to affairs of state? As the story turns out, it seems almost as if David had two choices: to make war—which was his duty as Yahweh's anointed—or to make love, which normally has the potential for new life but here will lead to death. David is portrayed as a man in the wrong place at the wrong time—hence a prime candidate for temptation and fall.

As the narrative continues, we are led into the corridors and bedrooms of the royal palace where we see unfolding the classic pattern of temptation, surrender to momentary passion, and far-reaching tragic consequences. What starts off as a fleeting sexual liaison turns into the decisive event of the second half of David's career—for him at least the second half would not be better! Here in microcosm we see all the significant bonded relationships under severe pressure, as the king violates one bond after the other.

The king breaks his bond with the army and subjects by a triple act of criminal irresponsibility. He stays home when he should have been at war, he sleeps with another man's wife, who becomes pregnant by him, he has the loyal, innocent third party murdered. We remember the tale, but we need to visualize it once again. When David arises from a nap and is pacing *(hithallēk)* on the roof of his palace, he sees the ravishingly beautiful Bathsheba. He inquires about her identity—after all, a powerful king could always add another wife to his harem! But a problem surfaces—she is another man's wife and so has a marital bond, which in Israel at least was sacred. Yet he is a king and she a subject; when summoned to the palace, she complies and sleeps with the king. We do not know Bathsheba's motives or feelings (though later interpreters will cast her unfairly into the role of seductress); we know only that the king wants her and takes her. Bathsheba's dilemma is clear: What to do when the king summons you to his palace—and his bed? David reveals no hint of any hesitation.

His action, however, was an egregious instance of the abuse of his royal power and position, a grim manipulation of one who was his subject. We recall the warnings about kingship in the prophet Samuel's mouth, warnings given prior to the rise of monarchy: "He will take the best of everything you have, and you will be his slaves" (1 Sam. 8:17). The king now unfortunately demonstrates the need for such warnings, for he takes another man's wife to the royal bed. But his one-night capitulation to passion does not end the affair. After due time Bathsheba sends back the brief message that every man in David's position has always feared to receive: "I am pregnant." The king now has a problem. How he chooses to solve this problem brings—to his mind at least—a form of harsh resolution, but as often happens such a resolution solves nothing and creates instead a deadly cycle of new problems. It unleashes the forces of crime and punishment, which take the form of a terrifying, ever-spreading nemesis.

David's first attempt at a cover-up is a reasonable ploy. He calls Uriah back from the front, ostensibly to bring information about the progress of the war, though he really wants him home so that Uriah can sleep with Bathsheba. The ploy does not work—note the spare style, especially the repetition of the key line, "he did not go down to his house" (2 Sam. 11:9, 10, 11, 13). The pace slows, as we hear a dialogue between David and Uriah:

> When they told David, "Uriah did not go down to his house," David said to Uriah, "Have you not come from a journey? Why did you not go down to your house?" Uriah said to David, "The ark and Israel and Judah dwell in booths; and my lord Joab and the servants of my lord are camping in the open field; shall I then go to my house, to eat and drink, and to lie with my wife? As you live, and as your soul lives, I will not do this thing." (2 Sam. 11:10–11)

Once again we find superb evidence of the narrative strategy of indirection and ironic contrast. Uriah is a Hittite, hence, like David's ancestress Ruth, a proselyte in the Israelite community, whereas David as Israelite king is, of course, to be the examplar of Hebrew tradition. Yet we have a reversal of roles—the one-time alien now instructs the native king in Israel's holy war traditions. But David does not give up easily, and he tries still another ploy. At a royal banquet, the king gets Uriah drunk, hoping that the stubbornly loyal proselyte will forget the old traditions and sleep with his wife. But the result is the same: "He did not go down to his house." Ever resourceful and persistent in devising new and harsher strategies, David conceives his third and final ploy, which he writes out in a letter to Joab; ironically he has the loyal Uriah carry his own death sentence in that sealed letter. Joab, who becomes a ruthless extension of his king, complies with the royal orders, setting Uriah in the forefront of the fighting so that he is killed. The murder plot works, Bathsheba is widowed, and after a proper time of mourning becomes David's newest wife and bears him a son. But now we find a break in the typical pattern. Normally, after a report of conception and birth we read about the name of the newborn child—here it is ominously missing; the child receives no name, thus symbolically has no identity and hence a clouded future. Instead, the narrator interrupts the story by inserting a jarring note: "The thing that David had done was evil in the eyes of Yahweh" (2 Sam. 11:27b).

Up to this point, Yahweh has been strangely absent from the scene, but according to the narrator he has not been unaware. Not only does Yahweh disapprove of David's action, but he sends Nathan, the same prophet who had announced the glorious dream of dynasty, to confront David. On this occasion, however, Nathan uses a strategy different from the typical prophetic speech. He resorts to the technique of indirection by telling the story of a rich man's seizure of the poor man's ewe lamb (2 Sam. 12:1–4), a story that on the surface is a simple case of injustice which the king as righteous judge is to decide. David believes the tale and gives the expected response: The rich man deserves to die! The story is a fiction in this case, a "juridical parable"[10] designed precisely to elicit royal judgment (after all, David was responsible for justice, cf. Sam. 8:15)—but a king famed for his wisdom falls into the trap, pronouncing unwittingly and ironically his own death sentence.

The prophet now abruptly drops the indirect mode—the prophetic application is brief but brutal in its directness: "You are the man" *(attâh hā'îš)*. What follows is Yahweh's announcement of the terrible future for the house of David: "The sword shall never be far from your house. . . . I will raise up evil against you out of your own house; and I will take your wives before your eyes, and give them to your neighbor, and he shall lie with your wives in the sight of the sun" (2 Sam. 12:10–11). In brief form this is the tragic plot line of the rest of David's story!

Like Saul, David as king is stripped of the veneer of any royal authority and reduced to the level of a common criminal, able to offer only the short confession: "I have sinned against Yahweh." No longer can he rationalize or cover up; he can only confess. The divine-royal bond has been violated as have all the other bonds. But in sharpest contrast to the damning response to Saul's confession (1 Sam. 15:26–29), God mysteriously forgives David, who is spared the death sentence for not one but two capital crimes: adultery and murder. To compound even more the complex, paradoxical turn of events we hear that the newborn son is to die—little "no name" will have no future.

At first glance the narrator describes a strange judicial action. In the name of justice a seemingly unjust penalty is handed down. The criminal is spared, but the child is to be killed by Yahweh. Why? What categories do we have for explanation? The human problem—adultery and murder—is age-old and the actions of the king are understandable, however reprehensible. Yet the response of Yahweh seems arbitrary and unjust to the extreme, though the narrator does not raise the issue of divine justice in the fashion of a Job or Ecclesiastes. It is simply assumed that Yahweh is within his prerogative as ultimate ruler. He can do what he will! David implores Yahweh for the stricken child, but it is no use. The child dies. When David perceives that the child is dead, he displays still another side of his many-faceted character: a hard-eyed realism that accepts life and death as they come. He bathes, puts on fresh clothes, and orders some food. To the queries of his anxious, incredulous servants who are astounded at the king's turnabout, he simply retorts: "While the child was still alive, I fasted and wept; for I said, 'Who knows whether Yahweh will be gracious to me, that the child may live?' But now he is dead; why should I fast? I shall go to him, but he will not return to me" (2 Sam. 12:22–23). Here in a nutshell is the fundamental Hebraic perception of life and death; all one can do is face the grim reality of death and continue with the business of living.

David's callous disregard for the varied traditions of bonding in Israel is all too apparent. We are initially heartened that Yahweh's king will not escape with impunity from his blatant crimes which have ruptured several bonds. The swift, sure prophetic word is welcome, and we feel that justice is served. The king is the one who truly deserves his own self-pronounced death sentence. But we are taken aback that the king's repentance is accepted and he is forgiven, whereas the baby is divinely stricken. Our reaction, however, is a typically modern response, though with Joban antecedents. Viewed from within Near Eastern and Israelite criteria of judgment, the child's death, harsh and horrifying though it is, does paradoxically affirm Yahweh's justice. Sin was committed, and sin must be punished—even though the resulting progeny—the child—and not the progenitor of the crime must die; yet it is a grim instance of the sins of the father being visited on the son.

When this child dies, David offers no moving lament, as on the occasion of Saul's and Jonathan's deaths, though a compassionate, tender note is added: "David consoled his wife, Bathsheba, and went into her, and lay with her; and she bore a son, and he called his name Solomon" (2 Sam. 12:24). Now for the second time we hear Yahweh's surprising response to this all-too-human chain of events: for reasons that are not disclosed, Yahweh loves this child—and once again sends his prophetic messenger with a new name, a second name for the second child, Jedidiah, "beloved of Yahweh." We will hear more about the second child at the end of the David story. For now young Solomon drops totally from view—but the perceptive reader will remember the significance of the child who bears two names. It is a small but subtle gesture of divine love, a love as arbitrary as it is touching, as mysterious as it is merciful. It stands in a story otherwise filled with the grim, violent events of betrayal, adultery, murder, and climaxed by the paradoxical forgiveness of the criminal and the divine execution of a baby.

The unnamed child, conceived in adulterous union and thus accursed, is but the first in David's family to feel the brunt of the prophetic announcement that death would never be far from the house of David. A dreadful, relentless nemesis will reach deeply into David's house and heart before it will be satisfied, creating a tragic pall over David's future. Yes, David was indeed spared, but he seems permanently changed after the Bathsheba-Uriah affair. He is marked by a sense of mortality and increasingly stands under an ever-lengthening shadow of death. He will die many times for his fateful act of passion and cold-blooded murder before he himself finally succumbs when he is old and full of days. His unnamed child is only the first to die—Amnon and Absalom will both fall to the "sword" before David dies; Adonijah will die shortly after David. Thus justice may seem to be compromised, and it may appear that David escapes with a softened penalty, but in fact he will feel the avenging sword again and again as it cuts down his sons. He will know bitterly what it means to experience death in life.

The second son (Jedidiah-Solomon), however, is a sign of Yahweh's equally enigmatic love that is now unexpectedly revealed. In light of Yahweh's covenantal bond with David (cf. 2 Sam. 7:14–15), it is not strange that Yahweh would give a sign that he has not abandoned the house of David. The child who will bear both a human and divine name signals the healing of the bond between Yahweh and king, showing that Yahweh accepts the chastened couple as forming a new and legitimate marital bond. The same prophet who was sent as the herald of death is now sent back to the king and his new wife to serve as herald of life and love—the new child will embody divine love in his second name, Jedidiah. Yahweh emerges as a God who both kills and makes alive—to echo Hannah's song of thanksgiving that had initiated the new era of kingship (1 Sam. 2:6). Yahweh reveals himself as a God of harsh enigmatic justice and yet mercy, of brutal judgment and yet compassion. So the house of David, like the human race, bears both curse and blessing,[11] hatred and love, death and new life. Yahweh fulfills his pledge to maintain his bond with the house of David—but he does so in the sordid, savage world of betrayal, violence, and bloodshed.

After the David-Bathsheba affair, the attention increasingly shifts to David's sons and we will again be struck by the fragile character of family bonds—especially the bond between father and sons. The next scene (2 Samuel 13) opens with a picture of a triangular bond involving a brother and a sister and a half-brother. Like Bathsheba, the sister, named Tamar, is stunningly beautiful; moreover, like Bathsheba she becomes the object of illicit desire. Her half-brother, Amnon, falls in love with her—indeed, his obsession makes him sick. Unlike David, however, Amnon lacks the imagination to conceive of a plan: "It seemed to Amnon impossible to do anything to her" (2 Sam. 13:2). But Amnon has a crafty friend—there always seems to be a friend in such circumstances. Jonadab gives him a plan of seduction, but a plan that, ironically, involves the unwitting connivance of King David. The plan is simple, its objective clear-cut, and its outcome brutal. Tamar complies with her father's command to prepare and serve food to Amnon, who has feigned illness; when they are alone, he asks her to sleep with him; when she refuses, he rapes her despite her pleas: "No, my brother, do not rape me, for such is not to be done in Israel. Do not commit this heinous crime. As for me, where will I carry my shame? And as for you, you will be as one of the base criminals in Israel. Now, speak to the king, for he will not withhold me from you" (2 Sam. 13:12–13). But he refused to listen to her, and he raped her. He has scarcely finished raping her when his obsessive love turns into its opposite: "The hatred he now felt for her was greater than his earlier love" (2 Sam. 13:15). The psychological perceptiveness of the narrator is striking; we seem to have a form of projection in which Amnon's self-hatred for being revealed by Tamar's just pleas becomes hatred for her. The incestuous rape, now compounded with hatred, is coupled with still another merciless act. The crown prince orders his attendant to throw her out—again despite her anguished plea (2 Sam. 13:16). No longer a virgin, the beautiful Tamar grows old and disconsolate before our eyes as she mourns her shamed condition—she is doomed to die a ravaged woman, bereft of any hope for a fulfilled future. Like Jephthah's daughter, like Michal, Tamar will suffer the curse of child-lessness. Hers will be that terrible destiny of enduring a life that is a form of living death; she is thereby denied opportunity for the bond of wife and mother.

The responses of father and brother mirror the fundamental problems of David's family. Father David is angered at Amnon's act, but he does nothing, for he loves his firstborn son; brother Absalom now hates his brother and refuses to speak to him, and at first he too does nothing. But his silence and inaction mask a patient man who is able to wait for an opportune time to seek his revenge. Two years pass before a royal banquet provides the occasion for Absalom's vengeance against Amnon. Thus a brother's rape of a sister begets fratricide. Thinking at first that Absalom has murdered all his sons, King David and his officers fall into mass mourning (2 Sam. 13:30–31). But the same Jonadab who had conceived the plot to seduce Tamar assures the king that Amnon alone is dead. Absalom now becomes an exile. The king mourns a long time for his slain son—apparently three years—but finally his heart turns toward his exiled son.

A partial rectification of the problem of the exiled Absalom, ostensibly the new heir of the throne, comes as a result of a parable. Under Joab's orders a wise woman brings before the king what appears to be her own tragic tale of the loss of her two sons, one to the murderous hand of his brother, and the other to forced flight out of fear of blood vengeance (2 Sam. 14:1ff.). The king gives the right judgment—bring back the exiled son—and in so doing again pronounces his own self-judgment (2 Sam. 14:12ff.). Though the king complies with his decision and brings back Absalom to Jerusalem, he refuses to see him for two more years until Absalom forces the issue; the reconciliation finally takes place and is sealed by a father's kiss of his son. A fragile bond is seemingly restored, and once again a delicate balance is achieved in David's kingdom.

With the sudden transitions we have come to expect from the narrator, we read in the next chapter (2 Samuel 15) that the reconciliation between father and son was in fact specious, for the crown prince harbors a desire to foment rebellion against his father. Absalom is not content to await his inheritance of the throne. Rather, he begins to engage in a conspiracy against his father's rule, ironically invoking the breakdown of justice as his argument against his father's administration (note the irony—the king had failed to maintain justice in regard to his own actions and the actions of his two sons!). Though Absalom asks only to be appointed "judge," thus evoking the image of old-time rule, he seeks to undermine the king, and succeeds—we are told that he "seduced the hearts of the men of Israel" (2 Sam. 15:6). Two bonds are broken: (1) the covenantal bond of king and people, which was to issue in a reign of justice and righteousness (cf. 2 Sam. 8:15); (2) the bond between father and son, which was designed not only for harmonious father-son relationships but above all for an orderly succession to the throne in keeping with the Davidic covenant (2 Sam. 7:12). Once again, the pressure becomes so severe as to stretch the fragile bonds of the kingdom to the breaking point. After four years Absalom gains sufficient support and goes to the old traditional city of Hebron to be crowned king. The conspiracy becomes open and he now forces his father into exile from Jerusalem. Yet David retains some servants loyal to the bond of service to the legitimate king. Ittai the Gittite, for example, is a newcomer to David's service, but he gives a stirring speech of loyalty to the exiled king: "As Yahweh lives, and as my lord the king lives, wherever my lord the king shall be, whether for death or for life, there also will your servant be" (2 Sam. 15:21). The ironic contrast is painful: the king who was always so successful in attracting the loyalty of his followers could not retain the loyalty of his own sons.

The revolt ultimately fails. But prior to the final battle, the king asks his soldiers to deal gently with Absalom for his sake. A father's compassion transcends the law and the king attempts to uphold the bond between himself and his son, even at the expense of his bond with God and the nation. Joab, the steely-eyed realist of the David stories, is not one to set aside strict justice and national welfare for the sake of a father's compassion; so he executes Absalom, directly contradicting the king's order but upholding the societal law governing the fate of rebels.

The scene of David's mourning over his fallen son Absalom is one of the most poignant in literature and brings to a climax the whole theme of bonded relationships in the story of David's reign and the tragic rupturing of those bonds. One perceives the split between the king's intense personal desire to spare his rebel son and the clear-cut demands of the public good. Joab, however, sees where the king's duty lies, and gives the mourning king a sharp rebuke for failing to honor his loyal servants (2 Sam. 19:5–7).

We cannot but be moved by how the father-son bond outweighs for David his public responsibility, notably his bond with his people and his soldiers. In a profound way the David who began to feel death when Jonathan died, a feeling intensified in the deaths of his unnamed son and Amnon, now wants desperately to die in the place of his beloved son Absalom: "My son Absalom! My son Absalom! Would that I had died instead of you! Absalom my son, my son!" (2 Sam. 18:33). David is reduced to bare repetition (cf. Lear's "Never, never, never . . ."). Contrast David's almost stuttering staccato of "My son, my son . . ." with his eloquent lament over Saul and Jonathan. The father is not granted his wish, but dies a worse form of death in that once again he has beheld the savage, relentless sword at work in his own house. David's tragedy is that he must continue to live.

In the aftermath of Absalom's failed revolt, David returns to Jerusalem amidst grave uncertainty as to the reception he can expect (2 Sam. 19:9ff.). The journey back to Jerusalem contains several moments of crisis and resolution as the king attempts to restore several key bonds that had either been broken or severely strained. First, to assure his welcome back by the men of Judah, his kinsmen, he appoints Amasa, apparently very popular with the Judeans, as the new commander of the army, demoting Joab in the process (2 Sam. 19:12–14). Second, he pardons Shimei, the Benjaminite of the house of Saul who had cursed David (2 Sam. 19:19–23), thus healing for the moment the threatened bond between the two rival houses. Third, he accepts (partially)

Mephibosheth's speech of self-defense against the slanderous charges of Ziba, thus upholding his bond with Jonathan (2 Sam. 19:24–30).

The return to Jerusalem, however, becomes the occasion for the smoldering discontent of the Israelites to be fanned into the fire of a new revolt. David had already compounded the problem of the always-latent sectional rivalry by appealing to his fellow Judeans on the basis of kinship bonds, an action that strained the covenant David had long ago concluded with the Israelites (2 Sam. 5:1–3) and that led in turn to an assertion of Israel's sense of superiority and priority (2 Sam. 19:43). The verbal dispute created the opportunity for still another Benjaminite named Sheba to call for open defection: "We have no portion in David, and we have no inheritance in the son of Jesse" (2 Sam. 20:2). Once again, however, the ever-vigilant and ruthless Joab intervenes to crush the revolt and restore the fragile union of North and South (2 Sam. 20:10b–22).

The next collection of texts has often been treated as an alien body that disrupts the smooth flow of the so-called Succession Narrative. Typically, it has been classed as an "Appendix," a catchall of texts dislocated from other contexts and set uneasily at the end of 2 Samuel. Yet a closer look presents another image, indeed, a picture of "artistic symmetry" and a profound commentary on the career of David. Childs, building particularly on the work of Carlson and Hertzberg, has offered a compelling revision of the usual view. He notes first that the symmetry is striking: "Two stories form the beginning and ending . . . then two lists of heroes are included (21:15–22; 23:8–39), finally, two poems are joined at the centre (chaps. 22; 23:1–7)."[12] After giving a sensitive interpretation of the texts' canonical significance, Childs concludes that "the final four chapters, far from being a clumsy appendix, offer a highly reflective theological interpretation of David's whole career adumbrating the messianic hope, which provides a clear hermeneutical guide for its use as sacred scripture."[13]

I would add to Childs's view the observation that 2 Samuel 21—24 corresponds functionally and even thematically to 2 Samuel 5—8, 9. Both sections serve a *climactic* and *anticipatory* role in the movement of David's story, in the first case standing between David's rise to kingship and his reign in Jerusalem and in the second instance between the end of David's reign and Solomon's rise to power (1 Kings 1—2). Moreover, we find a similar clustering of modes of legitimation in 2 Samuel 21—24, especially legitimation as grounded in central bonds between God, Davidic king, Jerusalem, and Judah and Israel. First, the narrator justifies David's act of handing over seven of Saul's sons to the Gibeonites for ritual execution in order to expiate Saul's bloodguilt for violating Israel's oath to protect the Gibeonites; at the same time he emphasizes how David spared Mephibosheth out of loyalty to his legal bond with Jonathan (2 Samuel 21; cf. 2 Samuel 9). Second, the military successes of David and his men against the Philistines are once more highlighted (2 Sam. 21:15–22; 23:9–17; cf. 2 Sam. 5:16–24). Third, we hear David recite a brilliant song of thanksgiving that serves as a poetic celebration of the mutual loyalty between God and king in upholding their divine-human bond (2 Samuel 22; cf. especially vv. 17–31). Fourth, in the so-called "last words of David," the king speaks as inspired prophet and shows the inner connections between just rule and Yahweh's covenantal bond with the house of David: "Does not my house stand so with God? For he has made with me an everlasting covenant, ordered in all things and secure. For will he not cause to prosper all my help and my desire?" (2 Sam. 23:5; see also vv. 2–4; cf. 2 Samuel 7). Finally, the narrator justifies Yahweh's sending a plague as punishment for David's act of taking a census, even though Yahweh "incited" David to do it in the first place (2 Sam. 24:1ff.). It is only when Yahweh's avenging angel turns toward Jerusalem to destroy it that Yahweh "repented of the evil" and commanded the angel to stop (2 Sam. 24:16). David is then given prophetic instructions to "rear an altar to Yahweh on the threshing floor of Araunah the Jebusite" (24:18), the place where the angel had stopped in his destructive advance toward Jerusalem. David complied with the prophetic command, buying the threshing floor, erecting an altar, and presenting burnt offerings and peace offerings (24:24–25). "So Yahweh heeded the supplications for the land, and the plague was averted from Israel" (24:25b). Thus the king's ritual action is implicitly a cultic etiology, dramatizing David's choice of the site of Solomon's temple (a connection made explicitly by the Chronicler; cf. 2 Chron. 22:1). In summary, most of the modes of legitimation initially represented in 2 Samuel 5—8 receive decisive reaffirmation here at the end of David's career. Hence these chapters function powerfully to bring to a climax central themes at work in David's reign and to set the stage for the Solomonic succession.

The last major act of the David story takes place explicitly in the process of working out the throne succession (1 Kings 1—2). It is another story of intrigue and conspiracy, this time pitting Adonijah against Solomon. When Adonijah attempts to seize the crown, the old prophet Nathan intervenes in Solomon's behalf. He instructs Bathsheba to remind the senile, dying David of a hitherto undisclosed oath to name Solomon as his successor. Bathsheba complies and is immediately followed by Nathan who reinforces her words. David then proclaims Solomon as his choice to be the legitimate successor.

The circle of the David-Bathsheba affair is finally closed. The king who so long ago had manipulated a beautiful young woman and seduced her, impregnating her and murdering her loyal husband, is now manipulated by her. Solomon, the second son of that fateful union, paradoxically favored by Yahweh's love as embodied in his divinely given name, becomes the new king. The succession to the Davidic throne takes place. Thus Yahweh has his way, keeping his word of promise, and Israel has her second Davidic king.

But what price success and succession? For David's house a frightful price indeed! Adultery, murder, rape, vengeance, conspiracy, rebellion, assassination, and plague have cut their grim course through the Davidic kingdom. Thousands of dead soldiers and four dead sons litter the stage of David's court. Yahweh's promise of a Davidic rule continues to be fulfilled, but at the price of shattered bonds and bloody acts. So ends the tragic story of King David. And so begins the story of his surviving son, successor to his throne, the fabled Solomon. The story goes on, but not without an awful toll. The tragedy may be mitigated, but it is hardly overcome.

III

The story of David's reign is rightly praised for its well-conceived plot line, its remarkably laconic style that tells so much by telling so little, its powerful, probing character portrayals, its psychological insight, and its theological sophistication. The narrative is often terrifying in its depiction of violated bonds, moving and even magnificent in its accounts of bonds upheld. Though all the significant relationships in David's kingdom come into the field of vision, the spotlight falls on the relationships between father and sons. The house of David in all its metaphoric extent is the central theater for action. David's sons, who embody all the hopes and fears of the future of David's house, become partial incarnations of their complex father, possessing some of his strengths but also some of his fatal weaknesses. Whatever the story's precise historical and theological purposes, it still retains that strange and illuminating power to transcend its ancient setting and speak with rare and universal language of those perennial but fragile bonds that hold human societies together. It is Israel's story of divine and human bonds in the time of David's reign, but it is also dramatically, even hauntingly, a deeply universal story as well.

NOTES

1. See esp. Brevard Childs's magnum opus, *Introduction to the Old Testament as Scripture* (Philadelphia: Fortress Press, 1979).

2. See the summary in P. Kyle McCarter, *II Samuel* (AB 9; New York: Doubleday, 1984) 142–43.

3. For the heated debate concerning the Deuteronomistic character of the redaction see McCarter's comments on 2 Samuel 5—8, *II Samuel,* 130–257.

4. See, e.g., ibid., 142, 174, 218, 230.

5. Martha Andresen, "David's House," unpublished lecture delivered at Claremont Congregational Church, September 21, 1986 (Pomona College, Department of English). See also Joel Rosenberg, *King and Kin: Political Allegory in the Hebrew Bible* (Bloomington: Indiana University Press, 1986) 121.

6. L. Rost, *Die Überlieferung von der Thronnachfolge Davids* (BWANT 3/6; Stuttgart: Kohlhammer Verlag, 1926).

7. See McCarter's summary, *II Samuel,* 7–16.

8. K. D. Sakenfeld, *The Meaning of Hesed in the Hebrew Bible: A New Inquiry* (HSM 17; Missoula, Mont.: Scholars Press, 1978).

9. On narrative strategies of the Hebrew Bible, see now R. Alter, *The Art of Biblical Narrative* (New York: Basic Books, 1981); M. Sternberg, *The Poetics of Biblical Narrative: Ideological Literature and the Drama of Reading* (Bloomington: Indiana University Press, 1985) 190–222.

10. U. Simon, "The Poor Man's Ewe-Lamb: An Example of a Juridical Parable," *Bib* 48 (1967) 207–42.

11. See esp. R. A. Carlson, *David, The Chosen King. A Traditio-Historical Approach to the Second Book of Samuel* (Stockholm: Almqvist och Wiksell, 1964).

12. Childs, *Introduction to the Old Testament,* 273.

13. Ibid., 275.

11

A Figure at the Gate: Readers, Reading, and Biblical Theologians

BURKE O. LONG

I

In the Books of Kings, the reign of Jehoram of Israel is largely accounted for with traditions about Elisha (2 Kings 3:1—8:15; 9:1–26).[1] The stories etch in high relief his miraculous powers of life and death (2 Kings 4:1–7, 38–43; 5:1–27; 6:1–7) and his preternatural sight into covert forces within human events (2 Kings 3:4–27; 6:8–23; 6:24—7:20; 8:7–15). Even his reputation had the power to move a monarch, presumably Jehoram, to deal kindly with one of his subjects (8:1–6).[2]

Curiously, Elisha's unrivaled claim to center stage is subverted in 2 Kings 4:8–37 by an unnamed woman from Shunem. She emerges to challenge Elisha's dominance in this storied world, briefly, as though playing before an audience charmed by Elisha-fixation (vv. 18–31); and then she abruptly effaces herself into mute humility and gratitude (v. 37). In that moment the lamp of the Shunammite diminishes Elisha's light, or at least dims the flame kept by the first tellers and editors of his tales.

One may harmonize or explain this incongruity in various ways, or simply ignore it (commentators have done all of these). But to honor the effect of the Dtr composition, that is, to respect this self-negating mode of narrating, requires us to hold to pluriform interpretations simultaneously. And that in turn raises far-reaching questions about what we do when we read the Bible and about the grounds for its theological interpretation.

The issues I see are made more pressing because growing numbers of biblical scholars seem willing nowadays to buy the tools of modern literary theory and practice, and it is in this marketplace of ideas that multiple interpretations of a text are encouraged, celebrated, deconstructed, and constructed again. For those who buy the tools of literary study, the purchase includes immanentalist metaphysics and a reader who is given great individual authority for actualizing meaning in texts. The spent coins bear the image of historically oriented Biblical scholarship and theology, which have systematically suppressed the reader in favor of textual objectivity and a metaphysics of transcendence.

Inevitably, such a transaction demands its own reckoning. These two ways of reading the Bible—the one dominated by historical approaches, the other largely by ahistorical methods—will have to deal substantively with each other. Although conversations are underway, as far as I can see the theological issues have not yet been confronted in their most disturbing form. From the city's tower, I peer along the dusty road and try to discern the markings on that shape bulking toward the gate. I offer this watchman's report with affection and gratitude to my teacher, Brevard Childs, who taught me to think clearly about method and to be captive of none.

Let us begin concretely, with the story of Elisha and the woman from Shunem and the ways in which this text simultaneously gives and takes away the prophet's pride of place.[3]

After a background exposition, which suggests something of the main characters and setting for incidents to follow (vv. 8–11), the drama plays itself out in three movements mostly built of speech and dialogue. In fulfillment of prophecy, a son is born to a Shunammite who was without child and married to old age (vv. 12–17); the son sickens and dies, creating a crisis for both mother and prophet (vv. 18–25aα); then Elisha's miraculous intervention restores the boy to life (vv. 25aβ–35). Dramatic intensity drains away in a brief and final meeting between prophet and woman (vv. 36–37).

This denouement in vv. 36–37 completes a thematic and structural symmetry in the narrative. The Shunammite appears first in deferential respect toward Elisha (vv. 8–10); she questions and pleads, even rebukes him, while demanding his help (vv. 16, 27–28), and now at the end, she falls at his feet (she had earlier grabbed hold of them in petitionary abandon, v. 27). Indeed, the woman seems nearly to worship this man of God (v. 37, *tištaḥū 'ārṣāh;* cf. Gen. 18:2; 19:1; 1 Kings 1:23; 2 Kings 2:15). At the close, Elisha in effect declares her son restored (v. 36bβ), as earlier he had announced his birth (v. 16). Occurring only as part of annunciation (vv. 14–17, 28) and restoration (v. 36), this "son" motif spans the narrative's main action: a son is given in promise, lost in sickness, and restored by the mother's pursuit of a holy man's power.

The narrative begins and ends by suggesting attitudes of admiration, respect, and awe. To put the matter another way, the narrator-writer's mode of telling leaves the impression that what finally counts is Elisha's status as a powerful and respected miracle worker.

The first support of that impression comes from the opening words of the tale, where the woman who so admires the prophet has no name. Elisha refers to her as "this (the) Shunammite" (vv. 12, 25, 36) and the narrator offers only the additional references to her as "mother" (v. 20; cf. the husband's reference, v. 19) or as "mother of the child" (v. 30a). Having no independent information, the reader can neither avoid the omission itself nor neutralize its power to encourage one to view the woman through the eyes of Elisha and Gehazi, who possess names, or through those of the narrator, who retains Adam's privilege of naming all creatures on the earth (cf. Gen. 2:19–23).

A second indication of the primacy given to Elisha comes in the intricately constructed opening exposition, vv. 8–11. One gains a sense of the Shunammite and her dealings with the prophet, but only as background filler placed in the midst of the primary action, Elisha's travel to Shunem. The latter is caught in repeated framing motifs, vv. 8aα and 11aα. One may visualize the literary device as follows:

FRAMEWORK v. 8aα	"one day Elisha crossed over to Shunem" *(wayĕhî hayyôm wayya'ăbōr . . .)*
	DESCRIPTION (vv. 8aβ–10) "and there, a wealthy woman . . ." etc. *(wĕšām 'iššāh gĕdôlāh . . .)*
FRAMEWORK v. 11aα	"One day he came there . . ." *(wayĕhî hayyôm wayyābô' šāmāh)*

Narrated time (v. 8aα) stops, then resumes in v. 11aα. In the pause, retrospective suggestions of character and past relationships emerge in a network of repeated images. (Note 1 Sam. 1: 3a, 7a; 2 Kings 7:5b,

8a—other examples of repetition that mark a place at which the narrator fills a gap in the reader's information.)[4] One hears of the Shunammite's customary actions in past days: "And she [habitually] urged him to eat food, and whenever he passed by, he would turn aside there to eat food" (v. 8b; note the durative temporal sense of *wayĕhî middê* + infinitive, *'obrô*, "whenever he passed by"; see 1 Kings 14:28a; 1 Sam. 1:7; 18:30). The verb "pass by" (*'br*) links the habitual past to the present with which the story began, v. 8aα. Then follows an explanation of how this habit developed: "and she [had] said to her husband . . ." (vv. 9–10). Note the repeated words that tie Elisha's customary action, v. 8b, to the Shunammite's plan to care for him: "pass by" (*'br*) "turn [go] in there" (*yāsūr šāmāh*), repeated in vv. 8bβ, 9, 10. Finally, with some of these same expressions, "turn in" *(wayyāsar)* and "there" *(šāmāh)*, the author turns habitual past into present, and slides back into the incident about to unfold in *this* moment, when Elisha "came there" *(wayyābô' šāmāh, v. 11aα)*. Note that the latter phrase recalls the Shunammite's intentions, who envisioned that he would "come" *(bô')* to her home, v. 10bβ. At the same time, this verb, along with *wayĕhî hayyôm*, marks the resumption of the main narrative sequentiality.

During this pause in forward movement, the narrator characterized the Shunammite. She is "wealthy" *(iššāh gĕdôlāh, v. 8aβ; cf. 1 Sam. 25:2; 2 Sam. 19:33)* but, one imagines, also greatly esteemed (cf. 2 Kings 5:1). In the main, however, one knows her as confessing her awe before Elisha ("this is a holy man of God"; cf. 1 Kings 17:24) and summoning the means to provide lavishly for him (note the narrator's descriptive fullness, "chamber with walls . . . a bed, a table, a chair, and a lamp . . ."). Man of God and Shunammite woman have thus come to a new narrative moment, v. 8aα + 11aα, with background, obligations, and relationship long since established. And for the reader, the rhetoric of flashback assures Elisha's preeminent position as one whose needs are attended.

Depiction of protocol also reserves a privileged status to Elisha. The narrator insistently enforces a respectful distance between Elisha and the Shunammite. In their first meeting, vv. 12–17, one must visualize a conversation between Elisha and Gehazi about, not with, the woman, as she stands by, having presented herself *(watta'ămōd lĕp-ānāyw).*[5] Nearly identical phrases in verses 12 and 15 bracket this conversation and set it forth as occurring while the frame action, the woman standing before the men, runs simultaneously.[6] Indeed, they speak as if she were not there at all. Elisha, groping for the raw materials of miracle, puts a musing question as a charge to Gehazi to ask the Shunammite if Israel's king or army commander might be of some help to her (v. 13). Apparently overhearing, the woman speaks, but the narrator suggests that she intrudes tentatively, as though addressing no one in particular: "I dwell among my own people" (v. 13b). Elisha refuses to acknowledge her declaration and inquires further of Gehazi, v. 14a, who nudges the man of God toward an answer to his own question. No one violates the protocol that separates Elisha from the Shunammite. Later, Elisha and Gehazi cling to the same conventions. Seeing the woman's approach, who by now has had the sorrow of her son's death thrust upon her, the prophet sends Gehazi with greetings (vv. 25–26), only to have the formal pleasantries cast aside in heedless and grief-stricken abandon (v. 27a). This violation of protocol, to which Gehazi strongly reacts (v. 27b), is surprising in view of its importance earlier. In fact, its breakdown testifies to the strength of the transformed Shunammite, who now challenges Elisha's dominance within the central section of the narrative, vv. 18–30.

However, in the end (vv. 36–37) the world is put right again. Just as Elisha's promise of conception and birth had its matter-of-fact fulfillment (v. 17), so the dead child is miraculously revived. Courtly convention returns (note that Elisha bids Gehazi call the Shunammite, v. 36; cf. vv. 12–15a, 25–26), and Elisha retains his position as miracle worker, summoner, and dispenser of gifts. This rhetoric of closure restores normalcy and renders the woman's brief exercise in forceful, direct action something of an aberration in the ordered world of prophet and layperson, prophecy and fulfillment, crisis and miracle.

Yet, one may ask if the alien is so easily made familiar, for the web of dialogue captures and holds ambiguity of perception. Already at their first meeting, the Shunammite strained against the norms governing her relationship with Elisha while the narrator upheld their validity (vv. 16–17). Hearing the promise that she, married to old age, would nonetheless enjoy a son, the woman reacted strongly with words that rebuked the prophet as much as conveyed her skepticism (v. 16b). On the other hand, having given the Shunammite her say, the writer immediately invoked the standard formula of conception and birth (v. 17) and thus counterweighted the emotional outburst with the disinterested tone of a reporter. Events occurred exactly as Elisha had said they would, despite the woman's momentary disruption of protocol.

This exchange warrants a closer look. It recalls a conventional annunciation scene (see Gen. 18:10–14; 16:11–14; Judg. 13:3–5; Luke 1:11–20; 26–36).[7] However, it is not an "angel" *(mal'āk)* or other supernatural emissary who announces imminent birth (as Gen. 16:11; Judg. 13:3; Luke 1:30), but Elisha, a "man of God," acting on his own initiative. Thus far, variation on the type guards the prophet's authoritative position. The Shunammite woman, true to type, is skeptical. She expresses doubt, even protest, at this promise and in so doing puts herself in the reader's ken on the side of Sarah, who laughed at her own similarly announced prospects (Gen. 18:12). But the fact of her protest, since it does not break with convention, does nothing to undermine expectations that the one who pronounces such tidings will be proven correct in the end.

It is Elisha himself who alludes to an element that eventually will work against his own authority in the narrative. Adapting the familiar annunciatory formula, he introduces an unusual image: she will "embrace" a son (cf. Gen. 29:13; 33:4; 48:10; Cant. 2:6; 8:3). This woman will not simply bear a child, and thus, meeting the requirements of literary convention, overcome barrenness or present the world a hero; her future will have something to do with the passions of motherhood—and this fact will prove troublesome to Elisha (vv. 18–30).

The Shunammite's protest adds yet another hint of what is to come. With outrage pressing against civility, she cries out, "No, my lord, O man of God, do not lie *('al těkazzēb)* to your maidservant," and infects the habitual decorum between prophet and hostess with moral standard. She hints at her own freedom and the terms on which she will choose to deal with this man of God, announcer of birth tidings.

The next scenes (vv. 18–25a; 25b–30) disturb the symmetry of promise and fulfillment and reorder the relationship between Elisha and the Shunammite woman. Brusque, action-verbed sentences depict childhood and death, entombment among the effects of the man of God, and urgent arrangements for a journey. The Shunammite is clearheaded and purposeful in her urgent concentration. Her husband, something of a foil, seems only a mystified bystander beside this newly visible "maternal passion."[8] She speaks only to get what she needs, to demand the haste she requires, and to deflect her husband's feeble objections in a one-word triviality, *šālôm*, "It will be well" (v. 23bβ).

Indeed, the Shunammite's intense pursuit of her aim propels her right past every obstacle, including those formalities that kept Elisha at some remove in vv. 12–15. Approaching the man of God on Mount Carmel, she brushes aside those ambassador-like greetings (v. 26), thrusts protocol aside, and "grabs hold of Elisha's feet" (v. 27). The expression *(wattaḥăzēq bĕraglāyw)* rescues the gesture of falling at a superior's feet from its more typical ethos of submissiveness (cf. v. 37; 1 Sam. 25:23) and turns it toward assertiveness. Her petition explodes into confrontational, accusatory questions (v. 28). Not even Gehazi, who rises to push her away, can restrain her. This mother denied will be satisfied only by direct dealings with Elisha. But he, like Gehazi, is ignorant of what lies behind this woman's newly found forcefulness and her headlong intrusion onto Mount Carmel. Acknowledging her distress, Elisha admits (to Gehazi) a blindness rarely confessed among the prophets: "The Lord has hidden it from me and has not told me" (v. 27; cf. 1 Kings 14:5–6).

One begins to see what the characters in the story do not, that the Shunammite is not merely pursuing her own design. She is, unwittingly, pressing an advantage against a prophet whose status has been diminished by ignorance. Moreover, her rebuke implies for us that the man of God, normally preeminent, lacks more than a tip-off from God. The mother has been wronged in this business; it is *her* son who is dead, and it is *this* man of God who somehow should assume responsibility. At the announcement of birth, she had pleaded, "Do not lie," but in the rhetorical recasting of that moment, she focuses on moral effect: "Did I not say, do not lead me astray?"[9] It is not the formerly generous and prophet-honoring Shunammite whom one now watches, but a mother demanding (without knowing Elisha's admission of withheld second sight) that the prophet accept the moral consequences of his miracle making.

In the Shunammite's extremity, Elisha seems to her like a god who holds sway over life and death. To the reader, he seems merely obtuse. Ironically, the aggrieved victim, like Job, has to break through crusty habits and raise the issue of moral accountability. Elisha's first response to her seems inadequate in its insistence on ambassadorial style: he sends Gehazi to heal the child. Even if the servant, armed with his master's staff and urgent charge, were able to harness apotropaic powers (cf. Exod. 7:20; 8:1–2, 12–13 [*RSV* 5–6, 16–17]; 17:5, 9), it may be too feeble a gesture. And in any case, sending an assistant fails to meet what her sense of moral restitution requires. The woman's second word to Elisha, formally an oath ("As the Lord lives, I will not leave you," v. 30a), thus in effect rejects the prophet's convention-bound response, and demands implicitly that he deal personally with the situation. She could not be thrust aside physically or procedurally (v. 27), and certainly she will not be ignored in this matter of moral accountability. Elisha seems to understand, although—as though clinging to formality even yet—he speaks nothing directly to the woman. The narrator notes simply, "He arose and followed her." However, one has been shown the contraries jostling one another: a clearheaded "mother of the child" (v. 30a), crowding convention and pressuring those who cling to it, and extracting from a somewhat obtuse, incompletely informed man of God a personal, direct action he seems not entirely to want.

Events finally vindicate the Shunammite's insistence. They also restore Elisha to his pedestal (vv. 31–37). While Elisha and the Shunammite are en route, Gehazi goes ahead, tries to revive the boy, and fails completely. Marking this incident as circumstantial "meanwhile" (in v. 31 the Hebrew word order and syntax shifts), the narrator depicts a valley of failure from which Elisha takes his ascent (vv. 32–35). One quickly enters the private world of healing magic. Set apart from ordinary space, locked away in the roof-chamber-become-tomb, Elisha prays to Yahweh, stretches himself like a curative template over the corpse, revives it, and presents the now-living son to his mother. His words, "Take up your son" (v. 37), not only announce the miracle but tap the memory of that annunciatory moment: "You shall embrace a son" (v. 16). In fact, the promise of birth and this short declaratory command are Elisha's only *direct* words to the Shunammite mother. Taken together, like a frame around events, the utterances express one interpretation of their relationship. In *giving* the son, Elisha played the part of the emissarial miracle worker who, with the help of his assistant, dispensed largesse among his patrons. In restoring the son, he merely worked his magic again. The Shunammite responds effusively, falling at Elisha's feet and "bowing to the ground" as though before royal or divine authority (v. 37; cf. 1 Sam. 25:24; Esther 8:3). The narrator quickly concludes: "She took up her son and went out." In the woman's mute approbation, Elisha holds onto his authority.

Through this selfsame closure, the writer keeps his admiring focus on Elisha.

Yet these concluding words seem only to suppress, not deny, the human transformations that have been demanded by the Shunammite's challenge to prophetic privilege. One imagines a reader—at least, I confess to being such a reader—who no longer can view her as she was first presented, as simply an awe-filled patron of this "man of God." She is a victor even if Elisha did not quite admit his blindness to her moral claim. While transformed by circumstance into an aggrieved mother pursuing restitution, she herself forced a change in Elisha. And her mute gestures of subservience at the end—as in the cases of Abigail with David (1 Sam. 25:23) or Esther before King Ahasuerus (Esther 8:3)—may have masked wily independence of mind and resourceful manipulation of authority. Even her demure intrusion into Elisha's and Gehazi's discussion of a suitable reward for her (vv. 13–14) in retrospect now admits of double readings. Did she piously refuse any reward for her admiring deeds? Or did she, even without having been given a name, announce her autonomy as an "esteemed woman" who needs nothing from the prophet, the king, or the king's men?

Indeed, from the beginning the Shunammite seems to have refused the agendas set by others. It was her initiative that established the wayside room for Elisha; she asked nothing when it was confidently suggested by the men that she must have some sort of need; and she pursued justice against thoughtless obstacles of convention thrown in her path by her husband and the prophets.

On the other hand, throughout the narrative Elisha is a man of power. This is his and the narrator's view, at least most of the time. Yet on this occasion Elisha is left without second sight, resists a moral claim, and finally turns the magic trick without confessing any shortcoming to his public. The reader shares a private knowledge of the prophet's vulnerability and thus perceives matters in ways that subvert other tendencies in the narration.

These contrary tendencies, Elisha-centered or Shunammite-centered, both which rest on one's response to items in the work, mitigate against any simplistic interpretation of the narrative. Metaphorically speaking, the text undermines itself; that is, the story bears two contrastive but coherent readings. Certain elements dissent against the untroubled praise of Elisha implied by other features in the story, the larger literary context, and even conventional scholarly interpretations, which have by and large filtered out the structures of contradiction in favor of an Elisha-centered interpretation.[10] There is no decisive reason for ruling out the one tendency in favor of the other, and no necessary call to lower readers' dissonance by invoking palliatives of hermeneutical harmony.[11] This view may be acceptable to readers who value the *plural* in pluriform interpretations, but possibly unsettling to others, such as Biblical theologians, who routinely seek unity in diversity and extract from the Bible definitive and normative guides for the faithful.

I take this simple opposition of pluriform to monoform as a handy way of raising questions about the assumptions, values, and claims for authority that shape the choices made by readers and inform their various strategies of interpretation. The next section of the essay explores some of these issues, especially as they relate to Biblical theology.

II

It may be helpful at the outset to mention some of the notions about texts and interpretation that are presupposed by many literary theorists today. I also confess that I share these views and that they have informed my reading of the Elisha-Shunammite story.

Although it has been commonly assumed that a reader confronts a written work as an autonomous object, many literary critics nowadays view a given document in terms of a transaction between writer and reader. A writer's effort to convey an idea or feeling through language is partially realized when a reader, in a similar act of imagination, construes meaning, or, in shorthand, interprets. Some theorists have defended extreme notions to privilege either the writer, the work itself, or the reader in setting the norms and limits of one's interpretation.[12] These disputes aside, it seems worthwhile to reclaim the commonsense thought that through acts of reading, which employ various conventions, a written work gains a signifying context. It takes on "meaning" in relation to a reader and the psychosocial world in which he or she lives. The object-for-reader that emerges in this process of interpretation may be called a "text," or, perhaps more precisely, the result of "text-making."[13]

Thus, the significance or meaning of a document is inextricably bound up with changing, problematic perceptions of readers.[14] From this vantage point, pluriform readings may be encouraged, celebrated, deconstructed, and constructed again. Critics may even expose structures of contradiction within text-making, as I did with Elisha and the Shunammite, and give full power to them.

This choice of theoretical perspective implies that essentialist notions, such as that some encoded, imperishable meaning awaits discovery within a literary document, have been given up along with their attendant metaphysical assumptions. Instead, one claims that readers configure the "is-ness" of the world as they construct meaning in a pluralistic universe of perceptions. If some metaphysical essence, property, or meaning inheres within a work, it seems unlikely that one can say unproblematically what it might be.[15]

Nevertheless, when many readers agree substantially about their interpretations, a given work may seem to possess a stable "meaning." But this may suggest only that such a consensus was wrought of shared assumptions and supporting analytical methods, or, in short, by a theory of textuality and strategies of reading held in common.

An apt example among Biblical scholars is the consensual use of historical inquiry to describe original authorial intent behind a particular Biblical text. Insofar as the originative act is taken as definitive for our understanding, the method privileges someone or something other than the reader: the author who wrote (source criticism), or the societal forces that transmitted stereotypically formed materials (form criticism), or the redactors who edited oral and written traditions (redaction criticism). To uncover any of these expressions of originally intended meaning is to reach a major goal of modern interpretation.[16]

For the most part, theological application of the Bible among scholars oriented to historical criticism submits to this hierarchy of original "meaning" and takes it as some kind of guide for religious belief and practice. Biblical theology and the religious communities it serves naturally are vested in trying to reach such a "text" stabilized by consensus. By granting theological and prescriptive privilege to a first author (or to one of the many authorial personae, such as the earliest recoverable manuscript reading, original writer, tradent, or even "canonical intention"[17]), one defers to a key theological axiom: revelation came definitively to human beings at a single moment in the past. Historical investigation into that moment not only allows a positive valuation of the human vehicles through which revelation comes, but—insofar as history can be correctly grasped—allows one to control errant teachings and identify inappropriate anachronizing of the Bible. A last stop along this path would be to claim God as author in some way (doctrine of inspiration, inerrancy of the scriptures, and the like). Intermediate stops, such as the idea of confronting the Word of God *through*, not *in* the human words of Scripture, disguise, perhaps, but do not relinquish the principle of divine transhistorical authority over meaning. Despite disputes over details among readers who develop similar competencies in reading historically, the Bible becomes, in effect, overdetermined as though one wished to grasp the thing itself, to lay hold of the Bible's definitive, holy meaning and religious injunction for its readers. Text-making hardens into text, and meaning settles down to normative theological interpretations rooted in common theory and privilege.[18]

In this heart of hearts beats the pulse that will resist pluriform readings of, say, Elisha's and the Shunammite's story. It will seek out historical explanations for diversity, and choose one variant point— usually the earliest recoverable one—as the definitive message. Or it may ameliorate the effects of plurality with higher abstractions.[19]

In the light of modern literary theory, such moves appear strained and diversionary, perhaps even temporizing. As secular literary competence makes its way into the tool kits of more and more Biblical scholars—who by and large continue to be interested in reaching theological results—and as such studies move increasingly from the margins of the field into established journals of historical and theological research, the really fundamental challenges posed by the newer theories of textuality can hardly be avoided. One may reject this and that, or borrow one thing and another from the modernists. But this is to take or reject some of the fruit without claiming as one's own the tree and the high technology that produced it. It is quite a step to take the literary paradigm whole. And yet that seems required if methodological rigor is to mean very much. If Biblical scholars would enjoy the satisfactions of finely tuned literary analysis, they must deal seriously with the linked philosophical views that shake the metaphysical certainties of *all* reading.

Reader-oriented theory robs us Biblical exegetes of our elegantly simple mode of scholarly objectivity—the text "out there" to which we submit. Text is "text-making" and meaning is construed by readers.

Reader-oriented theory undermines confidence in our ability to recover some historical "author" and original intention; and even if one could know the author, his or her privileged standing among various parties to text-making is discredited. At the very least, our liking for excavations into textual history (J E D and P; R^1 R^2 and the like) and our preference for the first among many (the original document, the real words of Jeremiah or Jesus as distinct from later accretions) seem more a matter of choice than necessity.

Reader-oriented theory relativizes distinct interpretations which result from the application of any one set of reading codes, including those highly refined diachronic methods current among deeply trained and highly competent Biblical scholars. No particular reading of a Biblical work may justifiably claim to be absolutely normative, as though rooted in some transcendental property or "truth."

Hence, reader-oriented theory gives a different point to the energy that has driven vast amounts of recent Biblical research—the drive to determine *normative* truth or meaning about a document, at least provisionally until a better formulation based upon the same historically oriented methods comes along. Truth in the reader-oriented mold has to do not with the comforts of absolutes, but with the persuasive power of a reader's language about his or her text-making. A truthful statement is a "text-making" which others acknowledge or fail to acknowledge. It does not describe an inherent property of a document that can be grasped through a series of increasingly precise investigations.

Assuming that reader-oriented theorists are telling us something right about our hermeneutical entrapments, theological use of the Bible as customarily seen among historical critics is, or will be, in trouble. Historical reconstructions embody a particular theory of reality, text, and strategies of reading. They are disabled and leveled to the extent that any reading is constrained by the walls of our language house. If historical reconstruction limps, so too historically grounded biblical theology—unless one can argue convincingly that interpreting the Bible theologically is free of the dynamics said to be associated with reading secular documents.

Traditionally, biblical theologians have done just that. They have relied upon a doctrine of canon, revelation, or divine inspiration to exempt the Bible from the full implications of secularist theories of reading, while borrowing from and contributing liberally to them.

For example, despite the display of historical wares, Biblical theology has seldom, if ever, actually invoked historicism to support its dearest claims. I adduce three cases as evidence.

In his *Elements of Old Testament Theology*,[20] Claus Westermann skillfully employs sophisticated investigations into the histories of Biblical traditions and redaction to expound the beginning of things, the historically situated first and authoritative statements about God in the OT.[21] However, in reflecting on the great (and late) historiographical statements made by Israel's writers (e.g., J and P), Westermann locates their unity and coherent message in the transcendental "reality of God" behind the documents. He asks:

> How is it possible that these historical works present a coherent whole? It is only possible because God is *one* for them and because this one is involved with *everything* that happens.[22]

God is the only author who counts, and he wrote a single "text." If such is the power of God, then the reality of Christ to Westermann guarantees a still more encompassing coherence to the whole Bible.

> Three stages can now be recognized in the history of God's saving acts: the rescue in the beginning, founded upon the mercy of God toward his suffering people; the deliverance from the Babylonian exile, based on forgiveness in light of the preceding history of apostasy; the deliverance from sin and death in Christ, which introduces the history of the new people of God and which took place for the benefit of all humanity. . . . In the history recounted by the Old Testament we can thus see a movement toward a goal which points to what the New Testament says about Christ. In the light of Christ a Yes and Amen are spoken to the Old Testament as the way which leads to this goal. At the same time, with Christ a No is spoken to that which, through the work of Christ, is overcome and now ended. . . . [23]

Jon Levenson, in a work of Jewish biblical theology, takes a somewhat different route to soothe the roughness historicism uncovers. As a historian of tradition, he demonstrates that the early traditions of Mosaic covenant *(tôrāh)* were not displaced in late monarchical Judah by the Zion/David traditions. Hence the canonical text, which now shows them side by side, accurately reflects a historical, originative context, and this fact weighs determinatively on his mind. For contrary theologies coexisted then, coexist now in the Bible, and from this transhistorical fixed point of canon address a religious Jew with equal authority.

In Jeremiah 7, Sinai demolishes the *hubris* of Zion; in Psalm 50, Zion demolishes the *hubris* of Sinai. The traditions correct each other. Each is fulfilled only in the presence of the other. The whole is greater than the sum of its parts.[24]

Levenson selects these themes for his "entry into the Jewish Bible" not solely because of their historical dimensions, including the post-Biblical developments in which Sinai/*tôrāh* were replaced with Paulinist interpretations of Jesus-Messiah. He seems to hear Sinai and Zion as twin calls because the classic rabbinic literature had already elevated them to imperishable, authoritative images around which Jewish religious life would be formed. In other words, these images speak with a power rooted in a shared strategy of reading, and like the reality of Christ for Westermann, they finally stand beyond historical modes of inquiry:

> The survival of these two ancient traditions endows the Jew with the obligation to become an active partner, in the redemption not only of his people, but of his world, to live in a simultaneous and indissoluble awareness of commandment and of promise. The two poles of Sinai and Zion thus delineate an entry not only into the Jewish Bible, but also into Jewish life.[25]

Among other things, one recognizes in Levenson his conversations with "canonical theology" and Brevard Childs. Most recently, Childs argued that OT theology should be frank about its confessional context, accept the self-imposed limits of a canon of scripture, and seek to be both descriptive and constructive. That is, one must recognize the task of "correctly interpreting an ancient text which bears testimony to historic Israel's faith," while exploiting the "intertextuality" of material made contiguous by its placement within a body of scripture.[26] This appears to mean that Childs submits to the authority of historical research and even to the "text" itself, which in its objective isolation stands over against the interpreter.[27] Childs wants to describe "correctly" the originative faith and its author, the "hermeneutical activity which continued to shape the material theologically in order to render it accessible to future generations of believers."[28] On the other hand, the canonical book arrived at over generations of interpretive activity and ratified by ecclesiastical decree, presses itself, complete and in need of no addition, on the theologian.[29] If I understand him correctly, Childs seems to imagine the canonical scriptures as something determined by historical authors and tradents, and yet free of history, as a poet's poem, once released into the world, is free of growth and decay. It simply is, and the reader submits to its internal patterns of truth while taking seriously the historical context out of which it grew. In some ways, Childs's concept would be quite familiar to a "new critic" of literature.

However, like Westermann and Levenson, Childs takes a further step. He acknowledges that "all of scripture is time-conditioned because the whole Old Testament has been conditioned by an historical people," and that the modern Christian reader is "just as historically moored as any of his predecessors."[30] Then, as though to rescue reading from privatism, Childs invokes the classic theological notion of transhistorical inspired *gnosis,* the ultimate authority for a reader's otherwise limited and subjectivistic interpretation.

> Fully aware of his own frailty, he awaits in anticipation a fresh illumination through God's Spirit, for whom the Bible's frailty is no barrier. Although such understanding derives ultimately from the illumination of the Spirit, this divine activity functions through the scriptures of the church; that is to say, completely within the time-conditioned form of the tradition. There is no one hermeneutical key for unlocking the biblical message, but the canon provides the arena in which the struggle for understanding takes place.[31]

In other words, there is a single book, and ultimately a single reader or at least there are readings aspiring to illumination by a single Spirit. Human perceptions may differ and thereby compete for consensus, but final authority for interpretation resides ultimately with God, beyond the reader.

As these examples demonstrate, Biblical theologians seem able to hold the line against secularist metaphysics and to claim in effect that interpretation of a scriptural text for theological purposes follows special rules and defers to transhistorical authority distinct from the reader. In short, theological interpretation is finally, where it counts, exempt from those troubles associated with reading all other documents. Definitive claims that override pluriform perceptions are not only possible, but desirable. And the way to unity is through historical conventions of reading, which are in the end swallowed by religious metaphysics.

But how long will this procedure suffice, as more and more Biblical scholars draw the waters of secular criticism and bring them inside the gates of Biblical exegesis? I have no answer. Perhaps the Shunammite woman will not be allowed to subvert admiration of Elisha or to impugn the prophetic voice with a question of moral obtuseness. Perhaps the disparities and contradictions among our readings of the Bible will never be allowed their due as symptoms of a problem in the dominant operative theories of textuality.

On the other hand, one aspect of Childs's program may hold promise for contributing to whatever life Biblical theology will have if and when the modernist approaches make their full impact. He stresses relation to the Spirit in the midst of radical historicality and echoes the sounds of H. Richard Niebuhr's "radical monotheism." One lives in faith with the absolute and transcendent God, but asserts, paradoxically, that one's perceptions about, and relation to, God are trapped absolutely in relativity.

> Radical monotheism dethrones all absolutes short of the principle of being itself. At the same time it reverences every relative existant. Its two great mottoes are: "I am the Lord thy God; thou shalt have no other gods before me" and "Whatever is, is good."[32]

This position, which of course accepts a conceptual and existential paradox as the condition of human life and religious faith, may offer a way for Biblical theologians to take reader-oriented methods whole, to rest comfortably with the relativism of textual interpretation, and even to accept that authority for one's statements must be lodged within oneself. The God beyond god cannot be claimed to legitimate one's reading; one may not invoke this God as author, even implicitly, or somehow align him or her—language fails—with a particular theory of text.

This God beyond gods is not the sort that religions call up to pronounce great clarifications or that prophets quote to gather their followers. But then again, reader-oriented theory is a child of the pluralisms of less certain times in which even biblical scholars must live. Perhaps a momentary stay against confusion is what one should expect and learn to live with, if and when biblical theology takes seriously the deepest challenge from literary studies.[33]

NOTES

1. Nested within the presentation are the regnal period of Jehoram of Judah (2 Kings 8:16–24) and the opening summary of the Judean Ahaziah's rule (2 Kings 8:25–27). Ahaziah's "slot" in the chainlike coverage of the reigns in 1

and 2 Kings—and this was apparently its main function in the author's literary plan—was given over to telling how both Jehoram of Israel and Ahaziah of Judah came to their deaths together in Jehu's rebellion (2 Kings 8:28—9:28). In these events, too, Elisha plays an important role (2 Kings 9:1–10).

2. Outside the literary boundaries of Jehoram's reign, Elisha's awesome powers are still the center of attention (2 Kings 2:1–24). Even his bones revive the dead (2 Kings 13:20–21).

3. For purposes of this paper, I set aside the disputes about the history of composition and redaction and take the work to be read as that which the Deuteronomistic writer of the early exilic period (including the additions of any supplementers) left to posterity. This move implies a theory of textuality and reading to be developed below and some choices about the contexts in which reading occurs. We shall in the end find ourselves closer on these matters to the assumptions upon which most modern Biblical theologians have worked, despite their reliance on heavily documented historical researches.

4. See Burke O. Long, "Framing Repetitions in Biblical Historiography" (forthcoming in *JBL*).

5. See J. Montgomery, *The Books of Kings* (Edinburgh: T. & T. Clark, 1951) 368.

6. Cf. vv. 25b, 27a; 1 Sam. 3:1, 19; 19:12, 18; 2 Sam. 13:34, 37; S. Talmon, "The Presentation of Synchroneity and Simultaneity in Biblical Narrative," *Scripta Hierosolymitana* 27 (1978) 9–26.

7. See R. Neff, "The Annunciation in the Birth Narrative of Ishmael," *BR* 17 (1972) 51–60; R. Alter, "How Convention Helps Us Read: The Case of the Bible's Annunciation Type Scene," *Prooftexts* 3 (1983) 115–30.

8. See A. Rofé, "The Classification of the Prophetical Stories," *JBL* 89 (1970) 433–34.

9. Heb. *šlh*, cognate with Aram. *šl'*, frequently used to translate Heb. *šgh* or *šgg*. See Deut. 27:18; 1 Sam. 26:21.

10. See, e.g., the entirely typical remarks by E. Würthwein (*Die Bücher der Könige. 1 Kön. 17–2. Kön. 25* [ATD 11, 2; Göttingen: Vandenhoeck & Ruprecht, 1984] 292–93), who pictured the woman as supporting cast, as a model of faithful and admiring devotion to a great religious figure. On vv. 8–17: "Thus will be rewarded whoever receives magnanimously the wandering man of God—who does not always meet with rightful respect and goodwill." He views the Shunammite as a person of such trust in Elisha that she elicits his power, as in the Gospel, "Her faith has helped her." Cf. J. Robinson, *The Second Book of Kings* (Cambridge: Cambridge University, 1976) 42: "This story is very similar to the one told of Elijah in 1 Kings 17:17–24. . . . Both stories make the same point, that life and blessing come from Yahweh and not from Baal, and that reverence for Yahweh's prophets and obedience to their teaching was what God wanted from his people."

11. For a sustained application of this deconstructionist position in Biblical interpretation of a number of texts, see P. Miscall, *The Workings of Old*

Testament Narrative (Chico, Calif.: Scholars Press/Philadelphia: Fortress Press, 1983).

12. E.g., "new criticism," which is still widely practiced, but less talked about by theoreticians today, views the literary work as an autonomous object whose meaning resides in a unique conjoining of form with content and, to a lesser extent, historical circumstance. Using properly honed tools of formal and aesthetic analysis, the work of the "new critic" reveals the text's meaning, which ultimately is independent of either the author—who may not have been aware of the work's fullest implications—or the reader, who tries as much as possible to minimize the distorting effects of personal bias. See the classic statement in R. Wellek and A. Warren, *Theory of Literature* (New York: Harcourt, Brace, 1942). At the opposite extreme is the radical "reader response" theorist, who posits a reader's subjective consciousness as the autonomous power which continually creates meaning, over against the illusion of an objective text. See, e.g., S. Fish, "Literature in the Reader: Affective Stylistics," *Reader-Response Criticism* (ed. J. Tompkins; Baltimore: Johns Hopkins University Press, 1980) 70–100.

13. See R. Scholles, *Textual Power: Literary Theory and the Teaching of English* (New Haven: Yale University Press, 1985) 112: "We neither capture nor create the world with our texts, but interact with it. Human language intervenes in a world that has already intervened in language." Cf. E. McKnight, *The Bible and the Reader: An Introduction to Literary Criticism* (Philadelphia: Fortress Press, 1985) 12: *"Readers make sense.* Even if the subject making sense is not autonomous, and even if the sense is not some final synthesis of meaning, a meaning is discovered or created that is satisfying for the present location of the reader" (italics his). For more technical discussions, see Paul Ricoeur, *The Rule of Metaphor: Multi-disciplinary Studies of the Creation of Meaning in Language* (Toronto: University of Toronto Press, 1971); Hans-Georg Gadamer, *Truth and Method* (New York: Seabury Press, 1975).

14. The situation seems analogous to what Heisenberg formulated as the principle of indeterminacy: certain variables in the physical order seem enmeshed with one another and the observer in such ways that approaching definitive measurement of one variable increases uncertainty about another. Our most fundamental perceptions about the world thus turn out to be problematic. Meaning, what we see and make of the world in its "is-ness," is a shifting, expanding, contracting, and finally linguistic thing forming and unforming of consensus, but perhaps not as stable as our gross hunches might suggest, or our ontologies proclaim.

15. This seems to be Miscall's point (*Workings of Old Testament Narrative,* 2), although he occasionally lapses into essentialist language, as though a text's "undecidability" were somehow an inherent metaphysical property. Consistency demands that one say that readings conflict because readers construe differently and in different contexts.

16. See J. Barton, *Reading the Old Testament: Method in Biblical Study*

(Philadelphia: Westminster Press, 1984). Barton very helpfully explains the various methods of Biblical analysis as ways to develop "literary competence."

17. See Brevard S. Childs, *Old Testament Theology in a Canonical Context* (Philadelphia: Fortress Press, 1985) 6: "Central to . . . [the formation of Canon] . . . was a hermeneutical activity which continued to shape the material theologically *in order to render it accessible to future generations of believers*" (italics mine). Cf. p. 11, where Childs writes of the "theological intention of the tradents."

18. Feminist criticism of the Bible offers a good example of a revolt against shared theory and masculine privilege, but insofar as new norms of theological application remain the goal of such work, feminist critics do not usually disturb the posited connection between original authorial intent (or historical referent) and contemporary religious authority.

19. For example, Würthwein, *Bücher der Könige,* 289ff.), treats all of the Gehazi material as secondary accretion, effectively eliminating many of the accents that give moral power to the Shunammite woman. Würthwein clearly sees his primary task as interpreting the resulting much simpler story. Elisha stands unrivaled at the center of events, and his great power is evoked (and supported) by the woman's great faith (p. 294). T. R. Hobbs, in *Word Biblical Commentary: 2 Kings* (Waco, Texas: Word Books, 1985), makes a synthesizing conceptual move. Acknowledging the historically determined composite character of the document, Hobbs grapples with the final edited form of 2 Kings 4. The elements that jostle one another in their contrariness are swept up into a discussion of higher principles. The varieties of prophetic experience are all presumably instructive; and more importantly, behind all these miracles, including the one Elisha performed with difficulty, 4:29–37, was a single motivation, the compassionate desire to respond to human needs (p. 54). With this, Hobbs domesticates dissonance, for in the end the story illustrates a single idea, the compassion of God himself, which finds its echoes in the ministry of Jesus (p. 55).

20. Claus Westermann, *Elements of Old Testament Theology* (Atlanta: John Knox Press, 1982); from the German edition, 1978.

21. E.g., the centrality of "covenant" (and along with it its religious claims) is rejected: "The concept of covenant between God and his people thus arose relatively late in Israel and was first used at an equally late time to refer to the mutual relationship between Yahweh and Israel; it is a subsequent interpretation intending to transform the relationship to God into a static concept" (p. 44). On the other hand, the so-called covenant formulation (you will be my people, I will be your God) originally had nothing to do with the (late) idea or ritual of covenant, but expressed something more determinative for Christian theology, a "reciprocating relationship [a saving process] open in the fullness of its possibilities" (pp. 45, 215). Furthermore, history of traditions study convinced Westermann that "fullness" of possibility did not include torah (law): "Exodus 19—34 thus represents a bracket between the saving at the beginning and the act of worship in the promised land. The Sinai pericope does not belong to the elements of the saving event and its expansions" (p. 51).

22. Ibid., 216. Paul D. Hanson, in *The People Called* (New York: Harper & Row, 1986) 354, seems to offer a similar view: "It would only invite despair if biblical theology were to commend to the communities it served an unordered set of dichotomies that seemed to imply blatant contradictions. On this level, the challenge is to describe the vision of divine purpose running through our confessional heritage ... to delineate the dynamic Reality active through all time and space...."

23. Ibid., 225, 231.

24. Jon D. Levenson, *Sinai and Zion: An Entry into the Jewish Bible* (Minneapolis: Winston Press, 1985) 209. See pp. 197–209 for the full argument.

25. Ibid., 217.

26. Childs, *Old Testament Theology*, 6–15, esp. pp. 12–13.

27. Childs envisions a continuing conversation between Jews and Christians such that "both religious renderings be continually forced to react to the coercion of the common text which serves both to enrich and to challenge all interpretations" (p. 10).

28. Ibid., 6.

29. "Even though historically Old Testament law was often of different age and was transmitted by other tradents from much of the narrative tradition, a theology of the Old Testament ... seeks to exploit theological interaction. Therefore, regardless of the original literary and historical relationship between the Decalogue and the narrative sections of the Pentateuch, a theological interchange is possible within its new canonical context which affords a mutual aid for interpretation," ibid., 13.

30. Ibid., 14.

31. Ibid., 15.

32. H. Richard Niebuhr, *Radical Monotheism and Western Civilization* (Lincoln, Neb.: University of Nebraska Press, 1960) 34.

33. See Robert Frost, "The Figure a Poem Makes," *Selected Poems of Robert Frost* (New York: Rinehart & Winston, 1962) 2.

Part III

THE INTERPRETATION OF PROPHETIC TEXTS

12

Patterns in the Prophetic Canon: Healing the Blind and the Lame

RONALD E. CLEMENTS

Few scholars in the contemporary Christian sphere have made a more concerted and constructive effort to enable the Christian church to recover a sense of the wholeness of scripture than has Brevard S. Childs. Out of an awareness of the seemingly endless tendency to divide and analyze the Bible into its assumed constituent sources and parts, Brevard Childs has sought to recover a sense of the wholeness and unity of the Bible. To what extent the rather all-encompassing method of canon criticism can achieve this is still engaging the minds of many scholars and theologians. In a practical sense the trend is clear: that the Bible is published as an intended unified collection of writings, that the Christian church has received the collection more or less in this form, and that the overwhelming majority of Bible readers seek to read and understand it as a unity. Only the specialized few who have been initiated into such techniques as source analysis and historical criticism are privileged to read the Bible in some other structural form than that offered by the traditional canonical shape. Two concomitant critical disciplines also point us firmly in the direction of giving heed to central aspects of the biblical tradition which canon criticism has sought to embrace. The first of these is redaction criticism, with its concern to understand how the extant biblical books came to acquire their present literary form and how they were intended to be interpreted in this form. The second relates to the realm of literacy and literality which recognizes that once written down language lays itself open to analyses and interpretations that could not conveniently be applied to it when left in its purely oral state. Comparisons can be made that would not have been considered had it not been possible to set one written text alongside another. Words can be studied in isolation from their original contexts and related to other contexts where the same, or a very similar, word occurs. It is not difficult to see how both of these aspects of interpretation have had a profound and widely popular appeal for biblical interpretation throughout the church's history.

I have endeavored in various essays published elsewhere to draw attention to the special relevance of these aspects of the literary form of the Bible for the understanding of OT prophecy.[1] Of all forms of human speech, that of the inspired prophetic individual is most susceptible to change and reinterpretation once it has been written down. The original historical context quickly becomes vague and indistinct until it may be wholly lost, while the high valuation of the prophet's words lends to it a special quality that leads to the search for new meanings within it. One prophecy is set alongside another, in order to be compared with it, and new meanings can be found in words that have acquired the fixation bestowed by writing. For this reason the edited structures of the four great literary collections of the OT prophetic canon are compositions of special interest. Furthermore, it is discernible that written prophecy did not emerge in a series of wholly self-contained collections. At a relatively early stage it is evident that prophecies from quite different individuals and periods have been brought together. In the post–587 period it is also noticeable that the whole prophetic corpus has been laid open to use in the formulation of new prophetic words of warning and assurance. The extent to which allusion to, and citation of, earlier prophecies is made in Isaiah 24—27, for example, is particularly noteworthy.[2] Nor did this wider basis of reference for the development of prophecy stop at the edges of the prophetic corpus, since it becomes clear that a wider spread of interpretive interest emerged as the corpus of canonical writings took on a firmer shape. Even in its formulative stages, therefore, the main corpus of the OT canon was affected by the principle that scripture could, and should, be interpreted by scripture.[3]

It is of interest in this regard to see how important, and revealing, this feature has become in respect of a quite fundamental aspect of the biblical teaching regarding the nature of the Kingdom of God. The ministry of Jesus of Nazareth in the New Testament is marked dramatically by works of healing that are interpreted as signs of this kingdom operating in the lives of men and women. We may leave aside in this context the question, much discussed among NT scholars, whether these works of healing are to be understood as implying that the Kingdom of God has already come, or is beginning to come, in the realm of human suffering and need. Mark's Gospel sets at the very outset of the ministry of Jesus a story of the healing of a man who had been paralyzed (Mark 2:1–12). This is followed by the healing of a person who suffered from withered limbs (Mark 3:1–6). Further stories tell of the recovery of sight by one who was blind (Mark 8:22–26; John 9:1–41), and of a healing of the deaf (Mark 7:32–37). This work of healing the sick "in the name, and by the power, of Jesus" continues in the life of the early church after Pentecost (cf. Acts 3:1–16). In this latter instance a lame man is able to recover full use of his limbs. The coming of the Kingdom of God is clearly the coming of an age when the healing of the sick can take place. We need say nothing here of the very considerable interest at the present time in the significance of healing in the name of Jesus for the life of the church. What is particularly striking from the point of view of the biblical interpreter is that, in the understanding of the coming of the Kingdom of God in the NT, the healing of the blind, the lame, and the sick generally has assumed a central importance. Against this we find that it occupies, or appears to occupy, a relatively peripheral place in the OT hope of the coming of that kingdom.

The passage where a promise of the healing of the lame, the recovery of sight for the blind, and the recovery of hearing for the deaf is most fully affirmed in the OT is Isa. 35:5–6. Almost all modern interpreters of Jesus' teaching concerning the coming of the Kingdom of God refer to this passage. However, it is very far from being a central one so far as the interpretation of OT prophecy is concerned, occurring as it does in a late and obscure literary context. Many standard volumes on the significance of Israelite prophecy fail to refer to it at all. Clearly, a passage that appears to stand at the very edge of prophetic teaching in the OT has been lifted in the NT into a prominence that it did not originally enjoy. The purpose of the present essay is to note that this verse in reality stands at the end of a long and very significant series of prophecies, suggesting that it has greater importance than may at first appear. In any case it illustrates very clearly the general principle that once the basis of interpretation of a passage is lifted beyond the question of its historical point of origin and its wider literary connections are considered, then its meaning becomes much clearer.

The passage itself is relatively straightforward:

> Then the eyes of those who are blind will be opened
>   and the ears of those who are deaf will hear again.
> Then the lame will leap about like the hart
>   and the tongue of the dumb will sing out joyfully.
> Isa. 35:5–6

The passage in which this occurs is a difficult one since the entire contents of Isaiah 34—35 stand rather awkwardly and uncertainly in the Book of Isaiah. Since the late nineteenth century several scholars have suggested that Isaiah 35, or perhaps both chapters 34 and 35, belong with the prophecies of Second Isaiah in chapters 40–55. Most recently, O. H. Steck has argued[4] that Isaiah 35 was composed specifically to facilitate the joining on of chapters 40ff. (not yet extended as far as chapter 66) to the earlier collection of Isaianic prophecies. Against this J. Vermeylen[5] has argued that Isa. 34:1—35:7 forms "The Little Apocalypse of Isaiah" and represents, like chapters 24–27, a significant stage in the development of the Isaianic prophetic tradition in the direction of apocalyptic. Similarly O. Kaiser regards Isaiah 34—35 as an independent collection of apocalyptic material.[6] The precise literary assessments vary over many details, but critical scholarship has found a fair unanimity over two important points: that Isaiah 35 is not from the eighth-century Isaiah of Jerusalem, but is of postexilic origin, and that it contains themes anticipating the message of chapters 40ff. as well as harking back to at least one major theme of Isaiah 1—33, that of opening the eyes of the blind and recovery of hearing for the deaf (cf. Isa. 6:9–10). I have noted elsewhere that this is sufficiently prominent throughout the Book of Isaiah for it to have constituted a significant point of connection in the growth of the book as a whole.[7] For our immediate concern it is sufficient to note that the promise of healing for the deaf, the blind, and lame—quite clearly intended literally—that is expressed in Isa. 35:5–6 occurs in a section that is strongly eschatological in tone, is postexilic in its origin, and has demonstrable connections with the theme of blindness and deafness that forms a central element in the original divine commission given to Isaiah:

Then he [God] said:
    "Go, and say to this people:
       'Listen carefully, but do not understand;
       look intently, but do not perceive.'
Make the heart of this people insensitive,
      and their ears heavy,
      and shut their eyes;
    lest they should see with their eyes,
      and hear with their ears,
and understand with their hearts,
      and repent and be healed."

Isa. 6:9–10

The entire commissioning address is clearly heavily ironic, but it no doubt does reflect that the prophet, in recording this account of his call, had had experience of the people's negative response to his message. The irony therefore reflects to some degree the prophet's frustration at the people's failure to respond to his words and is designed to goad them into a further and deeper reflection upon them. Clearly the imagery of blindness and deafness in this context is intended metaphorically to describe the situation of people who fail to sense the urgency and truth that lies within the prophetic message. The theme is taken up again later in passages that are almost certainly redactional in their origin (Isa. 29:9–10, linking up also with the Isaianic 28:7). Promises of the ending of this metaphorical blindness and deafness are then set in the reassuring sayings of Isa. 29:18; 30:20–21; and 32:3; it is noteworthy too that chapters 40ff. also develop this theme as a quite central one, namely, Isa. 42:18–21, which possibly has arisen by way of a literal understanding of "the blind" in Isa. 42:16; compare further Isa. 43:8; 44:18. Undoubtedly the theme of Israel's inability to understand the truth of the divine word given through the prophets has found in the imagery of blindness and deafness a convenient literary form of expression. All of these passages, which can be regarded as influenced in varying degrees by Isa. 6:9–10, understand the words in a metaphorical fashion. Isaiah 42:16 is an exception to this, where the notion of blindness is understood in a literal sense, as must also be the case in Isa. 42:7. In this latter case "blind eyes" refers to the temporary blindness of those who had been shut away in the total darkness of a prison dungeon for a long period. All of this would appear to indicate very strongly that the ironic terms of Isaiah's commission to render Israel blind and deaf have provided a convenient image with which to describe Israel living under judgment. Only when the judgment is past will the blindness and deafness come to an end. A literal understanding of blindness as a physical handicap eliciting the special mercy of God then appears in Isa. 42:7, 16 and has sparked off the further round of elaborations upon the theme in 42:18ff.

All of this might have been regarded as unexceptional and scarcely deserving of any greater attention than has already been given to the theme by scholars. Since blindness and deafness would have been, sadly enough, relatively commonly experienced physical disabilities in antiquity, it might not appear that the promise of Isa. 35:5–6 is related in any very direct way to what are almost certainly to be taken as earlier developments of the theme of Israel's blindness and deafness to the message of God. There is however a further passage, itself the subject of a rather disturbed textual tradition, that points us strongly in the direction of recognizing that the extended chain of imagery to be found in Isaiah concerning blindness and deafness has been brought to a climax in Isa. 35:5–6. This is to be found in Isa. 33:23 in a passage (Isa. 33:17–24) forming yet another of several apocalyptic-type additions made in chapters 32 and 33 of Isaiah.[8] The LXX clearly enables the more original text to be reconstructed:

> His rigging hangs loose; it cannot support the mast,
>   or keep the sail outspread.
> Then those who are blind will share out spoil in plenty,
>   even those who are lame will take booty.
> Then no inhabitant will say, I am sick;
>   the people who live there will be forgiven their wrongdoing.
>   Isa. 33:23 (cf. *BHS*)

The passage as a whole, with its mysterious references to ships with masts sailing through Jerusalem, has baffled commentators. Clearly a strong influence from the Zion psalms, particularly Psalm 46, has been exerted, as J. Vermeylen has seen.[9] So also however is it clear that the references to the taking of spoil and plunder from the enemy refer to Isa. 8:2, 4, with the probability that the "river" imagery has found further encouragement from Isa. 8:5–8. Further influence from Isa. 9:2 would also appear to be likely where the theme of rejoicing at the dividing up of spoil appears. But where has the unexpected reference to "the blind and the lame" arisen from? J. Vermeylen must surely be right in recognizing that it has come from 2 Sam. 5:6, 8.[10] The recorded tradition of the original capture of the Jebusite fortress of Jerusalem by David (2 Sam. 5:6–10) has a strange and not readily explicable mention of the blind and the lame who are hated by David. This is not the place to reexamine the many perplexities of this difficult passage, which has in any case been excellently dealt with by P. Kyle McCarter in his commentary on 2 Samuel.[11] A number of features are noteworthy and are relevant to the present discussion. Even today the references to "the blind and the lame" appear disconcerting and confusing to the expositor and have given rise to a wide variety of possible explanations. This was clearly so already in medieval times, as the contrived attempts at interpreting such references in a suitably negative fashion as idols, or suchlike, shows. Certainly too it must be held that the affirmation in 2 Sam. 5:8b ("Therefore it is said, 'The blind and the lame shall not come into the house' ") has been added by a redactor who already at a very early stage was nonplussed by the negative attitude toward such unfortunately handicapped persons. This would then be wholly in line with the evidence provided by the Chronicler, who omits all references to the lame and the blind (1 Chron. 11:6), undoubtedly because it already appeared strange and not susceptible of a ready explanation. We may simply note that modern commentators have generally sought to find a satisfactory interpretation in one of two ways. Either the reference to these physically handicapped persons belongs in connection with some kind of taunt such as "Even the blind and the lame will keep you out," or we may follow the attractive suggestion of McCarter that the original element of the tradition is that of 2 Sam. 5:8a and expresses idiomatically: "Go for a kill, do not leave any survivors (to be blind or lame)!" In this case, if McCarter is followed, then the reference to "the blind and the lame" in v. 6 has also come in secondarily as the earliest of the attempts to explain the hostile and uncompassionate attitude expressed in David's command.

Fortunately it is not our immediate concern in seeking to elucidate the prophetic promises of Isa. 33:23 and 35:5ff. to know for certain what the received tradition concerning David's first capture of the fortress of Jerusalem intended by the report of his saying about the blind and the lame. It is in fact more significant that there is an abundance of evidence to show that at a very early stage it caused interpreters great difficulty and came to be understood in various contrived ways. The fact of this difficulty of interpretation strengthens the contention of J. Vermeylen that the tradition concerning David's remarks has exercised a formative influence in Isa. 33:23. We have already noted that redactors of Isaiah's prophecies showed in Isa. 29:18; 30:20–21; and 32:3 a strong interest in reversing the judgment implied in Isaiah's commission to be a prophet. When the time of judgment was past and the age of salvation eventually dawned, then "the eyes of the blind would be opened and the ears of the deaf made to hear." Of course this was understood metaphorically, although it is characteristic of such midrashic-type elaborations on a pregnant poetic theme to interpret its imagery in more than one way. Since this is the case, then the scribal author of the promise of Isa. 33:17–24 has sought to find help for discerning in what manner the future salvation of Jerusalem would be brought about by seeking guidance from other parts of the canonical scriptural tradition. The author's first point of allusion was to the Zion psalms, especially Psalm 46, which has occasioned his quite unexpected and seemingly clumsy reference to the "broad rivers and streams" of the Jerusalem that will exist in the era of Israel's deliverance. He has taken this from Ps. 46:4ff., but has most probably been prompted to do so from the "river" imagery of Isa. 8:6–8. Having got this far, however, further influence has then come, as Vermeylen has noted, from the story of how David first captured the fortress of Jerusalem. But if this is the case, then how has he understood the blind and the lame and how has he understood the story of David's first capture of the city to provide illumination for the return to Jerusalem of Israel's scattered exiles in the coming New Age? One thing is clear: the affirmation "Then those who are blind will share out spoil in plenty, even those who are lame will take booty" (Isa. 33:23) takes up the message of the name Maher-shalal-hashbaz (Isa. 8:2) with the broad inference that it will be the righteous of Israel, returning to Jerusalem, who will share out the plunder. This has been associated with the mysterious reference to "the blind and the lame" of 2 Sam. 5:6, 8, and clearly with an inference that those who are blind and lame are to be numbered among the righteous of Israel. This presumably implies that the author assumed that 2 Sam. 5:6, 8 referred to David's men, or was taken as a taunt raised against them by the inhabitants of the Jebusite fortress and which could therefore be used to describe them. Probably this is to press the interpretation too far, since it could well have been the case that, like a host of interpreters after him, the author could not properly make out what was implied in the mysterious saying about the blind and the lame in the capture of Jebusite Jerusalem. He has simply fastened on its inherent mysterious oracular quality as a poetic image and attached it to the more fundamental image of the righteous of Israel as "the blind" who are soon to "see" again. What is important, and what has hitherto not been adequately recognized by commentators, is the complex midrashic style of elaboration that has been utilized in the composition of Isa. 33:17–24. What fails to receive any adequate explanation if its meaning is restricted to an examination of the circumstances and time of its origin becomes much clearer once a wider literary and canonical frame of reference is allowed to provide a key.

It may be argued that this type of elaborate technique of reinterpreting metaphors, reversing the original sense of specific poetic images, and of adducing new meanings on the basis of occurrences of the same word in another context is only typical of the midrashic techniques of Qumran and the rabbinic era of the first and second centuries A.D. However, it is clearly demonstrable at a much earlier stage than this, as current studies of both Jeremiah and Isaiah have shown. What is so strikingly evident is that such interpretive elaborations of a text are characteristic of certain types of literature, not only in ancient times but also in more recent years. They mark a sense of the magic that attaches to the written word and are highly typical of semiliterate societies in which a certain aura attaches to the skills of those who can write.[12] Even children's folklore can find great play in the mystery of an "unmentionable" word.[13] How much more did such a sense of wonder and mystery attach to those words that had been given through an inspired prophet and were formulated as the words of the Most High God!

In his rich and invaluable study on the development of an inner-biblical technique of interpretation Michael Fishbane has concentrated most heavily upon the areas of legislative and narrative interpretation.[14] He has however also drawn attention to the importance of mantological exegesis where the idea of oracular utterance from God is subjected to such development. The importance of this pattern of interpretation has received considerable attention on account of its prevalence at Qumran in various of the writings discovered there, and also on account of its centrality for the understanding of the OT adopted by the writers of the NT. Not least is it fundamental to the manner in which the apostle Paul understood the OT to provide a witness to the era of the Gospel.[15] The significance of this has all too often been set aside as though it points to an understanding of the OT writings in a manner foreign to the essential character and teaching of those writings themselves. Yet this is not the case, since the essential foundations of such a complex process of interpretation belong firmly within the emergent tradition of the OT canon.

However, we have not finished with tracing the pattern of the prophetic promise that in the coming era of Israel's salvation the blind, the lame, the deaf, and the dumb will all be healed (Isa. 35:5–6).

What has been important in establishing the intriguing exegetical background to the promise of Isa. 33:23 is that it marks a fusion of the original Isaianic warning about Israel's deafness and blindness, understood metaphorically, with the Davidic tradition about the blind and the lame, understood literally (whether or not this was the intended sense of 2 Sam. 5:6–10). Taken by itself Isa. 35:5, with its promise of recovery of sight for the blind and hearing for the deaf, could readily, and perhaps most easily, have been understood metaphorically, as is the case with Isa. 29:18; 30:20–21; 32:3. The continuation in Isa. 35:6 makes it clear that a literal healing of those who are sick is envisaged, and this point is also spelled out explicitly in Isa. 33:24. The age of salvation that will mark the coming of the Kingdom of God will be one in which the sick will be healed. What I have sought to show in tracing a pattern of connected development from Isa. 6:9ff. through to 35:5ff. is that a very significant basic theme concerning the spiritual and physical welfare of Israel has received careful elaboration. The dawning of the age of salvation will be a time when even the lame and the blind will enjoy the fruits of full physical health.

An objection to the foregoing attempt to show that the promise of Isa. 35:5ff. has an important, and even central, place in the development of the prophetic message of the OT could be that it simply draws attention to a kind of word game played by ancient scribes. It is true that an intricate process of word and context association has been utilized to fashion the overall message. To counter this, however, is that as strange as the exegetical techniques may appear to the modern reader, the sense conveyed through them was deeply felt and firmly rooted in the religious and human insights of righteous men and women in ancient Israel. Two fundamental facts about ancient Israelite society can be clearly inferred from a wide range of OT literature.

The first of these is that physical handicap, in which blindness and lameness formed very prominent categories, was a widely experienced feature of life. Much of this was undoubtedly the result of accident and war (cf. 1 Sam. 11:2; 2 Sam. 4:4; 2 Kings 25:7), but some was certainly also a consequence of malnutrition and other forms of disease. The other fact that was inseparably related to this was that God was the Great Healer (cf. Exod. 15:26). Many of the psalms were undoubtedly composed by those who were stricken, or who felt stricken, with illness, or who had suffered an injury needing time and care to heal (cf. esp. Isa. 38:9–22). Even though it would be easy to overplay this aspect of the much-discussed problem of what constituted the psalmist's cause of distress, illness must frequently have been high on the list.[16] Medical knowledge was clearly minimal in such a society and it was both natural and necessary to turn to God for the remedy. Moreover it is important to recognize that ancient Israelite society looked upon healing as one distinctive aspect of the mysterious powers of life. For Yahweh to be the "Living God" meant that he was the life-giving God and therefore, by the very same understanding, the healing God. It was not simply the intriguing words of the prophet Isaiah, or the narrator of the story of Jerusalem's capture by David, which raised the question about the fate of the lame and the blind and the possibility of their being healed. Fundamental aspects of the experience of life and of basic insights of Israel's faith in Yahweh as the life-giving Creator and Sustainer of the universe pointed to the importance of healing as a mark of God's power touching and entering into human lives. The purely scribal development of the theme of healing the blind and the lame, such as we have traced in the Book of Isaiah, was continually guided, shaped, and encouraged by this wider basis of experience and faith. It can be justly claimed therefore that the joyful outburst of Isa. 35:5–6 concerning the power of God to heal represents a desire and a basis of experience that was very central to ancient Israelite life. For NT Gospel writers to have taken this up and adduced it as a basic promise of the Kingdom of God that was fulfilled in the ministry of Jesus marks a very noteworthy and lastingly relevant feature of the biblical understanding of the work of God.[17] What appears to be merely peripheral, when viewed in isolation in a late passage in the Book of Isaiah, has become a foundation stone for the message of the Gospel in the NT. For biblical exegetes also this is a case where the truth of Ps. 118:22 holds firm.

NOTES

1. R. E. Clements, "Patterns in the Prophetic Canon," *Canon and Authority* (ed. G. W. Coats and B. O. Long; Philadelphia: Fortress Press, 1977) 42–55; idem, "Prophecy and Fulfilment," *Epworth Review* 10 (1983) 72–82; idem, "Prophecy as Literature. A Re-appraisal," *The Hermeneutical Quest: Essays in Honor of J. L. Mays for His 65th Birthday* (ed. D. G. Miller; Allison Park: Pickwick Publications, 1986) 59–76.

2. See H. Wildberger, *Jesaja 13–27* (BKAT X,2; Neukirchen-Vluyn: Neukirchener Verlag, 1978) 910.

3. R. E. Clements, *Old Testament Theology: A Fresh Approach* (London: Marshall, Morgan & Scott, 1978) 131ff.

4. O. H. Steck, *Bereitete Heimkehr: Jesaja 35 als redaktionelle Brücke zwischen dem Ersten und dem Zweiten Jesaja* (SBS 12; Stuttgart: Katholisches Bibelwerk, 1985).

5. J. Vermeylen, *Du prophète Isaïe a l'apocalyptique: Isaïe i-xxxv, miroir d'un demi-millénaire d'experience religieuse en Israel* (Paris: J. Gabalda, 1977) 439ff.

6. O. Kaiser, *Isaiah 13–39* (trans. R. A. Wilson; Philadelphia: Westminster Press, 1974) 353.

7. R. E. Clements, "The Unity of the Book of Isaiah," *Int* 36 (1982) 117–29; cf. also idem, "Beyond Tradition-History: Deutero-Isaianic Development of First Isaiah's Themes," *JSOT* 31 (1985) 95–113.

8. Cf. J. Vermeylen, *Du prophète Isaïe,* 433ff.

9. Ibid., 434ff.

10. Ibid., 434 n. 4.

11. P. Kyle McCarter, *II Samuel* (AB 9; New York: Doubleday, 1984) 137ff.

12. Interesting reflections on the awe and authority accorded to those who were modestly literate by those who were not are provided by Karen Blixen (Isak Dinesen) in *Out of Africa* (Harmondsworth, Eng.: Penguin Books, 1979) 65f.

13. An amusing recollection of a child's initiation into knowledge of "the worst word in the world" by the son of the second cattleman on an adjacent farm is to be found in A. Phillips, *My Uncle George* (London: R. Drew, 1984) 53.

14. M. Fishbane, *Biblical Interpretation in Ancient Israel* (Oxford: Clarendon Press, 1985). For mantological exegesis see esp. pp. 443ff.

15. See most recently D. A. Koch, *Die Schrift als Zeuge des Evangeliums* (BHT 69; Tubingen: J. C. B. Mohr, 1986).

16. See K. Seybold, *Das Gebet des Kranken im Alten Testament: Untersuchungen zur Bestimmung und Zuordnung der Krankheits-und Heiligungspsalmen* (BWANT 99; Stuttgart: Kohlhammer Verlag, 1973).

17. For the centrality of the theme in the NT preaching concerning the Kingdom of God, see G. R. Beasley-Murray, *Jesus and the Kingdom of God* (Grand Rapids: Wm. B. Eerdmans, 1986) 81ff.; R. H. Fuller, *The Mission and Achievement of Jesus* (SBT 12; London: SCM Press, 1954) 36ff.

13

The Law in the Eighth-Century Prophets

GENE M. TUCKER

What is the relationship between the prophets and the law? The answer has a bearing on a great many issues, including the role and message of the prophets, and implications for the history of Israelite religion and OT theology.[1] The traditional understanding of the relationship between the two, whether viewed as bodies of literature, religious ideas, or institutions, held sway in both synagogue and church until well into the era of critical biblical scholarship. According to that view, the law, given through Moses, came before the prophets, who were seen as its interpreters. Although Judaism and Christianity valued the law and the prophets differently, they agreed concerning their sequence.

All this changed, at least in critical circles, with the Graf-Wellhausen hypothesis and particularly with the publication of Wellhausen's *Prolegomena to the History of Ancient Israel* in 1878. The consensus that emerged in the next few decades entailed a different outline of the history of Israel's religion and a new image of the contribution of the prophets. They preceded rather than followed the law—at least in its final written form—and were the creative individuals who raised the national religion of Israel to a high moral plain. Wellhausen himself summarized what was to be repeated in numerous histories of religion to follow: "Thus, although the prophets were far from originating a new conception of God, they none the less were founders of what has been called 'ethical monotheism.' "[2] Wellhausen and his successors were concerned with more than law narrowly defined. They studied the contributions of prophets to biblical morality. For more than fifty years, most critical works on the prophets and Israelite religion would stress what was new at the expense of what was traditional in the prophets.

Based primarily upon form-critical and traditio-historical investigations of the Pentateuch, the emphasis seemed to shift in the decades following World War II. Since both the narrative and legal traditions of the Pentateuch were more ancient than the documents in which they were imbedded, the relationship between law and prophets had to be reassessed.[3] Gerhard von Rad's *Old Testament Theology,* Vol. II: *The Theology of Israel's Prophetic Traditions* popularized the view that the prophets depend on older traditions. Although this view sounds like the traditional precritical understanding, in many respects von Rad stressed the "break between the message of the prophets and the ideas held by earlier Jahwism."[4] In fact, what von Rad considered to be traditional in the prophetic proclamations was the particular, old election tradition in which each prophet stood, for example, the exodus traditions in the case of Hosea and the David-Zion traditions in the case of Isaiah. With regard to the law as such, he stressed what was new. The prophets took the old regulations and made them the basis of "an entirely new interpretation of Jahweh's current demands on Israel."[5]

While many recent scholars are prepared to acknowledge the dependence of the prophets upon legal traditions,[6] many others stress their independence. Although recognizing that Amos and Hosea in particular view themselves and their contemporaries as bound to the revealed law of God, Zimmerli likewise stressed the distance between the prophets and the law. Their interpretation of the law was so deep and comprehensive that it introduced a new stage in the history of religion.[7] John Barton's recent work concludes on a similar note: "For pre-exilic Israel, the classical prophets were eccentrics, strange and alarming figures who broke the mould of accepted beliefs and values but who, in the process, changed those values and altered the national religion into something scarcely paralleled in the ancient world."[8] While far more sophisticated than late nineteenth-century scholars, Bernhard Lang sees the prophets as formative forces in the development of monotheism and its morality. In an excellent discussion of the traditions available to the prophets, he demonstrates that their conventional repertoire included the national story (such as the exodus), specifically prophetic traditions (especially concerning the day of Yahweh), as well as historical and contemporary knowledge. Remarkably, he does not list legal or moral traditions, arguing that the prophets did not speak of the covenant because the Sinai covenant tradition probably was not created before the late monarchy.[9] Thus, although most scholars now recognize that the earliest prophets knew and depended upon prior tradition, many continue to stress the disjunction between the prophets and their specifically legal inheritance.

The broad question of the relationship between the law and the prophets could hardly be resolved in a brief essay. Our goals are more modest. We shall approach the question from the side of the earliest prophets by examining their moral inheritance. Focusing upon the eighth-century prophets, we shall attempt to draw a profile of the law, including specific legal sentences or broader moral teachings, which these prophets knew and used. What legal and/or moral tradition did the eighth-century prophets know, and how did they interpret it? In this process we hope to bring some clarity to the way the term "law" might be used in considering such questions.

There is abundant evidence that the prophets of the eighth century knew of expectations legally binding upon the people, and either reproached them for disobedience or—more commonly—listed the violations as reasons for judgment. In arguing that the primary function of the prophets was "the reassertion and application of the old traditions in ways which are relevant and compelling for the present community of faith," Walter Brueggemann assembled an impressive series of texts in which Hosea alludes to laws known elsewhere in the Hebrew Bible,[10] most of them from the Book of Deuteronomy. Likewise W. Beyerlin argued that the tradition of the amphictyonic law is the presupposition, the standard, and the leitmotif of Micah's prophetic complaint and criticism.[11]

One of the few detailed studies of prophetic use of the law is that of Robert Bach,[12] whose primary goal was to contribute to the history of Israelite law. Agreeing with Würthwein[13] that many of the reasons for judgment in Amos depend upon laws known elsewhere in the Hebrew Scriptures, he argued that a legal background was visible in some ten texts (2:6–8; 3:9–10; 4:1; 8:4; 5:11; 5:7; 5:10; 5:12; 6:12; 8:5), and in every case Amos depended upon apodictic rather than casuistic law. Bach is certainly correct in concluding that in these texts—as in some others—Amos presumed that his hearers knew what Yahweh expected of them, but in other respects his conclusions are unsatisfactory. In none of his examples does Amos actually quote a law as such, whether known elsewhere in the OT or not; his use is implicit rather than explicit.[14] Consequently, there is no way to know that the prophet limited himself to apodictically formulated laws. In fact, one of his clearest examples, the prohibition of keeping a garment taken in pledge overnight (Amos 2:8), depends not on an apodictic law but on a casuistic law with a parenetic expansion (Exod. 22:24–26).

Nevertheless, over and over again the prophets of the eighth century allude to regulations they consider binding upon their hearers. It is just as difficult to classify these assumed laws in terms of contents—for example, civil, criminal, religious—as it is to determine their form. Such distinctions seem to have been of limited significance in ancient Israel. Many of the binding expectations concern violations against the rights of other persons, some address specifically cultic affairs, and others are quite general. In some but not all cases their contents can be linked to laws known elsewhere in the OT.[15]

Specific Violations of the Rights of Others

One of the clearest instances of prophetic reliance upon old legal tradition is Hos. 4:1–3, which has definite links with the decalogue. The context is a distinct unit of prophetic discourse, introducing the collection of speeches in Hosea 4—14. It follows the typical structure of a prophecy of punishment and is identified as a *rîb,* Yahweh's lawsuit against the people of Israel. The introductory summons (1aα) is followed by the indictment or reasons for punishment (1aβ–2) and the speech concludes with an announcement of punishment (3). The allusions to the decalogue occur in the second part of the indictment, giving the specific crimes that follow from the failure of *'emet, ḥesed,* and "knowledge of God." "There is swearing, lying, killing, stealing, and committing adultery" *(RSV).* These five offenses correspond to half of the decalogue, although they are not in the same sequence found in Exod. 20:7–16 and Deut. 5:11–20. Only three of the five infinitives absolute correspond exactly to the verbs used in the decalogue: *rāṣōaḥ* (killing, Exod. 20:13), *gānōb* (stealing, Exod. 20:15; cf. also Hos. 7:1) and *nā'ōp* (committing adultery, Exod. 20:14; cf. Hos. 7:4). "Swearing" *('ālōh)* certainly alludes to the third commandment, "taking the name of Yahweh for evil purpose" (Exod. 20:7).[16]

"Lying," or "cheating," corresponds only broadly to the prohibition against bearing false witness in Exod. 20:16; the verb appears in an apodictic prohibition in Lev. 19:11 and a casuistic series in Lev. 6:3 (Hebr. 5:22). Consequently, it is not possible to determine whether or not Hosea and his audience actually knew the decalogue in the form that it has come down to us. However, he reflects here knowledge and acceptance of the substance of the decalogue's sentences concerning violations against the neighbor, and took it for granted that his audience did as well.

Hosea's allusions to such ancient law are typical of the eighth-century prophets. General accusations of sinfulness often are made more specific by references to offenses against other persons (cf. Hos. 6:9, "murder"; 7:1–7; 12:7–8; Isa. 1:21–23). Many of these offenses involve depriving other persons of their property. Amos 2:8 (discussed above) and Mic. 2:8 presume regulations limiting the possession of garments taken in pledge. The laws underlying such accusations are found in the Book of the Covenant (Exod. 22:24–26 [*RSV* 22:25–27]; cf. also Deut. 24:17). While the meaning of Amos's accusation that people are selling the righteous for silver and the needy for a pair of shoes (2:6; cf. 8:6) is far from clear, it probably refers to debtor servitude. In ancient Israel the practice was legal (cf. 2 Kings 4:1; Neh. 5:1–13), but it had limits. A series of casuistic laws in the Book of the Covenant spells out one version of those limits (Exod. 21:2–11). Deuteronomy 15:12 limits servitude to six years, and Lev. 25:39–46 specifies that Israelites in such circumstances must not be treated as slaves but as hired servants.

Likewise accusations concerning dispossessing people from their land presume that ancient law is being violated, possibly through the use of other laws, such as those that recognize the rights of creditors to take possession. Micah 2:2 is an explicit accusation against those who take away a person's land, identified as "his inheritance" *(naḥǎlātô)*. Micah 2:9 (cf. 2:4–5), an accusation against those who dispossess women of their houses, likely is such an instance; and some of Amos's more general indictments of those who expand their wealth at the expense of the poor probably also presume such a tradition concerning land ownership (Amos 4:1–3; 5:10–13). Isaiah 5:8 is another clear example: "Woe to the ones who are joining house to house, adding field to field. . . ." Assumed here is neither the prohibition against coveting another's property (Exod. 20:17) nor the curse upon one who "removes his neighbor's landmark" (Deut. 27:17) as Bergren suggested,[17] but the ancient tradition of familial and tribal land tenure reflected in Joshua 15—21 and provisions for inheritance in texts such as Num. 27:8–11; 36:7–12 (Hebr. 6–11) (cf. also the story of Naboth's vineyard, 1 Kings 21, especially v. 3).

Accusations of crooked business practices presume standards, if not explicit laws for fair transactions. In stating what it means to "trample upon the needy," Amos accuses his hearers of being eager to open the markets "that we may make the ephah small and the shekel great, and deal deceitfully with false balances" (8:5b *RSV*). These lines correspond quite closely to the law in Lev. 19:35–36 requiring fair measures and balances, and to the prohibitions against two kinds of weights and measures in Deut. 25:13–15.[18] The same standards of fair weights and measures are presumed in Mic. 6:10–11 and Hos. 12:7.

In none of these accusations of specific violations of others' rights do the prophets of the eighth century introduce new standards for equity but rather presume that their hearers already know what is right. While the prophets do not quote laws to their audiences—that does not correspond to their roles—it is clear that they allude to traditions that are both specific and accepted as authoritative.

Legal Institutions

It is remarkable how frequently the early prophets refer to the failure or misuse of the judicial system, showing that it was well established in their time. Amos indicts the people of Israel because "they hate the one who reproves in the gate [the court], and abhor anyone who gives an accurate testimony" (5:10). Moreover, they take a bribe and will not give the needy their day in court ("turn aside the needy from the gate," 5:12). When Amos calls for his hearers to "establish justice in the gate" (5:15), he is not asking for something new but only for the courts to function as they were intended. Both Isaiah and Micah also know that partiality and bribery have no place in the administration of justice: "Woe to the ones . . . who acquit the guilty for a bribe, and take away the right of the righteous" (Isa. 5:23; cf. also 3:9; 11:3–5; 29:21). "Its leaders give judgment for a bribe . . ." (Mic. 3:11; cf. also 7:3).

Behind such prophetic concerns stand the decalogue's prohibition of perjury (Exod. 20:16; Deut. 5:20), the Book of the Covenant's insistence upon honesty and fairness in the law court (Exod. 23:1–3, 6–8), and the substance of both the Deuteronomic (Deut. 17:18–20) and Priestly (Lev. 19:15–16) legislation concerning judges and the courts. What is particularly remarkable is the fact that all levels of tradition, both prophetic and pentateuchal, emphasize the role of the courts in the protection of the powerless, including the poor, the widow, and the orphan. According to Isaiah, those who love bribes "do not give justice to the orphan, and the case of the widow does not come before them" (Isa. 1:23). Moreover, those responsible for justice write decrees "to turn aside the needy from justice and steal the rights of the poor of my people, preying on widows and robbing orphans" (Isa. 10:2; cf. Amos 2:7; 5:10–11; 4:1–3).

There are, however, only brief allusions to the actual procedures and officials of the law courts known to the eighth-century prophets and their contemporaries. "The gate" refers to the site of the trial and suggests the traditional process in which all full citizens of the community participated.[19] By the time of Jehoshaphat a royal judicial system was in place in Judah (2 Chron. 19:4–11),[20] but it is not known how widespread this was, or whether such a system existed in Israel. The earlier mechanisms of judicial authority would have been related more directly to the clan and the tribe than to the central government.[21] Some of the prophetic accusations strongly suggest that there was a class of officials with specifically judicial responsibilities. Both Isaiah and Micah associate judicial responsibility with the "princes" or "leaders" (śārîm, Isa. 1:23; Mic. 3:9–11; cf. Isa. 1:26; 3:2).

Surprisingly, there are no direct accusations concerning abuse of the judicial system in Hosea, although the prophet's lawsuit against his unfaithful wife (2:2–15) presumes the traditional adversarial law court. However, Hosea alludes to another institution essential for the perpetuation of law and morality, the teaching office of the priest. In a speech (4:4–10) in which Yahweh acts as both prosecutor and judge, Hosea accuses the priests of having failed in one of their central responsibilities, teaching the law to the laity:

> My people are destroyed for lack of knowledge;
>> because you have rejected knowledge,
>> I reject you from being a priest to me.
> And since you have forgotten the instruction of God,
>> I will forget your children.
>
> (4:6; cf. 5:1–2)

It seems unlikely that the teaching responsibilities of the priests were limited to cultic questions concerning the distinction between clean and unclean (cf. Lev. 10:10–11). Rather, Hosea assumes that they have failed in teaching the people how to behave in accordance with the covenant.

Cultic Regulations

Often along with general indictments or accusations of specific violations against other persons, the prophets of the eighth century allude to particular cultic regulations and/or practices. While it is not always easy to separate them, we should attempt to distinguish between those practices or regulations the prophets take to be foreign and those they consider to be authentically Yahwistic. Only among the latter could we expect to find regulations that both the prophets and their hearers would consider binding; we shall take up the former in the next section. The prophetic use of and reaction to cultic regulations vary. In some cases, prophets simply take the existence of such rules for granted or even criticize their contemporaries for the violation or abuse of such regulations, implying their validity. In other instances they are explicitly critical of the practices and regulations themselves.

It is clear that the prophets presumed the validity of scheduled religious observances. Amos takes it for granted that business transactions were not allowed on the Sabbath or the "new moon," and implies that there are those who, in their eagerness to cheat others, do not respect the sacred times (8:4–6). When Hosea and Amos hear Yahweh announcing the end of all festivals as punishment, they presume that such practices are blessings that now will be removed: "I will bring an end to her joy, her feasts, her new moons, her sabbaths, and all appointed feasts" (Hos. 2:11 [Hebr. 2:13]; cf. 3:4; 9:3–5; Amos 8:9–10).

In Amos 2:6–8 the prophet does not criticize cultic practices as such but rather their abuse. He links crimes against persons, sexual corruption, and cultic activities:

> They stretch themselves out beside every altar
>   on garments taken in pledge;
> they drink in the house of their God
>   the wine of those they fined.
>
> (2:8)

The best-known texts, however, are those in which the prophets criticize the cultic practices of their day. At the top of the list stand

Amos 5:21–24, Isa. 1:10–17, and Mic. 6:6–8 (cf. also Hos. 8:11–14; 9:4–6; 12:11; 5:15—6:6). They are similar with regard to both form and content. All are modeled after the priestly torah,[22] with the prophet speaking in the name of Yahweh as if responding to a question from the laity concerning the appropriateness of sacrifices. The questions are explicit in Mic. 6:6: "With what shall I come before Yahweh?" Each of the texts includes a negative and a positive response. In all three instances Yahweh rejects a series of cultic activities, including all kinds of sacrifices, offerings, and various other acts of worship. The positive side is an exhortation to do justice, modified or expanded in slightly different ways.

It is not difficult to understand why interpreters have seen in these texts the outright rejection of the cult in favor of social justice. Here, for generations of commentators, beats the heart of the early prophets as the founders of "ethical monotheism." The contrasts between the negative and the positive responses are indeed dramatic. However, this popular interpretation must be qualified in several respects. First, the prophets have adopted a cultic model to criticize the cult, thereby remaining within the circle of the traditions they attack. Second, all these prophets show that the tradition of cultic regulations is an ancient one by their time. Third, in the fullest of our examples, Isa. 1:10–17, the continuation of cultic language is deeply significant: the prophet's positive response calls for purification (1:16), as in the cult. Fourth, it is highly unlikely that—as dramatic as they were—the prophets' calls for justice would have been heard for the first time in the eighth century.[23] When the justice and righteousness are given particular content, as in Isa. 1:17, it is in terms of traditional expectations, caring for orphans and widows. Moreover, the vocabulary of Mic. 6:8 (*ḥesed*) reflects ancient covenantal language. Thus these prophets have neither totally rejected the cult nor introduced a new morality.[24] The importance of social justice and corporate responsibility appears in virtually all levels of OT tradition. The prophets insist upon the integration of righteous behavior and cultic piety, and criticize an arrogance that divorces the two, such as lifting bloody hands to Yahweh in prayer (Isa. 1:15).

Faithfulness to Yahweh

With the consideration of faithfulness we come to the center of the prophetic understanding of what Yahweh expects of his people. While it underlies the thought of the other prophets as well, it is the dominant theme in Hosea. There is obviously a great deal that is innovative in the way Hosea addresses this question. His distinctive metaphors for the relationship between God and people are those of husband and wife, parent and child; and his main term for apostasy is prostitution. Hosea's marriage and children are symbolic actions "because like a whore the land is unfaithful to Yahweh" (1:2b). Israel has chased after other gods like a faithless wife has pursued her lovers for what they could pay her (2:7; cf. 4:10–14; 5:3; 6:10; 9:1–3). Hosea, under the influence of the Canaanite religion that he attacks so vigorously, has introduced the imagery of marriage into the language of the relationship between Yahweh and people. He also characterizes Yahweh's love and Israel's rebellion as that of a loving parent and a wayward child (11:1–9).

But what is traditional in the prophet's understanding of Israel's obligations of faithfulness to Yahweh? Hosea presumes at every turn that Israel had known its obligations to Yahweh from the very beginning of its history. It is widely accepted that Hosea and his contemporaries were steeped in the exodus traditions;[25] it is equally clear that they knew the obligations of covenantal faithfulness expressed in the Sinai traditions. In 13:4 he presumes knowledge of the opening of the decalogue and the first commandment.[26] He modifies it slightly, using a form of one of his favorite covenantal terms, *yd'* ("know"), instead of *yihĕyeh lĕkā* ("there shall be for you"):

I am Yahweh your God from the land of Egypt;
you know no God but me,
    and besides me there is no savior.
                    (cf. also 12:10)

Hosea persistently relates the obligation of faithfulness—represented in the first commandment—to the history of salvation, specifically to the exodus and wilderness traditions. In the divine soliloquy in chap. 11 he hears Yahweh contrasting his election of Israel with their failure to be faithful to him, specifically by participating in the cult of Baal (cf. also 9:10; 7:16; 2:4–13 [Hebr. 2:4–15]; 9:1–3). Moreover, he frequently uses the traditional language of covenant, including plays on one of its fundamental formulas, "You are my people . . . you are my God" (2:25 [Hebr. 2:23]; cf. 1:9; 2:1). In a rare prophetic use of the term *bĕrît* (8:1), breaking the covenant is equated with violating Yahweh's law *(tôrāh)*.

If these accusations of unfaithfulness presume violation of the first commandment, numerous others involve specific forms of participation in non-Yahwistic religious practices. Some entail the violation of the second commandment, the prohibition of images and idolatry: "With their silver and gold they made idols for their own destruction" (8:4b; cf. 13:1–2; 14:4, 8; 4:17; 10:1–2, 5; 11:2). Others refer to participation in the Canaanite fertility cult (2:15; 4:13; 10:5), including cultic prostitution (4:14). Still others concern prohibited means of revelation, such as consulting pagan cult objects for oracles (4:12).

Such concerns are by no means limited to Hosea. Although the issue of apostasy is not a central one for Amos, he does reproach Israel for acknowledging other deities (8:14; cf. 5:25–27), and alludes to Yahweh's covenant with Israel as a reason for announcing punishment (3:1–2). Both Isaiah (2:8, 18, 20; 10:10–11; cf. 1:29) and Micah (1:7; 5:13–14; cf. 4:5) accuse their people of idolatry, and criticize them for consulting mediums or the like (Isa. 8:19–20; Mic. 5:12 [Hebr. 5:11]).

These prophets were part of a continuing moral and religious dialogue concerning the precise meaning of faithfulness to Yahweh and its implications for all of life. For Amos the major problems were arrogance and social injustice. For Isaiah the heart of the problem was failure to trust Yahweh completely (7:9; 22:11; 29:15–16; 30:1–5). Hosea, more than any of the others, addressed the question of the practical meaning of the substance of the first commandment. The covenant tradition of allegiance to Yahweh alone certainly was known in Israel in his time. His major contribution to the ongoing interpretation of that tradition was the insistence that there could be no compromise, no acknowledgment of the validity of other deities and no participation in their cults.

Which of the expectations to which the prophets allude, if any, could be identified legitimately as law? The term is notoriously difficult to define in an ordinary sense, and becomes even more problematic when notions of divine law and the complexity of Hebrew terminology are brought into view. Some clarity can be achieved if one applies to the OT evidence categories developed in cultural anthropology for the comparative study of legal systems. Leopold

Pospisil's definitions, based on jurisprudence, philosophy of law, and ethnological research, are particularly helpful.[27] He begins by distinguishing broadly between folk legal systems—the categories of a given culture—and legal systems as determined critically and analytically by cross-cultural categories. In terms of its form, Pospisil defines law neither as a set of abstract rules—as in the Code of Hammurapi or the Justinian code—nor as principles abstracted from actual behavior—as do some ethnologists—but as principles abstracted from legal decisions in a given community or society.

He further defines law not in terms of a single feature but by means of a set of four attributes, all of which must be present for a phenomenon to be called legal rather than, for example, religious or political. These characteristics are authority, intention of universal application, obligation, and sanction. A decision has legal authority if it is accepted by the parties to a dispute or can be forced on them, and it requires a person or persons with powers of enforcement. A legal decision is distinguished from an ad hoc political pronouncement in that the authority intends for it to apply to all similar cases, at least within the particular group. Sometimes this intention of universal application is recognized by an appeal to precedent. Obligation, from the *obligatio* of Roman law, is the part of a legal decision that "defines the rights of the entitled and the duties of the obligated parties,"[28] and must concern living persons, not, for example, the dead or the gods. Finally, real but not necessarily physical sanctions are necessary for a matter to be considered law. Pospisil defines a legal sanction "either as a negative device—withdrawing rewards or favors that would have been granted if the law had not been violated—or as a positive measure for inflicting some painful experience, physical or psychological."[29]

The "folk legal system" of ancient Israel, its own theoretical frame of reference, would have been covenantal, for all law is ultimately brought under that heading. Properly "legal" matters such as the adjudication of disputes over property are understood as the will of Yahweh for his people. Whether law always and everywhere functioned that way would be a question for critical analysis. In order to understand Israel's legal system fully, we would look not so much to its codification but to the decisions rendered in juridical contexts, and the direct evidence for that is severely limited. However, our procedure of abstracting laws and legal principles from the prophetic allusions is an analogous one.

With Pospisil's definition of law in view, it is obvious that in no sense were the prophets legal authorities. While they may speak in the language of the law court, with accusations and announcements of punishment, they do not have the power to impose (human) sanctions upon the accused. In fact, although human instrumentalities such as Assyria may be involved, it is Yahweh who imposes sanctions. Moreover, although some of their speeches define the obligations of the parties, sometimes of human beings to one another, generally they are concerned about the relationship between Yahweh and his people. Nevertheless, some but not all of the violations to which the prophets refer were legal principles in use in the ordinary law court. This certainly would have been the case in the specific violations of the rights of others and the references to legal institutions mentioned above. All of these could meet the criteria for legal phenomena. What the prophets have in view with their references to such crimes is not necessarily codified legal sentences but the principles that guided judicial actions. It seems doubtful that any of the cultic violations could properly be called legal in the same sense. They could meet three of the criteria, but not the fourth. Such matters were in the hands of "legal" authorities, they had the intention of universal application, sanctions could be imposed, but the obligation was in no sense limited to human parties. The accusations concerning faithfulness to Yahweh do not refer to law, although all of Israel's legal principles eventually come under that rubric, articulated as it is in the first commandment.

Already in the eighth century B.C. there was a considerable body of legal, moral, and religious tradition that the prophets considered valid. While they did not actually quote laws known elsewhere in the OT, they frequently listed or alluded to specific violations of the rights of others as reasons for Yahweh's impending judgment. They were particularly concerned with the impartial administration of justice so that the courts could fulfill their traditional role of protecting the weak. They knew of a significant body of cultic regulations, criticizing a piety that ignored concerns with justice and righteousness; but they did not argue for the rejection of the cult. They upheld the ancient covenantal obligation of the people to Yahweh alone.

In no sense do the prophets view themselves as introducing new laws or a new morality or even reforming Israel's institutions.[30] They introduced neither ethics nor monotheism. At the point of their understanding of the people's obligations to Yahweh and to one another, they were neither radical nor revolutionary but conservative, at every point calling Israel back to its foundations. Thus the law, in the sense of authoritative and binding expectations for behavior, comes before even the earliest prophets. Their contributions to the continuing moral discourse were various, but all called attention to the legal will of Yahweh expressed in covenantal obligations. The effect of this analysis for understanding the thought of the OT is to stress the corporate rather than the individualistic factors in Israel's law and morality. All the prophets, however distinctive their language, saw themselves as standing in streams of thought inherited from the past, and in fact they did.

This discussion of the relation of the eighth-century prophets to the law should not be allowed to distort the interpretation of their fundamental role and message. The early prophets did not consider themselves, nor were they, primarily interpreters of the law. As we have seen, they do not teach or instruct in the law, but refer to violations of traditional expectations mainly to make it clear that Yahweh's judgment is reasonable. Those ancient expectations, along with the salvation traditions of the exodus, of the election of David and Zion, provide the background for the prophetic announcements. In the foreground are their announcements of the future, as judgment or salvation, not generally a distant, eschatological future, but the intervention of Yahweh in the immediate future.[31]

NOTES

1. Although Brevard Childs does not address the question directly in his *Old Testament Theology in a Canonical Context* (Philadelphia: Fortress Press, 1985), the issue is related to his interpretation of the role of the prophets (pp. 122–32), their relation to dominant institutions (pp. 180–81), and the interpretation of law (pp. 51–57, 63–91).

2. J. Wellhausen, *Prolegomena to the History of Ancient Israel* (Edinburgh: Adam & Charles Black, 1855) 474.

3. For a summary of recent work on the subject, see Gene M. Tucker, "The Prophets and the Prophetic Literature," *The Hebrew Bible and its Modern Interpreters* (ed. D. A. Knight and G. M. Tucker; Philadelphia: Fortress Press/Chico, Calif.: Scholars Press, 1985) 326–331.

4. G. von Rad, *Old Testament Theology* (New York: Harper & Row, 1965) 2.3.

5. Ibid., 2.400: cf. also 2.396ff.

6. A. Phillips argues that Amos, Micah, and Isaiah took over the tradition of the Book of the Covenant, the codification of Israelite law developed in Davidic court circles; "Prophecy and Law," *Israel's Prophetic Tradition: Essays in Honour of Peter R. Ackroyd* (ed. R. Coggins, A. Phillips, and M. Knibb; Cambridge: Cambridge University Press, 1982) 223.

7. W. Zimmerli, *The Law and the Prophets: A Study of the Meaning of the Old Testament* (New York: Harper & Row, 1965) 93, 67–70.

8. J. Barton, *Oracles of God: Perceptions of Ancient Prophecy in Israel after the Exile* (London: Darton, Longman & Todd, 1986) 268–69.

9. B. Lang, *Monotheism and the Prophetic Minority: An Essay in Biblical History and Sociology* (SWBAS 1; Sheffield, Eng.: Almond Press, 1983) 77–78.

10. W. Brueggemann, *Tradition for Crisis: A Study in Hosea* (Atlanta: John Knox Press, 1968) 13, 38ff.

11. W. Beyerlin, *Die Kulttraditionen Israels in der Verkündigung des Propheten Micha* (FRLANT 72; Göttingen: Vandenhoeck & Ruprecht, 1959) 87–88, 96.

12. R. Bach, "Gottesrecht und weltliches Recht in der Verkündigung des Propheten Amos," *Festschrift für Günther Dehn* (ed. W. Schneemelcher; Neukirchen-Vluyn: Neukirchener Verlag, 1957) 23–34.

13. E. Würthwein, "Der Ursprung der prophetischen Gerichtsrede," *ZTK* 49 (1952) 1–16.

14. Cf. M. Fishbane, *Biblical Interpretation in Ancient Israel* (Oxford: Clarendon Press, 1985) 295–96.

15. R. V. Bergren, who made a strong case for the reliance of the prophets upon legal traditions, assembled a list of parallels between prophetic accusations and pentateuchal legislative texts; *The Prophets and the Law* (MHUC IV; Cincinnati: Hebrew Union College, 1974) 182–83.

16. H. W. Wolff. *Hosea* (Hermeneia; Philadelphia: Fortress Press, 1974) 67–68.

17. Bergren, *Prophets and the Law*, 182.

18. Bach, "Gottesrecht und weltliches Recht," 27.

19. Cf. H. J. Boecker, *Law and the Administration of Justice in the Old Testament and Ancient Near East* (London: SPCK, 1980).

20. R. R. Wilson, "Enforcing the Covenant: The Mechanisms of Judicial Authority in Early Israel," *The Quest for the Kingdom of God: Essays in Honor of George E. Mendenhall* (ed. H. B. Huffmon, et al.; Winona Lake, Ind.: Eisenbrauns, 1983) 60–61.

21. Ibid., 71–75.

22. Cf. J. Begrich, "Die priesterliche Tora," BZAW 66 (1936) 63–88.

23. Cf. J. L. Mays, "Justice: Perspectives from the Prophetic Tradition," *Int* 37 (1983) 5–17, esp. 13, 16.

24. Cf. H. W. Hertzberg, "Die prophetische Kritik am Kult," *TLZ* 75 (1950) 219–26.

25. Wolff, *Hosea*, xxvi–xxvii.

26. Lang (*Monotheism and the Prophetic Minority*, 31) sees the lines of

influence running in the opposite direction, that Hosea's words have shaped the opening of the decalogue.

27. See esp. L. J. Pospisil, *The Ethnology of Law* (2d ed.; Menlo Park, Calif.: Cummings, 1978).

28. Ibid., 46.

29. Ibid., 51.

30. J. Blenkinsopp, *A History of Prophecy in Israel* (Philadelphia: Westminster Press, 1983) 25; cf. Mays, "Justice," 16.

31. G. M. Tucker, "Prophetic Speech," *Int* 32 (1978) 31–45; K. Koch, *The Prophets,* vol. 1, *The Assyrian Period* (Philadelphia: Fortress Press, 1983) 2.

14

Amos 3—6:
From the Oral Word
to the Text*

JÖRG JEREMIAS

The written form of the Book of Amos does not appear at first glance to present any great problem. Since, as a result of form-critical research, the distinction between the spoken word and the written text has increasingly concerned exegetes, it has been considered possible to hear the voice of the prophet more directly in Amos than in any other book of the classical prophets. And probably this conclusion was reached with at least some justification.

Nevertheless, the redactio-historical approach most recently has emphasized more and more that every presentation of a prophet's oral preaching rests on a reconstruction. The intention of the inherited written text is not at all to transmit as literally as possible the original contexts of the prophet's preaching. Rather, it changes the oral prophetic sayings in two basic ways. First, it broadens implicitly the circle of addressees. Not only are individual groups (e.g., politicians, priests, or prophets) to whom the prophet originally believed himself sent by God encountering God's word. Now, in the same way, people of other vocations, in later times, and with different experiences hear God's word. The oral word was intended, in the first instance, for a particular historical hour. The written word claims a validity extending beyond that hour. This is especially true when the prophet's speech had not achieved its aim among its first hearers and God's word seemed to have been spoken in vain. Second, the written text never

---

*Translated from the German by Stuart A. Irvine.

preserves a single prophetic saying alone but rather joins together originally independent sayings. Thereby it always relates at least to the complete sum of the prophet's preaching during a given period of his career (e.g., Isa. 8:16–18; Jeremiah 36), if not indeed to the sum of his entire prophetic message. This complete message of the prophet reflects in comprehensive fashion the will of Yahweh vis-à-vis his people. In both respects then, a growth in the validity and authority of God's word spoken by the prophet is to be observed when it is written down.

These considerations make it clear that the theological interpretation of the prophetic word requires that the overall intention of the prophetic book be illuminated as precisely as possible. This will be done here only in preliminary fashion for the middle part of the Book of Amos. This part of the book (chaps. 3–6) is framed by the two great literary blocks, the oracles against the nations and the vision reports. The formal distinctiveness of these two blocks is far easier to recognize than that of the middle section which, when superficially examined, appears loosely ordered and only structured in broad outline.

I

Reaching the above-mentioned goal is made quite difficult by the recognition that the Book of Amos has undergone not merely one but several editions and that the words of Amos must therefore be interpreted not merely in one but in several contexts. Synchronic questions pertaining to the surface of the text must thus be bound together with diachronic questions about the individual stages through which the book passed before attaining its final form.

These two kinds of questions need not be mutually exclusive, however, but can fruitfully complement and support one another. R. F. Melugin,[1] for example, has demonstrated this for Amos 3—6. With careful and cautious arguments, Melugin compares the two most important analyses of the Book of Amos in recent times, one proceeding essentially along diachronic lines, and the other moving essentially along synchronic lines: the most significant commentary on Amos in this century, by Hans Walter Wolff,[2] and a detailed monograph by Klaus Koch.[3] Melugin concludes that a redactio-historical analysis of the Book of Amos must reckon with different stages of the book's growth, as Wolff has done in detailed analyses, and with features of deliberate composing, to which Klaus Koch has directed his attention. If Wolff in his approach cannot avoid moving into hypothetical areas,

Koch's analysis stands in the even greater danger of proceeding un-historically where it departs from Wolff's approach. In the attempt to combine both types of questions, Melugin has made good progress for chapters 3–4. In what follows I will assume the results of these three authors and will try to build on them.

II

One can distinguish even in a cursory reading of Amos 3—6 two different signs of an intended broad division: the summons, "Hear this word," as an introduction in chapters 3–5, and the "doxologies," so conspicuous in context, in 4:13 and 5:8(9). The two organizing principles, however, do not lie on the same level. If the first is limited to Amos 3—6 (and is continued in 5:18 and 6:1 by a repeated "woe"[4]), the second has in view the doxology in 9:5–6 where the Book of Amos probably once concluded. The doxologies thus divide at least Amos 3:1—9:6, but more likely Amos 1:1—9:6, if one may assign Amos 1:2 to them as well, following Wolff and Koch.[5]

Consequently, chapters 3–6 apparently have undergone at least two editions, or even three editions, if one regards as separate the later conclusion in 9:7–15. One would have to reckon with four editions, if the deuteronomistic verses,[6] easily isolated on the basis of their language, were taken as indications of another edition. I myself am of the firm opinion (which I will substantiate in detail elsewhere) that the "doxologies" and the atonement liturgy connected with them in Amos 4:6–12 presuppose the fall of Jerusalem. To simplify matters, therefore, I would like, as a working hypothesis, to take the "Bethel-interpretation of the Josianic period" (that is, the doxologies) and the "deuteronomistic redaction" of the book of Amos, to use Wolff's terminology,[7] together as an exilic edition of the Book of Amos. To be distinguished from it is the older collection of the "words of Amos" (1:1) compiled by the prophet's followers. The present essay is devoted primarily to this older collection.

III

As matters stand, it is first of all unclear whether we still are able to reconstruct clearly the older collection of the "words of Amos," since the exilic edition of the book could have modified its arrangement. One need not, however, acquiesce in this general reflection. On the one hand, clear compositional features of the older collection are discernible, as will be shown soon in more detail. On the other hand, perspectives can also be identified, according to which sayings were rearranged in the exilic edition.

Two passages above all are to be mentioned, in which one can recognize how the new edition of Amos's words at the time of the exile made changes in the older arrangement, and therefore are not merely explanatory additions to an inherited text. The first case concerns Amos 4:4–5. In all probability this criticism of the cult, which is formally self-contained and which takes up and parodies priestly speech recognizable to contemporary readers, reflects the oral preaching of Amos, albeit condensed. In its present context, however, it is inextricably tied, both formally and with respect to content, to the later atonement liturgy in 4:6ff. The opening of the liturgy, "However I, for my part, have given you clean teeth," could not have formed an absolute beginning. Rather, it is meant in opposition to v. 5b: ". . . for so you love it, O Israelites." Moreover, with respect to content the liturgy needs such an introduction. It means to hold up before Israel the fact that the many punishments of God that have befallen his people and that aimed at effecting repentance were deserved. Amos 4:4–5 serves as evidence that the divine punishments were appropriate. Whether, however, Amos 4:4–5 already followed 4:1–3 in the older book of Amos assembled by his followers is highly uncertain. Indeed this is rather improbable, since Amos 3:9—4:3 presents exclusively sayings directed against the inhabitants of Samaria. The theme of divine worship is otherwise introduced only in chapter 5. There it is quite central and elaborated in detail.

That a new ordering of Amos's speeches has taken place also in chapter 5 is not so certain but still quite probable. As recognized in recent times with increasing clarity, Amos 5:1–17 is organized as an intricate chiastic composition.[8] The funeral lament anticipating the inevitable death of Israel forms the outer framework in this composition (vv. 1–3 and 16–17). The summons to "seek" Yahweh or the good forms an inner framework (vv. 4–6, 14–15). In the outer core is the demonstration of guilt (vv. 7, 10–12). At the center of the piece, toward which all thoughts lead and from which they are to be interpreted, stands the doxology (vv. 8–9). The structure appears schematically: A (vv. 1–3), B (vv. 4–6), C (v. 7), D (vv. 8–9), C' (vv. 10–12), B' (vv. 14–16), A' (vv. 16–17).[9] Naturally one cannot dismiss with absolute certainty the possibility that a chiastic composition formed out of parts A-B-C existed already before the insertion of the doxology. This assumption is doubtful, however, since the chiastic composition would thus be robbed of its center.

The examples of Amos 4:4–13 and 5:1–17 thus show that the exilic edition of the book of Amos did not merely add explanatory notes to a previous text but, at the very least, rearranged a few passages in order to show an unrepentant Israel that praise of the judging and punishing God is its principal task (cf. 1 Kings 8:33ff.).

IV

Despite this modification, the older organizational principles followed by Amos's disciples can be, on the whole, recognized clearly. The three initial summonses, "Hear this word," with which chapters 3–5 open, are upon closer inspection not of equal weight. In the first place, the middle summons in 4:1 lacks the relative clause characteristic of 3:1 and 5:1. In the second place, the ones addressed in the vocative are a limited group in 4:1—the aristocratic women of Samaria—in contrast to the sweeping form of address in 3:1 and 5:1.[10] Only when one has seen that 4:1 introduces only the small unit, 4:1–3, does the way become clear for a comparison of the introductions in 3:1 and 5:1 and thereby for a comparison of chapters 3–4, on the one side, and chapters, 5–6, on the other.

Amos 3:1 and 5:1 differ from one another in two respects.

Hear this word that *Yahweh* speaks over/against you,
you Israelites! (3:1)
Hear this word that *I* take up over you as a lament,
O *House of Israel!* (5:1)

The different forms of address are certainly striking. It is by no means explained by the need for stylistic variation. This follows clearly from the observation that chapters 3–4 use exclusively the address "you Israelites" (*běnê yiśrā'ēl:* 3:1, 12; 4:5) as a designation for the people of God, while chapters 5–6 employ "House of Israel" exclusively (*bêt yiśrā'ēl:* 5:1, 3, 4, 25; 6:1, 14). The LXX recognized this problem and adjusted 3:1 to the linguistic usage of 5:1ff. Why however are these different concepts employed?

This question can be answered only if the second difference is taken into account: *Amos 3:1 introduces divine speech; 5:1 opens prophetic speech.* The otherwise parallel form of the two introductions, each with a different address, shows that there is a programmatic difference here. It follows from this that Amos 3—4 belongs without question before Amos 5—6. The lament of the prophet is the response to God's word of disaster. Corresponding to this is Wolff's observation that "you [the] Israelites" (like the simple "Israel" and "my people Israel") is a designation for the people of God with whom God has dealt and continues to deal, whereas "House of Israel" refers primarily to the Northern Kingdom.[11] The state is heading toward its destruction because the people of God have not lived up to expectations, and this sequence of events is not reversible.

V

The programmatic distinction between divine and prophetic speech allows a series of individual sayings to appear in a new light. First of all, the distinction clearly explains the fact that chapters 3–4 contain, in 3:3–8,[12] a lengthy passage dealing with the legitimation of the prophet, while there is no corresponding passage in chapters 5–6. Here, however, it is not to be expected. If one has recognized the function of 3:3–8 as the legitimation of the prophet for the proclamation of God's word, Melugin's conjecture becomes certain, namely, that the preceding verse, Amos 3:2,

Only you have I known among all the families of the earth,
    therefore will I punish you for all your sins!

should be interpreted not as an individual speech of Amos, but rather as a thematic summary of God's word in chapters 3–4.[13] It thereby gains far greater emphasis. It does not merely summarize the individual speeches in 3:9ff., nor does it simply set their basic tone. It also establishes why the special legitimation of the prophet is required: not because he, like any other prophet, claims to speak God's word but rather because he claims that the hour of the divine *pqd*, or, to express the concept in Hosea's language, "the time [literally, the days] of *hapĕqūdâh*" (Hos. 9:7), has arrived. While this concept frequently has the neutral meaning of "official examination," it designates for the tradents of Amos and Hosea only the negative outcome of such an examination and with it the resulting consequences: God is forced to "punish" sin.[14] This sin is all the more incomprehensible when standing over against it is the unique affection of God directed exclusively toward Israel (v. 2a). Conversely, God's *pqd* follows all the more severely for the sake of this affection that aims at changing Israel and reforming its behavior.

The result is that Amos 3:1–8 is viewed altogether as a superscription for Amos 3–4. Verse 1 (more precisely, v. 1a) proclaims God's word, v. 2 summarizes it thematically, and vv. 3–8 provide the legitimation of the prophet for the proclamation of that word. God's word is then substantiated in vv. 9ff. with individual sayings of Amos. Further observations confirm the character of Amos 3:1–8 as a superscription:

First, as already observed several times, 3:1 and 3:8 form an inclusio. The "word" *(dabār)* that Yahweh "speaks," according to the opening verse 3:1, is identical with that "speaking" of God *(diber,* 3:8) that the prophet identifies with the lion's roar at the conclusion of his thought. This identification makes clear that the roar of the lion is the way in which Israel experiences the divine *pqd,* of which 3:2 speaks. The legitimation pericope, Amos 3:3–8, does not intend simply to establish the compulsory character of the prophetic proclamation generally, as has often been misunderstood. Rather, the pericope specifically intends to explain the pressure upon Amos to serve as a messenger of the divine *pqd.*[15]

The image of the lion linked to God's word in 3:8 is bracketed by two other applications of the image. These clarify its use in 3:8. By way of anticipation, the speech states already in 3:4 that the lion does not roar without prey. This sentence, if read superficially, could sound like an arbitrarily chosen example of cause-and-effect relationships. However, by means of the reference to God in 3:6 and 3:8, the sentence necessarily makes the association, namely, that Israel, to whom Yahweh's *pqd* applies, has become the "prey" of the "lion" which he "has captured" and will not give up. The third use of the image in 3:12 qualifies it in one final respect. When the lion snaps his jaws shut, as Yahweh now appears to Israel, "deliverance" is entirely out of the question. According to the ancient law of shepherds, the "legs" and "piece of an ear" that are "saved" are only evidence that a sheep was torn to pieces by a lion. Accordingly, the lion image in 3:4, 8, 12 is the essential interpretation of what Yahweh's *pqd* means for Israel.

Second, the image of the city in the legitimation pericope exhibits the same relationship to the text as the lion image. Where the passage reaches the first of its two climaxes, that is, where the realm of the animal world (3:4–5) is abandoned and attention turns to the human community, here unexpectedly the catchword "city" occurs twice (v. 6ab). The disaster that Yahweh brings occurs in the city. Therefore, it is in the city where the alarm is sounded, an alarm that makes human beings tremble, just as the roar of the lion does (v. 4). But why precisely "in the city"? The context clearly gives the answer. The "transgressions" that Yahweh as a roaring lion intends to "punish" are primarily the sins of the capital city. All the individual sayings of Amos, which in the older collection of Amos's speeches were introduced as divine speech by the opening sentence in 3:1, are sayings against the inhabitants of Samaria (3:9—4:3).[16] A conclusion about Amos 3:3–8 similar to that concerning 3:2 follows from these observations. Although the rhetorical form of the speech indicates that it derives from the oral preaching of Amos, this oral preaching can no longer be reconstructed. Amos 3:3–8 should no longer be read as a separate saying but as a saying inextricably connected to the proclamation of Yahweh's *pqd* (3:2) and its elaboration in 3:9ff. It defines the function of the prophet in *this* context.

VI

The analogous observations on the structure of the prophetic word in Amos 5(—6) are handicapped by a higher degree of uncertainty because the structure of the chapter reflects, as we saw, the later exilic edition's interpretation of Amos. Various observations, nevertheless, can claim at least high probability.

First, if the prophet introduces his own word in distinction from the divine speech in chapters 3–4 yet in response to it as a "funeral lament" *(qînâh),* then such a pronouncement might have been connected specifically to 5:2 in the oral preaching. In the present context, however, it applies to the whole, especially to the mourning by the farmers (5:16–17), the woe-cries raised in the funeral lament (5:18ff.; 6:1ff.), and the description of the houses full of corpses in 6:9ff. Death is the dominant theme of Amos 5—6, corresponding to the divine *pqd* of Amos 3—4.

Second, the woe-cries may not be related only to the immediately following verses that the woe-cries define formally. Rather, 5:18–27 and 6:1–14 are similarly constructed. After the woe-cry proper (5:18–20; 6:1–7), there follows in divine speech the concrete reason stating what Yahweh opposes ("I hate . . ." 5:21–24; 6:8–11). This leads into a didactic question, which aims at the reader's understanding (5:25; 6:12–13). Finally, the conclusion returns to the beginning, describing Yahweh as he executes the death sentence (5:27; 6:14).

Third, what is striking above all in the structure of the woe-speeches is the central position of the question. The prophetic funeral laments still hope for change of mind. They may aim (in dependence upon Hosea's message) at calling to mind the salvific beginnings of God with Israel in the wilderness (5:25), or at directing attention to the abrogated legal order (5:24; 6:12). A similar point holds true also for 5:1–17. There, in the middle of the funeral lament, the summons to "seek Yahweh" is made twice (5:4–6) and is picked up by the summons to "seek good." This "good" is essentially identical with the "establishment of justice in the gate" (5:14–15). While the possibility of deliverance is described very cautiously—it is effective with the proviso of the divine "perhaps" (cf. Zeph. 2:3; Jon. 3:9) and applies only to a "remnant of Joseph" (5:15b)—the form of the prophetic funeral lament clearly does not mark an absolute and definitive end, at least for the disciples of Amos who collected his words. It calls rather for serious reflection in the last hour.

Fourth, deserving attention in this connection is the fact that the theme of justice in the Book of Amos does not occur in the context of the divine *pqd* as its reason. It appears rather in the immediate or related context of those sentences that still look forward to the understanding of their listeners or readers (5:7, 10, 12; 6:12b). On the other hand, the enumeration of the transgressions in the capital city of Samaria, which binds divine speech (chaps. 3–4) and prophetic speech (chaps. 5–6) together, forms in chapters 3–4 the justification for the *pqd*. In chapter 6, however, it belongs to the more precise description of death (6:1–7, 8–11). To be sure, the tradents of Amos's speeches were also certain that an Israel that tramples justice further underfoot is lost without any hope of salvation. As long as the people of God, whom "God has known" (3:2), do not "know how to do right" (3:10), it remains condemned. Deliverance follows neither on the basis of election (3:2, 12; cf. 9:7) nor from increased worship (4:4–5; 5:4–5). If, however, Israel establishes justice, it may hope—"Deo volente" (5:14b)—to survive as a "remnant of Joseph."

VII

As it is described above, the intention of the collection of the "words of Amos" by his disciples apparently differs significantly from the orientation of the oral speech of Amos himself. By way of conclusion, that can be illustrated here only with examples for chapters 5–6 and 3–4, since a reconstruction of the spoken words of Amos is possible only in part and, in many instances, only in thoroughly complicated ways and with different degrees of probability.

The possibility, indeed the necessity, of tracing Amos 5:4–5 back to the oral preaching of the prophet follows from the differences between this saying and the analogous forms in 5:6 and 5:14–15, as Wolff has observed them more sharply than any of his predecessors. The command to seek Yahweh or the good in the latter two places is issued in extreme urgency as a summons to take advantage of one last chance for the "house of Joseph" or its "remnant." Furthermore, they take up the conceptuality of the surrounding context with which they are inextricably interwoven.[17] In contrast, Amos 5:4–5 (like 4:4–5) is conceived entirely out of the opposition between a genuine search for God and a search for God in the cultic pilgrimage. The passage (like 4:4–5) does not expound the possible salvation in greater detail. (As in more ancient times, "seeking Yahweh" presumably means turning to the prophets.[18]) Rather, 5:4–5 indicts a cultic search for God that soothes the conscience instead of evoking a confession of guilt (4:4). Therefore, there is good reason to believe that in 5:6, 14–15, disciples of Amos, living in a changed historical situation in which God's judgment already had been experienced,[19] listened anew to a harsh word of the prophet about Israel's lost contact with God,[20] with an ear for its hopeful implications. We know, therefore, nothing directly of Amos's proclamation of salvation. We can only infer it from the actualization by the disciples in later years.

In their formal and thematic integrity, the passages against Samaria that are assembled together in 3:9—4:3 quite probably directly reflect, to a large extent, the oral speech of the prophet. At least this is true for 3:9–11 and 4:1–3. These words were directed to a conspicuous upper class who lived in palaces (3:11), relaxed on luxurious beds (3:12, 15), and imbibed wine (4:1). By means of the summary of the chapter in v. 2, however, this sin of a numerically small group is now blamed on the entire people of God because they allow it. The extreme measure of oppression in Samaria, which according to v. 9 is to be noted with astonishment by Ashdod and Egypt as representatives of neighbors and superpowers who were rich in palaces (and who were experienced in acts of oppression),[21] is juxtaposed in 3:2 with the exclusiveness of Israel's election. In this way, every apologetic distinction between the guilty and innocent, the perpetrators and victims, is made impossible for the readers of Amos's words. What the upper class relaxing in Samaria does in their oppression of the poor, they do as representatives of Israel which also does not "establish justice in the gate" (5:15).

If I understand them correctly, the tradents of Amos's words, in a later era, did two things at once. On the one hand, they sharpened Amos's accusations, extended them to all Israel, and brought them into confrontation with Yahweh's saving acts. On the other hand, with the urgency of one last chance and with reference to Yahweh's "perhaps," they dared to call people to a new beginning in the establishment of justice even more clearly than Amos—according to all probability (at least in his public ministry)—dared to do.

VIII

The final form of the text has priority in every interpretation of a biblical book. The one who is celebrating his anniversary, and to whom I am indebted for an unforgettable and formative Exodus seminar, long ago impressed this upon those of us who are younger. The text, not the hypotheses, must be decisive for exegesis as well as for preaching. I would certainly add, and herein believe myself to be essentially in agreement with Brevard S. Childs,[22] that because the text must be interpreted as precisely as possible for the sake of the church that uses it, the attempt at a historical interpretation is indispensable. To be sure, this historical interpretation must acknowledge clearly the degree of certainty of its assertions. That is part of its integrity. In the case of Amos 3—6, the move backward from the postexilic form of the book to the exilic form is possible without great difficulties.[23] A move backward to the original written form of the book is possible only with considerable uncertainties, at least insofar as chapters 4—5 are concerned. To go behind this original form into the oral realm is, in contrast, feasible only with a degree of probability or even only possibility. Nevertheless, such a move backward does not cease thereby to be a part of the task of the exegete: for the sake of the text, which is handed down to the exegete as a living, often actualized, word of God, and for the sake of the church that lives by this text.

NOTES

1. R. F. Melugin, "The Formation of Amos: An Analysis of Exegetical Method," SBLASP (1978), I. 369–91. Cf. most recently esp. C. Coulot,

"Propositions pour une structuration du livre d'Amos au niveau rédactionel," *RevScRel* 51 (1977) 169–86; J. Vermeylen, *Du prophète Isaïe a l'apocalyptique* (Paris: Gabalda, 1978) 519ff.; R. B. Coote, *Amos Among the Prophets: Composition and Theology* (Philadelphia: Fortress Press, 1981).

2. H. W. Wolff, *Dodekapropheton 2 Joel und Amos* (3d ed.; BKAT XIV/2; Neukirchen-Vluyn: Neukirchener Verlag, 1985). English translation: *Joel and Amos* (Hermeneia; Philadelphia: Fortress Press, 1977).

3. K. Koch et al., *Amos: Untersucht mit den Methoden einer strukturalen Formgeschichte* (AOAT 30; Kevelaer: Verlag Butzon & Bercker/Neukirchen-Vluyn: Neukirchener Verlag, 1976).

4. The traditional view that a first "woe" is present already in 5:7 is based on an arbitrary conjecture; cf. below n. 9.

5. Cf. esp. K. Koch, "Die Rolle der hymnischen Abschnitte in der Komposition des Amos-Buches," *ZAW* 86 (1974) 504–37; 530ff.

6. Cf. esp. W. H. Schmidt, "Die deuteronomistische Redaktion des Amosbuches," *ZAW* 77 (1965) 168–93.

7. Wolff, *Joel und Amos,* 135–38.

8. Two names may serve here as representatives for work on this issue: J. de Waard, "The Chiastic Structure of Amos V 1–17," *VT* 27 (1977) 170–77; N. J. Tromp, "Amos V 1–17. Towards a Stylistic and Rhetorical Analysis," *OTS* 23 (1984) 56–84.

9. Because Koch fails to recognize this construction, he is able to explain the function of the second doxology in 5:8–9 only in a very unsatisfactory way. Also the traditional conjecture of a "woe" in 5:7 or even the transposition of entire blocks of speeches (W. Rudolph, *Joel-Amos-Obadja-Jona* [KAT XIII/2; Gütersloh: Gerd Mohn, 1971]) are measures that intend to respond to a text erroneously viewed as disordered.

10. Koch has already recognized this, *Amos,* 2. 107–8.

11. Wolff, *Joel und Amos,* 199–200.

12. More precisely: 3:3–6, 8; v. 7 is by common consent a component of the deuteronomistic redaction.

13. Melugin, "The Formation of Amos," 380–81.

14. Cf. J. Jeremias, *Der Prophet Hosea* (ATD 24/1; Göttingen: Vandenhoeck & Ruprecht, 1983) 32, and the literature cited there.

15. Cf. the interpretation by Wolff, *Joel und Amos.*

16. Regarding 4:4–5 as an introduction to 4:6–13, cf. above p. 220.

17. In the case of 5:15, cf. 5:10 for the concept of "hating"; for the "gate" in which justice is to be established, cf. again 5:10 and 5:12b; for "justice" itself, cf. 5:7; and finally for "Joseph," cf. 5:6.

18. For this meaning of *darāš* see, besides the newer lexicons, esp. C. Westermann, "Die Begriffe für. Fragen und Suchen im Alten Testament," *Forshung am AT: Gesammelte Studien* II (TBü 55; Munich: Chr. Kaiser Verlag, 1974) 162ff.

19. If Samaria itself had not already fallen, the concept "remnant of Joseph" then presupposes at least the reduction of the Northern Kingdom to a rump state in 733.

20. The harshness would be even more evident if 5:4–5 had been the basis for the funeral lament already in the prophet's oral preaching.

21. So Rudolph, *Joel-Amos-Obadiah-Jonah*.

22. Cf. B. S. Childs, *Introduction to the Old Testament as Scripture* (Philadelphia: Fortress Press, 1979) 399ff.

23. Once one looks away from the more frequently discussed verses or verse parts (5:9, 13, 22a; 6:5b) and from the plerophoristic divine predicates, only 3:13 is possibly a postexilic interpretation within Amos 3—6; cf. 9:8b.

15

"God with Us"—In Judgment and in Mercy: The Editorial Structure of Isaiah 5—10(11)

BERNHARD W. ANDERSON

A striking feature of the first part of the Book of Isaiah is the incorporation of the Memoirs of Isaiah (6:1—8:22), which set forth the theme of Immanuel ("God with us"), into the context of oracles in chapters 5—10(11) dealing with God's judgment upon his unrepentant people.[1] Probably the Memoirs, which reflect the Syro-Ephraimitic crisis of ca. 735–733 B.C.E., were edited basically by the prophet himself, and later were supplemented with other materials, including the poem about the birth of a *Wunderkind* who would one day ascend the throne of David (9:1–6; ET 9:2–7). At some point in the history of redaction, however, this document was inserted into a literary complex with its own editorial structure.[2] That this is an insertion is evident from the fact that it breaks the sequence of "woes" (5:8–10, 11–12, 18–19, 20, 21, 22–23; 10:1–4a) and interrupts the cluster of oracles culminating with the ominous refrainlike announcement that Yahweh's hand is "still outstretched" to strike (5:25b; 9:12, 17, 21; 10:4b).

The question is: How are we to understand the editorial arrangement of these materials? In the last analysis this is a theological question, as I hope to show in this essay.

I

A number of commentators have recognized that this part of the text of Isaiah has been disturbed, perhaps as a result of an error of transmission or of editing, and have proposed various reconstructions of the original.[3] The translators of the New English Bible attempt to resolve the problem by transposing 5:24–25 to a position after 10:1–4, thus locating the "woes" on one side and the "outstretched hand" oracles on the other side of the Memoirs. This solution is not altogether satisfactory, however, for the transposition leaves the "woe" *(hôy)* in 10:1 separated from the six "woes" in 5:8–23 and the "therefore" in the relocated 5:25 without an antecedent indictment. Another proposal is to leave 5:24 (a "therefore" saying) in its present place as the conclusion to the "woes" of 5:8–23 and to shift the "woe" speech of 10:1–4 to a place before this passage (thus: 10:1–4; 5:8–24, 25–29[30]). This makes good sense in terms of content, but necessitates saying that the "outstretched hand" formula in 10:4b was added when the passage was shifted to its present position at the end of a series of oracles having that refrain (9:7–20; ET 9:8–21). According to this view, the other "therefore" saying found in 5:25 and the ensuing poem about the summoning of Assyria (5:26–30) originally formed the conclusion to the "outstretched hand" stanzas (thus: 9:7–20 [ET 9:8–21] and 5:25–29[30]); hence all of this material is shifted to the other side of the Memoirs, just before the "woe" against Assyria in 10:5–15.[4]

In his recent commentary, R. E. Clements, following the lead of Hermann Barth,[5] proposes a redaction-critical reason for the dislocation. The removal of Isa. 5:25 (the first occurrence of the "outstretched hand" refrain) to its present place is said to reflect "a deliberate redactional decision." This verse, which now comes after the first indictment of Ephraim and Judah (5:8–24), indicates the consequent divine judgment that will take the form of invasion by Assyrian forces (5:26–30). Clements feels, however, that the decision of the redactors has created a problem. For the "therefore" at the beginning of 5:25 (following hard upon the "therefore" of 5:24) "shows clearly that some antecedent invective is required for the pronouncement of Yahweh's intended action given in this verse. One may infer from the content of 5:25, he concludes, "that it belongs at the end of 9:21, although something has been lost in the course of the transposition since the presence of the refrain shows that we do not have a full stanza here." Accordingly, Clements's discussion follows this sequence: 5:1–7 ("The Song of the Vineyard"); 10:1–4a; 5:8–24 ("Doom upon the Leaders of Jerusalem"); 9:8–21; 5:25–30 ("The

Continuing Anger of the Lord"). All this material is treated before the account of the call of Isaiah. Interestingly, this is the only place in the whole of Isaiah 1—39 where Clements finds it necessary to transpose material.[6]

Brevard Childs, in his monumental *Introduction to the Old Testament as Scripture,* proposes that we take seriously the present shape of the text. He notes that the date formula at the beginning of the inserted block of material (6:1) locates it at the beginning of the prophet's career, that is, "chronologically prior to the material both preceding and following." Clearly, then, something besides chronology has dictated the arrangement. "The significance of this editorial structure," he writes, "is that the words of judgment and of redemption are grounded in a divine decision regarding Israel which is made known to the prophet in his call." Overwhelmed by Yahweh's celestial majesty and purged of his guilt from association with a sinful people, the prophet "is commissioned as a messenger to deliver the verdict of divine judgment which has already been rendered in the heavenly council." Eventually, according to Childs, chapters 7 and 8, emanating from a completely different situation, were connected editorially to chapter 6 to show "the working out of the judgment in the crisis of the Syrian-Ephraimitic war of 734."[7]

This proposal has the merit of attempting to understand the significance of the text as it stands, rather than seeking the meaning in an "improved" text. However, it places heavy—perhaps too heavy—weight upon chapter 6, the opening part of the inserted document. If the significance of the "editorial structure," as Childs formulates it, is to ground "the words of judgment and of redemption . . . in a divine decision regarding Israel"—a decision made in the heavenly council to which the prophet was privy—it would have been more appropriate to place the account of Isaiah's call before, not in the midst of, oracles dealing with Yahweh's activity of judgment and mercy found in chapters 5–11 or even the larger context of chapters 2–12. This is the way editors proceeded in the Book of Jeremiah. Since the account of Jeremiah's call and commission (Jer. 1:4–19) introduces the theme of Yahweh's plan of judgment and mercy ("tearing down and rebuilding"), it was placed at the very beginning of the book.

Stimulated by Childs's suggestion, I propose to inquire whether there is an even larger significance in the editorial structure. In so doing, I wish to honor a colleague who, regardless of whether one follows him all the way in his canonical approach to Scripture, has induced all of us to ask new questions and, above all, has shown that scholarship can effectively serve the community of faith.

II

Let us begin by reexamining the editorial structure of chapters 5–10(11), leaving aside the Memoirs for the moment. In the present arrangement of the text, the theme of God's judgment upon both Ephraim and Judah ("the house of Israel and the citizens of Judah") is introduced powerfully in the Song of the Vineyard (5:1–7). Located editorially at this point, the song echoes a motif introduced in chapters 2–4 (see 3:14, "It is you who have devoured the vineyard"); and the reverberations of its punch line (5:7), with the wordplay ṣĕdāqāh ("righteousness")/ṣĕʿāqāh ("cry of lamentation"), are heard in the subsequent death-wails ("woes") for a people guilty of social injustice.

Divine judgment upon the vineyard is spelled out in the ensuing sections. First, we hear God's angry excoriation of "my people" (5:13) in a series of "woes" (5:8–25), four of which begin with a participle ("those who," 5:8, 11, 18, 20) and two with a nominal formulation ("wise in," "heroes at," 5:21, 22). Next, the prophet announces the execution of God's judgment by raising up "a nation afar off" (5:26–30). Then (jumping over the Memoirs) we find a sequence of stanzas culminating with the repeated refrain that God's hand is still outstretched to strike (9:7—10:4; ET 9:8—10:4). The momentum of the Assyrian advance is interrupted in 10:5–19, which like 10:1 begins with hôy ("woe"), for the purpose of rebuking the aggressor nation for its overweening pride. After an "in that day" passage with apocalyptic flavor (10:20–27), the Assyrian advance continues, though eventually Yahweh, the Divine Forester, will bring the huge tree down in crashing ruin (10:27b–34).

This brief overview is sufficient to indicate that (omitting the Memoirs) there is dynamic movement and thematic pattern in this whole section: divine rebuke for unjust life style, execution of judgment by means of a historical instrument, and the laying aside of that tool when Yahweh's "work on Mount Zion and in Jerusalem" is finished (10:12). A closer look at the rhetorical features of this section confirms the impression that this material has a deliberate editorial structure.

The first unit consists of two "woe" stanzas (5:8–10, 11–12), culminating in two brief "therefore" [*lākēn*] sayings (5:13, 14):

Assuredly [*lākēn*],
My people will suffer exile
For not giving heed,
Its multitude victims of hunger
And its masses parched with thirst.
Isa. 5:13 (NJPSV)

Assuredly [*lākēn*],
Sheol has opened wide its gullet
And parted its jaws in a measureless gape;
And down into it shall go
That splendor and tumult,
That din and revelry.
Isa. 5:14 (NJPSV)

For two consecutive sayings to begin with "therefore" is quite striking. This "double therefore" may well show that "the connection between verses 13 and 14 is questionable," especially in view of other textual problems such as the abrupt change from masculine to feminine suffixes in the two verses.[8] "Dass 5:14 nicht die urpsrüngliche Fortsetzung von 5:13 sein kann," observes Hermann Barth, "liegt auf der Hand."[9]

Here a distinction must be made, however, between the putative original text of Isaiah and the text that we have received from the hand of editors. Form critics have demonstrated convincingly that Isa. 5:1–30 + 9:7—10:34 is composed of independent literary units, each of which was originally addressed to a particular *Sitz im Leben:* the Song of the Vineyard, the sevenfold woes, the "outstretched hand" oracles, the Assyria texts (e.g., 10:5–34), and so on. For instance, the cry "woe" *(hôy)*, originally related to funeral rites, was used to show that the violation of God's order inevitably brings the consequence of "death."[10] A "therefore" was hardly necessary, though it was certainly appropriate, after such an outcry (as in Amos 6:1–7 or Isa. 30:1–3). The question arises, however, as to whether we are to view literary formulations primarily in terms of their *Sitz im Leben* (form criticism) or in terms of their function in the text itself (rhetorical criticism), that is, their *Sitz im Text,* as it has been called.[11] Recall James Muilenburg's famous address, "Form Criticism and Beyond," to the Society of Biblical Literature.[12]

When considered in terms of *function* in the text, the "double therefore" is not necessarily inelegant stylistically. This can be seen by considering a few examples, taken from different levels of Isaianic tradition. In Isa. 30:18, a poetic passage that seems to reflect a time after the fall of Jerusalem in 587 B.C.E., the repeated "therefore" gives emphasis to the promise of salvation.

Therefore [*lākēn*] Yahweh waits to be gracious to you,
Therefore [*lākēn*] he arises to show mercy to you;
    For Yahweh is a God of justice,
    Blessed are all those who wait for him.

Isa. 30:18

Similarly, in a passage from "Second Isaiah" the "double therefore" is used rhetorically to express the confidence of the Servant:

For the Lord Yahweh helps me,
    therefore [*'al kēn*] I am not confounded,
    therefore [*'al kēn*] I have set my face like flint,
And I know I shall not be put to shame.

Isa. 50:7

The same literary phenomenon is found in the so-called Apocalypse of Isaiah where it emphasizes the certainty of divine judgment because of violation of the "everlasting covenant" (cf. Gen. 9:4–6):

Therefore [*'al kēn*] a curse devours the earth,
    and its inhabitants suffer for their guilt;
therefore [*'al kēn*] the inhabitants of the earth are scorched,
    and few men are left.

Isa. 24:6 *(RSV)*

These rhetorical uses of the "double therefore" do not necessarily indicate that the present text of Isa. 5:13, 14 is original. At the least, however, they show that in the present editorial structure "verse 14 expands on verse 13"[13] by adding to the picture of exile the mythical view of the voracious appetite of Sheol and thereby emphasizing the inescapable consequence of divine judgment.

The unit we have been considering is followed by a small poem (5:15–16 [17]) that functions as a kind of coda or doxology, in which the poet pauses to extol the "Holy God" who "shows himself holy in righteousness," using language reminiscent of the "Day of Yahweh" poem in 2:6–21 (see esp. 2:9, 11, 17).

The divine rebukes are resumed in 5:18–23. This unit consists of four "woes," though it is approximately the same in length as the previous one containing only two "woes" and, like it, also culminates in two "therefore" sayings. The first one, with its climactic *kî* ("for"), serves as an editorial conclusion to all of the "woes" in 5:8–23. Previously the people were rebuked for failing to perceive the "action"/"work" *(pōʿal, maʿăśēh)* of Yahweh and for lack of "knowledge" *(daʿat)*; here the rebuke is based on rejecting the "teaching" *(tôrāh)*, despising the "word" *(ʾimrāh)* of Yahweh.

> Therefore [*lākēn*] as a tongue of fire consumes straw,
> and as dry grass sinks down in flame,
> so their root will be like rot,
> and their blossom vanish like dust;
> for [*kî*] they have rejected the teaching of Yahweh of hosts,
> and have depised the word of the Holy One of Israel.
>
> Isa. 5:24

The next verse (5:25) also begins with "therefore" *(ʿal kēn)*. The consecutive "therefore" sayings, corresponding to the "double therefore" of 5:13, 14, serve to emphasize the ominous destiny in store for God's people. In the former case, it was the hunger and thirst of exile and being swallowed up in the throat of Sheol; here it is a consuming fire that sweeps through the land and a seismic catastrophe that shakes the foundations.

In this unit, however, the second "therefore" saying—the one that is often regarded as a fragment belonging with 9:7—10:4—introduces a motif that serves as a transition to what follows. The ominous catastrophe is regarded as the expression of Yahweh's wrath.

> Therefore the anger of Yahweh blazed against his people,
> and he stretched out his hand against them and smote them,
> the mountains quaked, and their corpses
> were like refuse in the streets.
> For all of this his anger has not turned back,
> and still his hand is outstretched.
>
> Isa. 5:25

The hand of judgment is still held out to strike, as indicated by the concluding refrain. Hence this "therefore" saying not only emphasizes the inescapable consequence of the "woes" but points forward to what is taking place on the horizon of God's future: summoning the Assyrians to be the instrument of divine judgment (5:26–30).

The editorial structure of Isa. 5:1–30 may be outlined as follows at this point in the analysis:

5:1–7	A. Song of the Vineyard: Disputation with God's People
	B. The Rebuke of Israel for Social Injustices
5:8–12	1. Two "woes" followed by
5:13, 14	Two "therefore" sayings
5:15–16(17)	2. Coda: Yahweh's Exaltation in Righteousness
5:18–23	3. Four "woes" followed by
5:24, 25	Two "therefore" sayings with concluding "outstretched hand" refrain
	C. The Execution of Divine Judgment
5:26–30	1. Yahweh summons Assyria

Let us turn now to the material that lies on the other side of the Memoirs. This section continues the theme of the execution of God's judgment upon unrepentant Israel by re-sounding the refrain of Yahweh's "outstretched hand" (5:25). Four stanzas in sequence conclude with this ominous refrain. The first (9:8–12) announces that the people of Ephraim, situated in the path of the Assyrian advance, have not been fazed by the disaster but have boasted that they would rebuild in better style. The second (9:13–17) affirms that, instead of returning to "the One that smote them," the people put their trust in corrupt leaders. The third (9:18–21) describes civil strife which, fanned by moral decay, spreads through society like a consuming fire. The fourth (10:1–4) portrays the exploitation of the poor by a people who are careless of the ruin that will follow. This "woe" harks back to the "woes" in the previous section, but at the same time its form, especially its direct address ("you" pl.), differentiates it from the earlier material.[14]

What will you do on the day of punishment,
  when the calamity from afar comes?
Isa. 10:3

The threat "from afar" recalls the earlier poem about Yahweh's summons to "a nation afar off" (5:26); but it also provides a bridge to the next poem about Assyria, the "rod of Yahweh's anger." The connection

237

is further strengthened by the fact that the initial *hôy* ("woe") in
10:1–4 not only echoes the "woe" sequence in 5:8–23 but also links
with the ensuing apostrophe to Assyria, which likewise begins with
hôy. Assyria, the agent of God's "work on Mount Zion," is rebuked for
presuming that it acts autonomously by virtue of its own imperial plan
and power. After all, it is folly for the tool to magnify itself over the
One who uses it (10:15)! Because of Yahweh's overruling sovereignty,
Assyria's days are numbered (10:16–19)—an announcement that
prompted later editors to add a consoling passage that reflects an
apocalyptic hope.[15] The section concludes with a vivid description of
the Assyrian forces sweeping in from the north right to the outskirts of
Jerusalem (10:27b–32). However, the aggressors cannot escape the
sovereignty of Yahweh, who has the last word (10:33–34).

This section, which belongs essentially to the material in chapter 5,
may be outlined as follows, beginning with the last element of the
previous outline.

	C.	The Execution of God's Judgment
5:25		1. Transitional "therefore" saying
5:26–30		2. The summoning of Assyria
		3. God's Outstretched Hand of Judgment
9:8–12		a. Stanza 1
9:13–17		b. Stanza 2
9:18–21		c. Stanza 3
10:1–4		d. Stanza 4
10:5–19		4. The Rebuke of Assyria
10:20–27a		5. Apocalyptic Reinterpretation
10:27b–34		6. The Assyrian Advance and Ultimate Downfall

To avoid misunderstanding, a special word should be said. I do not
mean to say that the organization of the material, indicated in the two
outlines given above, was the original layout of the Isaianic text.
Perhaps a better, and conceivably more original, text can be reconstructed, though commentators have not reached a consensus on the
matter. The argument, rather, is that the present text, with its rhetorical features and editorial pattern, is designed to set forth the message
of God's judgment upon a people who do not "know" God (cf. 1:2–3)
and consequently are guilty of the most flagrant social injustice (cf.
1:12–17).

III

Let us consider now the editorial insertion of the Memoirs of Isaiah. I assume that this "book" has its own internal structure and existed as a separate literary unit before being placed here. In this redactional unit, the account of Isaiah's call in chapter 6 had already been placed before chapters 7 and 8, and the unit had been expanded to include the royal accession oracle (9:1–6; ET 9:2–7) and other material sometimes regarded as an addition, for example, 8:21–22, the description of the darkness upon the land. The structure and redaction of Isaiah's Memoirs is a separate matter that lies beyond the immediate purview of this essay.

Admittedly, the insertion of this document seems to interrupt the movement of the poems dealing with Yahweh's rebuke of the people and the execution of judgment upon them. Nevertheless, the editorial decision to locate the Memoirs where they now stand makes sense for several reasons.

Notice, first of all, the point at which this document is inserted: immediately after the first appearance of the motif of the "outstretched hand" (5:25) and Yahweh's invitation to "a nation afar off" (5:26–30). This is a proper place to put material dealing with the conspiracy of small nations—Ephraim and Syria in this case—to force Judah into a military coalition for the purpose of checking the Assyrian advance, as had happened more than a century earlier at the battle of Qarqar (853 B.C.E.). It matters not whether originally the poem on the summoning of Assyria (5:26–30), or the later one describing the invasion route (10:27b–32), originally referred to the invasion of Tiglath-Pileser III in 734–733 B.C.E. or to the march of Sennacherib in 701. In any case, the editorial insertion of the Memoirs has had the effect of locating Yahweh's summoning of Assyria at the beginning of Isaiah's career, sometime after his call and commission.

A second justification for the editorial insertion becomes evident when one looks at the oracles describing the execution of divine judgment found on the other side of the Memoirs. The initial oracle, culminating with its "outstretched hand" refrain, refers specifically to the Northern Kingdom: "Ephraim and the inhabitants of Samaria" (9:9). This presentation of the fate of the Northern Kingdom as an object lesson for Judah is consonant, of course, with the subject matter of the inserted document, where attention falls upon Ephraim, which lay in the immediate path of the Assyrian advance, and thus was the first to feel the effects of Yahweh's "decree of destruction" (cf. 10:22) announced in the heavenly council (6:11–13). The transition from the Memoirs to the royal accession oracle appropriately refers to the northern territories taken by Assyria after 734 B.C.E.: Zebulun, Naphtali, and Galilee (8:23; ET 9:1).

Finally, the inserted Memoirs and the framing editorial structure share a striking rhetorical feature. On one side we find a poem (5:26–30) that culminates with a frightening comparison of the Assyrian invaders to roaring lions and the consequent return of the earth to chaos.

> They will growl over it on that day,
>   like the roaring of the sea.
> And if one looks to the land [*'ereṣ*],
>   darkness and distress [*hôšek ṣar*],
> and the light is darkened by its clouds.
>   Isa. 5:30 *(RSV)*

At the very conclusion of the inserted material, this motif of "darkness and distress" reappears in strikingly similar language:

> And they will look to the earth [*'ereṣ*],
>   but behold, distress and darkness [*ṣārāh waḥăšēkāh*],
>   the gloom of anguish,
> And they will be thrust into thick darkness.
>   Isa. 8:22 *(RSV)*

In the present arrangement of the text, these passages serve as editorial sutures that connect the Memoirs on both sides. It is appropriate that the next poem begins with the well-known words:

> The people that walked in darkness
>   have seen a brilliant light;
> on those who dwelt in a land of gloom,
>   light has dawned.
>   Isa. 9:1 (ET 9:2) *(NJPSV)*

IV

Up to this point we have seen that the document containing Isaiah's Memoirs is integrally related to the surrounding editorial structure of the Book of Isaiah. The text moves from God's disputation (Song of the Vineyard), to God's rebuke of the people for their unjust ways, to the execution of God's judgment by summoning Assyria, to the final judgment upon Assyria when God's "work on Mount Zion and in Jerusalem" is finished. Let us return in conclusion to the question asked at the outset about the significance of the present shape of the text. We shall do so by considering the theological themes found in the inserted document and their relation to the framing editorial structure.

As indicated previously, Childs has already led the way by drawing attention to Yahweh's plan, announced in the heavenly council, which the prophet is commissioned to divulge to Israel. Indeed, the divine purpose/plan ('ēṣāh), which Yahweh announces in advance and brings to realization (Isa. 55:10–11), is a motif running through the whole Book of Isaiah.[16] In the final *relecture* of the Isaianic tradition, this theme is nuanced in the perspective of apocalyptic eschatology.[17]

Another theme, however, looms large in the Memoirs of Isaiah, and that is the theme of Immanuel, "God with us." So significant is this theme that the Jerusalem Bible aptly puts the material beginning with chapter 6 under the caption, "The Book of Immanuel."[18] The theme is accented especially in the material that reflects the Syro-Ephraimitic crisis. In chapter 7, Isaiah announces to "the house of David" that the imminent birth of a child with this theophorous name is a sign that God will bring deliverance from the threat of the two nations, Ephraim and Syria, even before the lad has reached the age of discretion (Isa. 7:13–17).

The same theme resounds twice in chapter 8 in passages often regarded as later interpretive expansions. Curiously, in 8:8 the reference to Immanuel's land, coming after the announcement of an ominous flood from Mesopotamia, indicates that the "outstretched wings" of God's presence involve the dark dimension of judgment. With this interpretation of Immanuel, Clements observes, "the redactor has fully brought out the implication of the prophecy of 8:5–8—the naming of Isaiah's child, *Maher-shalal-hash-baz* ('The spoil speeds, the prey hastes')."[19] The ensuing passage (8:9–10), perhaps from another hand, announces that God's word stands firmly or "abides forever" (Isa. 40:8), despite the contrary plans and raging of the nations (cf. Isa. 7:4–8; Psalm 46):

Make your plans, but they will be foiled,
propose what you please, but it shall not stand;
    for God is with us.

Isa. 8:10 *(NEB)*

These passages indicate that there is a strangeness in God's mercy.

For one thing, God's plan goes against the grain of human thinking or ideological attempts to legitimate the social order. According to royal covenant theology, the rule of Yahweh, the cosmic Creator and King, is mediated through the Davidic kingship and the Jerusalem temple, two sacral institutions that are presupposed in the account of Isaiah's call (Isa. 6:1). In popular piety then—as even now—the presence of God assures protection from hardship and an endorsement of human values. This popular view is reflected in the people's lament, quoted by the prophet Jeremiah:

> Hark, the cry of the daughter of my people
>   from the length and breadth of the land:
>   "Is the Lord not in Zion?
>   Is her King not in her?"
>
>   . . . .
>   "The harvest is past, the summer is ended,
>   and we are not saved."
>   Jer. 8:19–20 *(RSV)*

Isaiah stands within this Zion theological tradition, but sets forth a different understanding of what it means to live in the presence of the holy God. He lashes out against those who engage in revelry from morning until evening, but "do not regard the activity [*pōʿal*] of Yahweh or see the work of [*maʿăśēh*] his hands" (5:12). Elsewhere he speaks of Yahweh's *opus alienum:*

> For Yahweh will rise up as on Mount Perazim,
>   will become furious as in the valley of Gibeon,
> to do his deed [*maʿăśēhû*]—strange is his deed,
>   to perform his work [*ʿăbōdātô*]—alien is his work.
>   Isa. 28:21

Why is God's work "alien"? The historical allusions at the opening of this verse suggest a partial answer. The places mentioned recall battles in which Yahweh was "with Israel": at Perazim when David defeated the Philistines (2 Sam. 5:17–25) and in the Valley of Gibeon when Joshua defeated a coalition of Canaanite kings (Josh. 10:9–14). In holy wars, Yahweh was on Israel's side, defending them against their enemies and giving them the victory. What Yahweh is doing on Mount Zion, however, is "strange" precisely because Yahweh turns against his people, rebuking them for their failure and subjecting them to judgment. Yahweh's "enemies" are his own people, a theme found in the introduction to the book, where the Divine Warrior, Yahweh of hosts, speaks:

> Ah [*hôy*], I will vent my wrath on my enemies,
>   and avenge myself on my foes.
> I will turn my hand against you,
>   and will smelt away your dross as with lye
>   and remove all your alloy.
>   Isa. 1:24b–25 *(RSV)*

In short, Yahweh's plan, as interpreted by the prophet, is sharply critical of royal covenant ideology.[20]

There is, however, an even deeper strangeness about Yahweh's "work on Mount Zion and in Jerusalem." Isaiah announces the work of "the Holy One of Israel" who in the time of judgment—strange as it may seem!—is present redemptively in the midst of the people. This is the full meaning of the sign Immanuel, "God with us." Judgment (wrath) does not mean the absence of God, though it might seem so to a people who do not have the eyes to see or the ears to hear. On the contrary, the judgment of God signifies the strange presence of the Holy God who purges the dross in a cleansing fire and enables Jerusalem to become what it is intended to be in God's design: the faithful city, the city of God (cf. 1:24–26). In the perspective of prophetic faith Yahweh is "with us"—*mirabile dictu*—in judgment and in mercy.

Therefore, editors deemed it theologically appropriate to insert, at the point where the Assyrian advance is under way and Yahweh is executing his judgment, a "book" dealing with the mystery of Immanuel, "God with us." This insertion provides a pause in the momentum of the poems, allowing the reader to reflect theologically on the inexorable advance of Assyria as God's agent. The God who "dwells on Mount Zion" (8:18) is performing a "strange work" on Mount Zion. The present is the time when Yahweh is "hiding his face from the house of Jacob" (8:17), the time of God's wrath. Yahweh's ways are hidden, Yahweh's plan is inscrutable. Yet those who in faith perceive the God-given signs, including the sign of Immanuel, "wait for Yahweh and hope in him" (8:17; 40:31). They look forward to the redemption that is not only on the other side of the *Dies Irae* but which is also being accomplished through divine judgment. It is appropriate, then, that this section of the Book of Isaiah is rounded off and completed with two eschatological songs (chap. 12). The last word, addressed to the people symbolized as the City of Zion, is a call to worship the holy God who is present "with us":

> Shout, and sing for joy, O inhabitant of Zion,
> for great in your midst is the Holy One of Israel.
>
> Isa. 12:6

NOTES

1. This document is sometimes called the Book of Testimony on the assumption that it is the "testimony"/"torah" that, according to Isa. 8:16, Isaiah was commanded to "bind up" among his "disciples." Joseph Jensen, delimiting the Memoirs to 6:1—8:18, observes that the whole is bracketed by a literary *inclusio,* for "it begins and ends with a reference to Yahweh enthroned on Mount Zion (6:1 and 8:18)." See his commentary, *Isaiah 1–39* (Wilmington, Del.: Michael Glazier, 1984) 82–83.

2. Chaps. 2–4, headed with a separate superscription (2:1) and concluded with an eschatological "in that day" passage (4:2–6), constitute a separate redactional unit. The editorial unit under consideration, chaps. 5–10, is supplemented with material in chap. 11, including the messianic poem in 11:1–9. Chap. 12, with its two eschatological songs, is a doxological conclusion to the larger editorial structure, chaps. 2–12. Chap. 1 appears to be a separate introduction, not just to chaps. 2–12 but to the whole of chaps. 1–32(33), if not to the whole book. See G. Fohrer, "Jesaja 1 als Zusammenfassung der Verkündigung Jesajas," *ZAW* 74 (1962) 251–68. For a "structural overview" of the book as a whole, and special study of the opening chapters, see M. A. Sweeney, *Isaiah 1–4 and the Post-exilic Understanding of the Isaianic Tradition* (BZAW 171; Berlin: de Gruyter, 1988).

3. A long line of commentators has maintained that the original order of the text has been disturbed. The list includes Bernhard Duhm (HKAT, ⁴1922), K. Marti (KHC, 1900), G. B. Gray (ICC, 1912), O. Procksch (KAT, 1930), R. B. Y. Scott (*IB,* 1967; see 5. 158–59), G. Fohrer (ZBK, 1960–65), W. Eichrodt (BAT, 1967), O. Kaiser (OTL, 1972), H. Wildberger (BKAT, 1972–78). See also J. Vermeylen, *Du prophète Isaïe à l'apocalyptique. Isaïe I–XXXV, miroir d'un demi-millénaire d'expérience religieuse en Israël* (EB; Paris: Gabalda, 1977) 1. 159–86.

4. Jensen, *Isaiah 1–39,* 73–82, 114–21.

5. Hermann Barth, *Die Jesaja-Worte in der Josiazeit: Israel und Assur als Thema einer produktiven Neuinterpretation der Jesajaüberlieferung* (WMANT 48; Neukirchen-Vluyn:Neukirchener Verlag, 1977), 109–17.

6. R. E. Clements, *Isaiah 1–39* (New Century Bible Commentary; Grand Rapids: Wm. B. Eerdmans, 1980) 60–70.

7. Brevard Childs, *Introduction to the Old Testament as Scripture* (Philadelphia: Fortress Press, 1979) 311–41, esp. 331.

8. See J. A. Emerton, "The Textual Problems of Isaiah V 14," *VT* 17 (1967) 135–42.

9. Barth, *Jesaja-Worte in der Josiazeit,* 192.

10. See the excursus by Vermeylen, "Le discourse prophétique en hôy," *Du prophète Isaïe a l'apocalyptique,* 603–52.

11. The exegetical move to *Sitz im Text* is advocated by Edgar W. Conrad in his illuminating essay, "The Community as King in Second Isaiah," *Understanding the Word* (ed. J. T. Butler, Edgar W. Conrad, and Ben C. Ollenburger; Sheffield, Eng.: JSOT Press, 1985) 99–111.

12. James Muilenburg, "Form Criticism and Beyond," *JBL* 88 (1969) 1–18.

13. Jensen, *Isaiah 1–39,* 78.

14. As observed by Walther Eichrodt, *Der Heilige in Israel* (Stuttgart: Calwer Verlag, 1960), who, however, transposes the "outstretched hand" oracles (9:7–20; 5:25–30) to a position just after the Memoirs and before 10:1–4.

15. Passages with the cliché "in that day" (some thirty-six, according to my count) are found almost exclusively in Isaiah 1—33, suggesting that this part of the Book of Isaiah has undergone a special editing.

16. On the pervasive theme of the divine plan, see R. E. Clements's essay on the Book of Isaiah in the forthcoming Scribner's reference work, *The Books of the Bible.*

17. In my view the final *relecture* of the Isaianic tradition reflects proto-apocalyptic or apocalyptic eschatology. See my essay, "The Apocalyptic Rendering of the Isaiah Tradition," in *The Social World of Formative Christianity and Judaism: Essays in Tribute to Howard Clark Kee* (ed. J. Neusner, P. Borgen, E. S. Frerichs, R. Horsley; Philadelphia: Fortress Press, 1988).

18. Vermeylen (*Du prophète Isaïe a l'apocalyptique,* 187–249) also adopts this traditional appellation, though limiting the "book" to 6:1—9:6 (not to the end of chap. 12 as in *JB*).

19. Clements, *Isaiah 1–39,* 97.

20. In his essay "Unity and Dynamic in the Isaiah Tradition" (*JSOT* 29 [1984] 89–107), Walter Brueggemann observes that the dimension of Isaianic tradition found especially in so-called First Isaiah (chaps. 1–39) represents "a bold distancing between Yahweh's truth and Israel's fraudulently constructed social reality."

16

How Is the Word Fulfilled? Isaiah 55:6–11 within the Theological Debate of Its Time

ALEXANDER ROFÉ

The conviction that the Word of the Lord is always fulfilled was deeply rooted in the primary mantic character of prophecy in Israel.[1] Indeed, that is how an old Biblical legend described the people's view of Samuel (1 Sam. 9:6): "There is a man of God in this town, and the man is highly esteemed; everything he tells comes true." Admittedly, this legend, which describes Saul's anointing, conveys an additional aspect in Samuel's prophetic character: he commands the people by virtue of his intimate knowledge of the divine will, and is therefore entitled to appoint Saul as king. However, we may consider this function of Samuel as solely deriving from the position and authority he had attained by being a true prophet: a man of God whose word never fails.

To what extent this conception of prophecy prevailed in preexilic Israel is demonstrated by the narrative of Jehu's revolution (2 Kings 9:1—10:17). This sly usurper[2] tried time and again to prove to all that his deeds were nothing but the fulfillment of God's Word as spoken by Elijah.[3] Three times, in the course of the revolt, he refers to prophecies:[4]

> Jehu thereupon ordered his officer Bidkar, "Pick him up and throw him into the field of Naboth the Jezreelite. Remember how you and I were riding side by side behind his father Ahab, when the Lord made this pronouncement about him: 'I swear, I witnessed the blood of Naboth and the blood of his sons last night—declares the Lord, And I will requite you in this plot—declares the Lord.' So pick him up and throw him unto the plot in accordance with the word of the Lord." (2 Kings 9:25–26)

> So they went to bury her; but all they found of her were the skull, the feet, and the hands. They came back and reported to him; and he said, "It is just as the Lord spoke through His servant Elijah the Tishbite: . . . the carcass of Jezebel shall be like dung on the ground, in the field of Jezreel, so that none will be able to say: 'This was Jezebel.' " (2 Kings 9:35–36a, 37)
>
> In the morning he went out and stood there; and he said to all the people, "You, the righteous (be you judges).[5] True, I conspired against my master and killed him; but who struck down all of these? Know, then, that nothing that the Lord has spoken concerning the House of Ahab shall remain unfulfilled." (2 Kings 10:9–10a)

From the last of these quotations, it becomes clear how Jehu concealed his own part in the murder of Ahab's sons. All the more so he covered up the personal interest he had in the extermination of the former dynasty. Clearly he meant to depict the murder as an autonomous fulfillment of the word of the Lord in order to convince the people that these current events were necessary. Such a manipulation of the Word and its fulfillment is evidence of the cynical use Jehu made of prophecies to promote his own interest. This is a classic, perhaps the oldest case of Machiavellianism *ante litteram*: the extolling of religion while manipulating it for the sake of the prince's political aims.[6]

The editor who placed the story of Jehu in the Book of Kings could not keep silent about such a gross debasement of the Word of the Lord by the ill-bred general; he therefore summed up the story of the revolution with a saying of his own:

> The Lord said to Jehu, "Because you have acted well and done what was pleasing to Me, having carried out all that I desired upon the House of Ahab, four generations of your descendants shall occupy the throne of Israel." (2 Kings 10:30)

Thus Jehu is brought back to his right place: it was not the Lord, nor his prophets, who served Jehu; rather Jehu served the Lord, and served him well indeed, performing to the full all he desired. The editor also expresses this notion when he adds to the words of Jehu quoted above (2 Kings 10:10b): "But the Lord had done what he had announced through his servant Elijah."[7] It was not Jehu who acted, but the Lord, Jehu being no more than a tool in his hands.

The presentation of the events as fulfilling God's Word according to his will characterizes the history of the Kingdom of Israel as told in the Book of Kings. I refer to the verses that repeatedly describe the history of the kingdom as fulfilling the predictions of Ahijah of Shilo, Jehu son of Hanani, Elijah, Elisha, and Jonah.[8] This phenomenon was identified by G. von Rad.[9] In my opinion, however, different categories ought to be distinguished in his inventory.[10] I tend to explain the above group of verses as expressing the view that the various vicissitudes of the Northern Kingdom—the political ups and downs as well as the perennial internal strife—all follow a fixed prescript: God's Word as fulfilled in history. The Word is sovereign; it overpowers treaties, armies, chariots, and horses; it motivates personal ambition; by its very nature it is not greatly influenced by human reactions. This was already stated in an appendix to one of the first rejection prophecies: "Moreover, the Glory of Israel does not deceive or change His mind, for He is not human that He should change His mind" (1 Sam. 15:29).

After the fall of Samaria, refugees from the Northern Kingdom took their literary and spiritual heritage to Judah. Part of this legacy was, as far as I can see, the very concept of history as the fulfillment of the Word of the Lord. This would explain why, in the history of Judah, this concept is first evident in the story of Sennacherib's campaign, which took place in 701 B.C.E., some twenty years after the fall of Samaria. The first layer in the story, as identified by B. Stade,[11] was composed in the mid-seventh century, about fifty years after the actual events.[12] This stratum contains the first version about the Assyrian embassy, the one connected with the name of Rabshakeh (2 Kings 18:17—19:9a + 36–37). Now to be sure, this story as well emphasizes the postulate of the fulfillment of the Lord's Word in history, even if the point is made at the expense of a certain manipulation in the sequence of events. Isaiah says about Sennacherib (2 Kings 19:7): "I will delude him; he will hear a rumor and return to his land, and I will make him fall by the sword in his land"; therefore the narrator concludes by saying (2 Kings 19:9a, 36ff.): "And he [the king of Assyria] heard about Tirhakah, king of Nubia: 'Behold, he has set forth to fight against you.' So king Sennacherib of Assyria broke camp and retreated and stayed in Nineveh ... and his sons struck him down with the sword." Even if one leaves aside the question of the confrontation with Tirhakah, the presentation of events is puzzling: Hezekiah died soon after the siege of Jerusalem, in 698 B.C.E., while Sennacherib continued to rule and subdue all the fertile crescent until his assassination in 681 B.C.E. These minute details, however, did not count for much with our historian.

The Deuteronomistic (Dtr) historiography, composed in Judah in the seventh–sixth centuries B.C.E., inherited from its own sources the tenet of the fulfillment of the divine Word. Thus, this principle was inculcated by the Dtr school at three crucial points in its history of Israel: The fall of Jerusalem and the exile were viewed as the execution of the Word of the Lord spoken in the days of Manasseh (2 Kings 21:10–16; 24:2–4); the succession of Solomon to the throne and his building the temple were conceived as the fulfillment of Nathan's prophecy to David (1 Kings 8:18–20); and, last, the conquest of Canaan by Joshua was reckoned as the consummation of the promise to the patriarchs (Josh. 21:41–43; 23:14).[13]

In this way the doctrine of the Word's fulfillment stamped its mark on the whole corpus of the Former Prophets, usually designated as a major component of the Dtr historical work. Admittedly, this corpus contains, in its middle parts (Judges 3—16; 1 Samuel 1—12), the vestiges of an older edition, the late Ephraimite-Elohistic historiography,[14] which understood the function of the Word in a completely different way. Yet, the fact that the beginning and the end of the Former Prophets both expound the word fulfillment principle made it predominate. Moreover, this very rule was formulated in generic terms in a late appendix to the law concerning the prophet,[15] Deut. 18:21–22:

> If the prophet speaks in the name of the Lord and the word does not come true, that word was not spoken by the Lord, the prophet has uttered it presumptuously. . . .

The legal context required that a norm be established about the means of identifying a false prophecy, yet there is no doubt that the reverse was meant as well: every true prophecy is to be fulfilled in due time.

Second Isaiah was the prophet to adhere most strictly to the principle of word fulfillment.[16] He, or the compiler of his prophecies, put it at the beginning of his book: *ûdĕbar ʾĕlōhênû yāqûm lĕʿôlām* (Isa. 40:8). There can be little doubt about the meaning of this metaphoric expression, for its many parallels are unequivocal: to happen, to come to pass, to be fulfilled, to be realized.[17] Indeed, this principle dominates Second Isaiah's message, being repeated in no less than ten speeches: 41:21–29; 42:5–9; 43:1–10, 11–13; 44:6–23(6–8), 24–28; 45:18–25; 46:5–11; 48:1–11, 12–16. Such repetition is due to the function of this idea in the prophet's polemic against idolatry: The fact that only the Word of the Lord of Israel has come true proves that he is the only true god.

From a form-critical perspective, this polemic against the idols blends together two genres: litigation and hymn. To the latter apparently belongs the proclamation of the Lord's two attributes as creator and foreteller (42:5–9; 45:18–25; 48:12–16). This juxtaposition in turn sheds light on the premise behind Deutero-Isaiah's concept of the realization of the Word: the Word is infallible because the Lord has the power to realize it as he had the power of creating the universe (43:11–13; 44:24–28; 48:12–16). Indeed, in one passage, Deutero-Isaiah explicitly equates the Lord's foretelling with creation: *dibbartî ʾap ʾăbîʾennāh, yāṣartî ʾap ʾeʿĕśennāh* (46:11). Cyrus and his horde of conquerors, once announced by the Lord, are thereby created and exist; the only question is when are they going to appear on the historical stage before human eyes.

From this perspective, it appears that Second Isaiah develops here a dialectical attitude toward the hymns directed to the Babylonian gods, hymns that exalted them for the power of their word.[18] However, at the same time, the prophet seems to be familiar with part of the Israelite historical literature, which stresses the infallibility of the Word as uttered by the Lord's servants, the prophets. This is made evident by this passage in Isa. 44:25–26:

> Thus says the Lord, who annuls the omens of diviners and makes fools of the augurs, who turns sages back and makes nonsense of their knowledge, who confirms the word of His servants[19] and fulfills the plan predicted by His messengers. . . .

Both style and content echo Dtr passages such as 2 Kings 17:23; 21:10–15; 24:2; one may conclude that Second Isaiah continues the Dtr line of tradition.

These theological concepts may be described as sophisticated superstructures erected on the foundation of a rather primitive concept of the Word of God and of prophecy in general. The prophetic function is still conceived of as purely mantic, whereas the Word of the Lord retains a certain magical power. Yet, these primary notions allow the Deuteronomists to structure history as one flow of events through which the Lord manifests himself to his people.[20] As for the Second Isaiah, the fulfillment of prophecies becomes the first and foremost proof of monotheism.

Meanwhile, however, toward the end of monarchic times, a new conception of prophecy emphasizing its ethical principles and its admonitive character had made its appearance. This innovation should probably be connected with the emergence of the classical prophets such as Hosea, Amos, Isaiah, and Micah.[21] Yet, the ethical aspect of prophecy is already present in ancient northern literature: prophetic psalms, such as Psalm 81 and the Song of Moses (Deuteronomy 32), as well as the prophetic speeches composed by the Elohistic historiographers—Josh. 24:1–28; Judg. 6:7–10; 1 Samuel 12. In the historical epitome of 2 Kings 17:7–18, the prophets are considered (v. 13) not as predictors of the exile but as those who warn the people calling them to repent and observe the Lord's commands. This same view is present in the prose speeches of Jeremiah (e.g., chaps. 7; 21:1–10; 25; 26; 27; 29; 35; 44). The concept of the prophet as warner and castigator does not preclude others, because this role may go hand in hand with that of foretelling the future. Yet in the Book of Jeremiah, the mantic function of prophecy has been subordinated to the moral one. This feature is decisively stated in an editorial passage, Jer. 18:7–10[22]:

> At one moment I may decree that a nation or a kingdom shall be uprooted and pulled down and destroyed; but if that nation against which I made the decree turns back from its wickedness, I change My mind concerning the punishment I planned to bring on it. At another moment I may decree that a nation or a kingdom shall be built and planted; but if it does what is displeasing to Me and does not obey Me, then I change My mind concerning the good I planned to bestow upon it.

Forecasting the future is here a function of the prophets' ethical role. Insofar as the Word of the Lord uttered by the prophet leads to a change in the conduct of the people, the Lord's decision may be altered.[23]

The opinion expressed in Jer. 18:7–10 is similar to that found in Ezek. 3:17–21; 18:21–32; 33:12–20, the latter passage being the most significant for our present discussion. Here too it is stressed that the Word of the Lord disclosed to people is conditioned by the reaction of the addressee. Ezekiel, however, does not address a nation or kingdom, but an individual, whether righteous or wicked. An important innovation lies in the fact that here, for the first time, we hear a certain doubt concerning God's administration of justice. The doubt is expressed by the people in their response: *"lōʾ yittākēn derek ʾădōnāy"* (33:17, 20; cf. also 18:25, 29); often this has been taken to mean "the way of the Lord is unfair" or the like. However, it is better to follow Luzzatto and Tur-Sinai and interpret *yittākēn* according to its etymon: *tkn* = to measure, estimate, ponder; hence *lo' yittākēn* would mean "immeasurable, imponderable, inestimable."[24] The people, having heard Ezekiel's norms of retribution and how easily the Lord retracts, complain that there is no way of assessing the conduct of the Lord. To this the prophet answers, True, the conduct of the Lord is unpredictable, because it depends on human responses, which in turn cannot be foreseen and estimated, *wěhēmmāh darkām lō' yittākēn*. The Lord judges each person according to his conduct. Plausibly, Ezekiel's opponents, who expected the Lord's conduct to remain constant, represented the old popular (and Deuteronomistic) expectation that the will of God was immovable and his Word infallible.

In understanding the Book of Jonah as a parable dealing with this very question, I join contemporary commentators.[25] Indeed, the Book of Jonah does not deal with God's grace to the nations, because it bears no trace of controversy between Israel and the nations. Nineveh is not regarded as the capital of a heathen empire, but as just a far-off city.[26] Nor is repentance the message of the book, since in this case it could have ended describing the delivery of the penitent city. The book, in my opinion, deals with the problem of the attributes of the Lord: Should he be merciful, retract his Word, and change his mind concerning the calamity he had planned for the wicked? Jonah believed the Lord should not; therefore, he first tried to suppress the prophecy destined to be belied. The narrator, through the Lord's answer, deemed differently: the city of Nineveh and its hundred and twenty thousand inhabitants was dear to the Lord, as the gourd was to Jonah. Therefore the Lord was entitled to renounce his Word for the sake of Nineveh. With this as its message, the parable of Jonah should be construed as written by the disciples of the prophets, consistent with the books of Jeremiah and Ezekiel and opposing the view represented by the Dtr historiographical school.

Awareness of this acute theological debate may contribute to understanding the important passage in Isa. 55:6–11:

6. Seek the Lord since He may be found,
   call Him for He is near.[27]
7. Let the wicked give up his ways,
   the sinful man his plans,
   and let him return to the Lord, He will pity him,
   to our God, for He freely forgives.

8. For My plans are not your plans,
   neither are your ways My ways—says the Lord.
9. As[28] heavens are high above (the) earth,
   so are My ways high above your ways,
   and My plans above your plans.
10. For as the rain and snow come down from heaven
    and do not return there,
    until[29] they have soaked the earth
    and make it bring forth and bud
    and give seed to the sower and bread to the eater,
11. So is My Word that issues from My mouth:
    it does not return unto Me empty-handed,[30]
    but performs what I purpose,
    succeeds in what I send it to do.

These verses, in my opinion, comprise one complete unit,[31] which is made up of two parts: the call of the prophet for repentance (vv. 6–7) and a direct utterance of the Lord which motivates the appeal of the prophet (vv. 8–11). The distinction between the messenger and his sender is overt, stressed by the phrase *ně'um YHWH*,[32] which is placed after the opening words of the Lord in v. 8. From the point of view of form criticism, this structure is in keeping with the classical form of prophetic sayings that consist of two parts: an utterance of the prophet followed by one from the Lord.[33] A slight modification of the basic form has occurred here: the pronouncement of the Lord is not the usual prediction of the future, but a disquisition about the nature of the Lord's conduct.[34] Yet, it is possible that here again our passage follows a traditional literary pattern, according to which the Lord himself proclaims his own attributes, so in Exod. 34:6–7 (20:5–6); Num. 14:17–18; Ps. 103:7–8. At the same time, from the standpoint of literary criticism,[35] this address to the wicked, calling for repentance and promising him forgiveness, becomes all the more suggestive and persuasive when the Lord, having cast aside all barriers and intermediaries, directly turns to the wicked by revealing his own recondite attributes.

Verses 6–11 are quite distinct from the pericope preceding them. Verses 1–5 consist of a call to the entire nation (not to the individual) to obey the Lord and promise as a reward "the covenant of David," which, when reapplied to the whole nation, means a supremacy of Israel over all foreign nations. As for the following verses (55:12–13), these should again be taken as a separate unit;[36] the prophet speaks once more while the Lord is mentioned in the third person. The content of these verses is the return of Israel to its homeland (v. 12) and the reclaiming of its abandoned terrain (v. 13).[37] These promises do not relate to the theme of the preceding verses,[38] but seem to have been attached, at this point, because of the associative link with the image of fertility in v. 10.

The pericope in Isa. 55:6–11, the unity and coherence of which we have tried to establish, contains a call for the people to cleave to the Lord and to pray to him, relying on the very nature of the Lord's Word that grants everybody, even the wicked, permission to repent.[39] However, the train of thought in our passage is not easy to follow. The Lord says (v. 11): *kēn yihyeh děbārî 'ăšer yēṣē' mippî: lō' yāšûb 'ēlay rêqām, kî 'im 'āśāh 'et 'ăšer ḥāpaṣtî wěhiṣlîaḥ 'ăšer šělaḥtîw;* these words usually have been understood to mean the same as Isa. 40:8: *ûděbar 'ělōhênû yāqûm lě'ôlām,* namely, that the word of the Lord is always fulfilled.[40] But if the word sent by the Lord through his prophets is fulfilled verbatim, for what cause should the wicked repent? How then can the Lord have mercy and forgive? On the face of it there is a discrepancy between the demand for penitence and its supposed motivation, the nature of the Word.

This difficulty may be solved, I believe, by analyzing the simile in 55:10. The Word of the Lord is likened to rain and snow coming down from heaven: their result is not water returning to the skies; rather their function is saturating the earth, impregnating it, and offering abundance—a chain of effects. So too the Word of the Lord: its consequence is not its fulfillment verbatim—event following word—its effect is what people are made to do, their repentance and inner transformation. The Word is not to be fulfilled; the Word fulfills! That is why the prophet says that the conduct of the Lord differs from that of humans (v. 8): the Lord's deeds differ in their very essence; they are much loftier, most marvelous (v. 9).[41] A person's word can, at its best, be fulfilled, whereas the Word of the Almighty acts as a messenger to the Lord carrying out his hidden wish (v. 11b).

The theologumenon of Isa. 55:6–11 is dialectically related to both aforementioned positions. Following the Deuteronomistic historiography[42] as well as Deutero-Isaiah, it acknowledged the power of the Lord's Word;[43] while from the classical prophets and the editor of Jeremiah it accepted the principle of human freedom and the chance one has to repent and be accepted by God's mercy. The synthesis of both outlooks led our author to the assertion that the force of the Word of the Lord lies first and foremost in its causing people to repent.

Our interpretation of Isa. 55:6–11 affects the broader question of the authorship of Isaiah 40—66. Abraham Kuenen was the first to claim that the last portion of the Book of Isaiah was not composed by the Second Isaiah, but by later authors. This later portion encompassed, according to Kuenen, some fifteen chapters: Isaiah 50—51; 54—66. However, Kuenen's views, first published in Dutch and translated into German only after his untimely death,[44] all but fell into oblivion. As a result, the conjecture about Trito-Isaiah was connected with the name of Bernhard Duhm.[45]

The spell of Duhm's conclusions was not broken even after Karl Elliger subjected Isaiah 40—66 to a thorough study, reaching conclusions similar to those of Kuenen, namely, that Trito-Isaiah edited the oracles of Deutero-Isaiah in chaps. 40–53 whereas his own prophecies start in chap. 54.[46] The great majority of scholars still adhere to the position of Duhm, the only exception being the few who uphold the unity of the entire Deutero-Isaiah (chaps. 40–66).[47]

However, if we have rightly understood Isa. 55:6–11, the passage does not stand as the conclusion to the prophecy of Deutero-Isaiah, as has often been maintained. On the contrary, the conception of the Word in this passage is diametrically opposed to that of Deutero-Isaiah! The most natural explanation of this phenomenon is that here another voice is speaking; this is the prophet who repeatedly conditions his promises upon the people's behavior (55:1–5; 56:1–8; 58) or limits redemption to the righteous and those who repent (54:11–17; 57:13; 59:20; 65:8–15). The hypotheses of Kuenen and Elliger are hereby partially vindicated.

Who was Trito-Isaiah? What was his place in the history of prophecy and prophetic literature? Elliger regarded him as the editor of the words of Deutero-Isaiah. Zimmerli likewise viewed him as Deutero-Isaiah's disciple who paraphrased his master's sayings, lending them a new meaning.[48] In my view, the case of Isa. 55:6–11 confirms Elliger's and Zimmerli's conclusions, although the latter followed Duhm in attributing this passage to the master rather than to the disciple.

In 55:11b it is said about the Word that "it performs what I [the Lord] purpose, succeeds in what I send it to do"— 'āśāh 'et 'ăšer hāpaṣtî wĕhişlîaḥ 'ăšer šĕlaḥtîw; the verse echoes sayings of Deutero-Isaiah in 46:10: wĕkol hepṣî 'e'ĕśeh; and 48:14–15: YHWH 'ăhēbô, *ya'ăśeh ḥepṣô bĕbābēl ... hăbi'ōtîw wĕhiṣlîaḥ darkô.* However, Isa. 46:10 is one of the strongest statements about the infallibility of the Lord's Word and 48:14–15 refers to Cyrus who, as a good envoy, will execute the Lord's will in Babylon. Trito-Isaiah quotes here phrases of his predecessor, but gives them a new meaning: the Lord's envoy is not Cyrus (48:14–15), but the Word, which, no longer identical with the Lord's will *(ḥepṣî)* as in 46:10, is sent forth to execute that divine will,[49] destined not to be disclosed to men.

The same kind of reinterpretation took place in 55:11a: *kēn yihyeh dĕbārî 'ăšer yēṣē' mippî lō' yāšûb 'ēlay rêqām*—"so is My Word that issues from My mouth, it does not return unto me empty-handed." This is reported from 45:23: *bî nišba'tî: yāṣā' mippî ṣĕdāqāh dābār wĕlō' yāšûb*—"By Myself I swear: from my mouth has issued truth,[50] a Word that shall not come back." In the latter passage, the Word is not taken back, rather it is always fulfilled. Trito-Isaiah, quoting it, added two vocables, *'ēlay rêqām,* thus reversing the meaning: the Word of the Lord is like a messenger whose mission never fails. As a result, a new and deeper dimension has been given to Deutero-Isaiah's legacy by his disciple Trito-Isaiah.

NOTES

1. For the history of pre-classical prophecy, cf. the important contribution by I. L. Seeligmann, "On the History and Nature of Prophecy in Israel" (Hebrew), *Eretz-Israel* 3: *Dedicated to the Memory of M. D. U. Cassuto* (Jerusalem: Israel Exploration Society, 1954) 125–32.

2. This aspect of Jehu's character has been pointed out by B. Uffenheimer, *Ancient Prophecy in Israel* (Hebrew; Jerusalem: Magnes, 1973) 291–311. In my view, however, the story does not express abhorrence and condemnation of Jehu's actions.

3. The narrative was also expanded by an editor who tried to connect Jehu's revolt with the stories and prophecies of Elijah. His expansions are detectable in 9:7–10a, 36b. Yet the prophecies mentioned in 9:25–26, 36a, 37; 10:10a should be considered original. Literary layers must be distinguished not only on the basis of their style, but also by examining their organic cohesion with the flow of the narrative or, in the opposite case, with the tendencies of the redactor(s); *pace* H. C. Schmitt, *Traditionsgeschichtliche Untersuchungen zur vorklassischen nordisraelitischen Prophetie* (Gütersloh, W. Ger.: Gerd Mohn, 1972) 19–23. See the aforementioned volume for additional literature.

4. Translations throughout this article have been adapted from the *NJPSV.*

5. I construe Jehu's address to the people *ṣaddîqîm 'attem*—"you are righteous" as the litigants' appeal to a third party asking him to be their

arbiter; cf. O. Thenius, *Die Bücher der Könige erklärt* (KeHAT; Leipzig: S. Hirzel, 1873) 325. Hence the meaning (rare, but ascertained by the context) of *ṣaddiq* = "judge": Isa. 29:21; 45:21; Ezek. 23:45; Zeph. 3:5; Job 34:17; perhaps also Ps. 7:10.

6. Cf. H. Gunkel, *Geschichten von Elisa* (Berlin: K. Curtius, n.d. [1924]; repr. Jerusalem: Akademon, 1973) 81, 90.

7. Or was it already added by the author? A very similar parenthetic note occurs in 2 Sam. 17:14.

8. 1 Kings 11:35—12:15; 14:14—15:29; 16:1–12; 21:19—22:38; 2 Kings 7:1–2, 16–20; 13:19–25; 14:25.

9. G. von Rad, "The Deuteronomistic Theology of History in the Books of Kings," *Studies in Deuteronomy* (SBT 9; London: SCM Press, 1953) 74–84.

10. For details, cf. my *The Prophetical Stories* (Hebrew; Jerusalem: Magnes, 1982) 86–91.

11. B. Stade, "Miscellen," *ZAW* 6 (1886) 172–82. A later and thorough study of the story was offered by B. S. Childs, *Isaiah and the Assyrian Crisis* (SBS, 2d Ser. 3; London: SCM Press, 1967) 69–103.

12. I have tried to substantiate this view in my *Israelite Belief in Angels* (Jerusalem: Makor, 1979) 203–12.

13. Cf. I. L. Seeligmann, "From Historic Reality to Historiosophical Conception in the Bible" (Hebrew), *P'raqim* 2 (Jerusalem: Schocken Institute, 1969–74) 273–313.

14. See C. F. Burney, *The Book of Judges,* 2d ed. (London: 1918, 1920; repr. New York: Ktav, 1970) xli–1.

15. Cf. H. J. Kraus, *Die prophetische Verkündigung des Rechts in Israel* (Theologische Studien 51; Zollikon: Evangelischer Verlag, 1957) 15–16 n. 16; I. L. Seeligmann, in his classes at the Hebrew University, emphasized the similarities in form and content between Deut. 18:21–22 and Lev. 25:20–22; to these two I would add Deut. 15:9–11. All these secondary passages raise the question of the viability of biblical laws as asked by (future) Israelites. A stylistic similarity between Deut. 18:21–22 and Lev. 25:20–22 was already pointed out by A. B. Ehrlich, *Randglossen zur hebräischen Bibel* (Leipzig: Hinrichs, 1909) 2. 305.

16. Cf. W. Zimmerli, "Jahwes Wort bei Deuterojesaja," *VT* 32 (1982) 104–24. I differ from this very perceptive article in the basic understanding of phrases such as *dābār* + *qwm* (see below). Hence, on several points I have reached quite different conclusions.

17. The following list, mostly taken from BDB, s.v., is eloquent enough: 1 Kings 8:20; Isa. 7:7; 8:10; 14:24; 28:18; Jer. 44:28, 29; Prov. 15:22; 19:21; Job. 22:28. Late biblical and Rabbinical Hebrew substitute *'.m.d.* for *q.w.m.* as in Ps. 33:9, 11; cf. A. Hurvitz, *The Transition Period in Biblical Hebrew* (Hebrew; Jerusalem: Bialik, 1972) 173. In the same fashion the opposite idiom: *npl dābār* (fall of the word) means "fail to happen," as in Josh. 21:43; 23:14(2x); 1 Kings 8:56.

18. Yet, Sumerian and Akkadian hymns usually exalt the creative power of the divine words, including the strength of the words as commands. The

mantic aspect of these words is included in the other conceptions. See the rich material gathered by L. Dürr, *Die Wertung des göttlichen Wortes im AT und im antiken Orient* (Leipzig: Hinrichs, 1938).

19. Read *'ăbādāyw;* cf. Pseudo-Jonathan LXX[A]. The servants and messengers stand in contrast to the pagan sorcerers mentioned in the preceding verse.

20. Let me note in passing that, in my opinion, the so-called Dtr history is not a unified opus. Therefore I do not deem it possible to detect in it one single message; *pace* H. W. Wolff, "Das Kerygma des deuteronomistischen Geschichtswerks," *ZAW* 73 (1961) 171–86.

21. Koch's opinion that the Dtr historians opposed the classical prophets, because the latter denied any possibility of repentance, which was the kerygma of the former (so Wolff, preceding note), seems to me contrary to the evidence; cf. K. Koch, "Das Profetenschweigen des deuteronomistischen Geschichtswerks," *Die Botschaft und die Boten: Festschrift für H. W. Wolff zum 70. Geburtstag* (ed. J. Jeremias and L. Perlitt; Neukirchen-Vluyn: Neukirchener Verlag 1981) 115–28.

22. See the recent analysis by G. Wanke, "Jeremias Besuch beim Töpfer. Eine motivkritische Untersuchung zu Jer. 18," *Prophecy. Essays Presented to Georg Fohrer* (BZAW 150; Berlin: Walter de Gruyter, 1980) 151–62. Wanke distinguished, rightly in my opinion, between the original account in 18:1–6 and its later expansions, vv. 7–10, 11–12.

23. It should be noted in passing that both 2 Kings 17 as well as the prose sermons of Jeremiah are attributable to the Dtr school. This is a remarkable instance illustrating how misleading the term "Deuteronomistic" may be: by it we designate writings that do share a certain likeness of style and subject matter, but at the same time greatly differ in their theological outlook. Cf. I. L. Seeligmann, "Die Auffassung von der Prophetie in der deuteronomistischen und chronistischen Geschichtsschreibung (mit einem Exkurs über das Buch Jeremia)," *Congress Volume; Göttingen, 1977* (VTSup 29; Leiden: E. J. Brill, 1978) 254–84.

24. S. D. Luzatto (sic!), *Erläuterungen über einen Theil der Propheten und Hagiographen* (Hebrew; Lemberg: A. I. Menkes, 1876; *opus posthumum;* repr. Jerusalem: Makor, 1969) clvii; N. H. Tur-Sinai, *hallāšôn wĕhasseper* (2d ed.; Jerusalem: Bialik, 1954) 392.

25. S. D. Goitein, "Some Observations on Jonah," *JPOS* 17 (1937) 63–77; E. Bickerman, *Four Strange Books of the Bible* (New York: Schocken, 1967) 1–49; G. I. Emmerson, "Another Look at the Book of Jonah," *ExpTim* 88 (1976) 86–88; A. S. van der Woude, "Nachholende Erzählung in Buche Jona," *I. L. Seeligmann Volume* (Jerusalem: E. Rubinstein, 1983) 3. 263–72; Z. Shazar, *Mippardēs hattānāk* (Jerusalem: Kiryat Sepher, 1979) 207–15.

26. Cf. U. Cassuto, "Jona," *EncJud* (1932) 9. 268–72.

27. In my opinion the *b-* of *bĕhimmāṣĕ'ô—bihyôtô qārôb* is not temporal but causal; cf. BDB 91. This interpretation was already offered by Don Isac Abrabanel, *Commentary on the Later Prophets* (repr. Jerusalem: Torah Wada'at, 1955/6) cclx, who also pointed out the theological parallels in Deut.

4:7; Ps. 145:18–19. *qārôb*—"near" means "present, ready to intervene and assist," cf. Ps. 34:19; Lam. 3:57.

28. For *kî* meaning "as" in this verse, cf. U. Cassuto, "Note bibliche" *Rivista israelitica* 9 (1912) 30–34 and David Yellin apud A. Rofé, "The Completion of a Homoeuteleuton in David Yellin's Book on Isaiah" (Hebrew), *Kiryat Sefer* 51 (1976) 714; aliter A. Schoors, "The Particle *kî,*" *OTS* 21 (1981) 275–76.

29. Thus rightly the *NEB* translation; cf. S. D. Luzzatto, *Il profeta Isaia volgarizzato e commentato* (Padova, 1867; repr. Jerusalem: Akademon, 1966) 568.

30. *rêqām* = "empty-handed," cf. Gen. 31:42; Deut. 15:13.

31. Different layers, or units, have been distinguished by B. Duhm, *Das Buch Jesaja übersetzt und erlärt* (Göttingen: Vandenhoeck & Ruprecht, 1914) a.l.; J. Begrich, *Studien zu Deuterojesaja* (BWANT 77; Stuttgart: W. Kohlhammer, 1938) 14–15, 51–52, 73–74; cf. also Baltzer, n. 39 below.

32. Cf. S. Mowinckel, "Die Komposition des deuterojesajanischen Buches," *ZAW* 49 (1931) 111 n. 2.

33. Cf. H. Gressmann, "Die literarische Analyse Deuterojesajas," *ZAW* 34 (1914) 269–70.

34. The meaning of *derek* (sing. and pl.) = "conduct" is well attested in the Hebrew Bible; cf. Gen. 6:12; Deut. 32:4; Ps. 103:7. As for *maḥšābāh* (pl.), it is used by Trito-Isaiah (not by Deutero-Isaiah!) with the meaning of "plan" in parallelism with *ma'ăśîm* and *mĕsillôt,* cf. Isa. 59:7; 65:2; 66:18.

35. In the wake of the literary exegesis espoused by Meir Weiss, *The Bible from Within: The Method of Total Interpretation* (Jerusalem: Magnes, 1984).

36. In 1QIsa there is a *sĕtûmā'* between v. 11 and v. 12.

37. The *na'ăṣûṣ* (apparently a thorny bush, cf. the dictionaries) is mentioned in the description of the land desolation in Isa. 7:19; *sirpad* is a hapax in both Biblical and Rabbinical Hebrew. In Egyptian it means a kind of papyrus; cf. F. Buhl, *W. Gesenius' Handwörterbuch usw,* 15th ed. (Leipzig: F. C. W. Vogel, 1910) s.v. Neither plant belongs to desert vegetation, but instead to that of abandoned fields.

38. Admittedly, Jer. 29:11–14, which is coined in a similar style, ends its call to seek the Lord with the promise of redemption. The analogy is suggestive. Yet we do not know when this addition to the letter of Jeremiah against the prophets in Babylon was composed. Note also that in the LXX, only the first two words of 29:14 are represented.

39. This kind of argumentation is similar to that of some passages in Ezekiel (18:21–32; 33:10–20), though Ezekiel phrases his speech in casuistic form, as befits a priest-prophet and his school. Cf. the discussion by D. Baltzer, *Ezechiel und Deuterojesaja* (BZAW 121; Berlin: Walter de Gruyter, 1971) 118–30.

40. For this reason traditional commentators, such as Iben-Ezra, Radak, and Abarbanel, connected v. 11 with vv. 12–13. Among modern commentators, Gressmann and Begrich (nn. 31, 33 above) reckoned vv. 8–13 as one single unit.

41. Thus Maimonides interpreted it, conforming to his philosophy: "Between our knowledge and His knowledge there is nothing in common, as there is nothing in common between our essence and His essence ... it is truly necessary that His knowledge should differ from ours in substance, just as the substance of the heaven differs from the substance of the earth. The prophets have explicitly stated this saying: *kî lō' maḥšĕbôtay maḥšĕbôtêkem* ... (Isa. 55:8–9), *The Guide of the Perplexed* (trans. S. Pines; Chicago: University of Chicago Press, 1963) 482–83.

42. The relation of Isaiah 55 to the Dtr literature has recently been recognized by W. Brueggemann, "Isaiah 55 and Deuteronomic Theology," *ZAW* 80 (1968) 191–203. However, I differ from him in my understanding of the concept of the Word of the Lord in the present passage. The influence of the Dtr style on Trito-Isaiah was pointed out by Enno Littmann, *Über die Abfassungszeit des Tritojesajas* (Freiburg im Breisgau: J. C. B. Mohr, 1899).

43. Another recent development of this notion obtains in Deut. 8:3b, plausibly, a late expansion of the Deuteronomic text. Here what issues from the Lord's mouth, i.e., the Word, is attributed a creative power that sustains humanity, whether by dispensing bread, manna, or anything else. (A similar use of *lĕbad* may be noted in Deut. 29:13–14.) Cf. L. Perlitt, "Wovon der Mensch lebt (Dtn 8, 3b)," *Die Botschaft und die Boten* (see above, n. 21) 403-26.

44. A. Kuenen, *Historisch-kritisch onderzoek naar het ontstaan en de verzameling van de boeken des Ouden Verbonds 2* (Amsterdam: S. L. van Looy, n.d. [1886]) 134–50; German trans.: *Historisch-kritische Einleitung in die Bücher des Alten Testaments, IIer Teil: Die prophetischen Bücher* (Leipzig: Reisland, 1892) 128–44.

45. Duhm, *Jesaja.* There is no point in enumerating the many adherents to Duhm's position. The success obtained in Biblical research by the opinions of the latter scholar may be explained not only by their publication within a large commentary to Isaiah in a renowned German series, but also by their relative simplicity and their appeal to scholarly fashion of the time: one single author, Trito-Isaiah, composed Isa. 56–66; he is easily identified at the very beginning of his message by his call to observe the *šabbāt* (56:1–8). Hence not a universalistic prophet such as Deutero-Isaiah is speaking here, but a later representative of legalistic Judaism.

46. K. Elliger, *Deuterojesaja in seinem Verhältnis zu Tritojesaja* (BWANT 63; Stuttgart: Kohlhammer Verlag, 1933) 135–67; S. Mowinckel, "Neuere Forschungen zu Deuterojesaja, Tritojesaja und dem 'Äbäd-Jahvä-Problem," *Acta Orientalia* 16 (1938) 1–40.

47. F. Maas, "Tritojesaja?" *Festschrift L. Rost* (BZAW 105; Berlin: Walter de Gruyter, 1967) 153–63. This position is especially popular with Jewish scholars, probably as a reaction to Duhm's contrasting universalism with legalism as a criterion for differentiating Trito-Isaiah from Deutero-Isaiah; cf. Y. Kaufmann, *History of the Religion of Israel* (New York: Ktav, 1977) 4. 55–78; M. H. Segal, "Isaiah," *Encyclopaedia Biblica* (Hebrew; Jerusalem:

Bialik, 1958) 3. 926–30; M. Haran, *bên ri'šônôt lahădāšôt* (Jerusalem: Magnes, 1963); Y. Avishur, "Isaiah," *EncJud* 9. 61–66.
48. Cf. W. Zimmerli, "Zur Sprache Tritojesajas," *Gottes Offenbarung* (TBü19; Munich: Chr. Kaiser Verlag, 1963) 217–33. Brevard Childs drew my attention to this important article.
49. The concept of the Word as envoy occurs in a late Psalm: *haššōlēah 'imrātô 'āres 'ad mĕhērāh yārûs dĕbārô* (Ps. 147:15).
50. *sedāqāh* = truthfulness, so BDB 842 with references to Isa. 48:1; Zech. 8:8; Jer. 4:2. This meaning in Isa. 45:23 was already recognized by Iben Ezra.

17

True and False Prophecy within Scripture

GERALD T. SHEPPARD

Discerning true from false prophecy is presented in scripture as a matter of life and death. It lies at the heart of any claim of divine revelation within Judaism and Christianity. Brevard Childs has devoted an entire chapter to this subject in his *Old Testament Theology in a Canonical Context*. With his usual originality and appreciation for the wider implications, he explores how the context of scripture construed the older historical issue of finding criteria to discern true from false prophecy in a new way. As a small gesture of my appreciation for Childs, who has been both mentor and friend, I will seek to summarize his position, then try to press ahead to further implications of his proposal.

Prior to the modern period, the criteria in the Bible seemed compelling. However, the efficacy of these criteria has been repeatedly called into question by historical-critical investigations and, consequently, suspicions have been engendered regarding the traditional "moralistic" condemnation of "false" prophets. Most of these studies have focused on the account of Jeremiah's confrontation with Hananiah in Jeremiah 28. After one of the most thorough examinations of this problem, W. Zimmerli concludes that the rejection of the prophecy of Hananiah is ultimately based only on Jeremiah's subjective experience of God's presence. Childs summarizes what he calls Zimmerli's "psychological" or "existentialist" proposal:

> Apart from the witness evoked by the presence of God, there was no objective criterion by which a truth-claim could be demonstrated.[1]

When Childs reexamines Jeremiah 28 in its canonical context as a part of a book of "scripture," he emphasizes that it is set within an edited complex of traditions about true and false prophecy in Jeremiah 23—29, prefaced with the title: "Concerning the prophets" (23:9). His analysis is constantly attentive to the differences between original historical prophetic events, subsequent traditions about such events, and, still later, canonical "presentations" about the words and deeds of prophets in the context of Hebrew Scripture. Starting with a "literary analysis," Childs shows that the structure of the three judgment oracles against false prophets in Jeremiah 27 is identical to Jeremiah's prophecy against Hananiah in Jeremiah 28. This similarity establishes a "literary continuity" between the two chapters, implying that in both "the prophet delivered the same message." In traditio-historical terms, Childs concludes that the editor(s) of these traditions are responsible for a later "canonical construal" which shaped once-independent traditions in Jeremiah 28 "to conform to the previous chapter." If the tradition about Hananiah and Jeremiah was once primarily concerned with the criteria for discernment, the canonical context has shifted the perspective in a very different direction so that now the tradition offers, in concert with the more general treatment of Jeremiah 27 on the same subject, "a concrete illustration of the one message against false prophets."[2]

Collecting scripture in the postexilic period expressed "a new criterion" based on the recognition that "God had demonstrated by his action that Jeremiah was a true prophet."[3] Rather than inviting interpreters of scripture to "relive" the moment and to speculate regarding the criteria of discernment, the canonical context now casts the issue of true and false prophecy in thoroughly "theocentric" terms. What is retained psychologically in the narrative is only Jeremiah's initial uncertainty about the validity of Hananiah's prophecy because of the real possibility that God may have "changed his mind" regarding the fortunes of the king.

Attentive to the differences between the canonical presentation and a historical or sociological reconstruction of a prophetic event, Childs concedes to modern suspicions by observing, "If there had been confusion during Jeremiah's lifetime, there need be no longer." The effect of the canonical construal of older traditions is to establish "a scriptural norm for distinguishing the true from the false prophet."[4] The "scriptural norm" highlights "a unified message" in the biblical witness to the words and deeds of "my servants, the prophets" (26:5). Moreover, this norm is now accompanied by moral criteria for judging the character of false prophets (see Jer. 23:13f.), while "the faithful lives of true prophets are illustrated paradigmatically by Jeremiah and Uriah, who were killed for speaking the truth."[5] This application of older prophetic traditions goes beyond the original situation. It resists any modern attempt to draw a simple historical analogy between the present concern with correct biblical interpretation and the prebiblical concern with discerning a true prophetic word. Childs bluntly avers, "We are not prophets nor apostles, nor is our task directly analogous."[6]

Childs's analysis draws on conventional historical criticism to show that the editing of scripture has shifted the perspective and context of older traditions in a decisive manner. In this respect, his interpretation is not an exercise in a new discipline called "canon criticism," but applies conventional criticisms in service to a neglected vision of the biblical text as "scripture" within the religions of Judaism and Christianity.[7]

In Childs's assessment, evidence of a high degree of retention from the prebiblical period continues to be found. Though "new criteria" appear in scripture for distinguishing true from false prophets, "the original criterion of Jeremiah for prophetic truth" has still been applied in the canonical process of collecting and editing Jeremiah's oracles.[8] It is not that the old criterion is abolished, but it takes on a new dimension due to its "canonical construal." In my opinion, Childs's work lays the foundation for a more sophisticated understanding of the function of prophecy and its transformation in the postexilic period. Building on Childs's work, I will move in two different directions. First, I will seek to show how social-scientific insight into prophecy may further illuminate Childs's proposal about the criteria for determining true prophecy. Second, I will examine other aspects of the transformation of prophecy that participated in the development of a postexilic "scripture."

Criteria for Evaluating Prophecy in
Ancient Israel

Childs circumvents many of the modern problems in finding criteria for distinguishing true prophecy from false by focusing on how the later context of scripture framed the older issues in a very different way. He recognizes that many historical questions remain, agreeing with the modern view that "the criteria set up for distinguishing the true from the false prophet appear inadequate in practice."[9] At the same time, Childs does defend a degree of continuity between the criteria used in the original situation of prophecy and the criteria at work in the collection and formation of scripture. For this reason, he strongly objects to James Crenshaw's explanation for why prophecy declined in the postexilic period. According to Crenshaw:

> The tragedy of their existence was a failure to come up with an adequate means of self-validation that would lend weight to their authoritative word devoid of any means of self-authentication. Not a single one of the numerous criteria proposed for this purpose functioned in the present moment (cf. 1 Kings 13) either for the prophet or for his hearers, both of whom needed to know whether a spoken word carried any more weight than the authority of its bearer. The result was increased polarization of prophet against prophet, and people against prophet, followed by claim and counterclaim, self-assertion and inner turmoil. Such internal debate was heightened by the nature of the prophetic message, which contributed to the tension because of its diversity and its claim about history that was not borne out in daily experience.[10]

In a later study, Crenshaw claims that even the so-called true prophets offered only

> [an] embellished account of Israel's history, a story so far from the truth that it sowed seeds of skepticism at almost every telling. The disparity between present reality and grandiose confessions of God's mighty deeds in the past demanded an adequate explanation lest wholesale abandoning of the Lord took place.[11]

For Crenshaw, "skeptical wisdom" is the product of despair over this unresolvable conflict among prophets who often offered only a blatant falsification of history in order to affirm their fantasies of God's acts within it. So, "when the destruction of the temple and the subsequent Babylonian exile seemed to indicate Yahweh's impotence," wisdom with its creation doxologies, its proverbs based on experience, and its healthy suspicion of prophetic revelation could alone provide a viable faith for those who rightly felt betrayed by prophetic promises.[12] In Crenshaw's view, only wisdom literature could secure a proper place for God through its use of empirical observations of "order" in creation. Opposing the tendency in the Biblical Theology Movement to emphasize "salvation history," he proposes a more reliable "humanistic" project, a modern and scientific form of creation realism. Childs objects to Crenshaw's explanation in that it fails to "reckon with the formation of the Old Testament canon."[13] A better account regarding the role of criteria in ancient prophecy can be shown to lend support to Childs's position.

Anthropological/Sociological Insights into the Nature of "True" and "False" Prophecy

In the last decade or so, biblical studies have benefited enormously from fresh anthropological, sociological, and political interpretations of the ancient world. One of the most outstanding contributions on the subject of Israelite prophecy is Robert Wilson's *Prophecy and Society in Ancient Israel.* In my opinion, Wilson successfully demonstrates that there were different types of prophecy in Israel, with differing social determinants, utilitarian functions, and forms of prophetic speech. Relying heavily on the anthropological perspective of I. M. Lewis's *Ecstatic Religion,* Wilson argues that prophecy, though it could appear to be revolutionary and iconoclastic in moments of conflict, most characteristically performed a "social maintenance function" on behalf of some support group. In other words, Israelite prophets, like shamans in various cultures, "were able to regulate social, political, and religious change and thus preserve social stability."[14] Socially disruptive claims of a prophet emerge only when the continued existence or economic well-being of one group with its own terms of morality and/or political destiny conflicts with another group that seeks to limit or actively oppose it. For an anthropologist, the distinction between "true" and "false" prophets proves helpful because it defines the loyalty certain persons have to some particular group or groups in conflict. Canonization of "true" prophets at the end of a long and tumultuous social history similarly provides stability in the midst of change for a certain group or coalition of people.

Lewis argues that prophetic activity (or "shamanism") typically arises from oppressed or lower classes, from groups who depend on the power of spiritual/divine authority in order to make demands on the upper class. In societies with a strong patriarchal hierarchy, women figure prominently among prophets and through ecstasy can venture a socially acceptable intrigue against leaders or domineering husbands. In general, the social status of individual prophets is not rigidly fixed, but is negotiable both within the society at large and within his or her own group, where there may be more candidates for charismatic leadership than positions to be filled. Public fear or respect for the spiritual power(s) behind prophecy helps explain why Israelite prophets were so rarely killed by kings (cf. Jer. 26:14–15). In anthropological terms, the shaman with obvious ability to wield spiritual power is, simultaneously, a prime candidate for the charge of abusing this gift or of falling prey to its evil counterpart. Accordingly, a public accusation of "witchcraft" or "false prophecy" is the standard way to challenge a prophet's social status within the general typology of ecstatic religion. Lewis summarizes the situation:

> Hence it is they [shaman/prophets] who are held in check by accusations of witchcraft which seem designed to discredit them and to diminish their status. Thus, if possession is the means by which the underdog bids for attention, witchcraft accusations provide the countervailing strategy by which such demands are kept within bounds.[15]

Wilson seeks to demonstrate that in ancient Israel the "accusation of false prophecy" performs a social function similar to that of the charge of witchcraft in polytheistic cultures.

This way of assessing prophecy has the advantage of showing that adherents to the respective prophetic groups may at least *believe* that their own prophets are "true" and *assume* that they and their supporters have adequate criteria for distinguishing between those they will follow and those they will reject. In this regard, David Petersen's study of Israelite prophecy astutely suggests, "Fruitful study of what has been termed false prophecy or prophetic conflict might well ensue from the application of the categories of role expectation to the discussion."[16] Though Petersen, in my view, wrongly tries to remove the ecstatic element from Israelite prophecy, favoring instead the role of inspired poets for prophets, he does perceive that differing "role expectations" might pertain to each distinct group or to a coalition of related groups. In brief, the criteria for evaluating an instance of "prophecy" make sense only from within the domain of a socially defined support group and its marginal sympathizers, with their own recognized "true" prophets and idiosyncratic role expectations.

Therefore, from a strictly socioanthropological perspective, the various presentations of criteria for adjudicating prophetic claims, preserved in several places in the Old Testament, cannot be harmonized into a single system or reduced to a single hermeneutical principle (contra J. Sanders) consistent throughout the history of ancient Israelite prophecy.[17] The criteria could and did change over time and through social circumstance. So, Samuel could be expected to require payment from Saul for his prophetic insight about the lost asses, and the prophet could publicly confirm the divine word by selecting Saul to be a *nāgîd* through a divinatory casting of lots; but, in later periods, prophets who took money were held suspect, and the casting of divinatory lots fell away as a criterion of confirmation. No single "ideal" criterion can properly be isolated away from the discrete nexus of "role expectations" to which it once belonged in order to be tested independently (as Osswald and Crenshaw have done), thereby confirming or disconfirming its adequacy for distinguishing prophets in every age.[18]

Accordingly, one must be careful to separate two issues. The first concerns the specific regional and time-conditioned role expectations that served the needs of various types of prophets and their particular support groups. As the social performance of prophecy changed, so the criteria for evaluating it changed. The second issue is what need, if any, the presentation of criteria in scripture met for postexilic Judaism and later Christian prophecy. From a historical and social-scientific point of view, there is no such thing as a static conception of "biblical prophecy." Instead, we find in the Bible instances of changing prophetic phenomena to which pertain a variety of regional and social-historical differences regarding the criteria for prophetic role performance and the audience's discernment of legitimate prophecy.

A Canon Contextual Analysis of Jeremiah 28

Jeremiah 28 has become the *locus classicus* in the recent debate (i.e., Quell, Oswald, Crenshaw, Sanders, Zimmerli) regarding criteria for distinguishing "true" from "false" prophecy.[19] In Childs's work the focus is shifted from a historical reconstruction of original prophetic activity to a consideration of how prophets came to be depicted in the context of a later scripture. A close examination of the traditions surrounding Jeremiah 28 confirms that anxiety about finding a fixed set of objective criteria plays no significant role.

Jeremiah 26:3 states the problem clearly: Will the general public recognize the word of the prophet Jeremiah as God's word? The prophet hopes, "It may be that they [the people] will listen." Jeremiah's case is presented in deuteronomistic language in support of the view that the people do not recognize Jeremiah's message because they have failed to obey the laws of the "Torah" (v. 4), a "Torah" earlier prophets in the traditions of Jeremiah fully endorsed (v. 5). When Jeremiah's oracle of judgment threatens the house of the king, the princes and the people deliberate over the veracity of his prophetic claim (vv. 16–20). Arguments supporting his claim were based on parallels between his words and actions and those of other prophets—Micah of Moresheth and Uriah of Kiriath-jearim—who might be seen as of the same type as Jeremiah. Jeremiah's identification with this particular group of prophets served as confirmation of his trustworthiness for some people, while King Jehoiakim drew from this same evidence the opposite conclusion. Jeremiah belonged to a recognizable group of prophets whom the king stood against. Therefore, he pursued and killed Uriah. Only the intervention of Ahikam, the son of Shaphan, prevented him from killing Jeremiah as well. There was no room for ambiguity because the issues at stake were a matter of life and death. If a "disinterested" observer might have been confused by the options, Jeremiah's supporters were not.

In chapter 27, Jeremiah warns both king and priest that "your prophets, your diviners, your dream[er]s, your soothsayers, or your sorcerers" (v. 9) are telling "lies" (vv. 14, 16). The fivefold repetition of the pronomenal suffix, "your" (–km), makes explicit that the king *knows* who his prophets are and has clear expectations for them. Jeremiah is presented as appealing to other, different assumptions shared by his own followers but not by these royal prophets. He argues, "If they are prophets, and if the word of the Lord is with them, then let them *intercede* with the Lord of hosts, that the vessels which are left in the house of the Lord, in the house of the king of Judah, and in Jerusalem may not go to Babylon" (v. 18). Following the example of Moses, true prophets, according to the biblical Jeremiah, perform an intercessory function on behalf of the people. Lack of such activity violated the role expectations for a prophet of a public loyal to the presentation of Moses in the Torah.

The same confidence with which the characteristics of false prophets are described in the chapters preceding Jeremiah 28 is evident in the chapter that follows. A bold warning is directed against the king and his royal loyalists, including "your prophets and your diviners" (29:8), who announce new prophets raised up in Babylon (v. 15). Once more Jeremiah and his followers are portrayed in support of a particular set of known prophetic traditions (v. 19), precluding the sudden emergence of unknown prophets in Babylon. Because these prophets are familiar only to the king, not having found their legitimation among those loyal to Jeremiah and the prophetic tradition in which he stands, there is no doubt that they are imposters. The word of the Lord comes to Jeremiah later with punishment for one such prophet, "Shemaiah of Nehelam" in Babylon, who has prophesied among the exiles and sent letters in support of a rival priest in Jerusalem.

Public controversies regarding parties and politics charge the air. Nonetheless, there is no hopeless uncertainty presented in scripture about whether one should support or oppose the words of Jeremiah. The problem rests not on an abstract hermeneutical debate over criteria, but remains a highly political and clear-cut matter; namely, to what group or groups of prophets has God spoken and at what price is one ready to share allegiance to the "truth" treasured by that group? Within the scriptural depiction there is obvious continuity between those in preexilic Israel who supported the true prophets and the later postexilic believers who can live faithfully according to a newly formed scripture, with its canonical editions of "true" prophecy. For the postexilic adherents to scripture, the biblical prophets constitute a reliable and indisputable norm of God's word in ancient Israel, one that is continually applicable to future generations of believers.

This reexamination of the context surrounding Jeremiah 28 leads to two concluding observations, pushing Childs's proposal a step further. First, according to Childs's description of the canonical context, Jeremiah is depicted as recognizing that God could "change his mind" and Hananiah could deliver a true word diametrically opposed to what Jeremiah had previously given.[20] Implicit in this statement is the possibility that Hananiah might speak a true word, *even if* identified as a false prophet. That this possibility is a real one is validated by the larger canonical context and is an instance of the survival of an original complexity in the function of prophecy in ancient Israel. The biblical presentation of Hananiah seems to retain, even to build directly upon, the very recognition that a "false" prophet may say a true word and a "true" prophet may utter falsehood.

In social scientific terms, the one who is a channel for spiritual power is vulnerable to corruption by that power, and those guilty of witchcraft are still more familiar with the nature of true spiritual power than those with no ecstatic pretensions. Prophetic support groups regularly become accustomed to the need to cope with shamans that fall prey to witchcraft and witches or false prophets who might be healed or exorcised and, then, deliver "true" messages. Hence, the designation "true" prophet pertains to the social domain of a group of "true" believers, with its own normative traditions. This recognition does not, however, determine absolutely the freedom of God, gods, spirits, or demons to speak in unexpected ways and through unlikely persons, even through a "false" prophet associated with an opposing group.

As Childs interprets 1 Kings 13, the prophet at Bethel is not technically a "false" prophet, but lies to the young prophet from Judah and, later, speaks a true prophetic word. Conversely, in Numbers 22—24, God is shown to be able to speak through Balaam's donkey and even through this "false" prophet himself. In Jeremiah 28, Hananiah is described simply as "the prophet from Gibeon," with the possible implication that even Jeremiah expected true prophecy from him. Of course, possibilities in preexilic prophecy may cease to be live ones for the postexilic period. When these older prophetic traditions are taken up into the canonical context, Childs notes, as discussed earlier, the development of a new "scriptural norm for distinguishing the true from the false prophets."[21]

My point is to make clear that this later scriptural norm is not meant so much to solve an older, socio-anthropological problem of distinguishing true from false prophets as it is to offer guides to the interpretation of the words and deeds of the true "biblical" prophets in contrast to their adversaries. The biblical presentation is concerned "theocentrically" with depicting a specific group of "true" prophets who offer an allegedly "unified message" in the context of scripture. Historical figures who might not even qualify as "prophets" in a socio-anthropological sense may attain such a status within scripture. King David, for example, is depicted in parts of scripture as a prophet who prophesies through his hymnology instead of the usual prophetic speech. This prophetic hymnology is edited to become part of a larger inter-context of scripture with a resulting cumulative depiction of David.

Whole books, though deriving from different prophetic voices in different periods, are associated with the same true prophet. In the depiction of prophets such as Isaiah and Jeremiah, elements that distinguish true from false prophecy also indicate how to interpret these prophetic texts scripturally. The Mosaic Torah belongs to this new way of reading the prophetic texts. Certain approved prophets in scripture attain strong biographical proportion and serve as exemplars of the "true" prophets in the Bible. Some of these figures are connected with specific "books" within scripture and, by that association, lend a personal stamp to the unified message within the diverse traditions of these books. Words of promise and messianic hope now routinely accompany words of prophetic judgment. A new paradigm for understanding prophecy is established in scripture by this presentation of "true" prophets that goes far beyond a concern with social scientific questions about prophetic phenomena in ancient Israel.

Second, Childs argues for a "theocentric" focus to Jeremiah 28. This position may give the impression that the text is detached from the "flesh and blood" world of human history and is allowed to become a synchronic system of signs in service to abstract disputes about religion. In my opinion, the canonical context, as Childs describes it, resists just such an implication. One does not have to reconstruct the world behind the biblical text in order to ensure that reality itself is the object of interpretation. Scripture, in fact, makes a tyrannical claim about reality. Moreover, the biblical presentation is vividly realistic and can, on its own terms, be illuminated by social-scientific insights. A provocative Marxist analysis by H. Mottu entitled "Jeremiah vs. Hananiah: Ideology and Truth in Old Testament Prophecy" provides an example.[22]

Whether he realizes it or not, Mottu makes an appeal to the wider canonical context, rather than to a modern reconstruction of history, in his claims about the motives of King Zedekiah. The king wants God "to deal with us according to all his wonderful deeds" (21:2), in a manner like that familiar in the stories of Holy War, in order to "make him [Nebuchadnezzar] withdraw from us" (21:2). The mighty tyrant of Babylon stands on the verge of removing the present Judean leaders and of imposing on the Israelite population a more severe form of servitude. From the perspective of the biblical Jeremiah, if God intervenes and stops Babylon from pursuing the destruction of Jerusalem, the Judean leaders could stay on their thrones, the royal prophets would be further vindicated, the king's oppressive policies would appear to "work," and the peace promised by the king's prophets would rationalize the extremes of social injustice. Other prophetic traditions in the Book of Jeremiah state explicitly that Jeremiah *knows* the king is guilty of these crimes (21:12–13) and that God is about to punish the entire dynasty "according to the fruits of your doing"

(21:14). In other words, a "theocentric" distinction of a true prophetic word from a false one is never a purely "religious" matter, but asserts a discernment of "truth" as distinct from "ideology," a transcendent view of social and political realities as distinct from merely a solution to a syntactical problem in the grammar of faith.

In sum, this examination of Jeremiah 28 suggests some role, unexplained by Childs, for the use of social-scientific knowledge in interpreting the canonical context of scripture. It also confirms that adequate criteria for distinguishing "true" prophecy probably once existed for those who belonged to various prophetic support groups, and certainly they are portrayed as existing in the biblical traditions. This evidence counters on both levels the argument that exilic and postexilic "wisdom" was needed to replace unconvincing or indiscernible prophecy. Some other factor(s) must account for the decline of classical prophecy or, more accurately, its transformation into postexilic "deutero-prophetic" forms with their own need of different criteria for discernment.

The Cessation of Classical Prophecy

Besides the elements in Jeremiah 23—29 that retain older criteria alongside newer scriptural recommendations for distinguishing a true prophetic word, another tradition appears asserting that certain types of prophecy should no longer be practiced. Jeremiah 23:33–40 warns against people, priests, or prophets who seek any longer to hear a revelation called "The burden *(maśśa')* of the Lord" (vv. 33, 34, 36, 38). However, people should still be able to ask, "What has the Lord answered?" or "What has the Lord spoken?" (vv. 35, 37). Though the use of this term *maśśa'* as a *nomen technicus* is particularly difficult to reconstruct, it appears to have once indicated oracles of a particular genre (cf. Isa. 14:28; Ezek. 12:10; Lam. 2:14) and came to be employed as a superscription for either individual oracles (e.g., Isa. 13:1; 15:1; 17:1; 19:1; Zech. 9:1; 12:1; cf. Jer. 46:2; 48:1) or for oracular collections in prophetic books (e.g., Nah. 1:1; Mal. 1:1). In his *Late Israelite Prophecy: Studies in Deutero-Prophetic Literature and in Chronicles,* David Petersen concludes that Jer. 23:33–40 is a postexilic tradition added to Jeremiah's book, one in which "the use of classical formulae to legitimate new words as having prophetic authority is prohibited."[23]

Petersen thinks that the admonition to ask, "What has the Lord spoken?" implies one should consult canonical prophetic collections rather than expect more fresh prophetic revelation. For this interpretation Petersen stresses v. 35 as an explanation for v. 37 and its claim that one may seek "What the Lord says" from "a prophet." Zechariah 13:2–6, as scholars have long recognized, together with Petersen's more speculative interpretation of Isa. 40:1–11, also confirms that at least certain types of prophecy (but not necessarily all types) came to be condemned in the postexilic period. The development of this tradition coincides well with the decline of classical prophecy at that time. However, contrary to Petersen's conclusion, I do not see how the passage in Jer. 23:35 unequivocally advocates an end to *all* prophetic activity.

Following G. E. Wright's suggestion that classical prophecy is coterminous with monarchy, Petersen attempts to account for the gradual transformation from classical prophecy to a more learned, "bookish" deutero-prophecy by an appeal to a "trajectory" of changing prophetic views, in this case, predisposed by the demise of kingship during the Judean exile. In blunt terms Petersen asserts, "A prophet could not perform the old functions since the monarchic context no longer existed." There were no longer pretenders to the Davidic throne after 520 B.C.E. The "re-working of older (prophetic) speech forms" or so-called deutero-prophetic literature essentially resulted from that key social transition.[24]

Numerous problems have been raised about how well the mere existence of monarchy can account for the rise and decline of prophecy in Israel. The biblical traditions themselves regard some "judges" as "prophets"; Deborah is called a "prophetess," and certainly the prophetic activity of Samuel precedes the inauguration of Saul as "king." Also, recent historical investigations support the case for even more prophetic activity before the monarchy than these canonical prophetic traditions themselves suggest.[25] Furthermore, the Judean monarchy as a socially effective institution ended with the exile in 586 B.C.E., but prophets continued to be active up until the last royal claimant (ca. 520). Would the presence of mere figureheads or claimants be sufficient to explain the vitality of prophets in this period? Regardless, in the period from 520 to that of Ezra in the fourth century, classical prophecy continued to be robustly represented by prophets like Haggai, Zechariah, Malachi, and possibly Obadiah and Joel. For Petersen to dismiss this evidence of at least two generations of classical prophetic activity after the end of the Judean monarchy as simply the "last gasp" of a prophecy determined by the presence of kings is, in my view, unconvincing.

The mere fact that prophecy and monarchy coexisted for an extended period does not explain sociologically the interdependence of these two institutions. Moreover, the transformation of prophecy itself remains inadequately rationalized solely by an appeal to its association with monarchy. Long after the end of classical forms of prophecy, other types of prophetic activity appear to have thrived in the climate of postexilic Judaism and even in still later rabbinic Judaism.[26] In the biblical tradition itself, no sharp distinction is drawn between a later exilic "apocalyptic" and preexilic "genuine prophetic activity."[27]

Therefore, the cessation of a certain kind of prophetic speech and/or the transformation of it into another form apparently corresponds to a different set of social and religious needs than were previously common in Israel. From what can be known historically, this transition in prophecy took place fairly rapidly and decisively, breaking away from centuries of familiar and well-established role expectations for prophets within Israelite society. Klaus Koch cogently summarizes the little we know of these circumstances:

> After Ezra, we hear hardly anything more about a nābî'. Ezra's younger contemporary, Nehemiah, does mention people of the kind, but they play a dubious role and are open to the bribes of the political parties.[28]

In passages like Jer. 23:33–40 and Zech. 13:2–6, the biblical materials probably do bear witness to polemics against prophets around the time of Ezra or later in the postexilic period. Later Jewish adherents could look back on a former "time when prophets ceased to appear before men" (1 Macc. 9:27).

The Canonization of the Torah and the Transformation of Prophecy

Such a sweeping change in prophecy, coinciding with the appearance of Ezra as a leader in postexilic Judaism, requires a better explanation than simply a theory of prophecy's symbiotic relationship to monarchy. In my judgment, the key event that ended classical Israelite prophecy for the majority of Jewish believers in the fourth century was the promulgation of the Torah by Ezra. At present, the most plausible theory regarding the promulgation of Ezra's Torah is to view it as analogous to an arrangement which the Persians under Darius

275

(522–486 B.C.E.) inaugurated with their Egyptian subjects. As a concrete strategy to secure a commitment to orderly and law-abiding government on the part of his colony, Cyrus (539–530 B.C.E.) and, later, Darius sought to find a better legal arrangement of mutual benefit to the Egyptian religious leadership and the Persian military hierarchy. If the Egyptian priests would codify and make public their religious law, the Persians would honor the local administration of it in exchange for obedience to Persian civil and international law.

Simplifying this scenario for exiled Israelites, the policies of Cyrus and especially the specific plan inaugurated later by Darius and his successors involved a trade-off with the leadership of subjugated countries. In exchange for codifying and making public the secret Jewish religious laws, the Persian government would recognize the leadership of those involved in the process and would honor their local administration of that law. In this way, the likelihood of subversion based on secret religious traditions was minimized. The generosity of the Persians toward the colonial administration of its own regional religious laws would be reciprocated by strict Jewish obedience to Persian civil and international law. Those who participated in such a codification naturally received recognition by the Persian government as leaders in the new government, while groups outside of this agreement were subject only to its restraints.[29]

If, as now seems plausible, Ezra's Torah was approximately the same as the present Pentateuch, then its codification put into one collection the traditions maintained by Levitical priestly groups (with the so-called "P" edited materials found in Genesis through Numbers) together with the traditions of deutero-prophetic, deuteronomistic group(s). The composition of the Pentateuch supports this coalition of groups and related traditions. Each group retained distinct Torah traditions, which editorially now share a common emphasis on a Decalogue (cf. Exodus 20; Deuteronomy 5), along with other more substantially differentiated law *corpora*. Between the traditions concerned with the plight of the daughters of Zelophehad in Num. 27:1–11 and Num. 36:5–10, which mark the boundaries between the Levitical Torah and that of Deuteronomy, one discovers somewhat disordered traditions recalling similar materials found only in Joshua. Hence, some additional traditions were probably added at the time of the formation of the Pentateuch, including some which might have been left out of the Torah, when, in the deuteronomistic history,

Joshua was separated from Deuteronomy. The editors of this single Torah thus sought to give an overall "shape" to the collection, while respecting the individual contributions of each tradent group.[30] Other ancient traditions outside of this Torah undoubtedly retained their authority within this same coalition of religious groups, though the precise dimensions of their "scripture" beyond the Torah are not known. Editing prophetic collections appears to be at this late stage partially in response to the newly recognized Mosaic Torah and, eventually, the prophetic collections were viewed as commentary upon it (e.g., cf. Mal. 4:4).[31]

Prophecy after the Canonization of the Torah

Since the above scenario for the promulgation of the Torah entailed a political coalition of at least two major groups—probably deutero-prophetic, deuteronomistic tradents and the old Jerusalemite priestly families (cf. Neh. 10:1 [9:38])—one might expect to find both similarities and differences in their perspectives on the future of prophetic activity. The subject of prophecy certainly needed to be addressed, particularly if it were implied that older forms of prophecy ceased to be tolerated. After all, within just a generation prior to Ezra, Haggai and Zechariah had openly prophesied in a classical manner in support of efforts to rebuild the temple under the Davidide Zerubbabel and the Zadokite Jeshua. For purposes of this paper, the deutero-prophetic views will be considered first, then those of their priestly compatriots. Where many of these details are generally available in the contemporary scholarly literature, these comments are meant to be brief and representative.

Deutero-prophetic texts have already been noted that called for an end to a certain kind of prophecy, particularly in Jer. 23:33–40 in association with "the burden of the Lord." My suggestion is that the technical expression "burden" (maśśa') became a problem in the postexilic period because of its identification with the prophecies of the last classical prophets, especially those of Malachi (cf. Mal. 1:1) and Zechariah (Zech. 9:1; 12:1; cf. Nah. 1:1). The term is, likewise, familiar in the contemporaneous literature of Lamentations (2:14) and, especially, Ezekiel (12:10). Aside from the superscriptions to the oracles against the nations in Isaiah, this term only appears to gain its peculiar technical status in this late period prior to Ezra (cf. Prov. 30:1; 31:1). Consequently, the promulgation of the Torah must have helped to provoke a similar codification and fixation of "true prophets" who stood in the prophetic tradition of Moses (cf. Deuteronomy 13; 18; 34:10). In order to lend full support to the sufficiency of the Torah as the revealed law of God within Israel, collections of classical prophetic traditions were edited and expanded as commentary upon that same Torah. With the canonization of such prophecy, Ezra's Torah could be protected by ending the possibility that God might reveal a new and different Torah, such as that which had been offered by Ezekiel in Ezekiel 40—48.

In the place of classical prophecy, the sages within the deutero-prophetic schools added to their earlier editorial skills learned interpretations of older, authoritative prophecies. This augmentation of the classical prophetic traditions, often in deference to the Torah of Moses, provided a more appropriate conclusion to the canonical prophetic literature than would an anachronistic and potentially disruptive claim to fresh revelation in the manner of the earlier biblical prophets. Through a sort of charismatic exegesis (sometimes associated with later "midrash"), the biblical prophetic literature was eventually given its final canonical shape within a context attentive to future generations who would seek to be obedient to the Torah of Moses. Still later generations, like that of Ben Sira, could lay claim to their own synthesis of the Torah and the commentary of these biblical prophets, asserting that it constituted a "teaching like prophecy" for their own time (cf. Sir. 24:33).[32]

The other major group identified with the promulgation of the five-book Torah of Ezra was that of the "Levites" or old Jerusalemite priestly families who were probably tradents of the so-called P editions of the traditions in the Pentateuch (Genesis through Numbers) and authors of the so-called Chronicler's history. Despite continuing controversy over the exact date of Chronicles, its dependence both on P (the priestly code) and on the deuteronomistic history suggests that it belongs to the period immediately before or after the promulgation of the Torah and represents, in the words of P. Ackroyd, "the first Old Testament theologian, offering a unifying of strands and trends which may otherwise appear separate. . . ."[33] In essence, the books of Chronicles correspond from the side of the Levites, to the deutero-prophetic materials (what became the "Prophets") written or edited by the deuteronomistic tradents.

As already seen, the deutero-prophetic literature condemns the perpetuation of a professional office of prophecy like that of the classical prophets, but does not categorically rule out all possible forms of revelation and divination. The Chronicler is fully acquainted with the classical activity of prophets, including reference to certain figures not found in the deuteronomistic literature, for example, Eliezer (2 Chron. 20:37), Hanai (2 Chron. 26:7), Jahaziel (2 Chron. 20:14), Oded (2 Chron. 28:9), and so on. Yet, 1 and 2 Chronicles advocates its own deutero-prophetic modification of the familiar classical forms of prophecy by emphasizing the importance of prophetic hymnology in association with David and the Levitical singers. The Levites are portrayed as prophets in Israel's holy war (2 Chronicles 20) and the Levitical singers are depicted as prophets (2 Chronicles 34:20) originally appointed by David (1 Chronicles 25, cf. 2 Chron. 29:25–30). Among these "prophetic" Levitical singers 2 Chron. 20:1–30 mentions Korah and Asaph, whose hymnology has special authority. Their psalms now form a double inclusio around a collection of David psalms added to Psalms 3—41. They may well have been the ones responsible for the earliest editing of a "prophetic" Davidic psalter (Psalms 1—89), with an appropriate subscription at the end of Psalm 72, "The prayers of David, the son of Jesse, are ended."[34]

As a generalization about this history of prophecy, one might speak of differing types of classical Israelite prophetic activity (prophecy 1), with various kinds of divination as well as some stereotypical forms of prophetic speech (e.g., invective/threat oracles). When these types of prophetic speech ceased after the promulgation of the Torah, what remained was a less well-defined, more variegated set of deutero-prophetic activities (prophecy 2), including different forms of prophecy (hymns), editorial reformulation of prophecy, and highly visionary accounts, cast as pseudepigraphic re-presentations of earlier prophecy (e.g., Daniel 7ff., 1 Enoch, 2 Esdras, etc.). Finally, one can find within the late biblical and postbiblical traditions the hope for a future eschatological prophecy (prophecy 3) during the age of the Messiah, in which almost everyone could be a prophet (cf. Joel 3:1–2[2:28–29]; 1 Macc. 4:46; 9:27; 2 Bar. 85:3; etc.).

After the promulgation of the Torah under Ezra, any future occurrence of "prophecy" became in some sense postbiblical and of a different sort than what had preceded it. Any future prophetic phenomenon in Judaism, to the extent that it occurred in the shadow of the Torah, would be measured by a different norm and perform some different social functions than had prophecy before. In social-scientific terms, most of the social maintenance functions of classical prophecy had been taken over by the public promulgation of a religious canon. What made this canon different from the law promulgated by Josiah (presumably the core of Deuteronomy) was its ability to precipitate the codification and the canonization of *written* "prophecies," which pragmatically exhausted their foreseeable contribution. "Classical prophecy" could only confirm but no longer disconfirm the established consensus on the Torah, lest it become patently "false" and socially disruptive, in support of a different Torah (e.g., perhaps "The Temple Scroll" from Qumran).[35]

Because deutero-prophetic activity occurred in a different social configuration than had classical prophecy, other criteria must have arisen to test its legitimacy. The presence of an authoritative Torah and other normative ancient traditions encouraged midrashic-like interpretation and a canonical reshaping of some previous prophetic and nonprophetic traditions. The criteria for deutero-prophetic activity undoubtedly corresponded to the resulting "routinization" of ecstatic religion (Weber) within the new institutions which served a newly established hierarchy of "slaves" under the benevolent aegis of "kings whom thou [God] hast set over us because of our sins" (Neh. 9:36). The criteria for deutero-prophetic activity, more than for classical prophecy, became subject to expectations of competence in editing, in learned religious interpretation, and in the expertise of writing within the setting of schools.

The scripture itself includes in support of its authority both the older criteria of classical as well as later deutero-prophetic criteria of a "biblical" prophecy in relation to the Torah of Moses. By the time of Ezra, Israelite prophecy had taken an irreversible turn away from the past and moved on an uncharted path, leading eventually to rabbinic Judaism and Christianity. The context of scripture shows little interest in conveying a historical account of the history of prophecy. Instead, its concern is with an abiding word of God that is mediated through the prophets, with the assurance to its future readers: "In the latter days, you will understand it clearly" (Jer. 23:20).

NOTES

1. Brevard S. Childs, *Old Testament Theology in a Canonical Context* (Philadelphia: Fortress Press, 1985) 134. See W. Zimmerli, "Der Wahrheitser-

weis Jahwes nach der Botschaft der beiden Exilspropheten," *Tradition und Situation. Festschrift A. Weiser* (ed. E. Würthwein and W. Kaiser; Göttingen: Vandenhoeck & Ruprecht, 1963) 133–51.

2. Childs, *Old Testament Theology*, 138–9.

3. Ibid., 140.

4. Ibid., 142.

5. Ibid., 141.

6. Ibid., 137.

7. Brevard S. Childs, *Introduction to the Old Testament as Scripture* (Philadelphia: Fortress Press, 1975) 82–83.

8. Childs, *Old Testament Theology*, 140.

9. Ibid.

10. J. Crenshaw, *Prophetic Conflict* (Berlin: Walter de Gruyter, 1971) 111.

11. J. Crenshaw, *Old Testament Wisdom: An Introduction* (Atlanta: John Knox Press, 1981) 202. See R. Carroll, *From Chaos to Covenant* (New York: Crossroad Publishing Co., 1981) 183–89; and B. Long, "Social Dimensions of Prophetic Conflict," *Semeia* 21 (1981) 31–53.

12. J. Crenshaw, *Hymnic Affirmation of Divine Justice: The Doxologies of Amos and Related Texts in the Old Testament* (SBLDS 24; Missoula, Mont.: Scholars Press, 1975) 123.

13. Childs, *Old Testament Theology*, 140.

14. R. R. Wilson, *Prophecy and Society in Ancient Israel* (Philadelphia: Fortress Press, 1980) 300.

15. I. M. Lewis, *Ecstatic Religion* (Baltimore: Penguin Books, 1971) 122.

16. D. Petersen, *The Roles of Israel's Prophets* (Sheffield, Eng.: JSOT Press, 1981) 97.

17. J. A. Sanders, "Hermeneutics in True and False Prophecy," *Canon and Authority* (ed. G. W. Coats and B. O. Long; Philadelphia: Fortress Press, 1977) 21–41. See Childs's critique in his *Old Testament Theology*, 136–37.

18. See E. Osswald, *Falsche Prophetie im Alten Testament* (Tübingen: J. C. B. Mohr, 1962).

19. Cf. G. Quell, *Wahre und falsche Propheten* (Gütersloh: Bertelsmann, 1952).

20. Childs, *Old Testament Theology*, 139.

21. Ibid., 142.

22. H. Mottu, "Jeremiah vs. Hananiah: Ideology and Truth in Old Testament Prophecy," *The Bible and Liberation* (ed. N. K. Gottwald; New York: Orbis Books, 1983) 235–51.

23. D. Petersen, *Late Israelite Prophecy: Studies in Deutero-Prophetic Literature and in Chronicles* (SBLDS 23; Missoula, Mont.: Scholars Press, 1977) 29.

24. Ibid., 6.

25. Wilson, *Prophecy*, 146ff.; and see the abstract of Baruch A. Levine's paper on "The Balaam Inscription from Deir 'Alla—Historical Aspects," 38–39, *Abstracts* for "The International Congress on Biblical Archaeology," Jerusalem, 1–10 April 1984, sponsored by Israel Academy of Sciences and Humanities/Israel Exploration Society.

26. David E. Aune, *Prophecy in Early Christianity and the Ancient Mediterranean World* (Grand Rapids: Wm. B. Eerdmans, 1983) 103ff.

27. Wilson, *Prophecy,* 308.

28. K. Koch, *The Prophets* (Philadelphia: Fortress Press, 1984) 2.187.

29. G. Widengren, "The Persian Period," *Israelite and Judean History* (ed. J. H. Hayes and J. M. Miller; Philadelphia: Westminster Press, 1977) 514–23.

30. Brevard Childs, "The Old Testament as Scripture of the Church," *CTM* 43 (1972) 709–22.

31. J. Blenkinsopp, *Prophecy and Canon* (Notre Dame, Ind.: University of Notre Dame Press, 1977) 96–123.

32. G. T. Sheppard, *Wisdom as a Hermeneutical Construct* (Berlin: Walter de Gruyter, 1980) 136–44; and J. Neusner, *Midrash in Context* (Philadelphia: Fortress Press, 1983) 125–27.

33. P. Ackroyd, "The Chronicler as Exegete," *JSOT* 2 (1977) 101–16.

34. Childs, *Introduction,* 504–25; C. Westermann, "The Formation of the Psalter," *Praise and Lament in the Psalms* (Atlanta: John Knox Press, 1981) 250-58; and N. Sarna, "Psalm 89: A Study of Inner Biblical Exegesis," *Biblical and Other Studies* (ed. A. Altmann; Cambridge, MA: Harvard University Press, 1963) 29–46.

35. See J. Milgrom, "The Temple Scroll," *BA* 41 (1978) 105-20.

Part IV

THE INTERPRETATION OF
THE WRITINGS

18

Daniel 1 in the Context
of the Canon

W. SIBLEY TOWNER

Simple and straightforward as it is, the first chapter of the Book of Daniel nevertheless poses a challenge which seems most likely to be met if it is read in the larger canonical context.[1] The most important event of this "court tale of contest"[2]—Daniel's refusal to eat the king's "rich food" or to drink "the wine which he drank" (v. 5)—consistently is explained by modern commentators on the basis of a hypothetical reconstruction of Jewish dietary law derived in large part from practices known only from significantly later periods and from non-canonical sources. Moreover, the subject of the story is thrown into doubt by the "problem-solving" historical settings the scholars have provided for the stories.

The canonical perspective ought to provide just the right angle from which to cut through the tangle of interpretations that have overgrown the plain meaning of the text as it now stands at the beginning of the entire Book of Daniel and in the fictitious setting of the Babylonian exile. After all, while acknowledging that canon is a process, and that studies in the literary, redaction, and tradition-history of a text can illumine that process, the canonical stance positions itself on the claim that, as Brevard S. Childs puts it, the "crucial . . . move occurred when [the fruits of that process] were rendered into the form of Scripture to be used authoritatively by another generation."[3] The peculiar profile of the passage in its present form, its indigenous emphases and nuances, and particularly the larger sense of direction it has gained by being conjoined (even if secondarily) with the material that makes up the rest of the book in which it now stands, are all considerations that supersede in importance any aspects of its prehistory or the cultural and historical milieu of its origin. "To work from the canonical shape is to resist any method which seeks critically to shift the canonical ordering . . . [any] historical critical reconstruction [which] attempts to refocus the picture according to its own standards of historical accuracy."[4]

Childs does not give us a great many specific methodological guidelines on how to approach a specific small unit of scripture from the canonical perspective. He prefers to illustrate the approach in the actual event of interpretation rather than to talk about it in a theoretical way. However, we can discern at least two "rules" which appear to bear on Daniel 1. First, we are to watch for evidence that "material has been detached from its original historical mooring and provided with a secondary, theological context."[5] Such a thing has, of course, evidently happened in the Book of Daniel, as the essentially hagiographical and sapiental stories of Daniel A (chaps. 1–6) were combined with the apocalypses of Daniel B (chaps. 7–12). For Childs such a development in a text is crucially important since it is the kind of "actualization" that seeks "to transmit the tradition in such a way as to prevent its being moored in the past."[6] We should eschew all attempts, then, to bind the text too rigidly to this or that cultural or historical circumstance of its origin, for to do so would be to violate the very liberating function of the canon, in which the text already had been linked with circumstances not original to it.

Second, we are to be aware that "prophetic proclamation [can be] given a radically new eschatological interpretation by shifting the referent within the original oracles."[7] Childs thinks that the canonizers of Daniel B must have known that the "little horn" of the fourth beast (7:8) had been intended originally to signify Antiochus IV Epiphanes; however, they had already reactualized the prophecy into a reference to Rome. He even says, "There is strong evidence to suggest that the interpretation of the Book of Daniel has been sharply altered by those who edited it"![8] If this is the case (or even if—as I believe—it is not), the attachment of Daniel B to Daniel A has given the stories like that of chap. 1 an entire new vocation. They become interim ethics, illustrations of the way the saints who will soon inherit the everlasting kingdom (7:27) and who will be resurrected to shine "as the brightness of the firmament" (12:3) can conduct themselves in the meantime. Childs considers Daniel B to be a "midrash" on Daniel A (and therefore necessarily later) that legitimately draws out the true intent of the divine message in those earlier chapters.[9]

With these rules in place and Childs's general judgments regarding the "canonical shape" of the Book of Daniel in mind, I turn now to Daniel 1 to see what improvement over the standard results of historical-critical reading can be attained by assuming a canonical perspective.

In preparation for an initial "direct" reading, the canonical approach would, I suppose, reaffirm the principle always upheld by all good students of the Bible that the text must be understood with meticulous literalness. Every detail of the story is essential to its proper understanding. While it is not enough to say simply that the medium is the message, neither is it correct to suggest that the narrative is "merely framework, the décor of the literary form being used to convey the message"[10]—as though some timeless truth could be squeezed out of Daniel 1 and the dry rind of the narrative then thrown aside. No, story and theological content belong inextricably together. And if the story presents itself to us as a bizarre and time-bound "oriental court tale...full of miracles and what to us are glaring improbabilities,"[11] that is precisely the incarnate form in which the Word of God comes to us in this scripture. Our task is not to clean up the story to meet the theological needs of sophisticated modern readers; presumably the canonizers have already loosed it from its moorings in the long-vanished world of third or second century B.C.E. Palestinian Judaism precisely so that it can function in some way as "timeless truth" for other generations. Our task as interpreters is to discern how that liberation has taken place right in the midst of the medium of vivid and authentic cultural details that convey the message of this chapter.

Like other careful readings of scripture, a reading made from a canonical perspective will also value a structural analysis of the passage. The account of Daniel's refusal, the ordeal, and its success (vv. 8–16) constitutes a story within a larger story. The *RSV* demonstrates this in its paragraph divisions, and a number of commentators support the division: Dan. 1:1–7, prologue; 1:8–16, the trials of the faithful; 1:17–21, epilogue. The temptation always exists to suggest that vv. 8–16 are an insertion, and that the rest of Daniel 1 was the original story. Indeed, 1:1–7, 17–21 can be read coherently without vv. 8–16 as a larger, if somewhat duller story about the superiority of Jewish youths over all other wise men of Nebuchadnezzar's court. It must also be noted that the events of vv. 8–16 take place entirely privately within the household, that the refusal is known only to four Jews and one or two Babylonians (depending on whether the "steward" was conniving with the chief eunuch or acting on his own responsibility), and that no news of the trial by vegetables is reported to have reached Nebuchadnezzar's ears. No causal link is proposed between the miracle of vv. 8–16 and the warm reception that the four Jewish youths received from the Babylonian king. He liked them because "none was found like them" (v. 19), presumably in "wisdom and understanding," not in their ruddy, health-food appearance. They were "better in appearance" than all the other youths because of their vegetable diet (v. 15); but they were "ten times better than all the magicians and enchanters" (v. 20) because God made them that way (v. 17)! Thus the primary climax of the chapter is v. 15, the announcement of the victory of the four youths in their ordeal, which is the happy end of the story within the story. The rest is falling action, picking up threads already visible in vv. 3–6, with perhaps a secondary climax to the larger account of the superiority of the four Jewish youths over the other wise men occurring at v. 20. This analysis is crucial for the interpretation that follows because by suggesting that the chapter contains two concurrently running accounts, each of which makes its own point, it obviates the need to view it as a tightly integrated narrative whose only moral is that obedience results in divine reward.

For all this looseness of construction and lack of tight logical consistency in the story, however, a reader approaching this text in the context of the canon will treat it as a single story, respecting the literal terms of it as much as possible, on the grounds that the canonizers chose to preserve it in this form. No hypothetical reconstruction of the story into two separate accounts can ever surpass the theological importance of the form in which it now stands before us. This insight can hardly be termed a breakthrough, of course, because it simply reaffirms the conviction that was normative with all traditional pre-critical interpreters and is still standard with the rank and file of readers of the Bible in our own day. But insofar as it can help us hear more precisely the text's theological claim, this restoration of the status quo ante can in truth be considered an advance.

The basic plot of the story itself is familiar. Four Jewish lads are among the captives taken to Babylon by Nebuchadnezzar. This rather humane and befuddled king, evidently chronically in need of skilled court functionaries who can read omens and interpret the gods' guidelines for the royal decision-making process,[12] perceives these Jewish captives to be prime candidates for such duties. So he orders them enrolled in a three-year course in the royal academy of wisdom and places them under the kindly supervision of the chief eunuch Ashpenaz.[13] Judging from where they stood in their class and even in their new profession at the end of the three-year period (Nebuchadnezzar, it will be recalled, "found them ten times better than all the magicians and enchanters that were in all his kingdom," v. 20), things went very well for them in the classroom. But not so in the school cafeteria. Much to the dismay of Ashpenaz and the "steward" who had direct charge of Daniel and his three friends, they refused to partake of the standard fare. Even though this fare hit a very high standard indeed, considering that it was evidently the same food that the king himself ate (v. 5), the Jewish lads insisted upon eating nothing but vegetables (*KJV*: "pulse" = beans and lentils), and drinking nothing but water (v. 12). The school authorities acceded to this request only after Daniel ingeniously came up with the idea of a ten-day trial period which proved that, for the Jews at least, vegetables and water produced better body tone and color than that produced in all the others who preferred to take their chances on the rich food and wine (v. 15).

The men of God won the court contest, presumably because God, their silent partner, saw to it. The problem with the story is partly contextual and partly hermeneutical. In its own context, what led Daniel and the other three to conclude that the king's food would "defile" them (v. 8) and that they therefore should not eat it? In the later contexts of readers of scripture, beginning with that of the canonizers, and even including our own late in the twentieth century C.E., what conclusions does the story suggest about the contours that faithful obedience takes at the moment it sits down at the dinner table? God's respect for Daniel's voluntary act of religious discipline is a theme that believers can always affirm. But Daniel 1 is a story about people as well as God. They are people who—by the lights of canonical interpretation—are understood by the community that preserved their story in the pages of scripture not to be "moored in the past" but to be living and abiding illustrations of timeless theological truth. It is precisely when historical interpreters have sought to say exactly why the youths made the choice that they did and what the continuing implications of their choice might be that they have diverged unhelpfully. It is just here that a canonical reading might be most helpful.

We may begin with the objective problem of the king's food and wine. Without indulging in reconstructions of the historical and cultural milieus of the text and then interpreting *it* from *them,* does scripture itself give us any clue as to why Daniel would have understood himself to be "defiled" from eating the food and drinking the wine? All that the text actually tells us about the king's menu is contained in the single Hebrew word *patbag* (*RSV* "rich food") which is borrowed from the Persian (and ultimately Sanskrit) *patibaga,* "portion, ration." The Hebrew term probably means no more than this, though the evidence is too slim to be sure—the word occurs only in Dan. 1:8; 11:26. It is not pork. It is not oysters. As far as we can see, there is nothing defiling about a *patbag* as such! If the scene in Daniel 1 is a refraction of 2 Kings 25:30 (cf. Jer. 52:34), wherein the exiled Judean king Jehoiachin receives his "daily portion" at Nebuchadnezzar's table, it is worth noting that "defilement" is not at issue in that original. Jehoiachin seems to partake freely and without scruple in the royal provender.

It is the very notion of defilement, however, coupled with evidences of dietary scruples on the part of literary contemporaries of Daniel (cf. Esth. 14:17; Tob. 1:11; Jdh. 10:5; 12:1–4; 1 Macc. 1:63; 2 Macc. 6:18–20; 7:1–42) that has caused nearly all modern commentators to assume that Daniel's refusal to eat and drink from the king's victuals sprang from his religious allegiance to that set of dietary laws followed by observant Jews certainly since NT times and perhaps as early as the Maccabean period. He was, in some preliminary way, "keeping kosher." R. H. Charles states the case clearly. The youths demonstrate their loyalty to their religion—and consequently achieve superior physical condition—by observing "the laws of their religion regarding clean and unclean meats. The need of this loyalty was felt to be of supreme moment in the time of Antiochus Epiphanes, who was doing his utmost to hellenize the Jews. To eat of unlawful food in such circumstances was as sinful as idolatry itself."[14] Charles then goes on to distinguish two ways in which the food *might* have been unlawful: "Not only because the Levitical laws as to clean and unclean animals were not observed by the heathen in the selection and preparation of their food, but also because the food so prepared had *generally* been offered to idols (Exod. 34:15; Acts 15:29; 21:25; Deut. 32:38)." (This and following emphases are mine.) Montgomery takes a similar line, but stresses blood. He speaks of Daniel's "scruples against meat sacrificed 'with the blood' and *probably eidolothuta,* Acts 15:29 [i.e., offered to idols], and against wine as generally graced with a religious libation (cf. 1 Cor. 10:21)."[15] He goes on to reject any evidence of asceticism, early Essenism, or puritanic discipline (Josephus and Calvin), but argues that the practice is *logically* based on the Law. Porteous comments that Daniel's first crisis arose when he was expected "to eat the food and drink the wine from the royal table, which had *doubtless* been associated *in some way* with idolatrous worship. The food certainly would not have been prepared in the correct Hebrew fashion, and *might* even have consisted of animals regarded by Hebrew law as unclean." Porteous even takes account of the ostensible historical setting of the story when he continues, "It is true that scruples such as we are told the Jewish lads felt *might have* manifested themselves in the Babylonian exile, as they have been felt by the orthodox among Jews throughout Jewish history."[16] Among the most recent commentators, Lacocque assumes without reservation that "the central question of this chapter is that of a ritually pure diet," and he, like other commentators, compares Daniel's case above all with that of the Jewish hero Eleazar who (in 2 Macc. 6:18–31) preferred martyrdom at the hands of Antiochus's hellenizers to eating pork.[17]

Attention to the scriptural environment of Daniel 1 proves to be helpful here as one pushes farther into the question of what was wrong with the king's food (and by implication, whether the point of this story centers upon Daniel's obedience to known dietary law or upon something else). The issues of dietary law and the related matters of ritual cleanness of vessels, which were—as Jacob Neusner has shown[18]—hallmarks of "normative" Judaism even at its earliest period, are alluded to in the canon, but only in the NT. Texts such as Matt. 15:1–20; 23:25–26; and 1 Corinthians 8 show that dietary laws were already matters of concern among first century c.e. Pharisees. None of these texts suggests, however, that it had already become mandatory to eat only meat which had been butchered according to the later conventions of kosher slaughter, or that meat handled by gentiles was ipso facto unclean. The OT itself makes no mention of a prohibition on eating meat butchered by gentiles, although it is hard to see how a non-Jew could be depended upon to handle the required drainage of blood properly. That eating blood was something to be avoided clearly was generally accepted among Jews at an early date. The Priestly writers even made the prohibition incumbent upon gentiles in the so-called "Noachic covenant" (see Gen. 9:4). Even the semantics of the story in Daniel 1 warrant the suggestion that this might have been part of the problem with the king's food. Daniel's resolution not to "defile himself" (*yitgā'al*, v. 8) might well have had something to do with the forbidden presence of blood in meat coming from a non-Jewish kitchen. People are "defiled" (*něgō'ălû*) by blood in Isa. 59:3 and Lam. 4:14; on one occasion, Isa. 63:3, Yahweh testifies ('*eg'āltî*) that even the divine garments are subject to defilement by human blood.[19]

Concerning vegetables or bread prepared by gentiles, there seems to have been no scruple.[20]

Eating food in an exilic environment was obviously not forbidden. Eating unclean food in Assyria—Hos. 9:3—is not the same as eating food made unclean by Assyrians. The whole land and everything in it was unclean simply because it was not the land of Israel, yet life had to go on there.

In the category of forbidden foods, the OT includes blood (Gen. 9:4; Deut. 12:23; Lev. 7:27); certain fat (Lev. 3:17); the meat of a kid boiled in its mother's milk (Exod. 23:19; Deut. 14:21); certain unclean animals (esp. swine; cf. Isa. 65:4), fish, birds, insects, and reptiles (Deut. 14:3–21; Leviticus 11); and the meat of an animal that had died of itself (Deut. 14:21; Ezek. 4:14) or had been torn by predators (Exod. 2:31). The only other meat forbidden to be eaten by an ordinary Israelite was that part of a sacrifice reserved for use by priests (e.g., Lev. 7:28–36), or meat or wine originally offered to idols (Exod. 34:15; Deut. 32:28). The possibility that meat could be holy is affirmed in Hag. 2:11–12, but that holiness is not communicable to other food by contact.

Taking Daniel 1 in the context of the canon, and without playing the text off against a hypothetical reconstruction of the contemporary Jewish attitude towards diet based on extracanonical accounts, we cannot say that Daniel's refusal was an act of obedience to known law, or even an act of respect for ancient taboos against eating blood.

Another explanation of why Daniel demurred avoids the reconstruction of the dietary mores of observant Jews of that time but errs in the direction of speculation. This approach stresses the good health and sharpness of intellect which flow from simple vegetarian fare (that claim is in fact clearly made in Jdh. 8:6–7, Tob. 1:11, and in the T. Jos. 3:4)—thus making the story (or at least the story within the story) an illustration of the salutary effects of the self-discipline of godly people under the general rubric *mens sana in corpore sano*. Desmond Ford, for example, closes his discussion of v. 8 with some moralizations on diet added to the legal and cultic bases of refusal already mentioned. "A well-instructed Israelite," says he, "shunned rich, spiced foods on the basis that he was the property of God and should not defile his body or lessen its usefulness in any way. . . . It is also not too much to say that young men of the quality that these obviously were would be aware of the close connection between plain living and high thinking."[21] He then uses Daniel to teach this generation of "marshmallows" the importance of a low-cholesterol diet for combating heart disease, and returns to the text with the observation that "to shun 'the king's rich food' (v. 15) may have seemed an unnecessary cross, but the heroes of the story apparently knew that 'great eaters and great drinkers are rarely great at anything else.' "[22]

Among the many recent commentators on Daniel 1, Joyce Baldwin comes closest to offering an explanation of Daniel's great refusal that works strictly within the evidence of scripture itself. Neither citing a hypothetical *halakhah* of diet nor suggesting prudential health considerations as likely causes, she goes to Dan. 11:26, where the rare word *patbag*, "rich food," occurs again. Whoever eats the king's rich food becomes indebted to the king. It might be as simple as that.

Baldwin concludes, "It *would seem* [my emphasis] that Daniel rejected this symbol of dependence on the king because he wished to be free to fulfill his primary obligations to the God he served. The defilement he feared was not so much a ritual as a moral defilement, arising from the subtle flattery of gifts and favours which entailed hidden implications of loyal support, however dubious the king's future policies might prove to be."[23]

To conclude this discussion of the objective problem posed by the king's food and drink to Daniel—or rather, to the community that preserved this book as sacred scripture, that is, the canonizers—we can say that Daniel's refusal might have centered upon the issue of defilement by ingestion of blood. However, we cannot say even this with absolute certainty. If we take the story of Daniel 1 in the context of the canon, and without playing the text off against a hypothetical reconstruction of the contemporary attitude toward diet by observant Jews, based largely upon extracanonical texts and much later Tannaitic materials, how much less can we say that his refusal was an act of obedience to a set of dietary laws.[24] The slippage of this text away from its moorings to any specific dietary "halakhah" of the third and second centuries B.C.E., and the lack of any evidence of a remooring of the text to the dietary "halakhah" of the community of the canonizers, leave the reader and the interpreter free to make a hermeneutical bridge to the picture of integrity of character that this text draws rather than to objective details of ancient praxis which may or may not be important hallmarks of faith for readers of subsequent generations.

When we turn to the larger, hermeneutical issue in the interpretation of the act of four young Jews in Daniel 1, the connection between the refusal and its continuing implications for Jewish and Christian faith is quickly apparent. Take Lacocque's treatment as an example. He speaks for the many who see the issue to be a test of the lad's *obedience to God's will expressed in dietary law.* In fact, he pushes that reading to the limit. "The cause of the Jews is identified with that of God, and the ultimate consequences of one's alimentary diet at the Babylonian court are incalculable. It is a matter of God's victory or his defeat, of his life or his death."[25] Presumably obedience to expressions of the divine will past or future continue to have a life-or-death importance in the faith communities. Collins takes this basic understanding in the direction of reward-and-punishment (and finds the chapter—as others do—to be a lesson in works-righteousness), arguing that the *wisdom* that enables the Jews to succeed at the Babylonian court is in the last analysis a product of prior obedience: "Fidelity to the God of the Jews is an essential element of wisdom."[26] Does this, then, become a hermeneutical principle for him? Porteous admits the theological problems arising from a stress on rigid dietary law as an avenue to divine blessing, pointing out that obedience is not always met with success (cf. Psalm 91), and that in this case the principle being stood up for seems relatively unimportant to many believers. However, he continues to interpret the story as a validation to Jews (and Christians?) of a *stand on principle.*[27] Several see the moral of the story to be *loyalty to the faith while under trial;* others speak about the *pedagogical value of suffering.*[28] In addition to her other remarks already noted, Baldwin observes that the story has the flavor of a *theodicy*—"the Lord is in control and will in due course vindicate those who are loyal to Him because He must vindicate His own name."[29]

How can one simple story lead to so many potential hermeneutical applications? Can a canonical reading of this single passage help us to discriminate among them? In my opinion, the answer is yes. Reading this text in the context of the canon directs our attention to the function of Daniel's refusal, rather than to its motivation. Taken in its own terms, the text does not actually say why he did it. We are assured, however, that the four Jewish heroes of Daniel 1 refused the menu from the king's table. "The effect set the Jews apart in sharp relief from the common run of aliens and novices at the Babylonian academy of wisdom. In that sharp identity lay strength: the Jews were going to have to be reckoned with! A yes at this point would have resulted in a significant loss of identity for a man undefiled and obedient to the God of Israel: he would simply have been another man with a price. In Daniel's no lay his own sharp focus."[30] As the canonical setting suggests, this is the "eternal truth" which will bridge over from this text to believers in every generation. "Maintenance of sharp identity, uncompromised, unencumbered, and ramrod straight in the presence of the oppressive powers of the world, will prove to be a salient feature of the interim ethics to be practiced by the saints [in every generation] before the great day of vindication comes and the kingdoms of the world become that single kingdom in which integrity such as theirs prevails forever (2:44; 7:27)."[31]

This theological assessment of the subject of Daniel 1 draws upon the clarity achieved from a direct reading of the plain meaning of the text in its canonical setting without playing it off against any hypothetical cultural or historical background. This study may not actually have discerned anything about Daniel 1 that a Tannaitic rabbi or a Calvin or a Luther or a serious noncritical contemporary reader of the Bible might not also have discerned—even though this study does presuppose findings of critical exegesis in such matters of date, authorship, and the editorial coherence of the Book of Daniel. But if the significance of the text discerned by this kind of reading is both defensible, convincing, and theologically appropriable by our generation, perhaps its accessibility is also an asset.

NOTES

1. B. S. Childs, whose "canonical method" provides the guidelines along which this experiment with Daniel 1 will be run, rejects the term "canonical

criticism" as claiming too little for his program. The term was proposed for Childs's approach as well as his own by J. A. Sanders in *Torah and Canon* (Philadelphia: Fortress Press, 1972); see esp. p. ix, where he speaks of formulating "a sub-discipline of Bible study I think should be called canonical criticism." Childs is unhappy with this designation precisely because he does not see the canonical approach as a "sub-discipline," or "another historical critical technique which can take its place alongside of source criticism, form criticism, rhetorical criticism, and similar methods" (*Introduction to the Old Testament as Scripture* [Philadelphia: Fortress Press, 1979] 82). It is not a method or technique at all, but an orientation or stance toward the writings of the Bible which enables the interpreter to treat each of them as part of a vast collection understood as a whole to be sacred scripture, while at the same time applying standard critical methods to individual pericopes.

Since I am following Childs's guidelines in this essay, I too avoid the term "canonical criticism." However, I shall try to assume a canonical stance, allowing the interpretation of a specific small unit of scripture to take place in the environment of a larger collection of narratives, all of which reflect the convictions and hopes of the community that expressed them and preserved them as a sacred writ.

2. W. Lee Humphreys, "A Life-Style for the Diaspora: A Study of the Tales of Esther and Daniel," *JBL* 92 (1973) 211–23.

3. B. S. Childs, "The Exegetical Significance of the Canon for the Study of the Old Testament," VTSup 29 (1977) 67.

4. Ibid., 69–70.

5. Ibid., 70.

6. Ibid., 78.

7. Ibid., 75.

8. Ibid., 77. The same argument is advanced in his *Introduction,* 619. The only "strong evidence" he advances to show that this was in the mind of the canonizers is the fact that 2 Esdr. 21:10ff. (ca. 200 C.E.) understands the fourth beast and its horns to be Rome and its emperor.

9. Childs's argument that because the writer of Daniel B "understood the sacred writings of the past as the medium through which God continued to make contemporary his divine revelation" (*Introduction,* 618) he need not be charged with radical innovation and with employing the ruse of pseudonymity—but merely extending the implications of Daniel A—is a tour de force, in my opinion.

10. A. Jeffery in *IB* 6, 360.

11. Ibid., 359.

12. This interpretation of the phrase "the language and literature of the Chaldeans" (v. 4) has force when one notes that the term "Chaldeans" appears as one member of a list of four types of court sages in both Dan. 2:2 and 4:7.

13. Commentators have always spilled a good deal of ink on whether a "eunuch" (v. 3) was really a eunuch (citing Potiphar of Gen. 39:1, who was a married "eunuch"); whether the Israelite lads were made eunuchs in order to stand before the king; and whether the "steward" (*melsar*, v. 11) might not

have been a "guard" *(NEB, TEV, JB)*, a "guardian" (Moffatt), an "attendant" (Lacocque), or simply somebody named Melzar *(KJV)*. These are fascinating questions, but for the purpose of theological appropriation of the text, they may actually make it more—not less—remote from the world of our experience.

14. R. H. Charles, *A Critical Commentary on the Book of Daniel* (Oxford: Clarendon Press, 1929) 19.

15. J. A. Montgomery, *Daniel* (ICC; New York: Scribners, 1927) 130.

16. N. W. Porteous, *Daniel* (OTL; Philadelphia: Westminster Press, 1965) 29.

17. A. Lacocque, *The Book of Daniel* (trans. David Pellauer; Atlanta: John Knox Press, 1979) 25.

18. See, e.g., J. Neusner's discussion of the evidence mutually provided by Luke 11:38–41 (= Matt. 23:25–26) and M. Kelim 25:1 about the controversy over the cleanness of a cup, "'First Cleanse the Inside'; the 'Halakhic' Background of a Controversy Saying," *NTS* 22 (1975–76) 486–95; cf. his *History of the Mishnaic Law of Purities* (Leiden: E. J. Brill, 1974–77) 3. 374–81.

19. The term *gā'al* seems to have a priestly provenance, and perhaps we can see in Daniel's abstemiousness a reflection of the profound priestly concern with blood, with all of its ritual and cultic sacrificial dimensions. A number of scholars have pointed out priestly influence in OT apocalyptic literature, including recently John Gammie, "On the Intention and Sources of Daniel i–xi," *VT* 31 (1981) 282–92. Lacocque points out that the young men of Daniel 1 are "without blemish" (v. 4), as Israelite priests must be (Lev. 22:17–25).

20. G. F. Moore's remark that "the reason for the specification of 'pulse' is perhaps that, being dry, it did not contract uncleanness from contact with unclean hands" (cited by Montgomery, *Daniel,* 135) is completely anachronistic in that it refers to mishnaic law first articulated at least four centuries after Daniel 1 was written.

21. D. Ford, *Daniel* (Nashville: Southern Publishing Association, 1978) 80–81.

22. Ibid., 82.

23. J. Baldwin, *Daniel* (Tyndale Old Testament Commentaries; Downers Grove, Ill.: InterVarsity Press, 1978) 82–83.

24. See my discussion of this same point in my book, *Daniel* (Interpretation: A Bible Commentary for Preaching and Teaching; Atlanta: John Knox, 1984) 24–26. In a passing remark in "Daniel and His Social World" *(Int* 39 [1985] 131–43 n. 13), John J. Collins takes issue with this approach, contending that dietary laws self-evidently lie behind Daniel's policy in chap. 1. Taking a canonical approach seriously as I attempt to do here suggests that the matter is more complicated than that, and that, in their wisdom, both the writers and the canonizers of the story were willing to leave admonitions toward specific dietary praxis aside in order to allow the theme in the story that ought to be

seized upon and emulated to stand out in stark clarity, namely, the courage of individual conviction.

25. *Daniel,* Lacocque, 33.

26. J. J. Collins, *The Apocalyptic Vision of the Book of Daniel* (Missoula, Mont.: Scholars Press, 1977) 32.

27. *Daniel,* Porteous, 31: "The Jewish stand for principle was fraught with tremendous consequences for the future of the world and, in that moment of history, the very narrowness of the Jew was meritorious."

28. Including Charles's dubitable comment that "the vegetarian diet is helpful . . . in the direction of spiritual development," *Daniel,* 23.

29. Baldwin, *Daniel,* 85.

30. Towner, *Daniel,* 28.

31. Ibid., 29.

19

Psalm 118 in the Light of Canonical Analysis

JAMES LUTHER MAYS

In his *Introduction to the Old Testament as Scripture,*[1] Brevard Childs proposes a fundamental shift in the practice of criticism. Under the rubric of canon, he has laid out an approach to the books of the OT that relativizes the methodological questions and values of historical criticism. The consequences of this approach for the interpretation of particular texts are of the greatest importance for exegesis. In works that preceded and led to his *Introduction,* Childs provided examples of exegetical work;[2] but the *Introduction* brings his work to summation and lays out a full statement of its theoretical bases.

This paper is an attempt to interpret a text in light of the *Introduction.* It is certainly not meant to be an illustration of "How to practice Childs's method." The *Introduction* does not propose, strictly speaking, an exegetical method or model. Childs is quite clear that "a canonical Introduction is not the end, but only the beginning of exegesis ... the canon establishes a platform from which exegesis is launched. ... A variety of different exegetical models" can be based on canonical analysis. But canonical analysis of the books of the OT supplies the assumptions and directions with which exegesis should work.[3]

I

The Choice of the Text. Psalm 118 has been chosen as the text for exegesis because it has established liturgical settings in Judaism and

Christianity. From ancient times, Jews and Christians have recited and heard Psalm 118 in the hermeneutical context of special occasions. These liturgical settings show how the psalm has been used and understood. Judaism knows the psalm as the last in the "Hallel," Psalms 113—118, used in the celebration of the joyous festivals since before the turn of the era. Psalm 118 in particular had a prominent role in the festival of Tabernacles (Sukk. 4:1, 8) and in the ceremonies of Passover, both at the temple (*Pesah. 5:7*) and at the household meal (8:3; 10:6). In Christianity Psalm 118 was used from earliest times in worship on Sunday, "the day the Lord has made" (Ps. 118:24) by the resurrection of Jesus Christ. When the annual celebration of Easter Sunday developed, the psalm was recited in the order of the principal service, a practice that continues to the present time in the liturgy of most Christian churches. In both traditions the psalm functions as a text that speaks of the salvation that creates a religious community. For Jews, it is the exodus and all that symbol represents in their scripture and tradition; for Christians, it is the crucifixion and resurrection of Jesus Christ.

One of Childs's concerns, a point made repeatedly in his *Introduction,* is that modern historical criticism has tended to distance biblical texts from their use in theology and liturgy. The traditional liturgical uses of Psalm 118 provide a pole of comparison against which to view an exegesis undertaken on the basis of canonical analysis. As a result, one may ask, Is the resulting interpretation more helpful to the use of the psalm in a community of faith and practice?

Description of the Text. It is useful to begin with a description of the psalm drawn in as methodologically neutral a way as possible. Every approach begins with a unit of language that has a presumed logical structure. This logical structure consists of the arrangement of the clauses in a text by means of verbal meaning, syntax, and discourse style, elements accessible to any careful reading of the text.

Psalm 118 opens and concludes with plural imperatives invoking grateful praise of the Lord for the goodness of his everlasting *hesed* (vv. 1, 29). It is introduced by three jussive sentences (vv. 2–4) calling Israel, the house of Aaron, and those who fear the Lord to "say" that the Lord's *hesed* is enduring; these three addressees apparently comprising the aggregate group addressed by v. 1. The rest of the psalm can be read in two parts, vv. 5–18 and 19–25.

The first part is concerned with the salvation that has already happened. The psalmist speaks in the first person, referring to the Lord in the third person. Twice the speaker reports that the Lord delivered him from distress (vv. 5, 13). Each report is followed by statements about the Lord and about the situation created for the speaker by the Lord's help (vv. 6–12, 14–18). Whether vv. 10–12 are thus appropriately described depends on the full explanation of the text.

The second part of the text is concerned with an entry made by one who has been saved (vv. 19–20, 26, probably 27). The first-person style continues (vv. 18–20, 28) and becomes direct address to the Lord (vv. 21, 28). In vv. 23–27, the first-person singular language changes to plural. The psalm continues to make statements about and to the Lord, and about the situation in light of the Lord's deliverance (vv. 21–24, 27a, 28). There is also a prayer (v. 25), a blessing (v. 26), and an instruction (v. 27b).

Psalm 118 in Modern Criticism. Modern criticism has been primarily interested in psalms as individual texts and has viewed the book as the result of a process of collecting and expanding that has little significance for the interpretation of particular psalms. They are understood instead in terms of a genre and of cultic proceedings. For those who emphasize form criticism, genre analysis is likely to be decisive; proposals about *Sitz im Leben* tend to flow from classification; decisions about ambiguous verbal meanings follow. For those who emphasize the character of the psalms as cultic songs, a hypothesis about the cultic life of Judah in the preexilic period is decisive; proposals about the use of a particular psalm depend on its relation to the hypothesis; and the construal of obscure verbal meanings follows.

The two parts of Psalm 118 provide a purchase for each of these two critical emphases. Verses 5–18, with their report and celebration of deliverance from distress, are generally classified as the thanksgiving of an individual. Verses 19–22, with their mixture of entrance rituals, prayer, blessings, and shift between singular and plural are generally recognized as a liturgy for the completion of rites in which an individual gives praise for deliverance (vv. 19, 21, 28). For Herman Gunkel, genre was decisive.[4] The psalm is a thanksgiving of a private individual who has brought his celebration into the midst of the congregation. The trouble that threatened death was sickness. The apparent military language (vv. 10–12, 15–16) is used metaphorically. For Sigmund Mowinckel, the psalm is an entrance liturgy used in the fall festival for the enthronement of Yahweh.[5] The individual voice is that of a representative king or leader. The trouble from which the singer has been rescued—from life to death—is described using the typical threats of enemies, natural disasters, and so on, through which the nation has come. The interpretations of Gunkel and Mowinckel are illustrative of lines generally taken in contemporary criticism.[6] Overall, genre and cultic use in shifting relationships are decisive for the construal of verbal meanings. The psalm is understood and interpreted as an artifact of ritual proceedings in Judah.

The Psalm as Scripture. For the approach developed in Childs's *Introduction,* "scripture" is the controlling rubric. This approach subordinates both genre and cultic setting as directive concepts for exegesis. Scripture is *what* a text is, and *where* it is. "Canonical analysis" leads to exegetical practice, which recognizes that fact and follows its implications. The interests and concerns of such practice for an exegesis of Psalm 118 would include the following.[7]

First, the text is part of the Book of Psalms, which was shaped in its present arrangement and content to serve as scripture. The book is the first interpretive horizon for the psalm, rather than the genres of speech used in ancient Israel or the history of its cult. Exegesis will seek to read the language of the psalm according to the constraints and directives of the book.

Second, the Book of Psalms stands within a larger collection of scriptures, which forms a second interpretive horizon. The language of Psalm 118 will be understood in terms of possibilities offered by the canon, rather than those provided by proposed periods, reconstructed rituals, or precanonical views of God and his ways. For instance, such matters as the central importance of torah or prophetic eschatology may come into play when one attempts to make sense of the psalm's languages, even though such elements may not have been operative in the hypothetical precanonical context in which the psalm was written and used.

Third, Psalm 118 in the Masoretic text of the Book of Psalms is the text for interpretation.[8] The Masoretic text will be preferred over reconstructions based on earlier systems of language. The present form of the text, and not reference to possible reconstructed forms, will control the interpretation.

Fourth, the concept of scripture incorporates a reference to a community whose recognition of its authority and use as instruction about the way of God and the way to live belong to its identity. That community is the historical setting of Psalm 118, which exegesis has to consider.[9] Exegesis will attempt to understand the psalm as a reader would have in the historical group for whom the *těhillîm* (psalms) became scripture. It must be added that the focus on canon as context does not exclude consideration of the liturgical use of the psalm as scripture. This approach remains open to considering the use of the psalm in worship when its understanding is under the constraints and direction of its identity as scripture.

II

The Beginning and End of the Psalm. The psalm begins (v. 1) and ends (v. 29) with a summons to offer grateful praise to the Lord because of the goodness shown in his everlasting *ḥesed.* The parentheses of this summons interprets the whole psalm as testimony and response to a manifestation of the Lord's *ḥesed.* The summons appears in three psalms and in three other canonical books (Pss. 106:1; 107:1; 136:1; 1 Chron. 16:34; 2 Chron. 20:21; Jer. 33:11). These psalms tell how the Lord's *ḥesed* delivered Israel from faithlessness (Psalm 106), situations of distress (107), and the chaos of cosmos and history (136). The narrative settings locate the hymn in the celebration of the ark's entry into Jerusalem (1 Chron. 16:34) and in a battle against the nation's foes (2 Chron. 20:21). Jeremiah 33:11 uses it as the song of thanks that the gathered nation will sing in the time when the Lord restores the fortunes of the land. In every case the hymn appears in texts that speak of the Lord's actions that concern the community, rather than an individual. All three psalms end in language connecting the Lord's past saving acts with the situation of the congregation after the return from exile (106:44–47; 107:33–41; 136:23–24). The congregation is composed of delivered people who pray for the completion of salvation (106:47), as does Psalm 118 (see v. 25).

The Participants. Verses 2–4 give a threefold identification of those who are to speak of the Lord's *ḥesed:* Israel, house of Aaron, fearers of the Lord. The same inclusive list appears twice in a nearby psalm (115:9–13; also in 135:19–20) to identify first-person plural pronouns. Psalm 118 has no title attributing the psalm to anyone; hence, reader and singer of the psalm as scripture will take the group identified in vv. 2–4 as antecedent of the first-person pronouns in vv. 5–19, 21, 28 (note the combination of singular and plural pronouns for the recipients of blessing, v. 26). The designation "those who fear the Lord" will not be read simply as a term for cultic participants. The term will assume the meaning of torah—piety rehearsed endlessly in Psalm 119 (see v. 38), where response to and hope in Yahweh's *hesed* depends upon a relation to his torah. The understanding of *ṣaddîqîm* in vv. 15, 20 is also affected. The translation "victorious" used in some versions and commentaries assumes a military setting for the psalm. However, the setting of the book supports "righteous" and draws on the understanding of the righteous present in Psalms 1, 19, 111, 112, 119, among others.

The Salvation. The two reports of past distress and the Lord's help are composed in metaphors and general language. Verse 5 speaks of the distress of being hemmed in, which the Lord relieved by a widening out. Verse 13 tells of being pressed to the point of falling when helped by the Lord. The language, as is typical of the plasticity of psalmic poetry, could be used for a variety of predicaments and experiences. For guidance about the reference of these reports, the denotative and connotative import of the words, one can turn to the rest of the psalm read as a unit and to its connections with other scripture.

First, the psalm speaks about salvation in language that appears also in the song sung by Moses and the Israelites (Exod. 15:1–18) after "the Lord *saved* Israel *that day* from the hand of the Egyptians; and Israel *saw* the Egyptians dead upon the seashore. And Israel *saw* the great work . . . , and the people *feared* the Lord; and they believed in the Lord and in his servant Moses" (Exod. 14:30–31, *RSV*)—all this after the people had complained that they were about "to *die* in the wilderness" (Exod. 14:11). The italicized words in this introduction to Israel's song appear also in Psalm 118: *save* in vv. 14, 21, 25; *day* as the time of the Lord's action in v. 24; *saw* as the verb for looking on foes in confidence in v. 7; *feared the Lord* as the identification of the singers in v. 4; *die* as the fate of Israel in v. 17. Israel's song is spoken in the first-person singular.

Moreover, Psalm 118 uses crucial sentences from Exodus 15. "The Lord is my strength and song, and he has become my salvation" (Exod. 15:2a, *RSV*) appears in v. 14 and in part in v. 21. A version of Exod. 15:2b occurs in v. 28. Both songs praise "the right hand of the Lord" and his prowess (Exod. 15:6, 12; Ps. 118:15—16). Both speak of nations which can be faced in confidence because of the Lord's might displayed in salvation (Exod. 15:14—16; Ps. 118:10—12). All these repetitions and relationships can be taken as directives that Psalm 118 is to be read and understood in light of the situation of Israel and of Israel's song and story in Exodus 14—15. Song and situation are not identical with the psalm, but when the ambiguous language of the psalm is read in the light of the Exodus situation and song, much becomes clear.

Second, the grateful declaration of the psalm, that "I shall not die, but live; and I shall tell the works of YHWH" (v. 17), is to be understood in light of the prophetic proclamation that Israel would die (e.g., Amos 2:2; Hos. 13:1; Ezek. 18:31). As the claim of an individual, the declaration could be only temporary, for the time being. But as the statement of faith of the community restored from dispersion and exile, it could be unconditional. They know now that the people of the Lord will not cease to exist. The account of deliverance from death to life in Ps. 116:8—9 is to be understood in the same way, and it is in relation to this understanding of death that statements that "the dead do not praise the Lord" (115:17—18; 30:8—10; 6:4—5) are to be understood. It is a matter of concern in the psalms because the death of the people of God would bring the praise of the Lord from human voices to a total halt, and that would be a contradiction of the Lord's entire way with Israel and the world. No praise would mean no recognition of the kingship or the character of the Lord.

The Situation. In Psalm 118 the community that has been brought from death to life continues in predicament. Though they were saved, they pray for salvation (v. 25). Yet their situation has changed. Before the Lord's deliverance they faced death; now they face life. What they have learned from salvation is a faith with which they confront the threats of life. The psalm describes that faith in vv. 6—12 in a way suggesting that the psalm is as much a song of confidence for the present as praise for what has happened in the past. The statement unfolds in three parts (vv. 6–7, 8–9, 10–12), which are mutually interpretive and can also be read under the guidance of other texts.

First, the basic confession of faith is: "The Lord is for me; I am not afraid." Deliverance has brought knowledge ("This I know, that God is for me," Ps. 56:10 [Engl. 56:9]). And it has brought confidence: Those who have been saved are liberated from terror. This basic faith allows the community to view its situation in terms of a radical alternative laid out by putting the Lord in a contrasting pair first with "man/those who hate me" (vv. 6–7) and then with "man/leaders" (vv. 7–8). This theological stratagem of describing a situation by a contrast between the Lord and 'ādām is used in several other texts. In Isa. 31:3, the Egyptians are called "man/flesh" in contrast to "God" in a saying against those who trust Egypt instead of the Lord. Isaiah 51:7–8, 11–12 uses the contrast as a basis for a comforting call not to fear the human dangers that threaten Israel. Asa, facing war with the Ethiopians, prayed, "O Lord, you are our God; do not let man prevail against you" (see also Jer. 17:5–8; Psalms 9—10, 56, 124, 146). The stratagem is a way to raise the question of Israel's faith in history to the level of an issue between the Lord and "man." The deliverance of the community has disclosed the Lord's commitment, and now history is viewed from that vantage.

Second, a review of all these texts suggests that vv. 10–12 should be read as a continuation of the statement of confidence, rather than a report about a past victory over the nations. "*All* nations surround me"—that reports the community's ongoing situation. "It is by the name of the Lord that I can ward them off"—that affirms the community's confidence. The situation is: God-fearing, Lord-trusting Israel in the midst of the nations. The nations are spoken of under the terms "man . . . those who hate me . . . leaders," and in a life delivered from death but still lived among the nations the community in this psalm praises and prays.

Third, this clarification casts light on the saying in v. 22. "The stone which the builders rejected" is the community "hated" (in Hebrew, more an act than an emotion) by the nations. The Lord's salvation has revealed that the rejected are the focus and center of the Lord's way in the world. One notes how very near to Isaiah 53 these thoughts are.

Fourth, v. 18 draws another implication for the experience of distress, call on the Lord, and deliverance. The distress brought on by human historical agents is taken to be the chastisement and discipline of the Lord. Psalm 66 uses the same interpretation of "my/our" suffering from the violence of "men." The reasoning runs that because the affliction did not lead to death, it was the work not of God's final anger, but of his chastisement (see Pss. 6:2; 38:2; 119:67, 71). The Book of Jeremiah applies this way of thinking to Judah's affliction by the Babylonians (Jer. 10:24; 30:11; 31:18). This theological reading of the community's past distress casts light on a textual problem in v. 13. The Masoretic text reads "*You* pressed me hard" in a context in which there is no antecedent for this direct address. Some of the versions, followed by most translations, relieve the difficulty with a change to "*I* was hard pressed." But though the Masoretic text's style seems awkward, the thought makes perfect sense in this context: The Lord pressed his people to the point of falling in chastisement, but then helped them.

The Entry. Verses 19–28 are concerned with an entry (vv. 19, 20, 26). Demonstrative sentences indicate the place and the time. The place is the gates of righteousness (v. 19), so called because the gates belong to the Lord and may be entered by the righteous (v. 20). The gates open into the house of the Lord, a place of blessing for those who enter (v. 20). The time for the entry is "the day which the Lord has made" (v. 24). The purpose of the entry is to offer grateful praise directly to the Lord for his salvation (vv. 21, 28), the act that created the day (vv. 22–24).

First, the psalm itself offers no help in connecting this entry with any particular cultic occasion, festival, or historical event. The psalm has no title. There is no certain connection between its text and any probable setting. Its incorporation in the psalter as scripture (as Childs repeatedly reminds us in the *Introduction*) has loosed it from any particular historical context and blurred its relation to any specific cultic proceeding. To reconstruct an occasion or a ritual as a context for understanding the entry would be to resort to a form-critical or cult-functional hypothesis. What one can say about it as a text in the *těhillîm* is simply that those who read it and used it in the community of the canon would have understood it as a text of praise for the remembered salvation of exodus and return by which the community, corporately and individually, expressed gratitude and affirmed the faith by which they lived in the midst of the nations. Its connection with the temple as the place where one came to be in the presence of the Lord would have been obvious in the context of the other psalms.

Second, because the community of Psalm 118 lives in the midst of the nations, it also expresses its trust in a prayer: *'ānnā' YHWH hôšî 'āhnā'* (v. 25). The saved community still prays for and yearns for salvation yet to occur. This prayer is a reason to consider some connections between Psalm 118 and the Book of Isaiah. Isaiah 11 concludes with a prophecy (vv. 11–16) that "the Lord will extend his hand yet a second time to recover the remnant that is left of his people" who are scattered in a dispersion among the nations (v. 11). Then, chap. 12 follows with a song of grateful praise in two parts (vv. 1–3 and 4–6), each introduced by the phrase "and you will say in that day." The songs to be sung on the day when the dispersion comes to Zion use language found in Exodus 15 in much the same way that Psalm 118 does. Exodus 15:2a appears in Isa. 12:2b (see Ps. 118:14). Exodus 15:2b is reflected in Isa. 12:5. In these hymns the scenario of a future salvation is similar to that found in Psalm 118: The Lord's anger has ended; he has become their salvation in event and song; they trust rather than fear; the setting is the nations of the earth.

In Isaiah 26 there is a song that will be sung "on that day" in the land of Judah. The song celebrates a strong city with salvation as its walls (v. 1). Its *gates* are to open "that the *righteous* nation which practices faithfulness may *enter*" (v. 2). "That day" will arrive when the Lord has brought down the institution of human arrogance (v. 5) and vindicated "the way of the righteous" (v. 7).

These eschatological songs in Isaiah sketch a profile of the salvation prayed for in Ps. 118:25. They provide another interpretive horizon within the canon for the "entry" which takes place in vv. 19–28. The entry of the righteous through the gates of the temple anticipates the coming of the dispersed people to Zion. "The day that the Lord has made" is informed not only by the memory of salvation past but also by the hope of salvation to come. Psalmody and eschatological prophecy are brought together for the community by the interplay of scripture within the canon.

III

Conclusions. Reading the psalm under the direction and constraints of a canonical approach does result in an interpretation that has a distinctive profile.

First, the procedures followed and the conclusions reached in this exegesis overlap in certain details those found in almost all of the studies of Psalm 118 surveyed by the writer. Probably a common text and the basic requirements of understanding language would guarantee that much. But the interpretation as a whole does, when compared, have distinctive contours. The questions that arise in the process of exegesis resume those found in the commentaries of a Luther or a Calvin (and even at times of the Midrash on Psalm 118) more often than do modern critical commentaries. The procedures and conclusions find their closest kin in the work of those for whom "relecture" and "anthological" are themes of their approach.[10]

Second, Psalm 118 is understood as a song of grateful praise to the Lord for his salvation. The praise is rendered by testimony to that salvation and to its effect on the saved, and by coming into the presence of the Lord to thank him. The salvation is the marvelous work of the Lord by which he delivered his people from death. The deliverance is described and interpreted in terms used elsewhere in the Hebrew canon for exodus and for the return from exile. The purpose of the text is not so much to celebrate a specific occurrence as it is to express the situation in which the Lord's saving activity, known from the larger scope of the canon, has put those who study and sing the psalm.

Third, the historical context in which the psalm is read and used in this way is a religous community whose view of God, world, and self is created by the scriptures of the canon read in interrelationship. The thought-world of the community is reconstructed by undertaking to read the psalm as a unit prompted by the connections of its language and thought with other psalms in the final form of the psalter and with other texts in the canon. The interpretation is meant to be descriptive and historical for that context. The usual procedure of criticism is to set portions of the Hebrew Bible in different periods arranged in chronological sequence and to understand their individuality as a function of different times and social situtations. Canonical analysis locates the text at the conclusion of the whole process in a community for whom the whole is revelation. One cannot assume, on historical grounds, that there was only one way of reading scripture within the postexilic Jewish community at any time. In that sense, "the community of the canon" is an ideal, and it is reconstructed. But positing that community is the only way to think about a setting in life and in history for the genre "scripture" composed of the collection and final form of the books in the Hebrew canon.

Fourth, the "I" is understood in terms of the "we." The theological identity is corporate. Note the use of first-person songs for the people in narrative and prophetic contexts in the OT (e.g., Exodus 15; Isaiah 12). This does not cancel the function of the first-person style or eliminate the reading and use of the psalm by individuals. Psalm 56, which is similar in language and scenario, is attributed to a setting in David's life. What happens, in the interplay of scripture, is a correlation of corporate and individual identities. David's narrative is taken as illustration and instruction about the people's life under God. Through David and the first-person style of the psalms, individuals understand their own existence in terms of the faith of the community. The issue is not a mutually exclusive choice between individual or corporate readings. The issue is whether individuals and community are understood by means of God's way known through exodus and exile and the people's response as laid out in the canon of scripture.

Fifth, the ambiguous language in the psalm is construed in a way that is coherent with the psalm as a whole and meaningful in the context of the community of the canon. The talk about deliverance from death, the celebration in the tents of the righteous, the nations round about, and the prayer for salvation are not tied to a particular historical occasion or social setting or festival, but are read as functions of the canon. This opens the psalm to use and interpretation in later and other times by the community for whom the canon of scripture is the guide to faith and life. The testimonies to the salvation of the Lord in all the canon are echoed in this language. It is a reading that seems to be coherent with its use in the joyous festivals of Judaism. Its use by the church puts the event of Jesus Christ in the sequence of the Lord's marvelous works of salvation and provides language for the Christian community to speak of the meaning of that salvation for their present and future.

NOTES

1. Brevard Childs, *Introduction to the Old Testament as Scripture* (Philadelphia: Fortress Press, 1979).

2. Brevard Childs, *Biblical Theology in Crisis* (Philadelphia: Westminster Press, 1970); idem, *The Book of Exodus* (OTL; Philadelphia: Westminster Press, 1974).

3. Childs, *Introduction,* 83.

4. Herman Gunkel, *Die Psalmen* (HKAT II/2, 4th ed.; Göttingen: Vandenhoeck & Ruprecht, 1926) 504–11.

5. Sigmund Mowinckel, *The Psalms In Israel's Worship* (New York: Abingdon Press, 1962) 1.180–81.

6. For a convenient summary of recent work on Psalm 118, see Leslie C. Allen, *Psalms 101–150* (WBC 21; Waco: Word Books, 1983) 122–25.

7. See esp. Childs, "The Psalms," *Introduction,* chap. 33.

8. Ibid., 84–103.

9. Note Childs's emphasis on "the community of faith and practice which preserved and shaped it" as the historical setting of scripture (*Introduction,* 41, 71, 73, 76, 77, 83). He insists that canonical analysis is a *descriptive* task which holds the language of the Old Testament within the interpretive context of historic Israel, even though canon frees the texts from the past. What Childs means by "historic Israel" and "a community of faith and practice" is somewhat elusive, but it becomes an issue in working with a particular passage. Is exegesis also a *descriptive* task? The remarks on p. 83 leave uncertainty. This essay is written on the assumption that exegesis also should be descriptive.

10. For the first, see J. Becker, *Israel deutet seine Psalmen* (SBS 18; Stuttgart: Katholisches Bibelwerk, 1966) 56–57. For the second, compare the interpretation in A. Deissler, *Psalms* (Dusseldorf: Patmos Verlag, 1964).

20

Metastases in Canonical Shapes of the Super Song

MARVIN H. POPE

Early dissent on Solomon's Song focused on the issue of sanctity or canonicity. The matter had been debated with vigor among leading sages at Yabneh (Jamnia) where the definitive canon of Hebrew Scripture was finally decided some decades after the Romans destroyed Jerusalem.[1] Doubts had persisted with respect to Ezekiel and Esther and the three books attributed to Solomon (Proverbs, Ecclesiastes, and the Super Song). Opposition to Ecclesiastes was persistent, but eventually all the disputed writings were deemed canonical. Rabbi Aqiba was especially outspoken in defense of the sanctity of the Super Song. In response to a comment of Rabbi Judah concerning Qohelet and the Super Song (*M. Yadayim* 3:5) Aqiba said, "Perish the thought! No man of Israel ever disputed about the Super Song, that it did not defile the hands [i.e., is not holy].[2] The whole world is not worth the day on which the Song of Songs was given to Israel, for all the Writings are holy, but Super Song is holy of holies. If they disagreed, it was only about Qohelet." Aqiba also objected to the singing of verses of the holy song in the Banquet Houses and pronounced perdition on any who did so. This has been taken to refer to profanation of the sacred song, but the Banquet House was a place of worship, as is evident in Dan. 5:10.[3] If Aqiba was concerned about secularization of the most holy song, he would be spinning in his grave at the present-day use of the famous refrain "My love is mine and I am his who feeds on the lotus" as a filler on the radio Voice of Israel when there might otherwise be a moment of silence.

The sanctity or canonicity of a piece of literature obviously depends on interpretation and estimation of its purpose and theological significance. A booklet beginning with reference to kissing and continuing with dialogue of love, wine, and song, with not so much as a mention of the God of Israel, would naturally raise questions about the grounds for the sanctity attributed to it.

Aqiba's extraordinary esteem of the Super Song was doubtless due in large measure to the circumstance that he had immersed himself in esoteric or mystical speculation about the Song and the Chariot-throne matter of Ezekiel. According to rabbinic tradition,[4] there were four sages who entered Paradise (i.e., engaged in esoteric/gnostic/mystical speculation): Ben Azzai, Ben Zoma, Aher (Elisha Ben 'Abuyah), and Aqiba. Ben Azzai looked and died; Ben Zoma went out of his mind; Elisha uprooted the plants (i.e., became apostate); Aqiba alone emerged whole (i.e., was able to deal with the shattering data). What were these mind-boggling mysteries that destroyed other devotees but did not daunt Aqiba? It could not have been run-of-the-mill allegorical interpretation which identified the female protagonist of the Song with the nation Israel or found legal and historical allusions in the love-talk. The clue to these disturbing mysteries must surely be sought in the Tradition (Qabbalah) based on ancient lore, especially in the esoteric literature that speculated on the magnitude of the various members of the body of the deity and his consort. The measurements of parts of the divine body are given in millions of parasangs in the Shi'ur Qomah (Table of Stature). Even the deity's privy member is mentioned, though the dimensions are not divulged.[5] Such might be the sort of secret lore that could account for the unsettling impact on Aqiba's fellow explorers.

The amazing history of nearly two millennia of interpretation of the Super Song cannot be reviewed here,[6] but recollection of some major metastases in understanding and estimation of the Song may be helpful for perspective on latter-day reversals in viewpoint and the prognosis that further drastic changes may yet occur if Equity Action, long evaded, is evenhandedly applied in appraisal of the formidable female protagonist of the Super Song.

The official view of the Song both in Judaism and Christianity, *mutatis mutandis,* remained remarkably stable for centuries. For Jews generally the bridegroom was Israel's God and the Bride his chosen people. The implicit apotheosis of the nation need not give us pause.

That the Bride dominates the scene and is the aggressor in the wooing, grossly incongruous with Israel's record of apostases and indifference, did not bother the allegorizers. Similarly for Christians, the lovers were Christ and his church, or Christ and the individual soul. The mystical union of the individual soul with God or Christ was particularly cherished by religious celibates, both female and male. The identification of the Bride with the Virgin Mary made it possible for the medieval troubadours to sing of courtly love under the cloak of a kind of literary mariolatry. As J. Pelikan[7] put it, "Lyrics addressed to the Blessed Virgin Mary and lyrics addressed to a sweetheart often became interchangeable, with the devotional lines used to conceal—or rather, to conceal and thus reveal—the poet's true desire for his lady love." That the Marian interpretation comes closest to the original intent of the Super Song will be suggested below.

Toward the end of the fourth Christian century, Theodore of Mopsuestia[8] (Mupsh mentioned in the eighth-century B.C. Phoenician inscription from Kara Tepe) boldly rejected allegorical interpretation of Solomon's Song and presented it as human love songs assumed to be Solomon's answer to criticism of his liaison with an Egyptian princess. Not surprisingly, Theodore's treatment of the Song did not survive and is known only from attacks on it. The attacks came after Theodore's death, his great learning apparently discouraging opposition while he was able to answer. The Council of Constantinople in 550 condemned Theodore's view of the Song as unfit for Christian ears. Theodore's brother Polychronius is credited with a decent commentary identifying the bridegroom as Christ and the bride as the church. Theodoret of Cyrus obviously alluded to Theodore's views in castigating those who slander the Song and deny it to be a spiritual book, weaving fables unworthy of crazy old women, saying that Solomon the sage wrote it about himself and Pharaoh's daughter. Theodoret himself prudently followed Origen's line on the Song. A Roman monk named Jovinian[9] had earlier provoked censure by preaching the literal sense of the Song as sanctifying sex within marriage and abnegating the supreme value set by the celibate clergy on virginity and asceticism. Jovinian was assailed by both Augustine and Jerome, and Pope Siricius in 390 convened a synod to condemn Jovinian. When Jovinian and his followers fled to Milan, Ambrose called a synod to endorse Rome's condemnation.

The earliest Jewish exposition of the whole Song is the so-called

Targum. The Targum to the Song of Songs, dating probably to the seventh century of the common era, does not translate or even paraphrase the received text but uses it as a catapult for historical, legal, and soteriological flings in all directions, past, present, and future, with regard to Israel's history and hopes. Starting from the initial superscription, the Targum announces itself as a sort of history of salvation in an excursus on ten songs marking milestones in human and Jewish experience, from the first song composed by Adam (Psalm 92) after he had sinned and was pardoned by the intercession of the personified Sabbath (the Bride of God) on through seven other biblical songs—the Song of the Sea (Exodus 15), the Well-Song (Num. 21:17), Deborah's Song (Judges 5), Hannah's Song (1 Samuel 2), and David's Song (2 Sam. 22:1). The ninth and penultimate Song is Solomon's Super Song and the tenth and ultimate Song will be that sung by the returning exiles to celebrate Passover beginning the new messianic age (Isa. 30:29). Raphael Loewe[10] saw the Targum as an effort to reclaim the Song from Christian usurpation and virtual monopoly and to give it an authentic Jewish interpretation that would sustain the elect through the long wait for redemption. The message is to keep the faith and the Torah as the only human means that might speed the coming of the Messiah. In addition to echoes of Jewish-Christian dialogue in the early centuries of the church, Loewe found in the Targum allusions to difficulties with the descendants of Ishmael following the Muslim conquest of Palestine (636–638). Interpretation of Cant. 8:9 mentions payment of money to buy (permission to affirm) the Unity of the Name of the Lord of the World, which Loewe plausibly understood to refer to the poll tax *(jizya)* imposed on the People of the Book (Jews and Christians alike) for the privilege of continuing to practice their religion under Muslim rule.[11] Loewe also detected in the Targum subtle polemics against pursuit of esoteric speculation of the sort that had undone some devotees.[12]

Christians quickly took up the Targum's approach to the Super Song as an allegorical history of salvation.[13] In the late seventh century Aponius applied the first six chapters of the Song to the history of Israel from the Exodus to Christ and the last two chapters to the progress of the early church as far as the peace imposed by Constantine. In the fourteenth century Nicholas of Lyra, reputedly a convert from Judaism, revived the notion of kinship and continuity between the Jewish and Christian communities by adopting and adapting Aponius's view of the Canticle as presenting a history of salvation. In the seventeenth century, Thomas Brightman in London and John Cotton in Boston followed the line of Aponius and de Lyra to astounding extremes of historical allegory. Brightman found references in the Canticle to major figures in the development of Protestantism from Peter Waldo to Wycliffe and Huss. The pursuit of historical allegory in the Song continued well into the twentieth century. In 1909 the distinguished Jesuit Semitist P. Joüon interpreted Canticum Canticorum as an allegorical history of Israel from the exodus to the exile written to encourage the returning exiles. Again in 1928 G. Ricciotti also read history into El Cantico dei Cantici touching Israel's experiences up to the time of Ezra and Nehemiah. The latest and probably the last in this line of interpretation is largely the work of A. Robert,[14] posthumously edited and augmented by his pupils A. Feuillet and R. Tournay. Robert saw the Canticle as a sort of allegorical, historical midrash with numerous echoes of scriptural passages. The stakes in this effort were very high for Robert, who felt it imperative to validate this approach from Scripture or else surrender the holy Song to profanation at the hands of the "école naturaliste" or the "école voluptueuse," who persisted in viewing the songs as love poems. A doctoral dissertation by R. T. Loring[15] studied thirty-six Christian commentaries that follow more or less the line of the Targum, ending with the work of Robert. That this interpretation "should still be advocated by scholars with all the modern linguistic tools at their disposal" Loring found "curious." It does not seem likely that this line will be taken up again. What Robert feared has come to pass. The "école naturaliste" now prevails even in mainstream Catholic interpretation of Canticum Canticorum.

From early times the Song was regarded as a kind of drama.[16] Origen in the third century saw it as a nuptial poem in dramatic form. Codex Sinaiticus (fourth century) and Codex Alexandrinus (fifth century) supplied marginal notes indicating the speakers and the persons addressed. The Ethiopic translation divided the Song into five parts, possibly on the assumption that it is a drama in five acts. John Milton in his treatise against Prelatry noted that "the Scripture also affords us a Divine pastoral Drama in the Song of Solomon consisting of two persons and a double chorus, as Origen 'rightly' judges." The very limited potential of two-character drama was augmented by Ibn Ezra in the twelfth century, and this dramatic interpretation flourished in the eighteenth and nineteenth centuries. The three characters are supposedly a pair of rustic lovers and the royal lecher Solomon, who tries to take the girl from her shepherd swain. Christian D. Ginsburg[17] made this plot into a veritable Victorian melodrama celebrating the triumph of true love and womanly virtue over every temptation a dissolute king could offer. Ernest Renan[18] developed the drama to a cast of ten characters with two choruses, male and female. In the present century A. Hazan[19] rendered the Song in dramatic verse for stage presentation featuring the Beauty and the Shepherd with supporting cast of Solomon and a favorite concubine plus assorted minor characters. To generate drama from the Song requires highly imaginative stage directions approximating or exceeding the volume of the brief and repetitive text.[20] It is a blessing that Hollywood has not attempted a dramatic version of the Super Song with superstars.

Early in the nineteenth century a Catholic priest, J. L. von Hug,[21] taking his cue from Cant. 5:2, "I slept, but my heart [mind] was awake," interpreted the entire song as a dream composed of almost two score disordered fragments. The dreaming shepherdess represented the ten northern tribes longing to be reunited with Judah in reconstitution of the Solomonic state. In the middle of the present century S. B. Freehof[22] also understood the whole song as a series of dream sequences symbolizing Israel's quest for God. In recent years, Dr. Max Pusin,[23] a psychiatrist teaching at the New Jersey College of Medicine, has applied Freud's table of dreams to the Song of Songs to discover it a veritable dream book containing nearly every category of Freudian symbol with meanings nearly identical to Freud's meanings. The dreams are those of a woman searching for her beloved. More than 85 percent of the lines of the Song are the woman's and the male characters, her brothers and Solomon, are "mildly villainous." Pusin considered it unlikely that a man, no matter how great an artist, could know and present so vividly a woman's dream. Moreover, the dreams of the Song correspond remarkably to those of Pusin's own female patients.

In the latter part of the nineteenth century a scholarly Prussian consul in Damascus gave an account of peasant weddings in Syrian villages which has influenced interpretation of Solomon's Song ever since. The groom and the bride were enthroned on a threshing sledge as king and queen in a week-long celebration with dance and songs describing and praising the royal pair. J. G. Wetzstein's[24] report in a journal of ethnology was taken up and applied to the Super Song, and for decades this was supposed to solve virtually all the mysteries of the Song. The songs accordingly were taken to be simply epithalamia. The metaphors and similes, however, remained passing strange as applied to any mortal couple.

The idea broached by Theodore, Bishop of Mupsh that Solomon's Song relates to human love, though condemned by both synagogue and church, persisted through the centuries, as attested by sporadic reactions and protests. Rabbi Ben Ezra, or Ibn Ezra, pronounced the idea repugnant: "Abhorred, abhorred be the idea that the Song of Songs is in the category of love songs, but rather it has the character of a parable; and were it not for the greatness of its excellence it would not have been incorporated in the corpus of sacred writings."[25]

The Protestant divines of the Westminster Assembly in annotations to the Song of Solomon observed that "both among them [i.e., the Jews] as well as other Readers, there were some that had lower conceptions of it [the Song], and received it as an hot carnall pamphlet, formed by some loose Apollo or Cupid, rather than the holy inspiration of the true God. But this blasphemy hath perished with the father of it."[26] (The father of this allegedly defunct blasphemy would be Theodore, Bishop of Mupsh.)

The learned William Whiston in 1723 boldly asserted that the Song "exhibits from beginning to end the marks of folly, vanity, and looseness" and that "it was written by Solomon when He was become Wicked and Foolish, and Lascivious, and Idolatrous." With respect to the allegorical and mystical view Whiston wrote, "I venture to affirm, as to the internal Composition and contents of this Book itself; that so far as the common Meaning of Words and critical Judgment of the Nature of the Book can guide us, this Evidence is wholly on the other side; and this so certainly and plainly, that 'tis next to a Demonstration against its allegorical meaning and consequent Authority."[27]

Such sentiments have persisted down to the present day. One reviewer of the Anchor Bible Song of Songs referred to the Song as "that cuckoo in the biblical nest." Nevertheless, the Song, no matter what interpretation is laid on it, remains a part of canonical Scripture and will continue to exercise and confound exegetes until the crucial issue of the nature and identity of the dominant female protagonist is settled.

In Christian shuffling of traditional order of biblical books the Song was removed from its place among the five scrolls of the Hagiographa of the Jewish canon (Ruth, Song of Songs, Lamentations, Ecclesiastes, Esther) and put with the Wisdom Books. The idea that the protagonists of the Super Song are Solomon and Wisdom was developed by the first Jewish humanist of the Renaissance, Judah Abravanel or Leone Medigo Ebreo in his Dialogues on Love, in which Philo (the Lover, i.e, Solomon) engages in conversation with Sophia (Wisdom) on love as the universal principle governing all existence.[28] This idea takes on new interest in light of the Qumran text[29] of the acrostic poem of Sirach 51:13–30, which presents Solomon's ardent love affair with personified Wisdom in language capable of double and multiple entendre suggesting more than merely Platonic intimacy. There are, however, scholars of great erudition but greater verecundity who refuse to recognize any intentional sexual suggestiveness.

Brevard Childs[30] regards Solomon's Song as wisdom, noting that the canonical editors did likewise. (Presumably the canonical editors meant are Christian rather than Jewish.) By assigning these love poems to the category of wisdom, the canonical editors, in Childs's view, do not alter the quality of the Song as poem of human love. "Wisdom, not human love, is divine," according to Childs. Yet love between a man and a woman is of inestimable value, a power stronger than death (8:6ff.). The witness of the Song to the reality of human love prevents this experience from being assigned either to the past or the future. "Yet within the context of the entire Old Testament canon the mysterious joy of human love which continues to erupt as an unquenchable flame is balanced by the threat of that same human love to destroy and twist its beauty." "The Old Testament bears witness to the reality of human love as a gift of the creator for human benefit, but one which carries with it both the promise of enriching joy as well as the threat of egoistic destruction." Childs's admonitions, written shortly before the onset of the alarming epidemic of deadly acquired immune deficiency syndrome, take on prophetic quality in all senses of that term. Oracular condemnations of the distortion of God's intention for humanity through abuse of sex and/or drugs, unfortunately, will be dissuasive only for those who take them to heart. In this connection, it is interesting to note that the Sublime Song has inspired pedophiliac poetry[31] since the Middle Ages, and long before that time Greek and Latin laments of locked-out lovers were about evenly divided between opposite and same-sex orientation.[32] The estimate that roughly 10 percent of populations have been and will continue to be homosexually inclined, whether innately or induced, makes expectation for elimination of homosexual activity dubious.

Conservative or evangelical Protestants began a few decades ago to focus on the Super Song, which had for a time been ignored in embarrassed silence, and to commend it for indoctrination to preserve the eroding sanctity of marriage and the stability of home and family life. E. J. Young[33] saw the Song as celebrating the dignity and purity of human love within the bonds of marriage and therefore as didactic and moral in purpose. Its very inclusion in the canon, according to Young, reminds us of a love purer than our own. R. B. Dempsey[34] polled a hundred priests, rabbis, ministers, and seminary teachers on their understanding and use or neglect of the Song in teaching, preaching, and counseling and went on to recommend that the Song be used for marital and even premarital counseling and for prayers and wedding ceremonies. R. B. Laurin[35] stressed that the modern message of the Song is the wholesomeness of sex—pure, passionate, hungry sexual love within strictly monogamous marriage. The meaningful ingredients of this mix are "exclusiveness" and "steadfastness," according to Laurin. Efforts to derive these lessons from the text were at times a bit contrived. The metaphor of the lady's towering neck (4:4) and nose (7:5d) Laurin took to signify purity, virginity, faithfulness, inaccessibility, and insurmountability, the picture of a maiden with head held high, standing aloof from all advances. The consideration that this demure damsel gets out of bed and takes to the streets to search for her lover who failed to appear as expected (3:1–4) was passed over without comment. The Tower of Lebanon overlooking Damascus, to which the maiden's nose is compared (7:5d, e), must be Mount Hermon, which rises more than nine thousand feet, commanding a view not only of Damascus some thirty miles away but of the entire area, including the Golan Heights and the Hauran of Transjordan. A lass with so prominent a nose might not need to scorn advances. The significance of this prodigious proboscis will be pondered anon.

The good news of healthy sex in marriage based on the Super Song has been developed and given practical application by J. C. Dillow[36] of Dallas, at the buckle of the Bible belt, where he and his wife operated a marital therapy program incorporated under the title "Inherit-a-Blessing," using Solomon's Song as interpreted by Dillow for a guidebook. Dillow's manual charts the path to marital bliss in a dozen steps to remedy female sexual dysfunction. The nonorgasmic wife begins with overcoming inhibitions through saturating her mind with "God's viewpoint on sex" by memorizing biblical passages on that topic and advances to exercising the P.C. (pubococcygeus) muscle to induce orgasm. The biblical solution to what Betty Friedan called "the problem that has no name," Dillow asserted, is total submission or "yieldedness" on the part of the female. In love, as in life, man is the actor and woman is acted upon. The Women's Liberation Movement, in Dillow's view, only aggravates the very problem it seeks to solve by balking at the prerequisite total submission to divinely ordained male domination. It seems unlikely that Solomon's wisdom, as mediated by Dillow, will be widely accepted by the sisterhood seeking liberation. Dillow himself had some initial misgivings about Solomon's qualification to discourse on the merits of monogamous love while enjoying the services of a harem of a thousand women. But the fact that a man is a hypocrite does not disqualify him to write on ideal feminine conduct. Perhaps Solomon wrote when he was young, before he had degenerated into lustful polygamy. But then it was that very longtime experience with polygamy that proved the same unsatisfactory. One need not worry unduly about whether Solomon was young or old when he wrote because in Dillow's understanding the Song consists of fifteen reflections by Solomon's true love as she looked back on her marriage, wedding night, and early years with Solomon. Thus, the actual insights were a woman's, but Solomon gets the credit. That, presumably, accords with divine predilection. The woman receives her reward the only possible way, through subordination and submission.

It is ironic that the view of the Song as dealing with human love, an opinion condemned by both Synagogue and Church for nearly two millennia, has in these latter days become the common view both in Judaism and Christianity. Only in the most orthodox and conservative circles of Judaism and Catholicism has the allegorical and mystical interpretation survived. Evangelical Protestants have outstripped all others in practical application of the Song for cultivation of robust sex in strictly monogamous marriage. Among Catholic biblical scholars in the U.S.A., Roland Murphy[37] early took the lead in criticizing some aspects of traditional Catholic views of Canticum Canticorum and in championing the interpretation as human love songs. The introduction to the Song of Songs in the New Jerusalem Bible regards the exegetic justification advanced in favor of the allegorical meaning as forced and artificial and notes that literal interpretation is now widely accepted and supported by the most ancient tradition, which is the absence of any sign of allegorical interpretation before the Christian era. Apart from the old attribution to the sage Solomon, the literal interpretation is held to justify the Song's place in the Catholic Canon among the Wisdom Books because it deals with human nature and treats one of its most vital aspects, teaching the excellence and dignity of the love that draws man and woman together. Over and above the literal meaning, it is permissible to apply the Song to the relationship between Christ and the church and the union of individual souls with the God of Love, thus vindicating the way the Song has been used by such mystics as St. John of the Cross.

There is a problem that has been ignored by those who suppose they are following literal interpretation of the Super Song, from the time of Theodore of Mupsh to the present, and that is the matter of the limits of hyperbole as applied to mere mortals. Generations of devout and learned exegetes who identified the male protagonist of the Song with the God of Israel or with apotheosized Christ were well aware that the description of the male lover with head and arms of gold, torso of sapphire-encrusted ivory, and alabaster legs set on gold bases, looking like Lebanon (5:10–16), could hardly represent mere flesh and blood. For nearly two millennia Jewish and Christian interpreters agreed at least that the Bridegroom of the Super Song must be superhuman. There was, however, a large blind spot with respect to the far more remarkable and formidable female protagonist with neck (i.e., necklace) like the Tower of David built in courses on which hang a thousand warriors' shields (4:4). Waterman's[38] facetious quip that "her neck is described in a manner to suggest the earliest recorded case of goitre" does not begin to do justice to the supposed hyperbole. Our Lady's towering nose is even more impressive, "like the Tower of Lebanon overlooking Damascus" (7:5d, e). The only eminence overlooking Damascus and much more is Mount Hermon, which towers over the region. The argument that "nose" here does not mean "nose," but indignation (a high dudgeon indeed!) is absurd on the face of it. The supposition that a big nose was considered beautiful can hardly be extended to include a human nose of the magnitude of Mount Hermon. Any anthropoid bodily feature grossly out of proportion with other parts, particularly a nose, would be grotesque. In the Shi'ur Qomah the dimensions of parts of the divine body are given in millions of miles, but the point is made that all proportions are in accord with the human form, the normal length of the nose corresponding roughly to that of the little finger.[39] Some exaggeration is to be expected and tolerated in praise of one's ladylove, but there are limits, as Shakespeare reminded his fellow poets in Sonnet 129. It is remarkable that those who perceived that the Bridegroom of the Canticle was more than mere mortal could not perceive that the Bride is far more impressive. A. Robert[40] recognized the Tower of Lebanon as Mount Hermon, but took the salient nose to suggest powerful and haughty surveillance in defiance of the successors of traditional enemies who continue to hold Palestine in thrall. (This fits the current situation with Israeli forces holding the heights of Hermon overlooking Damascus and the Golan since the Six-Day War.) But in spite of Robert's geopolitical insight or foresight, it is still our Lady's prodigious proboscis that confronts us (even if we go along with Robert to see her navel as Jerusalem, her belly as the mountain of Judah, and the breasts as the twin mountains Ebal and Gerizim!). If the Lady of the Canticle is the Great Goddess of Love and War, of Life and Death, equal and even superior to her divine consort, we can get over her monumental nose more easily than if she is taken to be a normal-sized human being.

We have touched only a few of the Protean metamorphoses in canonical shapes of the Super Song. The crucial question for the exegete is posed in the Song itself (7:1c) *mah tehĕzū baššulammît?* which for the present purposes we may translate, "What will you see in the Shulammite?"[41] The supposed hyperbole which gets far out of control with the nose falls into proportion only if the Lady is superhuman. This must be the crux of the stupendous mystery that devastated three of the four sages of old who ventured into the orchard of esoteric lore. Rabbi Aqiba was able to cope with the shattering news that the Holy One had a consort, but apparently Aqiba thought it prudent not to talk about it. It would have been helpful to Aqiba and to posterity if he had spoken freely of what he saw in the garden. If modern exegetes would calmly contemplate the nose of our Lady of the Canticles in perspective with due appreciation of proportion and symmetry, the conclusion that she is superhuman is as obvious as the nose on one's face. The impact of this holy mystery need not be so catastrophic as it was to Aqiba's associates.

Those who choose to read the Super Song as Wisdom would still be able to find, or, more precisely, to bring there, as much didactic and homiletic substance with as much validity as was done before the nature and identity of the divine virgin bride was admitted. Those who seek historic identifications of the Lady can find multiple choices in her prototypes and congeners, Inanna, Ishtar, ʿAnat, Athena, and the black and beautiful, tender and violent, licentious yet pure, virgin mother Kali of India. The most vivid portrait we have comes from pre-Israelite Syria-Palestine of the second millennium before our common era in the mythological poems from ancient Ugarit depicting the exploits of Virgin Anat on behalf of her brother/consort, Mighty Baal. The Lady of the Canticle may be the same whose name was linked to that of the God of Israel by descendants of Judeans who fled to Egypt during the attack by Nebuchadnezzar and there continued to swear by the entity ʿAnat-Yahu *(ᶜnt yhw)*.[42] She is the "queen of heaven," to whom the Judeans in Jeremiah's day baked cakes in her form, poured libations, and burned incense (Jer. 7:18; 44:17, 18, 19, 25). At Kuntillet ʿAjrud, in northern Sinai, in a syncretistic Israelite shrine of the ninth century B.C.E. she is depicted standing arm in arm with her mate and over their heads is the legend "To YHWH of Samaria and his AŠRT (place/consort)."[43] She is the Shekinah (dwelling place) or Malkut (royalty), the divine feminine principle through whom the created world is sustained in Jewish mystical or gnostic tradition (Qabbalah).[44] She is in effect the embodiment of the people Israel. Everything that happens to Israel on earth affects Israel's divine counterpart, the consort of YHWH, who responds to every good deed and every sin of every Israelite individually and collectively. Moreover everything that happens to the Shekinah in her sexual union with her masculine counterpart, which union was originally constant but later broken by Israel's sin, is also reflected in Israel's status on earth. Accordingly the goal of Jewish piety in the thought of Buber and Rosenzweig is to reunite YHWH and his consort, the Shekinah, representing his people.[45] Though the name of the God of Israel is not mentioned in the Super Song, the only excuse for inclusion of the Song in Jewish Scripture was the assumption that he is the Bridegroom. For both Jews and Christians, the crucial problem remains the identity of the formidable Bride.

When F. X. Kugler[46] sixty years ago called attention to parallels between the warlike bride of the Song and the goddess Ishtar, he was on the verge of recognizing connections that would have clarified numerous related phenomena. To mention only a few interesting interconnections, the first Christian heretics persisted in baking cakes for the Virgin just as the Judeans in Jeremiah's day had baked cakes for the Queen of Heaven (Ishtar-Anat). These Collyridians (so named after the cakes) also admitted women to the priesthood following a tradition more than four thousand years old, going back at least to Enheduanna, daughter of Sargon of Akkad, priestess of the goddess Inanna (or Ishtar) and notable also as the first identifiable author in history. The *labarum* of Constantine, the potent symbol of victory revealed after the first "Christian" emperor worshiped Athena-Victoria and Apollo-Mars on the eve of the crucial battle of Milvian Bridge, turns out to be the crossed chest bands of the war goddess (the same as the harness of an ordinary soldier), a symbol that survives on flags and military uniforms to this day.[47] The dedication of the seventh day of the week to the Virgin Mary, and in Jewish pietism the devotion of the night of Sabbath eve to marital duty in emulation of the Holy One and his consort both find their explanation in connection with the ancient goddess in whose honor the day was called Love-day, *Veneris die* or Fri(gg)-day (after the name of the queen of the gods in Norse myth).[48] The martial aspect of the Lady of the Canticle has parallels not only in her prototypes Inanna, Ashtart, ʿAnat, Atargatis, Athena, and her successors such as the Shekinah-Matronit of the Zohar and the black, beautiful, and horrendous Kali-Durga of India, but also in Byzantine war banners featuring the black Virgin supposedly painted by Saint Luke.[49]

Roman Catholic interpreters who have boldly identified the Bride of the Song with the Virgin Mother of God ought to be able to cope with whatever theological adjustments might be required by acceptance of the insight that behind the formidable Bride of the Super Song looms the imposing figure of the great virgin goddess of love and war of the ancient Near East. Her constancy and devotion to monogamy was not always what one might wish, but in Ugaritic myth she retains her title Virgin through a thousand torrid couplings with her brother-consort Mighty Baal and on through pregnancy and birth. This offers the thoughtful a mystery to contemplate in connection with the background of the idea of perpetual or renewable virginity and immaculate conception. For Jews and Christians of whatever persuasion, sexual or theological, rightist, leftist, or middle of the road, patriarchalist or militant feminist, admission of the superhuman quality of the Bride of the Super Song could be accepted with equanimity in keeping with the ancient pattern of the divine image emphatically specified as (both) male and female. The goal of getting the Holy One (Blessed be He) reunited with his spouse, with all attendant benefits, would receive a boost with recognition that the Shulammite (a title that has something to do with pacification) in the Super Song is that consort, the Shekinah, Virgin Bride, Sorrowing Mother, Wisdom personified as the principle of creation, or whatever other titles she may have.

The depatriarchalizing of biblical theology, a consummation devoutly desired in some circles,[50] would receive impetus from adoption and adaptation of some aspects of the concept of the Shekinah as the feminine hypostasis of deity, as portrayed in R. Patai's book *The Hebrew Goddess.* The Goddess most anciently was not "Hebrew" or even "Semitic" (the two terms are not quite synonymous); she was already fully developed in the world's oldest literature, Sumerian, under the name Inanna, centuries before Israelites came on the historical scene. The earliest canonical shape of the Super Song which in both synagogue and church recognized the male protagonist as divine should be restored and preserved and relieved of distortion by Equity Action with respect to the better half of the pair. Those who have difficulty, emotional or rational, with this eminently logical step can solve the problems with far less contortion than has accompanied efforts to identity the Bride as Israel, the church, Wisdom[51] personified, the individual soul, or a rustic shepherd lass. Recognition of the female as superior to the male, often the case in the natural world, will also correct the distortion in the traditional shape of the Song. Those who think to solve the problems by making both protagonists mere mortals will need to offer better explanations of the supposed hyperbole than that the lady's neck is long and her nose straight.[52]

NOTES

1. Cf. S. Z. Leiman, *The Canonization of Hebrew Scriptures: The Talmudic and Midrashic Evidence* (Hamden: Archon, 1976).

2. On sanctity and hand defilement see ibid., 102–20.

3. M. Pope, *The Song of Songs: A New Translation with Introduction and Commentary* (AB 7c; New York: Doubleday, 1977) 19, 210–25. Hereafter cited as Pope, *SoS.*

4. Cf. M. S. Cohen, *The Shi'ur Qomah: Liturgy and Theurgy in Pre-Kabbalistic Jewish Mysticism* (Lanham, Md.: University Press of America, 1983) 5ff., 9f., 84f.

5. Ibid., 210 n. 47; 217 n. 6.

6. For a survey see Pope, *SoS,* 89–229.

7. J. Pelikan, *Jesus Through the Centuries: His Place in the History of Culture* (New Haven: Yale University Press, 1985) 130.

8. Pope, *SoS,* 90, 119, 126, 184, 192, 237.

9. Ibid., 119ff.

10. R. Loewe, "Apologetic Motifs in the Targum to the Song of Songs," *Biblical Motifs: Origins and Transformations* (ed. A. Altmann; Philip W. Lown Institute of Advanced Judaic Studies, Brandeis University, Studies and Texts, 3; Cambridge: Harvard University Press, 1966) 159–96.

11. Pope, *SoS,* 94, 682.

12. Ibid., 96–101.

13. Ibid., 124–28.

14. A. Robert, R. Tournay, and A. Feuillet, *Le Cantique des Cantiques: traduction et commentaire* (EBib, 1963).

15. R. T. Loring, "The Christian Historical Exegesis of the Song of Songs and Its Possible Jewish Antecedents: A Chapter in the History of Interpretation" (diss., General Theological Seminary, New York, 1967).

16. Pope, *SoS,* 35–37.

17. On Ginsburg's melodramatic interpretation and Women's Liberation, see Pope, *SoS,* 205–10.

18. Ibid., 35.

19. Ibid.

20. Ibid., 132–34.

21. Ibid.

22. Ibid.

23. Ibid.

24. J. G. Wetzstein, "Die syrische Dreschtafel," *Zeitschrift für Ethnologie* 5 (1873) 270–302.

25. Pope, *SoS,* 103ff.

26. Ibid., 192.

27. Ibid., 129f.; 249.

28. Ibid., 110.

29. J. A. Sanders, *The Psalms Scroll of Qumran Cave II* (Discoveries in the Judean Desert of Jordan 4; Oxford: Clarendon Press, 1965) 79–85; cf. his *The Dead Sea Psalms Scroll* (Ithaca, N.Y.: Cornell University Press, 1967) 113–17.

30. B. S. Childs, *Old Testament Theology in a Canonical Context* (Philadelphia: Fortress Press, 1985) 192–95.

31. N. Roth, " 'My Beloved Is Like a Gazelle': Imagery of the Beloved Boy in Religious Hebrew Poetry," *Hebrew Annual Review* 8 (1984) 143–65.

32. Cf. F. O. Copley, *Exclusus Amator: A Study in Latin Love Poetry* (American Philological Monographs XVII, 1956).

33. E. J. Young, *An Introduction to the Old Testament* (Grand Rapids: Wm. B. Eerdmans, 1949) 327.

34. R. B. Dempsey, "The Interpretation and Use of the Song of Songs," (Diss., Boston University School of Theology, 1963).

35. R. B. Laurin, "The Life of True Love: The Song of Songs and Its Modern Message," *Christianity Today* 6 (1962) 1062–63.

36. J. C. Dillow, *Solomon on Sex* (New York: Nelson, 1977).

37. For Murphy's views, see Pope, *SoS,* 37, 44, 188–91, 200ff., 275.

38. L. Waterman, "The Role of Solomon in the Song of Songs," *JBL* 44 (1923) 180.

39. On the correspondence of the length of the nose to the little finger, see M. S. Cohen, *Shi'ur Qomah,* 217 n. 8. A nose longer or shorter than one's "pinky" finger was considered a defect sufficient to disqualify one for priesthood.

40. Cf. Pope, *SoS,* 626–27.

41. On other possibilities, see ibid., 601.

42. See A. Cowley, *Aramaic Papyri of the Fifth Century* (Oxford: Clarendon Press, 1923) text 44 line 3.

43. See Z. Meshel, *Kuntillet 'Ajrud: A Religious Center from the Time of the Judaean Monarchy* (Jerusalem: Israel Museum, 1978); and M. Weinfeld, "Kuntillet 'Ajrud Inscriptions and Their Significance," *Studi epigrafici linguistici* 1 (1984) 121–30.

44. See *EncJud,* s. v. "Kabbalah," "Zohar"; R. Patai, *The Hebrew Goddess* (New York: Ktav, 1967).

45. See *EncJud,* s. v. "Shekkinah."

46. F. X. Kugler, "Von Hohen Liede und seiner kriegerischen Braut," *Scholastik* 2 (1927) 38–52. See also W. Wittekindt, *Das Hohelied und seine Beziehungen zum Istarkult* (Hannover: Heinz Lafaire, 1926); and Pope, *SoS,* s. v. Wittekindt.

47. Cf. M. Pope, "The Saltire of Atargatis Reconsidered," *Near Eastern Archaeology in the Twentieth Century: Essays in Honor of Nelson Glueck* (ed. J. A. Sanders; Garden City, N.Y.: Doubleday, 1970) 178–96.

48. On the Sabbath as the Bride of God, see Pope, *SoS,* 171, 173, 175, 178.

49. On Gory Goddesses, Black Beauties, and Violent Virgins, scc ibid. 307–22.

50. See ibid., 205–10 ("On The Song of Songs and Women's Liberation").

51. On the pedigree of Lady Wisdom, see R. Murphy, "Wisdom and Creation," *JBL* 104 (1985) 8–9. On the striking word play in Prov. 31:27, see Al Wolters, "*Şôpiyyâ* (Prov. 31:27) as Hymnic Participle and Play on *Sophia,*" *JBL* 104 (1985) 577–87.

52. See M. V. Fox, "Love, Passion, and Perception in Israelite and Egyptian Love Poetry," *JBL* 102 (1983) 225–26.

Brevard Springs Childs:
A Bibliography

JOHN B. TROTTI

1953 *Der Mythos als theologisches Problem im Alten Testament.* Inaugural-Dissertation zur Erlangung der Doktorwürde der Theologischen Fakultät der Universität Basel, 1953.

1955 *A Study of Myth in Genesis I–XI.* Plymouth, Wis.: The Author, 1955.
"A Study of Glory." *Mission House Seminary Bulletin* 2 (1955): 34–43.

1958 "Jonah: A Study in Old Testament Hermeneutics." *Scottish Journal of Theology* 11 (1958): 53–61.
"Prophecy and Fulfillment: A Study of Contemporary Hermeneutics." *Interpretation* 12 (1958): 260–71.
Review of *A Companion to the Bible,* edited by J. J. Von Allmen. *Princeton Theological Bulletin* 52 (1958): 25–26.

1959 "The Enemy From the North and the Chaos Tradition." *Journal of Biblical Literature* 78 (1959): 187–98.
Review of *An Outline of Old Testament Theology,* by Th. C. Vriezen. *Journal of Biblical Literature* 78 (1959): 256–58.
Review of *Rabbinic Stories for Christian Ministers and Teachers,* by William B. Silverman. *Journal of Religious Education* 54 (1959): 80.

1960 *Myth and Reality in the Old Testament.* London: SCM Press, 1960.
Review of *Bibliography of the Dead Sea Scrolls 1948–1957,* by William S. LaSor. *Journal of Biblical Literature* 79 (1960): 196.
Review of *A Christian Theology of the Old Testament,* by G. A. F. Knight. *Interpretation* 14 (1960): 202–4.

1961 Review of *Congress Volume, Oxford, 1959* (Supplements to Vetus Testamentum, Vol. 7). *Journal of Biblical Literature* 80 (1961): 192.
Review of *Jahwes Eigentumsvolk,* by Hans Wildberger. *Interpretation* 15 (1961): 206–7.

Review of *The Old Testament: Its Origins and Composition,* by C. Kuhl. *Theology Today* 18 (1961): 282–83.

Review of *Religion in the Old Testament,* by Robert H. Pfeiffer. *Journal of Biblical Literature* 80 (1961): 294.

Review of *The Semantics of Biblical Language,* by James Barr. *Journal of Biblical Literature* 80 (1961): 374–77.

1962　*Memory and Tradition in Israel.* London: SCM Press, 1962.

"Adam," "Eden, Garden of," "Eve," "Orientation," "Tree of Knowledge, Tree of Life." In *The Interpreter's Dictionary of the Bible,* edited by George Arthur Buttrick et al. Nashville: Abingdon Press, 1962.

Review of *Die essenischen Schriften vom Toten Meer,* by A. Dupont-Sommer. *Journal of Biblical Literature* 81 (1962): 106.

Review of *Exodus: A Commentary,* by Martin Noth. *Journal of Biblical Literature* 81 (1962): 428.

Review of *Genesis: A Commentary,* by Gerhard von Rad. *Journal of Biblical Literature* 81 (1962): 103.

Review of *The Old Testament: Its Formation and Development,* by Artur Weiser. *Journal of Biblical Literature* 81 (1962): 211–12.

Review of *Studies on the Books of Samuel. Journal of Biblical Literature* 81 (1962): 326.

Review of *Theology of the Old Testament,* vol. 1, by Walther Eichrodt. *Interpretation* 16 (1962): 311–14.

Review of *The Way of Israel,* by James Muilenburg. *Journal of Biblical Literature* 81 (1962): 74–76.

1963　"A Study of the Formula 'Until this Day.' " *Journal of Biblical Literature* 82 (1963): 279–92.

Review of *The People of the Covenant,* by Murray Lee Newman, Jr. *Journal of Biblical Literature* 82 (1963): 134–36.

Review of *The Prophets,* by Abraham Heschel. *Journal of Biblical Literature* 82 (1963): 328–30.

1964　"Interpretation in Faith: The Theological Responsibility of an Old Testament Commentary." *Interpretation* 18 (1964): 432–49.

Review of *Gedenken im Alten Orient und im Alten Testament,* by W. Schottroff. *Journal of Biblical Literature* 83 (1964): 447–48.

Review of *The Hebrew Passover,* by J. B. Segal. *Journal of Biblical Literature* 83 (1964): 94–95.

1965　"The Birth of Moses." *Journal of Biblical Literature* 84 (1965): 109–22.

"A Survey of Recent Books in Old Testament." *Yale Divinity News* 62/3 (March 1965) 13–14.

Review of *All the Kingdoms of the Earth,* by Norman K. Gottwald. *Andover Newton Quarterly* 57 (1965): 40.

Review of *The Anchor Bible: Genesis,* by E. A. Speiser. *Religious Education* 60 (1965): 154–55.

Review of *The Book of Genesis: A Jewish Interpretation,* by Julian Morgenstern. *Journal of Biblical Literature* 84 (1965): 338.

Review of *History, Archaeology and Christian Humanism,* by W. F. Albright. *Interpretation* 19 (1965): 59–60.

Review of *Interpreting the Old Testament,* by Walter Harrelson. *Religious Education* 60 (1965): 168.

Review of *The Method and Message of Jewish Apocalyptic,* by D. S. Russell. *Journal of Biblical Literature* 84 (1965): 98.

Review of *Tetrateuch-Pentateuch-Hexateuch,* by Sigmund Mowinckel. *Journal of Biblical Literature* 84 (1965): 309–10.

Review of *Vatke und Wellhausen,* by Lothar Perlitt. *Journal of Biblical Literature* 84 (1965): 470.

1966　Review of *Die Bearbeitungen des "Retterbuches" in der deuteronomischen Epoche,* by Wolfgang Richter. *Journal of Biblical Literature* 85 (1966): 390–91.

Review of *Hebrew Union College Annual, Vol. 36,* edited by Elias Epstein. *Journal of Biblical Literature* 85 (1966): 269–70.

Review of *Israelite Religion,* by Helmer Ringgren. *Journal of Biblical Literature* 85 (1966): 497.

Review of *Kaf-Hē, 1940–1965,* edited by P. A. H. de Boer. *Journal of Biblical Literature* 85 (1966): 270.

Review of *The Old Testament: An Introduction,* by Otto Eissfeldt. *Journal of Biblical Literature* 85 (1966): 130.

Review of *The Problem of The Hexateuch and Other Essays,* by Gerhard von Rad. *Journal of Biblical Literature* 85 (1966): 390.

1967　*Isaiah and the Assyrian Crisis.* London: SCM Press, 1967.

"Deuteronomic Formulae of the Exodus Traditions." In *Hebräische Wortforschung. Festschrift zum 80. Geburtstag von Walter Baumgartner.* Supplements to Vetus Testamentum, vol. 16, pp. 30–39. Leiden: E. J. Brill, 1967.

Review of *Der Erzvater Israel und die Einführung der Jahweverehrung in Kanaan,* by Horst Seebass. *Journal of Biblical Literature* 86 (1967): 120.

Review of *Old Testament Theology,* vol. 2, by Gerhard von Rad. *Theology Today* 23 (1967): 575-78.

Review of *Studia Biblica et Semitica, Theodoro Christiano Vriezen dedicata,* edited by W. C. van Unnik and A. S. van der Woude. *Journal of Biblical Literature* 86 (1967): 484–85.

Review of *Studien zur Alttestamentlichen Prophetie (1949–1965),* by Georg Fohrer. *Journal of Biblical Literature* 86 (1967): 364–65.

Review of *Understanding Genesis,* by Nahum M. Sarna. *Interpretation* 21 (1967): 244–45.

1968　Review of *Archeo-Biblical Egypt,* by Robert North. *Journal of Biblical Literature* 87 (1968): 117–18.

Review of *A Commentary on the Book of Job,* by E. Dhorme. *Journal of Biblical Literature* 87 (1968): 114–16.

Review of *Creation Versus Chaos,* by Bernhard W. Anderson. *Religious Education* 63 (1968): 145.

Review of *Das Ferne und Nahe Wort. Festschrift Leonhard Rost,* edited by Fritz Maass. *Journal of Biblical Literature* 87 (1968): 355-56.

Review of *Jahwe, Jerusalem und die Völker,* by Hanns-Martin Lutz. *Journal of Biblical Literature* 87 (1968): 461–62.

1969   "Karl Barth as Interpreter of Scripture." In *Karl Barth and the Future of Theology: A Memorial Colloquium Held at Yale Divinity School January 28, 1969,* edited by D. L. Dickerman, pp. 30–39. New Haven: Yale Divinity School Association, 1969.

"Psalm 8 in the Context of the Christian Canon." *Interpretation* 23 (1969): 20–31.

Review of *Asylie und Schutzorakel am Zionheiligtum,* by L. Delekat. *Journal of Biblical Literature* 88 (1969): 104–5.

Review of *Hermann Gunkel: Zu seiner Theologie der Religionsgeschichte und zur Entstehung der formgeschichtlichen Methode,* by Werner Klatt. *Journal of Biblical Literature* 88 (1969): 508–9.

Review of *History and the Gods,* by Bertil Albrektson. *Journal of Semitic Studies* 14 (1969): 114–16.

Review of *Isaiah 40–66,* by Claus Westermann. *Journal of Biblical Literature* 88 (1969): 368.

Review of *Der königliche Messias im Licht der Immanuel-Weissagungen des Buches Jesaja,* by Martin Rehm. *Journal of Biblical Literature* 88 (1969): 365–66.

Review of *Mose. Überlieferung und Geschichte,* by Herbert Schmid. *Journal of Biblical Literature* 88 (1969): 245.

Review of *Numbers,* by Martin Noth. *Journal of Biblical Literature* 88 (1969): 244–45.

Review of *Studies in Sin and Atonement in the Rabbinic Literature in the First Century,* by A. Büchler. *Interpretation* 23 (1969): 107.

Review of *Words and Meanings: Essays Presented to David Winton Thomas,* edited by Peter A. Ackroyd and Barnabas Lindars. *Journal of Biblical Literature* 88 (1969): 370.

"The Rise and Fall of Biblical Theology." Sound cassette. New Haven: Paul Vieth Christian Education Service [1969?].

1970   *Biblical Theology in Crisis.* Philadelphia: Westminster Press, 1970.

"Should Theological Education Be Professional?" *Reflection* 67/2 (January 1970): 3–5.

"A Traditio-Historical Study of the Reed Sea Tradition." *Vetus Testamentum* 20 (1970): 406–18.

Review of *The Psalms: Their Origin and Meaning,* by Leopold Sabourin. *Journal of Biblical Literature* 89 (1970): 233–34.

1971   "Psalm Titles and Midrashic Exegesis." *Journal of Semitic Studies* 16 (1971): 137–50.

Review of *Das Todesrecht im Alten Testament,* by Hermann Schulz. *Journal of Biblical Literature* 90 (1971): 214–15.

1972 "Midrash and the Old Testament." In *Understanding the Sacred Text: Essays in Honor of Morton S. Enslin on the Hebrew Bible and Christian Beginnings,* edited by J. Reumann, pp. 45–59. Valley Forge, Pa.: Judson Press, 1972.

"Old Testament as Scripture of the Church." *Concordia Theological Monthly* 43 (1972): 709–22.

"A Tale of Two Testaments." Review of *Die biblische Theologie. Ihre Geschichte und Problematik,* by Hans-Joachim Kraus. *Interpretation* 26 (1972): 20–29.

1973 "The Old Testament as Scripture of the Church." *Reflection* 70/2 (January 1973): 3–6.

Review of *Essential Books for Christian Ministry: Basic Reading for Pastors, Church Staff and Laymen,* by the Faculty of Southwestern Baptist Theological Seminary. *Interpretation* 27 (1973): 498–500.

Review of *Jewish Biblical Exegesis,* by Louis Jacobs. *The Review of Books and Religion* 3/3 (November-December 1973): 12.

Review of *Torah and Canon,* by James A. Sanders. *Interpretation* 27 (1973): 88–91.

1974 *The Book of Exodus, A Critical Theological Commentary.* Philadelphia: Westminster Press, 1974.

"The Etiological Tale Re-examined." *Vetus Testamentum* 24 (1974): 387–97.

Review of *Genesis: A Commentary,* revised edition, by Gerhard von Rad. *Religious Studies* 10 (1974): 360–62.

Review of *The Laws of Deuteronomy,* by Calum M. Carmichael. *The Review of Books and Religion* 4/2 (October 1974): 14.

Review of *A Theology of the Old Testament,* by John L. McKenzie. The Review of *Books and Religion* 3/9 (June 1974): 16.

1975 "The Old Testament as Narrative." *Yale Alumni Magazine* 38/4 (January 1975): 30–32.

Review of *Lutherstudien,* by Gerhard Ebeling. *Interpretation* 29 (1975): 328–29.

1976 "God Leads a People to Freedom: Studies in Exodus." *Enquiry* 9/1 (September-November 1976): 1–33.

"Reflections on the Modern Study of the Psalms." In *Magnalia Dei: The Mighty Acts of God: Essays on the Bible and Archaeology in Memory of G. Ernest Wright,* edited by Frank M. Cross et al., pp. 377–88. Garden City, N.Y.: Doubleday & Co., 1976.

"The Search for Biblical Authority Today." *Andover Newton Quarterly* 16 (1976): 199–206.

"The Sensus Literalis of Scripture: An Ancient and Modern Problem." In *Beiträge zur Alttestamentlichen Theologie. Festschrift für Walther Zimmerli zum 70. Geburtstag,* edited by Herbert Donner, pp. 80–93. Göttingen: Vandenhoeck & Ruprecht, 1976.

Review of *The Prophets and the Law,* by Richard Victor Bergren. *Journal of Biblical Literature* 95 (1976): 314.

Review of *Two Old Testament Theologies: A Comparative Evaluation of the Contributions of Eichrodt and von Rad to Our Understanding of the Nature of Old Testament Theology,* by D. G. Spriggs. *Journal of Biblical Literature* 95 (1976): 281–82.

"The Present Confusion in the Church's Use of the Bible." Phonotape. Dallas: Forum Tapes [1976?].

1977 *Old Testament Books for Pastor and Teacher.* Philadelphia: Westminster Press, 1977.

"New Work on the Old Testament." *The New Review of Books and Religion* 1/6 (February 1977): 6.

Review of *Eusebius Werke, Neunter Band: Der Jesajakommentar,* edited by Joseph Ziegler. *Journal of Biblical Literature* 96 (1977): 439.

Review of *Introduction to the Old Testament,* by Otto Kaiser. *Journal of Semitic Studies* 22 (1977): 220–21.

Review of *The Old Testament and the World,* by Walther Zimmerli. *Theology Today* 34 (1977): 130–32.

1978 "Background Material on Exodus." In "Studies in Exodus and Psalms," by John A. Bowe. *New Ventures in Bible Study* 1/2 (Winter 1978–79): 3–64.

"The Canonical Shape of the Book of Jonah." In *Biblical and Near Eastern Studies: Essays in Honor of William Sanford LaSor,* edited by G. A. Tuttle, pp. 122–28. Grand Rapids: Wm. B. Eerdmans, 1978.

"The Canonical Shape of the Prophetic Literature." *Interpretation* 32 (1978): 46–55.

"The Exegetical Significance of Canon for the Study of the Old Testament." In *Congress Volume, Göttingen, 1977.* Supplements to Vetus Testamentum 29, edited by Walther Zimmerli et al., pp. 66–80. Leiden: E. J. Brill, 1978.

Review of *On Genesis: A New Reading,* by Bruce Vawter. *The New Review of Books and Religion* 2/6 (February 1978): 14.

Review of *Das überlieferungsgeschichtliche Problem des Pentateuch,* by Rolf Rendtorff. *Journal of Biblical Literature* 97 (1978): 272–73.

1979 *Introduction to the Old Testament as Scripture.* London: SCM Press, 1979/ Philadelphia: Fortress Press, 1979.

"The Recovery of Biblical Narrative." *Catalyst* 11/8 (May 1979): 2, 5.

"The Recovery of Biblical Narrative: The Samson Cycle." *Catalyst* 11/9 (June 1979): 4–5.

Review of *The Book of Job:.Commentary, New Translation and Special Studies,* by Robert Gordis. *Judaism* 28 (1979): 248–49.

Review of *The Early History of Israel,* by Roland de Vaux, *Interpretation* 33 (1979): 193–95.

Review of *The Elusive Presence: Toward a New Biblical Theology,* by

Samuel Terrien. *Journal of the American Academy of Religion* 47 (1979): 441–42.

Review of *Er spaltete das Meer. Die Auszugsüberlieferung in Psalmen und Kult des alten Israel,* by Stig L. Norin. *Journal of Semitic Studies* 24 (1979): 116–17.

1980 "On Reading the Elijah Narratives." *Interpretation* 34 (1980): 128–37.

"A Response" [to J. L. Mays, J. A. Sanders, B. C. Birch, D. P. Polk, and D. A. Knight]. *Horizons in Biblical Theology* 2 (1980): 199–221.

"Response to Reviewers of *Introduction to the Old Testament as Scripture.*" *Journal for the Study of the Old Testament* 16 (1980): 52–60.

1981 "Differenzen in der Exegese. Biblische Theologie in Amerika." *Evangelische Kommentare* 14 (1981): 405–6.

Review of *Gerhard von Rad,* by James L. Crenshaw. *Journal of Biblical Literature* 100 (1981): 460.

Review of *The Past, Present, and Future of Biblical Theology,* by James D. Smart. *Journal of Biblical Literature* 100 (1981): 252–53.

Review of *Die Vorfahren Israels in Agypten. Forschungsgeschichtlicher Überblick über die Darstellungen seit Richard Lepsius (1849),* by Helmut Engel. *Journal of Biblical Literature* 100 (1981): 269.

1982 "Anticipatory Titles in Hebrew Narrative." *Isaac Leo Seeligmann Volume: Essays on the Bible and the Ancient World,* edited by A. Rofé and Y. Zalovitch, pp. 57–65. Jerusalem: E. Rubinstein, 1982.

"Some Reflections on the Search for a Biblical Theology." *Horizons in Biblical Theology* 4 (1982): 1–12.

1983 "On Using the Old Testament Theologically." 4 sound cassettes. Nils W. Lund Memorial Lectureship, October 25–26, 1983. Chicago: North Park Theological Seminary, 1983.

"Wellhausen in English." *Semeia* 25 (1983): 83–88.

1984 *The New Testament as Canon: An Introduction.* London: SCM Press, 1984/ Philadelphia: Fortress Press, 1984.

Review of *Holy Scripture: Canon, Authority, Criticism,* by James Barr. *Interpretation* 38 (1984): 66–70.

1985 *Old Testament Theology in a Canonical Context.* London: SCM Press, 1985/ Philadelphia: Fortress Press, 1985.

1986 "Gerhard von Rad in American Dress." In *The Hermeneutical Quest: Essays in Honor of James Luther Mays on his Sixty-Fifth Birthday,* edited by Donald G. Miller, pp. 77–86. Allison Park, Pa.: Pickwick Publications, 1986.

1987 "Die Bedeutung des jüdischen Kanons in der alttestamentlichen Theologie." In *Mitte der Schrift? Ein jüdisch-christliches Gespräch,* edited by M. Klopfenstein, U. Luz, et al., pp. 269–81. Bern, 1987.

"Death and Dying in Old Testament Theology." In *Love & Death in the Ancient Near East: Essays in Honor of Marvin H. Pope,* edited by

John H. Marks and Robert M. Good, pp. 89–91. Guilford, Conn.: Four Quarters Publishing Company, 1987.

1988 "Biblische Theologie und der christliche Kanon." *Jahrbuch für biblische Theologie* 3 (1988).

"The Struggle for God's Righteousness in the Psalter." In *Festschrift James Torrance*. Aberdeen, 1988.

"Die theologische Bedeutung der Endform eines biblischen Textes." *Theologische Quartalschrift* (Tübingen, 1988).

Index

337

Index

Index

Index